AMERICA AND
THE WORLD

AMERICA AND THE WORLD

Jolyon P. Girard

Major Issues in American History
Randall M. Miller, Series Editor

GREENWOOD PRESS
Westport, Connecticut • London

Library of Congress Cataloging-in-Publication Data

Girard, Jolyon P., 1942–
    America and the world / Jolyon P. Girard.
        p. cm.—(Major issues in American history, ISSN 1535–3192)
    Includes bibliographical references (p.   ) and index.
    ISBN 0–313–31292–3 (alk. paper)
    1. United States—Foreign relations.   2. United States—Foreign relations—
Sources.   I. Title.   II. Series.
E183.7.G45   2001
327.73—dc21   00–069132

British Library Cataloguing in Publication Data is available.

Library of Congress Catalog Card Number: 00–069132
ISBN: 0–313–31292–3
ISSN: 1535–3192

First published in 2001

Greenwood Press, 88 Post Road West, Westport, CT 06881
An imprint of Greenwood Publishing Group, Inc.
www.greenwood.com

Printed in the United States of America

The paper used in this book complies with the
Permanent Paper Standard issued by the National
Information Standards Organization (Z39.48–1984).

10 9 8 7 6 5 4 3 2 1

Copyright Acknowledgments

The author and publisher are grateful to the following for granting permission to reprint from their materials:

George F. Will, "The Opiate of Arms Control," originally appeared in *Newsweek* magazine, April 27, 1987. Reprinted with permission.

Excerpt from anti-war speech by Dr. Martin Luther King, Jr., reprinted by arrangement with The Heirs to the Estate of Martin Luther King, Jr., c/o Writers House, Inc. as agents for the proprietor. Copyright 1970 the estate of Dr. Martin Luther King, Jr.

"The Truth about Vietnam" (Editorial), *New York Times*, February 14, 1962; Senator Albert Gore, "But Arms Dangers Lurk" (Op-Ed article), *New York Times*, November 24, 1985; Richard Pipes, "Why Hurry into a Weapons Accord" (Op-Ed article), *New York Times*, October 10, 1986; and Tom Wicker, "The March of Folly" (Editorial), *New York Times*, October 17, 1986. Reprinted with permission.

ADVISORY BOARD

To
Wayne S. Cole

Contents

Series Foreword by Randall M. Miller   xi

Preface and Acknowledgments   xv

Chronology of Events   xvii

1. Introduction   1

2. Neutrality and the Farewell Address: Founding Principles in American International Relations   9

3. The Monroe Doctrine: The United States and the Hemisphere   27

4. The *Trent* Affair: International Affairs during the Civil War   45

5. The Open Door Notes: America and Asia   65

6. The Fourteen Points: Woodrow Wilson, the United States, and World War I   85

7. The Kellogg-Briand Pact: Pacifism in the 1920s   103

8. The Good Neighbor Policy   125

9.   The Neutrality Acts and American Entry into World War II   145

10. Potsdam: The Last Wartime Conference   167

11. Joseph McCarthy and the Red Scare   189

12. Vietnam and the Paris Peace Accords: America's Longest
     War   209

13. The Camp David Accords: The Search for Peace in the
     Middle East   231

14. The Reagan-Gorbachev Summit in Reykjavik: The End of
     the Cold War   255

15. Epilogue   277

Annotated, Selected Bibliography   285

Index   299

Series Foreword

This series of books presents major issues in American history as they have developed since the republic's inception to their present incarnation. The issues range across the spectrum of American experience and encompass political, economic, social, and cultural concerns. By focusing on the "major issues" in American history, the series emphasizes the importance of an issues-centered approach to teaching and thinking about America's past. *Major Issues in American History* thus reframes historical inquiry in terms of themes and problems rather than as mere chronology. In so doing, the series addresses the current, pressing need among educators and policymakers for case studies charting the development of major issues over time, so as to make it possible to approach such issues intelligently in our time.

The series is premised on the belief that understanding America demands grasping the contentious nature of its past and applying that understanding to current issues in politics, law, government, society, and culture. If "America" was born, and remains, as an idea and an experiment, as so many thinkers and observers have argued, issues inevitably have shaped whatever that America was and is. In 1801, in his presidential inaugural, Thomas Jefferson reminded Americans that the great strength of the new nation resided in the broad consensus citizens shared as to the rightness and necessity of republican government and the Constitution. That consensus, Jefferson continued, made dissent possible and tolerable, and, we might add, encouraged dissent and debate about critical issues thereafter. Every generation of Americans has wrestled with such issues as defining and defending freedom(s), determining America's place in the world, waging war and making peace, receiving and assimilating new peoples, balancing church and state, forming a "more perfect union," and pursuing "happiness." American identity(ies) and interest(s) are not fixed. A nation of many peoples on the move across space and up and down the socioeconomic ladder cannot have it so. A nation charged with ensuring that, in Lincoln's words, "government of the people, by the people, and for the people shall not perish from the earth" cannot have it so. A nation whose heroes are not only soldiers and statesmen but also ex-slaves, women reformers, inventors, thinkers, and cowboys and Indians cannot have it so. Americans have never rested content locked into set molds in thinking and doing—not so long as dissent and difference are built into the character of a people that dates its birth to an American Revolution and annually celebrates that lineage. As such, Americans have been, and are, by heritage and habit an issues-oriented people.

We are also a political people. Issues as varied as race relations, labor organizing, women's place in the work force, the practice of religious beliefs, immigration, westward movement, and environmental protection have been, and remain, matters of public concern and debate and readily intrude into politics. A people committed to "rights" invariably argues for them, low voter turnout in recent elections notwithstanding. All the major issues in American history have involved political controversies as to their meaning and application. But the extent to which issues assume a political cast varies.

As the public interest spread to virtually every aspect of life during the twentieth century—into boardrooms, ballparks, and even bedrooms—the political compass enlarged with it. In time, every economic, social, and cultural issue of consequence in the United States has entered the public realm of debate and political engagement. Questions of rights—for example, to free speech, to freedom of religion, to equality before the law—and authority are political by nature. So, too, are questions about war and society, foreign policy, law and order, the delivery of public services, the control of the nation's borders, and access to and the uses of public land and resources. The books in *Major Issues in American History* take up just those issues. Thus, all the books in this series build political and public policy concerns into their basic framework.

The format for the series speaks directly to the issues-oriented character of the American people and the democratic polity and to the teaching of issues-centered history. The issues-centered approach to history views the past thematically. Such a history respects chronology but does not attempt to recite a single narrative or simple historical chronology of "facts." Rather, issues-centered history is problem-solving history. It organizes historical inquiry around a series of questions central to understanding the character and functions of American life, culture, ideas, politics, and institutions. Such questions invariably derive from current concerns that demand historical perspective. Whether determining the role of women and minorities and shaping public policy, or considering the "proper" relationship between church and state, or thinking about U.S. military obligations in the global context, to name several persistent issues, the teacher and student—indeed, responsible citizens everywhere—must ask such questions as "how and why did the present circumstance and interests come to be as they are" and "what other choices as to policy and practice have there been" so as to measure the dimensions and point the direction of the issue. History matters in that regard.

Each book in the series focuses on a particular issue, with an eye to encouraging readers and users to consider how Americans at different times engaged the issue based on the particular values, interests, and political and social structures of the day. As such, each book is also necessarily events-based in that the key event that triggered public concern and debate about a major issue at a particular moment serves as the case study for the issue as it was understood and presented during that historical period. Each book offers a historical narrative overview of a major issue as it evolved; the narrative provides both the context for understanding the issue's place in the larger American experience and the touchstone for considering the ways Americans encountered and engaged the issue at different times. A timeline further establishes the chronology and place of the issue at different times. A timeline further establishes the chronology and place of the issue in American history. The core of each book is the series of between ten to fifteen case studies of watershed events that defined the issue, arranged chronologically to make it possible to track the development of the issue closely over time. Each case study stands as a separate chapter. Each case study opens with a historical overview of the event and a discussion of the significant contemporary opposing views of the issue as occasioned by the event. A selection of four to nine critical primary documents (printed whole or in excerpts and introduced with brief headnotes) from the period under review presents differing points of view on the issue. In some volumes, each chapter also includes an annotated research guide of print and non-print sources to guide further research and reflection on the event and the issue. Each volume in the series concludes with a general bibliography that provides ready reference to the key works on the subject at issue.

Such an arrangement ensures that readers and users—students and teachers alike—will approach the major issues within a problem-solving framework. Indeed, the design of the series and each book in it demands that students and teachers understand that the crucial issues of American history have histories and that the significance of those issues might best be discovered and recovered by understanding how Americans at different times addressed them, shaped them, and bequeathed them to the next generation. Such a dialectic for each issue encourages a comparative perspective not only in seeing America's past but also, and perhaps even more so, in thinking about its present. Individually and collectively, the books in the *Major Issues in American History* thereby demonstrate anew William Faulkner's dictum that the past is never past.

Randall M. Miller
Series Editor

Preface and Acknowledgments

America and the World developed from my professional and personal interest in foreign policy and a course in American diplomatic history that I have taught during the past twenty-eight years at Cabrini College. It serves as an introduction to some of the key events in U.S. foreign relations. My hope is that it will provoke discussion and further interest in the complex world of international relations and America's part in that global concern. The book considers thirteen specific issues in the history of U.S. foreign policy that influenced not only United States international relations, but world affairs as well. Other historians might have chosen different topics, equally important, but I find the selections in this text significant for students to examine, and I hope they will agree.

The documents in each chapter offer a look at the views of people involved in the decisions, actions, and criticisms of each of the events and issues discussed. Along with the text, they provide a basis for students and teachers to engage in a challenging dialogue on the various problems that have faced the United States in international affairs. To encourage readers to consider the broad variety of participants and positions found in the foreign policy arena, I have sought to include a wide range of viewpoints, with different levels of complexity. Selections include personal and official letters, memoirs, treaties, books, and magazine and newspaper articles. They are drawn from a variety of resources, including primary published works and secondary sources, and suggest the many options available for locating documents. The selected bibliography is designed to help readers seek further information and ideas on American foreign policy. While not exhaustive, it does represent comprehensive and quality material.

I have many people to thank for helping me with *America and the World*. Dr. Randall Miller and Dr. Barbara Rader provided careful, experienced, and positive assistance as editors. So, too, did Betty Pessagno and Barbara Goodhouse. Professors James Hedtke, Michael Edmondson, and Antoinette Iadarola, at Cabrini College, read chapters and gave insightful comments and criticisms. Ann Schwelm, Rosemarie DeMaio, Ruth Richardson, and Alan Silverman, in Cabrini College's library, were wonderful resources with research advice, Internet sources, and copyright assistance. Donna Schaeffer and Marie Aragona assisted with the editing and proofreading and offered a student's perspective on the text.

My wife, Marilyn, gave quiet encouragement and patient tolerance throughout the process. My son and daughter, Geoffrey and Traci, read the text, pointed out errors, and said they would stick by me no matter what readers might think.

I am finally and particularly indebted to Professor Wayne S. Cole, my mentor at the University of Maryland. His strong influence and kind concern made whatever positive contributions I have made as a teacher and historian possible.

Chronology of Events

EIGHTEENTH CENTURY

1776	July: Declaration of Independence. Revolutionary War in progress.
1778	June: France allies with United States against Great Britain.
1783	September: Treaty of Paris signed. Britain recognizes American independence.
1787	Constitutional Convention.
1788	Constitution ratified.
1789	July: French Revolution begins.
1793	England and France at war. European conflict begins. President Washington proclaims U.S. neutrality in European conflict.
1794	John Jay's Treaty with Britain.
1795	Thomas Pinckney concludes treaty with Spain regarding U.S. navigation of the Mississippi River.
1796	Washington's Farewell Address.
1798	XYZ Affair. Crisis with French government.

NINETEENTH CENTURY

1803	Louisiana Purchase. Thomas Jefferson purchases territory from France.
1807	Embargo Act.
1812	War of 1812 begins. James Madison asks Congress for declaration of war against Britain.
1814	Treaty of Ghent ends war with Britain.
1819	Adams-Onis Treaty. Spain cedes Florida to the United States.
1823	Monroe Doctrine. Delivered in James Monroe's State of the Union message.
1835	Texas revolts against Mexico.
1842	Webster-Ashburton Treaty establishes U.S.-Canadian border.
1845	United States annexes Texas.
1846	Oregon boundary question settled with Britain. Mexican War begins.
1848	Treaty of Guadalupe Hidalgo ends Mexican War.
1853	Gadsden Purchase. Commodore Matthew Perry "opens" Japan to U.S. commercial relations.
1861–1865	American Civil War.
1867	Secretary of State William Seward negotiates purchase of Alaska from Russia.
1898	War declared against Spain. United States annexes Hawaii. United States annexes the Philippines, Guam, and Puerto Rico.
1899	Secretary of State John Hay issues Open Door Notes regarding China.

TWENTIETH CENTURY

1904	Theodore Roosevelt's Roosevelt Corollary to the Monroe Doctrine.
1914	World War I begins in Europe. President Woodrow Wilson announces U.S. neutrality. Panama Canal opens.

1917	April: America declares war on Germany.
1918	January: President Wilson announces Fourteen Points. November: Armistice ends World War I.
1919	June: Versailles Treaty signed in Paris. Senate rejects American entry into the League of Nations.
1928	Kellogg-Briand Pact.
1933	Franklin D. Roosevelt announces Good Neighbor Policy.
1935–1937	Congress legislates the Neutrality Acts.
1936	Spanish Civil War breaks out.
1939	September: Germany invades Poland. Beginning of World War II.
1940	September: Tripartite Pact—Germany, Italy, and Japan sign treaty aimed at the United States.
1941	March: Lend-Lease aid begins. August: Atlantic Charter issued. December: Japan attacks Pearl Harbor. United States enters World War II.
1945	February: Yalta Conference. May: Germany surrenders. War in Europe ends. July: Potsdam Conference. August: Japan surrenders. World War II ends. United Nations Charter signed.
1947	Truman Doctrine announced. Marshall Plan created.
1948	Berlin Airlift.
1949	China "falls" under Communist leadership of Mao Zedong. North Atlantic Treaty Organization (NATO) created.
1950	Senator Joseph McCarthy begins anti-communist crusade. Korean War begins.
1953	Armistice ends fighting in Korea.
1954	Geneva Conference is held regarding Southeast Asia.
1956	Suez Crisis. Hungarian uprising.
1961	Bay of Pigs fiasco in Cuba.
1962	Cuban Missile Crisis.

1964   Gulf of Tonkin Resolution.

1973   Paris Peace Accords signed, ending U.S. involvement in
            Vietnam War.

1978   Camp David Accords. Middle East Peace Treaty signed
            March 1979.

1987   United States and Soviet Union sign INF Treaty.
            United States signs Panama Canal Treaty.

1990   Iraq invades Kuwait. United States and UN respond
            with military buildup.

AMERICA AND
THE WORLD

1

Introduction

What's past is prologue.

—William Shakespeare
The Tempest, Act II, Scene 1

For wee must Consider that wee shall be as a Citty upon a Hill, the eies
of all people are uppon us.

—Jonathan Winthrop
1630

In 1923, the U.S. ambassador to Great Britain, George Harvey, informed a reporter that "the national American foreign policy is to have no foreign policy." That oft quoted remark appeared to make sense then. Many observers believe it remains appropriate today.

U.S. international affairs often seem to critics to have neither rhyme nor reason. Perceived as a young, unsophisticated nation by some, America seems to have stumbled through the world community like a bull in a china shop, using its economic and military power recklessly. Other observers sense an underlying arrogance to U.S. foreign policy. They argue that America abuses its power and behaves with an unclear sense of what remains important or proper in the conduct of affairs between nations. Still others conclude that the United States is well meaning and powerful, but naïve and idealistic. At the beginning of the twenty-first century, America is the most powerful, influential nation within the international community. If Ambassador Harvey was correct, that seems an amazing history of good fortune.

In fact, the United States has always defined broad, basic principles as its foreign policy goals and objectives. While debatable as to their intent and success, most of those principles have proven not only effective, but thoughtful. Since the beginning of the republic, key ideas have evolved to form the basis of U.S. relations with the international community. In Thomas A. Bailey's *Diplomatic History of the American People*, the distinguished diplomatic historian lists those objectives as isolationism, freedom of the seas, the Monroe Doctrine, Pan-Americanism, the Open Door, and the peaceful settlement of disputes.[1]

While those concepts developed from basic goals, they have altered and evolved with time and circumstance. *Isolationism* emerged as a foreign policy device to protect a young, weak America from aggressive and threatening European superpowers in the late eighteenth century. U.S. policy makers feared that military alliances with states like France or England could drag the young republic into dangerous entanglements that America lacked the strength to control. In 1919, isolationism took a new form when senators rejected President Woodrow Wilson's effort to join the League of Nations. At that point, America had concluded World War I as a powerful nation. Yet, many senators sought to guard that power unilaterally and avoid tying the United States to a weak international organization. The basic concept remained similar, but America's posture had shifted dramatically between the eighteenth and the twentieth centuries.

During most of U.S. history, the nation's leaders worked to protect America's right to sail the seas safely. Designed to enhance trading options, and aimed at the strong European naval blockades that prowled the oceans during the Napoleonic Wars, that early *freedom of the seas* stance led to a war with Britain in 1812. England, with little fear of American strength, refused to acknowledge the principle on American terms. A century later, the same concept created a crisis with the German government and its U-boat attacks on "neutral" shipping. Little had changed in theory, but America's power in 1914–1916 had grown significantly. Again, the basic principle persisted, but the U.S. response altered, as did the German government's actions compared to England's in the early 1800s.

The *Monroe Doctrine* and the idea of *Pan-Americanism* have developed as two of the most abiding American foreign policy principles. Yet, the two ideas, while linked, create an ambivalent relationship between the United States and its neighbors in the Western Hemisphere. President James Monroe's 1823 State of the Union message warned Europeans that a "hands off" principle existed in the Western Hemisphere. The New World differed from the Old, and the United States and the recently independent Latin American states hoped to keep it that way. Europe should stay out! In a spirit of Pan-American unity, the United States became the first nation to recognize the independence of its Latin American neighbors as those countries won their freedom from Spain.

At the same time, however, President Monroe and his secretary of state, John Quincy Adams, had no intention of seeing the United States abide by the same rules as Europe. America refused to keep its hands off. Simon Bolivar, the Venezuelan independence leader, recognized that ambivalence and realized that a true partnership between the Latin America nations and the United States might prove difficult if not impossible. Still, the ideal and the reality have merged and created fundamental issues and concerns for U.S.–Latin American relations. The two remain neighbors, yet the United States can act, and has acted, as a "Yankee Colossus," imposing its policies unilaterally.

Secretary of State John Hay announced the *Open Door* policy of the United States in 1899. He sent several notes to European governments to articulate America's belief that China should remain free of European colonization and open to free trade. While specific in their intent, the Open Door Notes actually spoke to a larger U.S. policy principle. As a competing force in international trade and commerce, American diplomats and business leaders sought to prevent any one nation or group of nations from establishing control of a geographic area to block U.S. access to any potential market. The concept served as a self-interested conclusion that trade barriers and restricted access to global markets threatened American prosperity. Recent policies of the United States, such as the North American Free Trade Agreement (NAFTA) and American dissatisfaction with Japanese "protectionism" regarding its products, continue to reflect U.S. attitudes about the Open Door.

So-called new left scholars like William Appleman Williams have argued that our economic drive for free markets really expressed an ironic form of Open Door imperialism. America, Williams maintained in *The Tragedy of American Diplomacy*, used the free trade concept to exploit and dominate commercial markets with its superior capital and products. Thus, what some viewed as a noble concept to free the international marketplace, he and other critics saw as a provocative and unfortunate example of U.S. greed and aggression.

Beginning with the Revolution, the United States has experienced ten wars. If one includes the series of conflicts with Indian peoples and the "banana wars" in Central America, the history of U.S. military action is broader. Yet, the United States enters war reluctantly, and the diplomatic record shows that America has preferred the *peaceful settlement of disputes*. As Walter Millis noted in *Arms and Men*, the United States can act with militancy, but distrusts militarism.

Throughout U.S. history, both the public and politicians have hesitated to create substantial military budgets to "provide for the common defense." In most circumstances America responded to a brewing conflict with a hurried reaction and a rapid, sometimes confused, arms buildup. Any study of the years prior to the world wars of the twentieth century suggests that clearly. In virtually every instance, a flurry of diplomatic activity preceded the military response as the United States sought a resolution at the bargaining table.

In international relations, America seeks to enhance its interests peacefully and has tended to negotiate resolutions to its concerns. Whether constructing systems like the Organization of American States or the United Nations, the United States prefers to advance its international interests diplomatically. That does not suggest that America always follows its own principles. Nation-states, like people, may espouse principles, and those may determine generally their behavior. Yet, they often violate or alter their own fundamental tenets when it suits them. Time and circumstance directly affect foreign affairs, and U.S. diplomacy provides no exception to that reality.

No nation reaches the position of power and influence that the United States has in the twentieth century through ignorance, folly, or simple good fortune. The ability of the American "experiment" to survive its infancy and childhood in the eighteenth and nineteenth centuries also speaks to that conclusion. Nations develop and prosper through a combination of factors, responding to a set of guidelines, and reacting to particular issues on the international scene as they occur. While human behavior cannot reduce itself to a simple equation, key themes do offer a lesson to examine.

If the concepts that Professor Bailey suggested served as key elements in America's foreign policy actions, the nation had a founding and rooted belief in its special circumstance within the world community. Throughout its history, the United States derived, from its colonial origins, a belief in its "exceptionalism." America provided an extraordinary religious, political, cultural, and social opportunity. New England Calvinists, as they arrived to settle the Massachusetts Bay Colony, wrote about a "Citty upon a Hill" in the early seventeenth century. Revolutionary War patriots extolled the virtues of American liberty and the republican experiment the new nation had committed to create. The United States sought a "separate sphere" from the rest of the world and needed to defend, and then expand, that goal. To its leaders and the general American public, that grave responsibility underpinned its relations with the world community.

The principles discussed above, then, did not develop in a vacuum, nor did they evolve accidentally. They emerged, and Americans began to articulate and pursue them, based on two broad concerns. Domestic influences and external issues married to generate U.S. foreign policy.

The deadly struggle between France and England in the early 1800s served as an *external* issue that motivated U.S. international relations. Their ships seized American vessels and sailors on the high seas and provoked an angry response in the United States. But the *domestic* factors involving commercial profits and a political battle between Federalists and Republicans also drove the foreign policy engine. War Hawk congressional leaders like John C. Calhoun and Henry Clay considered Indian problems on the frontier, territorial acquisition in Canada and Florida, and a bitter conflict with Federalist opponents equally influential in their decision making. Obviously, had no war raged in Europe between France and England, no naval blockade would have existed in the early 1800s. There would therefore have been no pressing need for the United States to defend its principle of freedom of the seas. The impact of external events clearly influenced international relations between the United States and Great Britain. But the domestic issues described above also worked to shape America's position. While the idea of external-domestic influences appears obvious, examining the specific impact each has on particular issues remains important if one seeks to understand how foreign policy evolves.

In international relations, nations operate to advance or protect their self-interest. While they may seek to "do the right thing," in moral or ethical terms, states will act in their own best interests. In *Politics Among Nations*, Hans Morgenthau focused on that realism. He argued that nations failing to devise principles and policies based on the reality of self-interest face a dangerous and potentially disastrous future. Between 1776 and the present, America's principles have articulated U.S. foreign policy from a posture of self-interest. That has helped the nation to survive, grow, and prosper within the international community. America is a world power. As the new century begins, it may be the only world power. Part of the pleasure and challenge in studying international relations hinges on the interplay of the various concerns discussed above. As one looks at a specific foreign policy issue, all of those basic factors help in understanding how and why things happen in the international arena.

In its beginnings, the nation lacked the strength and influence to do anything other than guard those objectives. In clear terms America devised defensive policies designed to protect itself against stronger European powers. In the course of time and events, however, America evolved as a powerful, expansive state. Its earlier defensive goals may have appeared the same, but U.S. influence and authority enabled the nation to apply its basic concepts much differently. Exceptionalism defended remains very different from exceptionalism on the offensive.

The various topics in the book examine not only the particular incidents and events that mark America's international affairs, but explore, as well, the themes discussed above. They also seek to describe a pattern of growing power and influence in America's diplomatic conduct. George Washington clearly expressed his early concerns about the war in Europe and domestic political factions squabbling over that conflict in his Farewell Address. To the president, the new nation, faced with the threat of powerful European aggression, lacked the luxury of misguided actions.

A century later, during World War I, similar issues, both at home and abroad, provoked a different response from President Woodrow Wilson. Defending the same principles that Washington had defined defensively, Wilson confronted the global conflict from a position of strength. The European combatants feared U.S. involvement against them in World War I. Thus, the interrelationship created a different dialogue between the European powers and a potentially powerful U.S. opponent.

When President James Monroe issued the Monroe Doctrine during his 1823 State of the Union message, he appeared concerned that the European monarchs might intervene in Latin America and elsewhere in the hemisphere to threaten U.S. interests. Monroe recognized that the United States lacked the independent strength to prevent such intervention, and, in that respect, his warning counted upon the backing of the British. At the beginning of the twentieth century, however, President Theodore Roosevelt's corollary to the Monroe Doctrine served notice, to both Europe and Latin America, that the United States would act unilaterally and aggressively to enforce the 1823 policy in a different manner altogether. The principle may have appeared basic, but its application had changed with an evolving American worldview and the U.S. position within the international community.

The United States confronted the dilemma of its newfound influence following World War I. In the struggle between President Wilson and the Senate over the League of Nations, both policy makers and the American public came face to face with the altered status of the United States in world affairs. Should America defend its interests against the threats of international crisis by clinging to the warning of Washington or confront them as the leading member of an international organization? During Franklin Roosevelt's battle over neutrality legislation, in the 1930s, Americans debated the same basic concerns. How much had the power of the United States shifted its stance and its responsibilities?

The nation appears to have always believed in its "exceptional" status, and it has tended to accept the broad principles developed early in its history of foreign relations. Yet, every generation of policy makers, and the American public, confronts the changing nature of world events and the U.S. response to those events differently. Thus, the study of American foreign policy requires a fundamental understanding of the principles and the ability to weave those broad goals into the pattern of change that has also influenced the conduct of U.S. international affairs.

The story, tritely, should begin at the beginning. America's colonial origins and the experiences learned during the Revolutionary War prompted the first key expression of U.S. international affairs. That lesson taught an abiding distrust of Europe, a concern that the nations there threatened American interests. The new nation's leaders concluded that the United States had to avoid political involvement with the countries of Europe. From George Washington's administration to Thomas Jefferson's, a generation of development, the United States sought to create a policy to protect the nation in the dangerous shoals and eddies of international affairs. Isolationism and neutrality served to guarantee that end. Those qualities also defined the first key American principle in international relations.

NOTE

1. Thomas A. Bailey, *A Diplomatic History of the American People*, 10th ed. (Englewood Cliffs, NJ: Prentice-Hall, 1980), p. 2.

2

Neutrality and the Farewell Address: Founding Principles in American International Relations

> The great rule of conduct for us, in regard to foreign nations, is, in extending our commercial relations, to have with them as little political connexion as possible.
>
> —George Washington
> Farewell Address, 1796

On April 22, 1793, President George Washington issued a Proclamation of Neutrality, stating that the United States would take no sides in an exploding European war. That decision established a major American international policy for the next century and a half. In his Farewell Address in 1796, the president reexamined the concept of neutrality in light of the ongoing war in Europe and political debates about that conflict at home.

As the new nation took life, Americans swam in dangerous waters, confronted with powerful, contentious European states. Neutrality, as a basic policy position, surfaced quickly to safeguard U.S. interests. Its roots, a distrust of the Old World, came from colonial history. Its practice began in Washington's first term.

A variety of problems had sent thousands of settlers from Europe to America in the seventeenth and eighteenth centuries. While those colonists may have remained loyal to their mother country and appreciated qualities of English culture and heritage, they also had left, even fled, the Old World for the New, bringing with them skeptical attitudes about

Britain's rulers and policies. The relationship seemed ironic—obedience coupled with distrust. Additionally, large numbers of immigrants came from places other than England, and while they tended to accept English authority, they were also wary of the Old World's impact on their lives.

A series of wars in Europe between 1688 and 1763 enhanced the ambivalent relationship between settlers and the government in London. Most of the wars were dynastic in origin, battles among monarchs for territory or royal succession. Invariably, England and France found themselves enemies. Colonial competition mattered, because Anglo-French commercial and territorial ambitions in North America grew in importance. Additionally, both sides sought Indian allies to assist their efforts, and the Huron and Iroquois, traditional enemies, used the Europeans with equal dexterity to protect their interests. In all, a dicey, confused, and dangerous set of circumstances marked colonial diplomacy in English America.

Ultimately, as loyally as one might act, the Anglo-French wars came to frustrate American provincials. The conflicts left a legacy of cynicism and added to the growing conviction that Europe remained different and dangerous to the hopes of the men and women living in the colonies. At the end of the French and Indian War (1763), many Americans had reached a point of potential rupture over policy decisions that King George III's ministers made to benefit the British Empire. The evolving sense of "exceptionalism" and the special place that America had become to the provincial population fueled the move toward separation.

In a sense, the American Revolution began in 1763, when the English ousted France from Canada. Victory led Parliament to tax Americans to help pay for the new costs of administering a larger North American empire. Parliament also forbade the colonials to develop settlements or to reap real estate profits in the Ohio Valley, a major incentive for colonial speculators. The new costs and the presence of a standing British army in America added to the problems colonials faced. Between 1763 and 1776, a serious debate developed over the benefits continued association with England might have, and George Washington grew to political maturity during that crisis, along with other prominent Americans. In basic terms, in 1776 revolutionary leaders decided that the defects of English authority outweighed the benefits.

The Revolutionary War (1775–1783) fed the general conclusion that Europeans posed dangers to American security. Even while the new United States allied with France and had help from Spain and Holland, American diplomatic agents knew that those states operated in their own interests, not the interests of a new republican government. The Europeans wanted to harm England. U.S. diplomats utilized that belligerence to gain help and ultimate victory, but the three principal American diplomats in Europe, Benjamin Franklin, John Adams, and John Jay, had few illusions. They recognized that their new, sovereign nation would confront a host of European threats in the future. The proof came quickly.

Between 1781 and 1788, under the Articles of Confederation, the United States placed major authority in individual state governments and created a weak central government. In foreign policy, the concept failed. British troops occupied forts in the Ohio Valley (American territory) and refused to leave. The government proved unable to negotiate a treaty with Spain allowing access to the Mississippi River. Trade relations with foreign governments languished. Few leaders in Europe took the United States seriously. Those concerns, plus others, prompted the calling of the Constitutional Convention, held in Philadelphia in 1787.

The Constitution created a stronger central government and gave the Senate and the president authority to conduct foreign relations with a clearer sense of direction and authority. George Washington swore the oath of office as president on April 30, 1789, at Wall and Broad Streets in New York City. Fewer than three months later, Paris mobs attacked the Bastille, the hated prison, setting in motion the French Revolution.

Initially, many Americans applauded the events in France as imitative of their own struggle. French leaders sent Washington a key to the Bastille as a symbolic gesture of unity. The situation, however, escalated. In 1793, the revolutionaries in Paris executed Louis XVI, the Bourbon monarch, and a Reign of Terror convulsed France. It also provoked a European war that saw England and France engaged, once more, as deadly enemies.

President Washington's administration faced a critical situation. The United States had a treaty with France, from its own revolutionary era, and the French would surely call upon America to honor that commitment. The president also faced a cabinet, and country, with different views on the conflict, a split that would create two political factions. As policy discussions began, the differences surfaced.

Thomas Jefferson, the secretary of state, favored the French Republic. Alexander Hamilton, the secretary of the treasury, supported Great Britain. The two men clashed on a variety of other issues, both foreign and domestic, and those differences created factions. Jefferson represented and spoke for Southern and Western rural, agrarian interests. Hamilton advanced the objectives of the urban, manufacturing Northeast. They also disagreed about the central government, states' rights, and the power of the presidency. The politics created Federalists and Republicans, America's first two parties.

Concerning the war in Europe, however, both men appeared willing to put their biases aside. Neither wanted to see the United States honor the French alliance, nor would Hamilton's Federalists have desired a military treaty with England. The current danger, and a history of skepticism regarding Europe, led to Washington's response. On April 22, 1793, he issued a Proclamation of Neutrality announcing that America would follow a "conduct friendly and impartial toward the belligerent Powers." The United States would avoid becoming a pawn in a deadly game of "super states."

Between 1793 and 1812, four presidential administrations sought to apply the neutrality principle to relations with Europe, even while the conflict there grew in intensity. A variety of issues threatened America's position, yet for almost two decades the United States avoided direct involvement in the war.

The neutrality position that Washington claimed not only prevented unfortunate alliances with particular European nations, it also allowed the United States exceptional trade opportunities in the war zone. As neutrals, American merchants could claim that freedom to sell goods and products to the various belligerents without fear of having their ships and cargoes seized. Under general guidelines, the idea of neutral vessels having that protection existed in the international community. Unfortunately, neither Britain nor France saw any need to respect U.S. neutrality when it came to commercial shipping.

In a series of incidents, European warships began to harass U.S. merchant vessels and confiscate cargoes, and in some instances the British impressed American sailors right off the decks of U.S. ships. The issue of neutral rights on the high seas, and Anglo-French disregard for that principle, served as the major foreign policy concern for President Washington and his cabinet.

Additionally, domestic politics also frustrated the situation. When Citizen Edmond Genet arrived in America in 1793 as an emissary from the French government, he violated all diplomatic tact. He roamed through the South and West, appealing to wildly pro-French, Republican crowds to back his country's war against England. Jefferson refused to encourage Genet's behavior, but Washington's critics attacked his neutrality position and demanded action against Great Britain. Genet finally came to Philadelphia, the new capital, to a chilly presidential reception. Ultimately, Washington would regain public support, and Genet's brash behavior led to his dismissal and recall to France. Instead, he married the daughter of a wealthy New York business leader and lived safely in the United States.

At the same time, James Monroe, a pro-French Republican, arrived in Paris as U.S. minister. His prejudice led him to underestimate the president's commitment to neutrality, and time after time he gave the French bad advice on what America might do. Ultimately, Monroe, too, failed to serve the interests of his nation, and Washington recalled him in 1796.

During two terms as president, George Washington had managed to avoid a direct clash with either England or France. The U.S. government had also concluded several key treaties demonstrating the strength of the new constitution. In the Treaty of San Lorenzo (1795), Spain granted the United States rights to navigate the Mississippi River and use the port of New Orleans as a shipping facility. Jay's Treaty (1794) saw England agree to evacuate forts it had occupied in the Ohio Valley since the end of the American Revolution. Yet, the domestic issue between Federalists and Republicans, and the inability to have either France or England respect U.S. neutrality, prompted Washington's Farewell Address.

He made his warnings clear: the political divisions in America harmed U.S. foreign policy interests. Partisan politics had to stop "at the water's edge." The nation needed to present a united front in its diplomatic agenda. Washington also restated his belief in neutrality, "no permanent alliances," as the best direction for the young nation. Then and now, some have misunderstood the president's caution. "The course that Washington advocated so chimed in with America's isolationist instincts," Thomas Bailey wrote, since it went "back deep into colonial times, [and] was bound to be a major, if misunderstood, foundation stone of future American foreign policy."[1]

The three presidents who followed Washington pursued the same basic policy that he had defined in 1793 and reemphasized in 1796. During the presidency of John Adams, the Federalist-controlled government almost went to war with France over the infamous XYZ Affair. Angry crowds and critics were after France, but Adams kept a cool head and resisted popular pressure for war. It may have lost him the presidency in 1800, but Adams realized that a war with France could cost the country a great deal more. Still, the domestic struggle between Federalists and Republicans continued, and Thomas Jefferson brought the Republicans to the highest office in 1801.

Jefferson pledged a new direction in international relations, but confronted the same basic crisis. Anglo-French conflict intensified with the emergence of Napoleon Bonaparte as a powerful leader in France. As the war in Europe expanded in the 1800s, French and British policy toward the United States hardened. Jefferson pulled off a fortunate diplomatic coup when he purchased the Louisiana Territory from Napoleon in 1803. That dramatic land acquisition, however, failed to nudge the French or English to alter their positions on neutral shipping. The president tried a number of tactics to persuade the Europeans to respect U.S. neutrality, but he left office in 1809 with things much the same.

When James Madison became America's fourth president, he, too, pledged to follow a path of diplomatic neutrality. By 1812, however, that became untenable. English maritime actions, particularly the impressment of American seamen, had become impossible for many in the United States to accept. The government also had evidence that British military officers in Canada had armed Indians in the Ohio Valley and encouraged them to resist American settlement there. An angry, tough-minded Tenth Congress, known as the Warhawk Congress, called for action. They also sensed that the United States might take advantage of a war with England to seize territory in Canada and Florida (Spain owned Florida and was a British ally). Finally, the Republican president and Congress saw war with Britain as a clear test of Federalist "loyalty." Would their pro-British opponents support the conflict? On June 17, 1812, the United States declared war on Great Britain. Perhaps ill-advised, it drew to a close two decades of American neutrality.

Many in the United States (certainly not the Federalists) believed that their country had done everything diplomatically possible to protect American rights and principles. Three presidents had tried to follow Washington's "farewell wisdom." England had brought this war on itself.

NOTE

1. Thomas A. Bailey, *A Diplomatic History of the American People*, 10th ed. (Englewood Cliffs, NJ: Prentice-Hall, 1980), p. 91.

DOCUMENTS

2.1. George Washington's Neutrality Proclamation, April 22, 1793

In many respects, the Neutrality Proclamation established the first formal U.S. policy regarding European affairs and America's response to them. It laid the groundwork for more than a century of U.S. unilateral foreign policy and concern over "entanglements" in Europe's crises.

Whereas it appears that a state of war exists between Austria, Prussia, Sardinia, Great Britain, and the United Netherlands, of the one part, and France on the other; and the duty and interest of the United States require, that they should with sincerity and good faith adopt and pursue a conduct friendly and impartial toward the belligerent Powers.

I have therefore thought fit by these presents to declare the disposition of the United States to observe the conduct aforesaid towards those Powers respectfully; and to exhort and warn the citizens of the United States carefully to avoid all acts and proceedings whatsoever, which may in any manner tend to contravene such disposition.

And I do hereby also make known, that whatsoever of the citizens of the United States shall render himself liable to punishment or forfeiture under the law of nations, by committing, aiding, or abetting hostilities against any of the said Powers, or by carrying to any of them those articles which are deemed contraband by the modern usage of nations, will not receive the protection of the United States, against such punishment or forfeiture; and further, that I have given instructions to those officers, to whom it belongs, to cause prosecutions to be instituted against all persons, who shall, within the cognizance of the courts of the United States, violate the law of nations, with respect to the Powers at war, or any of them.

In testimony whereof, I have caused the seal of the United States of America to be affixed to these presents, and signed the same with my hand. Done at the city of Philadelphia, the twenty-second day of April, one thousand seven hundred and ninety-three, and of the Independence of the United States of America the seventeenth.

GEORGE WASHINGTON
April 22, 1793

Source: Ruhl J. Bartlett, ed., *The Record of American Diplomacy*, 4th ed. (New York: Alfred A. Knopf, 1964), p. 90.

2.2.   George Washington's Farewell Address, September 17, 1796

The Farewell Address deals with other issues besides foreign policy and is not reprinted in full here. The international affairs issues discussed in the president's address dwell considerably on the domestic need to avoid party politics in the conduct of diplomacy. Washington lays down the principle that "politics should cease at the water's edge." Additionally, the president restates the basic positions regarding neutrality that guided his policy toward the war in Europe.

To the People of the United States.
September 17th, 1796
Friends and Fellow-Citizens:
The period for a new election of a citizen, to administer the executive government of the United States, being not far distant, and the time actually arrived, when your thoughts must be employed designating the person, who is to be clothed with that important trust, it appears to me proper, especially as it may conduce to a more distinct expression of the public voice, that I should now apprize you of the resolution I have formed, to decline being considered among the number of those out of whom a choice is to be made.

The unity of Government, which constitutes you one people, is also now dear to you. It is justly so; for it is a main pillar in the edifice of your real independence, the support of your tranquillity at home, your peace abroad; of your safety; of your prosperity; of that very Liberty, which you so highly prize. But as it is easy to foresee, that, from different causes and from different quarters, much pains will be taken, many artifices employed, to weaken in your minds the conviction of this truth; as this is the point in your political fortress against which the batteries of internal and external enemies will be most constantly and actively (though often covertly and insidiously) directed, it is of infinite moment, that you should properly estimate the immense value of your national Union to your collective and individual happiness; that you should cherish a cordial, habitual, and immovable attachment to it; accustoming yourselves to think and speak of it as of the Palladium of your political safety and prosperity; watching for its preservation with jealous anxiety; discountenancing whatever may suggest even a suspicion, that it can in any event be abandoned; and indignantly frowning upon the first dawning of every attempt to alienate any portion of our country from the rest, or to enfeeble the sacred ties which now link together the various parts.

For this you have every inducement of sympathy and interest. Citizens, by birth or choice, of a common country, that country has a right to concentrate your affections. The name of american, which belongs to you, in your national capacity, must always exalt the just pride of Patriotism, more than any appellation derived from local discriminations. With slight shades of difference, you have the same religion, manners, habits, and political principles. You have in a common cause fought and triumphed together; the Independence and Liberty you possess are the work of joint counsels, and joint efforts, of common dangers, sufferings, and successes.

I have already intimated to you the danger of parties in the state, with particular reference to the founding of them on geographical discriminations. Let me now take a more comprehensive view, and warn you in the most solemn manner against the baneful effects of the spirit of party, generally.

This spirit, unfortunately, is inseparable from our nature, having its root in the strongest passions of the human mind. It exists under different shapes in all governments, more or less stifled, controlled, or repressed; but, in those of the popular form, it is seen in its greatest rankness, and is truly their worst enemy.

The alternate domination of one faction over another, sharpened by the spirit of revenge, natural to party dissension, which in different ages and countries has perpetrated the most horrid enormities, is itself a frightful despotism. But this leads at length to a more formal and permanent despotism. The disorders and miseries, which result, gradually incline the minds of men to seek security and repose in the absolute power of an individual; and sooner or later the chief of some prevailing faction, more able or more fortunate than his competitors, turns this disposition to the purposes of his own elevation, on the ruins of Public Liberty.

Without looking forward to an extremity of this kind, (which nevertheless ought not to be entirely out of sight,) the common and continual mischiefs of the spirit of party are sufficient to make it the interest and duty of a wise people to discourage and restrain it.

It serves always to distract the Public Councils, and enfeeble the Public Administration. It agitates the Community with ill-founded jealousies and false alarms; kindles the animosity of one part against another, foments occasionally riot and insurrection. It opens the door to foreign influence and corruption, which find a facilitated access to the government itself through the channels of party passions. Thus the policy and the will of one country are subjected to the policy and will of another.

There is an opinion, that parties in free countries are useful checks upon the administration of the Government, and serve to keep alive the spirit of Liberty. This within certain limits is probably true; and in Governments of a Monarchical cast, Patriotism may look with indulgence, if not with favor, upon the spirit of party. But in those of the popular character, in Governments purely elective, it is a spirit not to be encouraged. From their natural tendency, it is certain there will always be enough of that spirit for every salutary purpose. And, there being constant danger of excess, the effort ought to be, by force of public opinion, to mitigate and assuage it. A fire not to be quenched, it demands a uniform vigilance to prevent its bursting into a flame, lest, instead of warming, it should consume.

It is important, likewise, that the habits of thinking in a free country should inspire caution, in those intrusted with its administration, to confine themselves within their respective constitutional spheres, avoiding in the exercise of the powers of one department to encroach upon another. The spirit of encroachment tends to consolidate the powers of all the departments in one, and thus to create, whatever the form of government, a real despotism. A just estimate of that love of power, and proneness to abuse it, which predominates in the human heart, is sufficient to satisfy us of the truth of this position. The necessity of reciprocal checks in the exercise of political power, by dividing and distributing it into different depositories, and constituting each the Guardian of the Public Weal against invasions by the others, has been evinced by experiments ancient and modern; some of them in our country and under our own eyes. To preserve them must be as necessary as to institute them. If, in the opinion of the people, the distribution or modification of the constitutional powers be in any particular wrong, let it be corrected by an amendment in the way, which the constitution designates. But let there be no change by usurpation; for, though this, in one instance, may be the instrument of good, it is the customary weapon by which free governments are destroyed. The precedent must always greatly overbalance in permanent evil any partial or transient benefit, which the use can at any time yield.

Observe good faith and justice towards all Nations; cultivate peace and harmony with all. Religion and Morality enjoin this conduct; and can it be, that good policy does not equally enjoin it? It will be worthy of a free, enlightened, and, at no distant period, a great Nation, to give to mankind the magnanimous and too novel example of a people always guided by an exalted justice and benevolence. Who can doubt, that, in the course of time and things, the fruits of such a plan would richly repay any temporary advantages, which might be lost by a steady adherence to it? Can it be, that Providence has not connected the permanent felicity of a Nation with its Virtue? The experiment, at least, is recommended by every sentiment which ennobles human nature. Alas! is it rendered impossible by its vices?

In the execution of such a plan, nothing is more essential, than that permanent, inveterate antipathies against particular Nations, and passionate attachments for others, should be excluded; and that, in place of them, just and amicable feelings towards all should be cultivated. The Nation, which indulges towards another an habitual hatred, or an habitual fondness, is in some degree a slave. It is a slave to its animosity or to its affection, either of which is sufficient to lead it astray from its duty and its interest. Antipathy in one nation against another disposes each more readily to offer insult and injury, to lay hold of slight causes of umbrage, and to be haughty and intractable, when accidental or trifling occasions of dispute occur. Hence frequent collisions, obstinate, envenomed, and bloody contests. The Nation, prompted by ill-will and resentment, sometimes impels to war the Government, contrary to the best calculations of policy. The Government sometimes participates in the national propensity, and adopts through passion what reason would reject; at other times, it makes the animosity of the nation subservient to projects of hostility instigated by pride, ambition, and other sinister and pernicious motives. The peace often, sometimes perhaps the liberty, of Nations has been the victim.

So likewise, a passionate attachment of one Nation for another produces a variety of evils. Sympathy for the favorite Nation, facilitating the illusion of an imaginary common interest, in cases where no real common interest exists, and infusing into one the enmities of the other, betrays the former into a participation in the quarrels and wars of the latter, without adequate inducement or justification. It leads also to concessions to the favorite Nation of privileges denied to others, which is apt doubly to injure the Nation making the concessions; by unnecessarily parting with what ought to have been retained; and by exciting jealousy, ill-will, and a disposition to retaliate, in the parties from whom equal privileges are withheld. And it gives to ambitious, corrupted, or deluded citizens, (who devote themselves to the favorite nation,) facility to betray or sacrifice the interests of their own country, without odium, sometimes even with popularity; gilding, with the appearances of a virtuous sense of obligation, a commendable deference for public opinion, or a laudable zeal for public good, the base or foolish compliances of ambition, corruption, or infatuation.

As avenues to foreign influence in innumerable ways, such attachments are particularly alarming to the truly enlightened and independent Patriot. How many opportunities do they afford to tamper with domestic factions, to practise the arts of seduction, to mislead public opinion, to influence or awe the Public Councils! Such an attachment of a small or weak, towards a great and powerful nation, dooms the former to be the satellite of the latter.

Against the insidious wiles of foreign influence (I conjure you to believe me, fellow-citizens,) the jealousy of a free people ought to be constantly awake; since history and experience prove, that foreign influence is one of the most baneful foes of Republican Government. But that jeal-ousy, to be useful, must be impartial; else it becomes the instrument of the very influence to be avoided, instead of a defence against it. Excessive partiality for one foreign nation, and excessive dislike of another, cause those whom they actuate to see danger only on one side, and serve to veil and even second the arts of influence on the other. Real patriots, who may resist the intrigues of the favorite, are liable to become sus-pected and odious; while its tools and dupes usurp the applause and confidence of the people, to surrender their interests.

The great rule of conduct for us, in regard to foreign nations, is, in extending our commercial relations, to have with them as little political connexion as possible. So far as we have already formed engagements, let them be fulfilled with perfect good faith. Here let us stop.

Europe has a set of primary interests, which to us have none, or a very remote relation. Hence she must be engaged in frequent controversies, the causes of which are essentially foreign to our concerns. Hence, therefore, it must be unwise in us to implicate ourselves, by artificial ties, in the ordinary vicissitudes of her politics, or the ordinary combinations and collisions of her friendships or enmities.

Our detached and distant situation invites and enables us to pursue a different course. If we remain one people, under an efficient government, the period is not far off, when we may defy material injury from external annoyance; when we may take such an attitude as will cause the neu-trality, we may at any time resolve upon, to be scrupulously respected; when belligerent nations, under the impossibility of making acquisitions upon us, will not lightly hazard giving us provocation; when we may choose peace or war, as our interest, guided by justice, shall counsel.

Why forego the advantages of so peculiar a situation? Why quit our own to stand upon foreign ground? Why, by interweaving our destiny with that of any part of Europe, entangle our peace and prosperity in the toils of European ambition, rivalship, interest, humor, or caprice?

It is our true policy to steer clear of permanent alliances with any portion of the foreign world; so far, I mean, as we are now at liberty to do it; for let me not be understood as capable of patronizing infidelity to existing engagements. I hold the maxim no less applicable to public than to private affairs, that honesty is always the best policy. I repeat it, therefore, let those engagements be observed in their genuine sense. But, in my opinion, it is unnecessary and would be unwise to extend them.

Taking care always to keep ourselves, by suitable establishments, on a respectable defensive posture, we may safely trust to temporary alli-ances for extraordinary emergencies.

Harmony, liberal intercourse with all nations, are recommended by policy, humanity, and interest. But even our commercial policy should hold an equal and impartial hand; neither seeking nor granting exclusive favors or preferences; consulting the natural course of things; diffusing and diversifying by gentle means the streams of commerce, but forcing nothing; establishing, with powers so disposed, in order to give trade a stable course, to define the rights of our merchants, and to enable the government to support them, conventional rules of intercourse, the best that present circumstances and mutual opinion will permit, but temporary, and liable to be from time to time abandoned or varied, as experience and circumstances shall dictate; constantly keeping in view, that it is folly in one nation to look for disinterested favors from another; that it must pay with a portion of its independence for whatever it may accept under that character; that, by such acceptance, it may place itself in the condition of having given equivalents for nominal favors, and yet of being reproached with ingratitude for not giving more. There can be no greater error than to expect or calculate upon real favors from nation to nation. It is an illusion, which experience must cure, which a just pride ought to discard.

In offering to you, my countrymen, these counsels of an old and affectionate friend, I dare not hope they will make the strong and lasting impression I could wish; that they will control the usual current of the passions, or prevent our nation from running the course, which has hitherto marked the destiny of nations. But, if I may even flatter myself, that they may be productive of some partial benefit, some occasional good; that they may now and then recur to moderate the fury of party spirit, to warn against the mischiefs of foreign intrigue, to guard against the impostures of pretended patriotism; this hope will be a full recompense for the solicitude for your welfare, by which they have been dictated.

How far in the discharge of my official duties, I have been guided by the principles which have been delineated, the public records and other evidences of my conduct must witness to you and to the world. To myself, the assurance of my own conscience is, that I have at least believed myself to be guided by them.

In relation to the still subsisting war in Europe, my Proclamation of the 22d of April 1793, is the index to my Plan. Sanctioned by your approving voice, and by that of your Representatives in both Houses of Congress, the spirit of that measure has continually governed me, uninfluenced by any attempts to deter or divert me from it.

After deliberate examination, with the aid of the best lights I could obtain, I was well satisfied that our country, under all the circumstances of the case, had a right to take, and was bound in duty and interest to take, a neutral position. Having taken it, I determined, as far as should depend upon me, to maintain it, with moderation, perseverance, and firmness.

The considerations, which respect the right to hold this conduct, it is not necessary on this occasion to detail. I will only observe, that, according to my understanding of the matter, that right, so far from being denied by any of the Belligerent Powers, has been virtually admitted by all.

The duty of holding a neutral conduct may be inferred, without any thing more, from the obligation which justice and humanity impose on every nation, in cases in which it is free to act, to maintain inviolate the relations of peace and amity towards other nations.

The inducements of interest for observing that conduct will best be referred to your own reflections and experience. With me, a predominant motive has been to endeavour to gain time to our country to settle and mature its yet recent institutions, and to progress without interruption to that degree of strength and consistency, which is necessary to give it, humanly speaking, the command of its own fortunes.

Though, in reviewing the incidents of my administration, I am unconscious of intentional error, I am nevertheless too sensible of my defects not to think it probable that I may have committed many errors. Whatever they may be, I fervently beseech the Almighty to avert or mitigate the evils to which they may tend. I shall also carry with me the hope, that my Country will never cease to view them with indulgence; and that, after forty-five years of my life dedicated to its service with an upright zeal, the faults of incompetent abilities will be consigned to oblivion, as myself must soon be to the mansions of rest.

Relying on its kindness in this as in other things, and actuated by that fervent love towards it, which is so natural to a man, who views it in the native soil of himself and his progenitors for several generations; I anticipate with pleasing expectation that retreat, in which I promise myself to realize, without alloy, the sweet enjoyment of partaking, in the midst of my fellow-citizens, the benign influence of good laws under a free government, the ever favorite object of my heart, and the happy reward, as I trust, of our mutual cares, labors, and dangers.

George Washington

United States September 17th, 1796

Source: Ruhl J. Bartlett, ed., *The Record of American Diplomacy*, 4th ed. (New York: Alfred A. Knopf, 1964), pp. 86–88.

2.3. Thomas Jefferson to Thomas Pinckney, November 1796

In November 1796, Thomas Jefferson wrote to Thomas Pinckney of South Carolina giving his impression of the problems that Citizen Genet caused within the administration.

The [yellow] fever [epidemic] which at the time has given alarm in Philadelphia became afterward far more destructive than had been apprehended, & continued much longer from the uncommon drought & warmth of the autumn. The 1st day of this month . . . began the first rains which had fallen for some months. They were copious, & from that moment the . . . disease terminated most suddenly. The inhabitants who had left the city, are now all returned, & business going on again as briskly as ever. . . .

Our negotiations with the Northwestern Indians have completely failed, so that war must settle our difference. We expected nothing else, & had gone into the negotiations only to prove to all our citizens that peace was unattainable on terms which any one of them would admit.

You have probably heard of a great misunderstanding between Mr. Genet & us. On the meeting of Congress it will be made public. . . . We have kept it merely personal, convinced his nation [France] will disapprove him. To them [the French] we have with the utmost assiduity given every proof of inviolate attachment. We wish to hear from you on the subject of M. de la Fayette, tho we know that circumstances [the increasing radicalism of the French Revolution, which put the lives of moderates like Lafayette in danger] do not admit sanguine hopes.

Source: Andrew Libscomb, ed., *The Writings of Thomas Jefferson*, vol. 9 (Washington, DC: Government Printing Office, 1903), p. 349.

2.4.   George Washington to Jonathan Trumbull, July 1799

In an interesting letter dated July 21, 1799, five months before his death, George Washington wrote to his former personal secretary, Governor Jonathan Trumbull of Connecticut, regarding Jefferson's Republicans and attempts on the part of the French to use that faction's pro-French sympathies to influence domestic politics in the United States.

No well informed and unprejudiced man, who has viewed with attention the conduct of the French Government since the Revolution in that Country, can mistake its objects, or the tendency of the ambitious projects it is pursuing. Yet, strange as it may seem, a party, and a powerful one too, among us, affect to believe that the measures of it are dictated by a principle of self preservation; that the outrages of which the Directory [the governing body in France] are guilty, proceed from dire necessity; that it wishes to be upon the most friendly & amicable terms with the

United States; that it will be the fault of the latter if this is not the case; that the defensive measures which this country has adopted, are necessary & expensive, but have a tendency to produce the evil which, to deprecate, is mere pretense in the Government; because War with France they say, is its wish; that on the Militia shd. Rest our security; and that it is time enough to call upon these, when the danger is imminent & apparent.

With these, and such like ideas, attempted to be inculcated upon the public mind (aided by prejudices not yet eradicated) and with art and sophistry, which regard neither truth nor decency; attacking every character; without respect to persons, Public or Private, who happen to differ from themselves in Politics, I leave you to decide the probability of carrying such an extensive plan of defense as you have suggested in your last letter into operation; and in the short period which you have supposed may be allowed to accomplish it in.

I come now, my dear Sir, to pay particular attention to that part of your Letter which respects myself. . . .

Let that party [Jeffersonian Republicans] set up a broomstick, and call it a true son of Liberty, a Democrat, or give it any other epithet that will suit their purpose, and it will command their votes in toto! Will not the Federalists meet, or rather defend their cause on the opposite ground? Surely they must, or they will discover a want of Policy, indicative of weakness & pregnant of mischief, which cannot be admitted. Wherein then would lye the difference between the present Gentlemen in Office and Myself?

It would be a matter of sore regret to me, if I could believe that a serious thought was turned towards me as his successor; not only as it respects my ardent wishes to pass through the vale of life in retirement undisturbed in the remnant of the days I have to sojourn here. Unless called upon to defend my country (which every citizen is bound to do), but on Public ground also; for although I have abundant cause to be thankful for the good health with which I am blessed, yet I am not insensible to my declination in other respects. It would be criminal therefore for me, although it should be the wish of my Countrymen, and I could be elected, to accept an Office under this conviction, which another would discharge with more ability. . . . That I should not draw a single vote from the Antifederalist side; and of course, should stand upon no stronger grounds than any other federal character well supported; & when I should become a mark for the shafts of envenomed malice, and the basest calumny to fire at; when I should be charged not only with irresolution, but with concealed ambition, which wants only an occasion to blaze out, and, in short, with dotage and imbecility.

Source: John C. Fitzpatrick, ed., *The Writings of George Washington*, vol. 7 (Washington, DC: Government Printing Office, 1940), p. 312.

2.5.   John Adams to Benjamin Rush, September 1807

In September 1807, former President John Adams wrote Dr. Benjamin Rush a letter critical of Jefferson's policies on British impressment of American seamen. The letter reflects the broad New England, Federalist dissatisfaction with Republican foreign policy.

War? Or No War? That is the question. Our Monarchical, anti-republican administration conceal from us, the People, all that Information which I a zealous Republican was always prompt to communicate. . . . If an express stipulation is demanded . . . that our Flag on board Merchant as well as Ships of War shall protect all British subjects; Deserters from their Navy and all others, I will apprehend the English will not agree to it. . . . Prudence would dictate that our government should forbid all its Naval officers to recruit a Deserter from any Nation, in any case; and if the President has not the power to enact it, Congress should enact it. But our People have such a Predilection for Runaways of every description except Runaway Negroes that I suppose Congress would think it too unpopular to abridge this right of man. How we will get out of this Scrape I know not . . . tho' I carry the Principle by the Law of Nations, to as great an extent as Mr. Jefferson does. If the English fly into a Passion and with or without declaring War Seize every ship and Cargo we have at Sea, I don't believe our present Congress would declare War against them. I am sure they cannot consistently, with their avowed system . . . defend Nothing but our Farms.

Source: The Works of John Adams, vol. 9 (Freeport, NY: Books for Libraries Press, 1969), pp. 600–601.

3

The Monroe Doctrine: The United States and the Hemisphere

The American continents . . . are henceforth not to be considered as subjects for future colonization by any European powers.

—James Monroe
State of the Union Message, December 1823

Go West Young Man!

—Horace Greeley
Editor, *New York Tribune*, 1867

In December 1814, the Peace of Ghent ended the War of 1812, and the
United States subsequently experienced a generation of peace and prosperity. A surge of nationalism marked the decade immediately following
the war. That sentiment helped prompt President James Monroe's famous 1823 State of the Union message to Congress that included what
became known as the Monroe Doctrine. At the same time, the United
States began to expand westward, a migration that supporters justified
broadly as Manifest Destiny. Both the Monroe Doctrine and Manifest
Destiny evolved as complementary parts of a key principle in America's
relations with the international community in general and the Western
Hemisphere specifically.

The wars of the French Revolution and Napoleon (1792–1814) produced explosive results in Latin America. Most of Spain's colonies rebelled against their mother country, and, at the end of the Napoleonic

Wars, revolutionary leaders fought vigorously to win their independence all across Latin America.

At the Congress of Vienna (1815), the major European powers met to decide the postwar fate of their continent, and they examined the rebellions in the Western Hemisphere against Spain as a minor part of that discussion. Alexander I, the Russian tsar, proposed a Holy Alliance of monarchs seeking to restore the "Old Order," a phrase that defined broadly a return to pre-republican, aristocratic authority. In simple terms, it sought the elimination of any of the republican, nationalistic, or liberal ideas created as a result of the American Revolution, and particularly the French Revolution.

With Spain locked in a battle with its colonies in Latin America, some of the European monarchs considered a joint military venture to restore Ferdinand VII, the Spanish king, as the rightful ruler of his rebellious territories. To that end, they sought the support of Britain, which saw little benefit to restoring Spain as ruler of South America. That would harm British commercial interests in the region. The English planned to develop profitable trade with the independent nations, and a restored Spanish monopoly would block English access to Latin American markets.

In August 1823, the British foreign minister, George Canning, asked Richard Rush, the U.S. minister in London, whether America might side with Great Britain in a joint declaration warning the Europeans to stay out of Latin America. It appeared an odd suggestion considering previous Anglo-American relations, but it flattered Rush. The U.S. minister sent the request to Washington, where the idea also impressed President Monroe. Secretary of State John Quincy Adams, however, disagreed. In his famous conclusion, Adams suggested that the United States should not "come in as a cock-boat in the wake of the British man-of-war."[1] He argued for a *unilateral* U.S. response, one not tied to England.

Adams recognized that his country would seem a weak partner in any Anglo-American statement. He guessed, too, that Europe would prove unable to reclaim Spain's colonies in any event. The secretary of state also determined, correctly, that England would use naval force to prevent a European move into Latin America no matter what the United States did or failed to do. Finally, other concerns besides Latin America were involved. Adams wanted to warn the Russians, who had a colony in Alaska, to forego any southward movement of their own. For all of those reasons, the secretary of state convinced President Monroe to announce a unilateral U.S. position in his December 1823 State of the Union message.

In clear terms, the president's statements "closed" the Western Hemisphere to further European colonization or territorial acquisition of any kind. The Americas would no longer serve as a hunting ground for the ambitions of the Old World. Monroe also stated that the United States would avoid involvement in European affairs. As in the past, policy expressed an Old World–New World dichotomy that perceived the Western Hemisphere, and America's special role in it, as exceptional. It seemed a prideful warning, one that U.S. postwar nationalism helped stimulate. Whether anyone believed the United States had the military power to stop a combined European venture remained dubious. It didn't matter. Monroe's doctrine resounded positively throughout the nation, even while Europeans attacked its arrogance and questioned its sincerity.

Unknown to either Monroe or Adams, the French government had already informed Britain that it would take no role in any European coalition involving Latin America. The Polignac Memorandum (October 1823) had circulated through the courts of Europe and effectively ended any possibility of a military alliance to help Spain.

In Europe, critics attacked the president's remarks as ineffective, cowardly, and stupid. Major newspapers editorialized that the United States remained unable to enforce the policy and would hide behind a wall of British ships. It appeared just the type of statement that a young, arrogant country might make—thoughtless and inappropriate.

In fact, Tsar Alexander I considered challenging Monroe's warning in 1824, but reconsidered, faced with Britain's disapproval. French and British diplomats dismissed America's arrogance as immature. Yet, except in minor ways, the European powers never challenged the president's toothless warning, and the concept that Monroe had pronounced in December slowly grew to encompass a major U.S. policy regarding the Western Hemisphere.

While most Americans supported the president's announcement, for both patriotic and practical reasons, some attacked Monroe for meddling in affairs that were none of the country's business. They argued, too, that rash, unenforceable threats created potential dangers if challenged. Yet, in the 1820s, a decade of political stability in foreign policy, few serious domestic challenges developed. Most Americans saw the hemisphere, Europe, and America in terms similar to those expressed in Monroe's message.

The Latin American reaction proved ambivalent. U.S. support and recognition exhilarated the new governments, but that attitude was dampened somewhat when Secretary Adams refused to consider any kind of defensive alliance with those nations. Additionally, Simon Bolivar expressed concern about U.S. intentions and advantages. The noted Venezuelan revolutionary leader, El Liberator, did not trust the United States. Bolivar envisioned some form of Pan-American goal that might draw the Hispanic peoples of the hemisphere into a confederation to advance and protect their interests. To him, the North Americans did not belong in that coalition. Predominantly Anglo and Protestant, the United States lacked cultural and historic similarity with its neighbors to the south. With a head start as a government and a nation, the United States also posed a threat to the new Hispanic states. The United States failed to attend the Panama Conference in 1826, a meeting designed to consider Pan-American unity. Ongoing diplomatic discussions made clear that the Monroe Doctrine aimed to protect U.S. interests more than those of its neighbors. Bolivar's concerns proved accurate.

Ultimately, the Monroe Doctrine sought to define U.S. self-interest in the hemisphere. Once again, concern about Europe's threat to American security provoked the president's message. A European coalition that restored Spain's control of Latin America would surely harm those revolutionaries, but it would also threaten U.S. economic and security objectives as well. Then, too, if Russia extended its Alaskan colony south toward Oregon and California, that would block any further American expansion toward the Pacific Coast. If criticisms came, they remained principally foreign in origin. Very few Americans saw Monroe's policy as anything less than a pronouncement of an emerging sphere of influence for the United States.

The United States failed to enforce or even refer to President Monroe's policy statement until 1865. Europeans even violated its warnings on occasion. For the most part, however, the grand design of restoring Ferdinand VII collapsed. The former Spanish colonies emerged as more than a dozen new nations. Britain became a major commercial force in the region, and the United States turned to territorial expansion in North America. Bolivar's concern lingered and escalated. Throughout the nineteenth century, the United States sought aggressively to establish a sphere of influence in the Western Hemisphere to include both commercial and national security hegemony. Some evidence suggests that Secretary Adams, President Monroe, and other American policy makers had that in mind from the start. In the early 1800s, however, territorial expansion dominated their thinking.

Manifest Destiny, an American belief that God had ordained the nation to spread across the continent, served as the flip side of the Monroe Doctrine. In that respect, it acted as the basis for, and the ongoing application of, the idea that President Monroe had stated in 1823. If the president forbade Europeans to acquire new colonies, nothing blocked U.S. territorial ambitions. In point of belief, God required territorial expansion. The roots of the idea, along with many principles of American thought, grew in the colonial era—a land "ordained by God" for righteous settlers. Again, the fundamental idea of "exceptionalism" and America's special purpose motivated deep convictions in the view of policy makers. So, too, did the more prosaic interests in economic growth and profit. It always seems beneficial when God and self-interest work together!

By the early 1800s, with the acquisition of the Louisiana Territory, the concept took clearer form. In February 1819 (Adams-Onis Treaty), the United States purchased Florida from Spain. With all its territory east of the Mississippi River secured, America looked west for more. Neither Indian peoples, European plans, nor Mexican sovereignty blocked the coming migration. Between 1820 and 1850, the United States secured control of the transcontinental United States, while American policy makers defined and defended the action in terms of Manifest Destiny under the rubric of the Monroe Doctrine.

Who else deserved the land? Not Indians—they failed to use the land "properly." Certainly not Europeans—the Old World–New World divider made their claims unjustified. Americans seemed the only people able to spread democracy and freedom across the broad continent. Whether the United States violated treaties, made war, or negotiated legitimate purchases, nothing would stop its drive for territory.

Both then and now, observers have questioned the motivation and ethics of U.S. expansion between 1815 and 1850. Most European diplomats viewed America's position with regard to Manifest Destiny as arrogant and self-serving. While a number of European states showed interest in challenging U.S. territorial expansion, none did so. Between the 1820s and the 1840s, America and Great Britain resolved touchy boundary disputes along the U.S.-Canadian border. For years, those concerns had damaged Anglo-American relations, but by mid-century treaties had ended the possibility of a major confrontation.

Threats that Russia, France, or some other nation might block Manifest Destiny diminished and disappeared. Europeans may have thought American policy arrogant, but it worked, because the Old World found itself focused on other concerns. If President Monroe and Secretary Adams failed to see that specific protection in 1823, they certainly understood its implications. Europeans always seemed to stew in their own crises, and America generally benefited from those squabbles by staying out of them.

U.S. attitudes regarding Indian peoples saw the various tribes as independent states and dealt with them "diplomatically." Americans showed a callous disregard for Indian rights throughout the era of expansion and violated treaties cavalierly. While at the time few critics questioned those violations, some did. Even the U.S. Supreme Court ruled in favor of the Cherokee Indians. In *Cherokee Nation v. Georgia* (1831) and *Worcester v. Georgia* (1832), Chief Justice John Marshall challenged the Indian Removal Act (1830), which expropriated Cherokee land. Unfortunately, President Andrew Jackson refused to back the Court's action. The government moved the tribe to "Indian territory" (in the present state of Oklahoma). If it suited U.S. interests, treaties and ethics be damned!

Expansion of the United States, 1783–1898

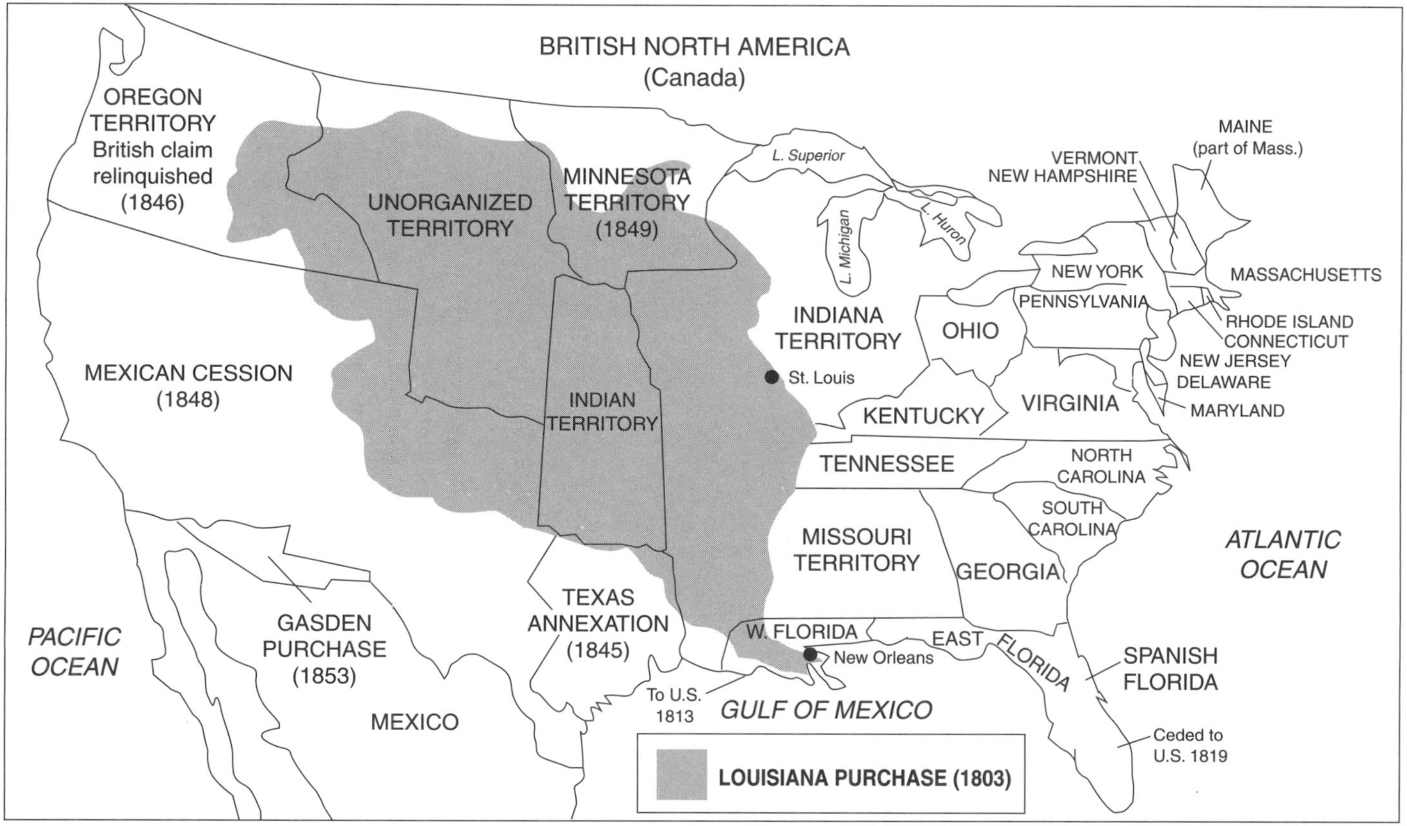

As the United States expanded westward and came into conflict with Mexico, the self-serving quality of the Monroe Doctrine and Manifest Destiny crystallized. Texas independence, in 1836, and American annexation of that former Mexican province in 1845, laid bare U.S. interests in its own growth. The issue, however, created a serious dispute in Congress.

Antislavery advocates in the North saw the Texas annexation as an attempt on the part of slaveholders to extend their power westward. The Missouri Compromise of 1820 limited squabbles over slavery's expansion into the western territories by drawing a line across the continent at 36°30′. If Texas, below that line, were carved into several new slave states, that would enable proslavery defenders to add congressmen and senators in increased numbers to the battle. As a result, antislavery politicians blocked the annexation of Texas for almost a decade as the domestic debate over expansion continued.

When James K. Polk assumed the presidency in 1845, American strategy sought to incorporate California as well as resolve a boundary dispute in Oregon with Great Britain. The United States hoped to create a transcontinental nation. Polk resolved the Oregon boundary peacefully, but when he tried to buy California from Mexico, that diplomatic bid failed. Promptly, with both sides spoiling for a fight, the United States provoked a war with Mexico.

Angry critics challenged Polk's decision. Abraham Lincoln, a junior Whig congressman from Illinois, attacked the president and hinted that Polk had caused the unnecessary conflict. Henry David Thoreau went to jail rather than pay a tax to support what he considered an unjust war. The antiwar, anti-expansion protest, however, failed to block the conclusion of a successful U.S. war. In March 1848, Mexico signed the Treaty of Guadalupe Hidalgo, ceding California and large areas of the Southwest to the United States.

Ironically, America's victory reheated a domestic confrontation that ignited the slow fuse toward the Civil War. Throughout the nineteenth century, the domestic debate over slavery evolved into a regional struggle of increasing emotion and resolve. Northerners grew to oppose the extension of slavery westward, while proslavery Southerners demanded access to the frontier. When Representative David Wilmot, a Pennsylvania Democrat, introduced a resolution in 1846 to do away with the Missouri Compromise line and ban slavery in any of the territory gained in the Mexican War, the struggle began anew. The resultant Compromise of 1850 pleased few and led many Southerners to consider secession as an alternative to what they feared was increased abolitionist authority in the government.

The ongoing debate over slavery even had significance when some proslavery advocates sought to annex territory in Central America and the Caribbean. While business interests in the Northeast, led by a New York financier, Cornelius Vanderbilt, hoped to expand trade markets in Latin America, they saw no real interest in territorial acquisition there. While Americans moved west, debating the extension of slavery, they also argued over the question of territory versus trade in Central America and the Caribbean.

Ultimately, the business position won. After the war with Mexico, the United States resisted any further major land acquisition (with the exception of Alaska). At the same time, U.S. commercial expansion in Latin America exploded in the last half of the 1800s. The functional sense of the Monroe Doctrine and Manifest Destiny had merged. As America grew stronger following the Civil War, it would come to view the hemisphere as a U.S. sphere of influence for both commercial and security reasons. The nation had the territory it needed. It would then consolidate its economic and security position within the framework of the Monroe Doctrine as it chose to define that 1823 pronouncement.

NOTE

1. Thomas A. Bailey, *A Diplomatic History of the American People*, 10th ed. (Englewood Cliffs, NJ: Prentice-Hall, 1980), p. 182.

DOCUMENTS

3.1. Letter from George Canning, British Foreign Secretary, to Richard Rush, United States Minister to Great Britain, August 20, 1823

Following the Napoleonic Wars, British interests hoped to expand their trade and commerce into increasing global markets. If the Latin American colonies could secure their independence from Spain, the English could trade manufactured goods for raw resources in a profitable environment. If Spain, with European help, reclaimed its colonies, the Spanish would block English access to that market. Canning's motivations, then, seemed purely self-serving. Yet, he wanted the United States to join Great Britain to add some hint of propriety to the policy.

My Dear Sir:

Before leaving Town, I am desirous of bringing before you in a more distinct, but still in an unofficial and confidential, shape, the question which we shortly discussed the last time that I had the pleasure of seeing you.

Is not the moment come when our Governments might understand each other as to the Spanish American Colonies? And if we can arrive at such an understanding, would it not be expedient for ourselves, and beneficial for all the world, that the principles of it should be clearly settled and plainly avowed? For ourselves we have no disguise.

1. We conceive the recovery of the Colonies by Spain to be hopeless.

2. We conceive the question of the recognition of them, as Independent States, to be one of time and circumstances.

3. We are, however, by no means disposed to throw any impediment in the way of an arrangement between them, and the mother country by amicable negotiation.

4. We aim not at the possession of any portion of them ourselves.

5. We could not see any portion of them transferred to any other Power, with indifference.

If these opinions and feelings are as I firmly believe them to be, common to your Government with ours, why should we hesitate mutually to confide them to each other; and to declare them in the face of the world?

If there be any European Power which cherishes other projects, which looks to a forcible enterprize for reducing the Colonies to subjugation, on the behalf or in the name of Spain; or which meditates the acquisition of any part of them to itself, by cession or by conquest; such a declaration on the part of your government and ours would be at once the most effectual and the least offensive mode of intimating our joint disapprobation of such projects.

It would at the same time put an end to all the jealousies of Spain with respect to her remaining Colonies—and to the agitation which prevails in those Colonies, an agitation which it would be but humane to allay; being determined (as we are) not to profit by encouraging it.

Do you conceive that under the power which you have recently received, you are authorized to enter into negotiation, and to sign any Convention upon this subject? Do you conceive, if that be not within your competence, you could exchange with me ministerial notes upon it?

Nothing could be more gratifying to me than to join with you in such a work, and, I am persuaded, there has seldom, in the history of the world, occurred an opportunity when so small an effort, of two friendly Governments, might produce so unequivocal a good and prevent such extensive calamities.

I shall be absent from London but three weeks at the utmost: but never so far distant but that I can receive and reply to any communication, within three or four days.

Source: Ruhl J. Bartlett, ed., *The Record of American Diplomacy*, 4th ed. (New York: Alfred A. Knopf, 1964), pp. 173–174.

3.2.   John Quincy Adams's Notes on November 7, 1823, Cabinet Meeting

---

Secretary Adams had a clear sense of what motivated Canning's letter. His conclusion to go it alone stemmed from a realization that the world community would see the United States as a second-class participant in a joint Anglo-American statement. Additionally, the idea to offer a unilateral policy expressed Adams's sense of nationalism and his desire to continue the separation that existed between Europe and America.

Washington, November 7th.—Cabinet meeting at the President's from halfpast one till four. Mr. Calhoun, Secretary of War, and Mr. Southard, Secretary of the Navy, present. The subject for consideration was, the confidential proposals of the British Secretary of State, George Canning, to R. Rush, and the correspondence between them relating to the projects of the Holy Alliance upon South America. There was much conversation, without coming to any definite point. The object of Canning appears to have been to obtain some public pledge from the Government of the United States, ostensibly against the forcible interference of the Holy Alliance between Spain and South America; but really or especially against the acquisition to the United States themselves of any part of the Spanish American possessions.

Mr. Calhoun inclined to giving a discretionary power to Mr. Rush to join in a declaration against the interference of the Holy Allies, if necessary, even if it should pledge us not to take Cuba or the province of Texas; because the power of Great Britain being greater than ours to seize upon them, we should get the advantage of obtaining from her the same declaration we should make ourselves. I thought the cases not parallel. We have no intention of seizing either Texas or Cuba. But the inhabitants of either or both may exercise their primitive rights, and solicit a union with us. They will certainly do no such thing to Great Britain. By joining with her, therefore, in her proposed declaration, we give her a substantial and perhaps inconvenient pledge against ourselves, and really obtain nothing in return. Without entering now into the enquiry of the expediency of our annexing Texas or Cuba to our Union, we should at least keep ourselves free to act as emergencies may arise, and not tie ourselves down to any principle which might immediately afterwards be brought to bear against ourselves. Mr. Southard inclined much to the same opinion.

The President was averse to any course which should have the appearance of taking a position subordinate to that of Great Britain. . . .

I remarked that the communications recently received from the Russian Minister, Baron Tuyl, afforded, as I thought, a very suitable and convenient opportunity for us to take our stand against the Holy Alliance, and at the same time to decline the overture of Great Britain. It would be more candid, as well as more dignified, to avow our principles explicitly to Russia and France, than to come in as a cock-boat in the wake of the British man-of-war.

This idea was acquiesced in on all sides, and my draft for an answer to Baron Tuyl's note announcing the Emperor's determination to refuse receiving any Minister from the South American Governments was read.

Source: Charles F. Adams, ed., *The Memoirs of John Quincy Adams*, vol. 6 (Freeport, NY: Books for Libraries Press, 1969), pp. 177–180.

3.3.   The Monroe Doctrine, December 2, 1823

*President Monroe's remarks were a minor aspect of his broad
State of the Union message, and, at the time, had little impact on
American public opinion. The significance of the Monroe Doctrine emerged as U.S. influence and power evolved in the last
half of the 1800s.*

... At the proposal of the Russian Imperial Government, made
through the minister of the Emperor residing here, a full power and
instructions have been transmitted to the minister of the United States
at St. Petersburg to arrange by amicable negotiation the respective rights
and interests of the two nations on the northwest coast of this continent.
A similar proposal has been made by His Imperial Majesty to the Government of Great Britain, which has likewise been acceded to. The Government of the United States has been desirous by this friendly
proceeding of manifesting the great value which they have invariably
attached to the friendship of the Emperor and their solicitude to cultivate
the best understanding with his Government. In the discussions to which
this interest has given rise and in the arrangements by which they may
terminate the occasion has been judged proper for asserting, as a principle in which the rights and interests of the United States are involved,
that the American continents, by the free and independent condition
which they have assumed and maintain, are henceforth not to be considered as subjects for future colonization by any European powers. ...

It was stated at the commencement of the last session that a great effort
was then making in Spain and Portugal to improve the condition of the
people of those countries, and that it appeared to be conducted with
extraordinary moderation. It need scarcely be remarked that the results
have been so far very different from what was then anticipated. Of
events in that quarter of the globe, with which we have so much intercourse and from which we derive our origin, we have always been anxious and interested spectators. The citizens of the United States cherish
sentiments the most friendly in favor of the liberty and happiness of their
fellow-men on that side of the Atlantic. In the wars of the European
powers in matters relating to themselves we have never taken any part,
nor does it comport with our policy to do so. It is only when our rights
are invaded or seriously menaced that we resent injuries or make preparation for our defense. With the movements in this hemisphere we are
of necessity more immediately connected, and by causes which must be
obvious to all enlightened and impartial observers. The political system
of the allied powers is essentially different in this respect from that of

America. This difference proceeds from that which exists in their respective Governments; and to the defense of our own, which has been achieved by the loss of so much blood and treasure, and matured by the wisdom of their most enlightened citizens, and under which we have enjoyed unexampled felicity, this whole nation is devoted. We owe it, therefore, to candor and to the amicable relations existing between the United States and those powers to declare that we should consider any attempt on their part to extend their system to any portion of this hemisphere as dangerous to our peace and safety. With the existing colonies or dependencies of any European power we have not interfered and shall not interfere. But with the Governments who have declared their independence and maintain it, and whose independence we have, on great consideration and on just principles, acknowledged, we could not view any interposition for the purpose of oppressing them, or controlling in any other manner their destiny, by any European power in any other light than as the manifestation of an unfriendly disposition toward the United States. In the war between those new Governments and Spain we declared our neutrality at the time of their recognition, and to this we have adhered, and shall continue to adhere, provided no change shall occur which, in the judgement of the competent authorities of this Government, shall make a corresponding change on the part of the United States indispensable to their security.

The late events in Spain and Portugal show that Europe is still unsettled. Of this important fact no stronger proof can be adduced than that the allied powers should have thought it proper, on any principle satisfactory to themselves, to have interposed by force in the internal concerns of Spain. To what extent such interposition may be carried, on the same principle, is a question in which all independent powers whose governments differ from theirs are interested, even those most remote, and surely none of them more so than the United States. Our policy in regard to Europe, which was adopted at an early stage of the wars which have so long agitated that quarter of the globe, nevertheless remains the same, which is, not to interfere in the internal concerns of any of its powers; to consider the government de facto as the legitimate government for us; to cultivate friendly relations with it, and to preserve those relations by a frank, firm, and manly policy, meeting in all instances the just claims of every power, submitting to injuries from none. But in regard to those continents circumstances are eminently and conspicuously different. It is impossible that the allied powers should extend their political system to any portion of either continent without endangering our peace and happiness; nor can anyone believe that our southern brethren, if left to themselves, would adopt it of their own accord. It is equally impossible, therefore, that we should behold such interposition in any form with indifference. If we look to the comparative strength and resources of Spain and those new Governments, and their distance from each other, it must be obvious that she can never subdue them. It is still the true policy of the United States to leave the parties to themselves, in hope that other powers will pursue the same course. . . .

Source: Ruhl J. Bartlett, ed., *The Record of American Diplomacy*, 4th ed. (New York: Alfred A. Knopf, 1964), pp. 181–183.

3.4.　Response by Prince von Metternich, Prime Minister of Austria, to President Monroe's Message, January 19, 1824

Klemens von Metternich, the Austrian minister, represented and spoke for the reality of the Old Regime following the Napoleonic Wars. He was one of the principal architects of the plan to support Ferdinand VII's bid to reclaim Spanish colonies in Latin America with European support. His note to Count Karl Robert Nesselrode, in St. Petersburg, reflects the general disdain and distrust he and other European conservatives had for republicanism in general and its dangerous reflection in the Monroe Doctrine.

These United States we have seen arise and grow, and which during their short youth already mediated projects which they dared not then avow, have suddenly left a sphere too narrow for their ambition, and have astonished Europe by a new act of revolt, more unprovoked, fully as audacious, and no less dangerous than the former. They have distinctly and clearly announced their intention to set not only power against power, but to express it more exactly, altar against altar. In their indecent declarations they have cast blame and scorn on the institutions of Europe most worthy of respect, on the principles of its greatest sovereigns, on the whole of those measures which a sacred duty no less than an evident necessity has forced our governments to adopt to frustrate plans most criminal. In permitting themselves these unprovoked attacks, in fostering revolutions wherever they show themselves, in regretting those which have failed, in extending a helping hand to those which seem to prosper, they lend new strength to the apostles of sedition, and reanimate the courage of every conspirator. If this flood of evil doctrines and pernicious examples should extend over the whole of America, what would become of our religious and political institutions, of the moral force of our governments, and of that conservative system which has saved Europe from complete dissolution?

Source: Dexter Perkins, *Hands Off: A History of the Monroe Doctrine* (Boston: Little, Brown, 1963), pp. 56–57.

3.5.   John L. O'Sullivan on Manifest Destiny, 1839

John L. O'Sullivan was a journalist whose editorials concerning territorial expansion came to symbolize the American sense of righteousness and conviction regarding the drive across the continent. If he did not invent the concept of Manifest Destiny, O'Sullivan certainly defined it for Americans in the 1800s. His position dovetailed neatly with both Monroe's policy statement and the broader elements of territorial acquisition. In a sense, he became the great "huckster" for the transcontinental movement.

The American people having derived their origin from many other nations, and the Declaration of National Independence being entirely based on the great principle of human equality, these facts demonstrate at once our disconnected position as regards any other nation; that we have, in reality, but little connection with the past history of any of them, and still less with all antiquity, its glories, or its crimes. On the contrary, our national birth was the beginning of a new history, the formation and progress of an untried political system, which separates us from the past and connects us with the future only; and so far as regards the entire development of the natural rights of man, in moral, political, and national life, we may confidently assume that our country is destined to be the great nation of futurity.

It is so destined, because the principle upon which a nation is organized fixes its destiny, and that of equality is perfect, is universal. It presides in all the operations of the physical world, and it is also the conscious law of the soul—the self-evident dictates of morality, which accurately defines the duty of man to man, and consequently man's rights as man. Besides, the truthful annals of any nation furnish abundant evidence, that its happiness, its greatness, its duration, were always proportionate to the democratic equality in its system of government. . . .

What friend of human liberty, civilization, and refinement, can cast his view over the past history of the monarchies and aristocracies of antiquity, and not deplore that they ever existed? What philanthropist can contemplate the oppressions, the cruelties, and injustice inflicted by them on the masses of mankind, and not turn with moral horror from the retrospect?

America is destined for better deeds. It is our unparalleled glory that we have no reminiscences of battle fields, but in defence of humanity, of the oppressed of all nations, of the rights of conscience, the rights of personal enfranchisement. Our annals describe no scenes of horrid carnage, where men were led on by hundreds of thousands to slay one another, dupes and victims to emperors, kings, nobles, demons in the human form called heroes. We have had patriots to defend our homes, our liberties, but no aspirants to crowns or thrones; nor have the American people ever suffered themselves to be led on by wicked ambition to depopulate the land, to spread desolation far and wide, that a human being might be placed on a seat of supremacy.

We have no interest in the scenes of antiquity, only as lessons of avoidance of nearly all their examples. The expansive future is our arena, and for our history. We are entering on its untrodden space, with the truths of God in our minds, beneficent objects in our hearts, and with a clear conscience unsullied by the past. We are the nation of human progress, and who will, what can, set limits to our onward march? Providence is with us, and no earthly power can. We point to the everlasting truth on the first page of our national declaration, and we proclaim to the millions of other lands, that "the gates of hell"—the powers of aristocracy and monarchy—"shall not prevail against it."

The far-reaching, the boundless future will be the era of American greatness. In its magnificent domain of space and time, the nation of many nations is destined to manifest to mankind the excellence of divine principles; to establish on earth the noblest temple ever dedicated to the worship of the Most High—the Sacred and the True. Its floor shall be a hemisphere—its roof the firmament of the star-studded heavens, and its congregation an Union of many Republics, comprising hundreds of happy millions, calling, owning no man master, but governed by God's natural and moral law of equality, the law of brotherhood—of "peace and good will amongst men." . . .

Yes, we are the nation of progress, of individual freedom, of universal enfranchisement. Equality of rights is the cynosure of our union of States, the grand exemplar of the correlative equality of individuals; and while truth sheds its effulgence, we cannot retrograde, without dissolving the one and subverting the other. We must onward to the fulfilment of our mission—to the entire development of the principle of our organization—freedom of conscience, freedom of person, freedom of trade and business pursuits, universality of freedom and equality. This is our high destiny, and in nature's eternal, inevitable decree of cause and effect we must accomplish it. All this will be our future history, to establish on earth the moral dignity and salvation of man—the immutable truth and beneficence of God. For this blessed mission to the nations of the world, which are shut out from the life-giving light of truth, has America been chosen; and her high example shall smite unto death the tyranny of kings, hierarchs, and oligarchs, and carry the glad tidings of peace and good will where myriads now endure an existence scarcely more enviable than that of beasts of the field. Who, then, can doubt that our country is destined to be the great nation of futurity?

Source: John L. O'Sullivan, "The Great Nation of Futurity," *United States Magazine and Democratic Review* 6 (November 1839): pp. 2–3, 6.

4

The *Trent* Affair: International Affairs during the Civil War

"It don't seem hardly right, John
When both my hands was full,
To stump me to a fight, John—
Your cousin, tu, John Bull!"

—James Russell Lowell
Poet

The Civil War was America's bloodiest conflict. Between April 1861 and April 1865, North and South suffered a million casualties fighting over union and slavery. While historians tend to focus on the significant battles of that struggle, international affairs played a key role in the outcome of the American Civil War.

When eleven Southern states seceded from the Union and established the Confederate States of America, they hoped to win recognition and support from European countries, particularly England and France. Those two nations used large amounts of Southern cotton for their textile industries. Many Confederate leaders believed that "King Cotton" would compel the two major powers to recognize and back the South, if only to keep their textile profits and employment expanding.

Abraham Lincoln, America's new president, worked to prevent that Confederate objective. To preserve the Union and defeat the "rebels," he acted to block foreign involvement or intervention, indeed, any outside interference in what he defined as a domestic rebellion against the legal authority of the United States. Northern policy, therefore, sought to keep England and France out of America's private conflict.

Around those two positions, a number of complex, tense issues developed that made unclear, until well into 1863, whether England or France would intervene in America's war. The *Trent* Affair served as an example of the kind of episode that defined the tension. Both before and after the event, it tended to explain the evolving positions of the various governments during the Civil War. The *Trent* Affair also suggested that in the field of foreign affairs, Union leadership responded to issues carefully and successfully.

On April 19, 1861, a week after Southerners fired on Fort Sumter, President Lincoln issued a Proclamation of Naval Blockade around the Southern states "in rebellion" against the Union. (Those states included Alabama, Florida, Georgia, Louisiana, Mississippi, South Carolina, and Texas. After the attack on Fort Sumter, Arkansas, North Carolina, Tennessee, and Virginia joined the Confederate States of America.) It seemed an odd policy decision. If, as the president claimed, the Confederates were rebels, they had no legal status, and therefore, what need was there to issue a blockade order? Yet, privateers and merchant vessels slipping out of Confederate ports concerned the North, as did the possibility that foreign vessels might ship arms and equipment into the Confederacy.

The blockade order produced two conflicting results. Britain and France honored the proclamation. But at the same time it enabled both European governments to recognize Confederate belligerency formally. International maritime convention did not require that a government issue formal blockade notices against rebels. Essentially, a rebellion remains an internal affair. The president's proclamation, therefore, made the status of the Confederacy unclear. Lincoln was pleased with European recognition of the blockade, but disturbed at Britain and France's recognition of the Confederacy as a belligerent.

Great Britain, particularly, planned to remain neutral, despite mixed public attitudes in the country, but self-protection required England to alert its vessels of the "war environment" defined as a result of the Union's official maritime blockade. Accordingly, the English announced, on May 6, 1861, that they would pursue a policy of neutrality, but recognize that the Confederate states had belligerent status. President Jefferson Davis, in his offices in Richmond, represented a "government."

Giving official status to the rebels angered public opinion in the North. Secretary of State William Seward and Charles Francis Adams, the U.S. minister in London, feared the next step might lead to formal English recognition of the Confederacy, followed by support in the form of arms and equipment.

The British policy elated the South, and President Davis instructed James M. Mason and John Slidell to sail for London and Paris, respectively, to begin diplomatic discussions there. Confederate leaders sensed that England's recognition of belligerency and its dependence on cotton created a favorable environment for positive discussions. Davis and others also believed that Napoleon III, the French monarch, had an even stronger interest in a pro-Confederate position. France was in the process of backing a government in Mexico that might revive French influence in the hemisphere. A weakened United States, split as a result of the Civil War, would only help that French effort.

Mason, a former U.S. senator, had served as chairman of the Foreign Affairs Committee. He seemed an experienced person well able to represent the Confederacy's views in England. Slidell had minimal diplomatic experience. He had served as James Polk's minister to Mexico prior to the Mexican War. But he was a friend of Davis and spoke French fluently. His assignment was to convince Napoleon to help the Confederacy.

The two men left Charleston, South Carolina, on October 12, eluding the Union blockade and arrived in the Bahama Islands. Hoping to find English vessels to transport them, they learned that the closest ships were in Cuba. Off they went. The two diplomats had to wait until November, when they finally arranged passage on the British mail ship *Trent*, bound for St. Thomas, then England.

While Mason and Slidell waited to sail, U.S. Navy Captain Charles Wilkes sailed into the Caribbean aboard the U.S.S. *San Jacinto*. After stops in Jamaica and the Grand Caymans, Wilkes cruised to Cuba and learned that two important Confederate diplomats were about to leave on the *Trent*. The Union officer decided to take them off the British mail ship when it left Spanish territorial waters. On November 8, 1861, the *San Jacinto* intercepted the English vessel and fired two shots across its bow, forcing the mail ship to stop. Wilkes ordered Lieutenant D. M. Fairfax to take a boarding party, find out if Mason and Slidell were aboard the *Trent*, and, if so, take them off it.

Fairfax confronted an angry British captain, James Moir, and a tense crew and passengers, many of them Southerners. After some heated verbal exchanges that threatened violence, Mason and Slidell agreed to leave the ship with Fairfax. Returning to the *San Jacinto*, the young officer faced a dissatisfied Wilkes, who wanted to seize the British ship as a prize of war. Instead, after a terse conversation with Fairfax, Wilkes allowed the *Trent* to depart, and the *San Jacinto* sailed for the United States with its prisoners.

Wilkes telegraphed news of the capture immediately. When newspapers began publishing the story, public opinion in the North heralded the officer as a new hero of the war. In Washington, enthusiasm initially greeted the incident. Lincoln's cabinet needed some good news after several military setbacks. Additionally, a degree of anti-British sentiment existed in the United States, and twisting the tail of the British lion always seemed to please Americans. That positive atmosphere changed, however, when the president and Secretary Seward realized that the *Trent* incident could provoke a serious diplomatic rupture with England. It did.

News of the *Trent* Affair reached London at the end of November. The British prime minister, Lord Palmerston, decided, with sound legal advice, that Wilkes had taken Mason and Slidell illegally, unless he had also seized the *Trent* itself and brought the ship to an American prize court to determine whether his actions were legal under maritime law. At a cabinet meeting, he yelled at a colleague, "[Y]ou may stand for this but damned if I will!"[1] British newspapers and the British public tended to agree with Palmerston. Editorial outrage and serious talk of war with the United States echoed through London. Britain reinforced its fleet in the Caribbean, and additional English troops sailed for Canada to buttress regiments along the border.

The fact that Wilkes had "kidnapped" Mason and Slidell from a neutral vessel sailing peacefully in international waters created the legal maritime issue. It was proper to stop such a ship and search it for contraband, and if such contraband existed, the ship could be hauled into an American port. One might make the argument that Mason and Slidell were contraband, but even so, Wilkes should not have removed them from the *Trent*. He should have taken the English ship to the United States for a prize court to decide the question. Legalisms aside, the *Trent* Affair also served as a sharp slap in the face to British pride and honor.

As England rattled its saber, the British cabinet drafted a tough ultimatum demanding the immediate release of Mason and Slidell and a formal diplomatic apology for Wilkes's actions. In Richmond, Southern leaders waited happily for the outbreak of war, a conflict that they recognized could only aid their cause. Unfortunately for the Confederacy, the tension began to ebb. Palmerston softened the ultimatum when Charles Francis Adams and Seward convinced him that Wilkes had acted independently, without Washington's knowledge or direction.

As much as Secretary Seward hated giving in to England, he realized that the Union had no choice. Neither government wanted war. On Christmas Day, President Lincoln drafted a note stating that Captain Wilkes had acted without the knowledge of the government in Washington. The note added that the *San Jacinto* had improperly failed to seize the *Trent*, making it impossible for a prize court in the United States to determine whether Wilkes had acted legally.

To preserve American pride, Seward added that his government would release Mason and Slidell, not as a result of British demands, but because of U.S. concern for maritime law, which Seward reminded the British that President James Madison had asked England to obey in 1804.

The secretary of state closed his note with a feisty challenge. "If the safety of this Union required the detention of the captured persons it would be the right and duty of this government to detain them."[2]

As the new year began, the *Trent* Affair moved off the front pages and out of cabinet rooms as a concern. The Confederacy had hoped the incident would provoke a confrontation, driving England and the North into war. But Lincoln, Seward, and Adams avoided the danger, regardless of the patriotic newspaper editorials around the country attacking British demands and calling for a tough response. Instead, they defused the crisis, even though Seward may have responded a bit too impudently in his note.

In the same vein, Prime Minister Palmerston suppressed his initial anger and finally toned down British demands. Again, the press in England called for tougher action against the "upstart Yankees," but Palmerston had no interest in a war with the United States. By the time Mason and Slidell finally arrived in London, Adams wrote to Seward that the incident had lost steam. Yet, the *Trent* Affair lingered as a concern in Anglo-American relations during the remainder of the Civil War. If another incident sparked a confrontation, it might fail to defuse as readily as this crisis had.

Battles between North and South made it clear that the war would continue to be destructive and indecisive. On September 17, 1862, the bloodiest one-day battle of the war occurred in the cornfields near Antietam Creek, Maryland. Over 4,000 men died and 18,000 fell wounded. The Union had turned back the South's first major invasion of the North. Its forces, however, failed to pursue the Confederate army of Robert E. Lee as he retreated back to Virginia. On the battlefield, bloody stalemate continued into 1863.

Prior to Antietam, Palmerston had considered an Anglo-French-Russian effort to mediate an end to the conflict in America. A series of earlier Southern victories, particularly the Second Battle of Bull Run (August 1862), convinced him that Europe had to intercede to end the slaughter. If the North refused the offer, he concluded, it would force England and France to recognize the Confederacy as an independent nation. Antietam changed Palmerston's mind. It persuaded him that the Union could win the war. The prime minister concluded, "We must continue merely to be lookers-on till the war shall have taken a more decided turn."[3]

Other factors had also begun to persuade England to maintain its neutrality policy. The threat that lack of Southern cotton would damage British and French industry never materialized. Both nations made strong profits in the cotton textile business. Some estimates suggest that 20–25 percent of those employed in the two countries worked in the industry. But in 1861, the European nations had a healthy surplus of raw cotton, and they began to develop new resources in Egypt and India.

At the same time, the farmers in the Northern states produced bumper crops of grain at a time of low harvests in Europe. Made available in the European market, Queen Wheat may have "seduced" King Cotton. The Union also purchased significant arms and munitions from British manufacturers during the Civil War. That added to an increased economic interest in Northern dollars, at the expense of Southern support. In the end, the Confederacy's total diplomatic commitment to King Cotton diplomacy failed.

Finally, a significant part of the public in Great Britain opposed the institution of slavery and could never justify supporting the Confederacy in any way. That antislavery element, however, remained perplexed that President Lincoln and the Union had taken no steps to free African American slaves.

Lincoln hesitated to act on abolishing slavery at the beginning of the Civil War for important reasons. He thought the issue of union a cause more apt to gain support for military action against the South, and he wanted to keep as many border states as possible loyal to his government. It worked. Delaware, Maryland, Missouri, and Kentucky, all slave states, stayed with the Union. The president's policy drew criticism, both at home and abroad.

In England and France, antislavery supporters could hardly argue for pro-Union neutrality for their cause when Lincoln had failed to address the issue. It became an embarrassment that led some to conclude that the president had no intention of eradicating the evil of slavery. English Liberal Party leaders like John Bright and Richard Cobden communicated regularly with Secretary Seward and prominent Northern abolitionists. They appeared confused and frustrated that the cause of the conflict in America focused so obviously on union rather than slavery. It made defending the North difficult in Britain and France.

The president began to think about an Emancipation Proclamation as early as the spring of 1862. He waited for events on the battlefield to provide a favorable opportunity. Antietam provided that timing. The *Trent* Affair had disappeared from the front pages, both at home and in Europe. No international or domestic storm clouds threatened. And, if his Army of the Potomac had failed to deliver a death blow to the Confederacy, it had at least won a key, if costly, victory.

Lincoln published a preliminary statement in September 1862, indicating his intention to act against slavery. That early draft may have had as much impact on European opinion as the formal statement later. After some careful drafting and internal debates within his own government, Lincoln issued the Emancipation Proclamation on January 1, 1863. Essentially, it freed slaves only in the states in rebellion against the government. An odd "law," a critic concluded. The president seemingly had liberated African Americans where he could not secure their actual freedom (in the Confederacy) and kept them enslaved where he could guarantee their freedom (in the border states). That irony served as the basis for an ongoing critique of the Emancipation Proclamation. Yet, in legal terms, it was unfair to Lincoln. The law protected slavery in the border states, and only an amendment to the Constitution could alter that condition. The Thirteenth Amendment, ratified in December 1865, did so.

Oddly, the president and Seward remained unaware that Palmerston had come close to accepting a French proposal to pressure the North and South to mediate an end to the Civil War. No evidence exists to suggest that Lincoln issued the Emancipation Proclamation to influence international relations, but pro-Union defenders in Palmerston's cabinet certainly used both Antietam and the Emancipation Proclamation to persuade the prime minister to stay the course of neutrality.

While a number of newspapers and abolitionists in England and France attacked Lincoln's belated and obviously political move, others reacted favorably to the Emancipation Proclamation. A series of public meetings took place in Great Britain, with leading antislavery spokesmen and women applauding the president's decision and condemning the Confederacy. In any event, as soon as Lincoln sensed that the issue had a significant influence in international affairs, he acted quickly to capitalize on his policy.

Throughout 1863, the president instructed Adams in London, and William Dayton, the U.S. minister in Paris, to explain and defend the action. Lincoln also enlisted the support of a number of key Northern business leaders who traveled to Europe and used their connections in London and Paris to discuss and applaud the president's policies. Lincoln may have arrived in Washington an inexperienced diplomat, but he possessed common sense and learned quickly. In similar fashion, Seward evolved as an effective, careful secretary of state after some initial mistakes and stubbornness. Adams and Dayton, too, served the Union cause intelligently and effectively.

The United States would confront other diplomatic issues, with both England and France, between 1863 and 1865. English manufacturers built a number of ships for the Confederacy that would cause damages leading to postwar U.S. claims against Great Britain. Napoleon backed a government in Mexico under the monarchy of Archduke Maximilian. The French sent troops to support the regime against Mexican "freedom fighters." Secretary Seward could not invoke the Monroe Doctrine while the Union focused on its own deadly struggle, but the United States would respond aggressively to the French threat in the hemisphere as soon as the Civil War ended. Neither of those issues disrupted the clear Union goal. Between 1861 and 1865, the United States maintained a blockade that hurt the Confederacy and avoided any effort on the part of England or France to intervene on the side of the South in the conflict. Neither by recognition and aid nor through forced mediation could Europe influence the outcome of the war.

The resolution of the *Trent* Affair, followed by Antietam and the Emancipation Proclamation, ended the serious possibility that any European state would try to use its influence to stop the war or support the South. Given all of the domestic and external variables—wheat versus cotton, antislavery attitudes, munitions purchases, and other factors—it appears, in some sense, that the Union also had better diplomats serving its interests. Neither Jefferson Davis nor Judah P. Benjamin, the Confederacy's secretary of state, possessed the personal style or ability to counter Lincoln and Seward. And the South had no diplomats in Europe to compare with Adams or Dayton. Mason and Slidell finally arrived in London and Paris, but they remained unable to counter the effective work of Adams and Dayton. From the top down, Union diplomats outclassed their Confederate colleagues.

The careful manner that the Union government adopted in the *Trent* Affair indicated a growing maturity in international relations and a keen appreciation that small but dangerous events, if mismanaged, could cause serious problems. Had Lincoln's government reacted too belligerently, as some newspapers and political critics demanded, Prime Minister Palmerston may have had little choice but to respond similarly. A British military action against the United States might well have guaranteed the success of the Confederacy and changed American history.

NOTES

1. Quoted in J. G. Randall and David H. Donald, *The Civil War and Reconstruction* (Lexington, MA: D. C. Heath, 1969), p. 361.

2. Quoted in ibid., p. 362.

3. Quoted in James M. McPherson, *Ordeal by Fire* (New York: McGraw-Hill, 1993), p. 300.

DOCUMENTS

4.1. Abraham Lincoln's Blockade Proclamation, April 19, 1861

President Lincoln's Blockade Proclamation was a mixed blessing. While it aimed to limit and threaten Southern trade and commerce, it also hinted that the federal government considered the Confederacy a legal entity, something Lincoln had vigorously denied. Great Britain and France agreed to respect the blockade for their own reasons, but also used the president's proclamation to recognize the belligerency of the Confederacy.

BY THE PRESIDENT OF THE UNITED STATES OF AMERICA: A PROCLAMATION.

Whereas an insurrection against the Government of the United States has broken out in the States of South Carolina, Georgia, Alabama, Florida, Mississippi, Louisiana, and Texas, and the laws of the United States for the collection of the revenue cannot be effectually executed therein comformably to that provision of the Constitution which requires duties to be uniform throughout the United States:

And whereas a combination of persons engaged in such insurrection, have threatened to grant pretended letters of marque to authorize the bearers thereof to commit assaults on the lives, vessels, and property of good citizens of the country lawfully engaged in commerce on the high seas, and in waters of the United States: And whereas an Executive Proclamation has been already issued, requiring the persons engaged in these disorderly proceedings to desist therefrom, calling out a militia force for the purpose of repressing the same, and convening Congress in extraordinary session, to deliberate and determine thereon:

Now, therefore, I, Abraham Lincoln, President of the United States, with a view to the same purposes before mentioned, and to the protection of the public peace, and the lives and property of quiet and orderly citizens pursuing their lawful occupations, until Congress shall have assembled and deliberated on the said unlawful proceedings, or until the same shall have ceased, have further deemed it advisable to set on foot a blockade of the ports within the States aforesaid, in pursuance of the laws of the United States, and of the law of Nations, in such case provided. For this purpose a competent force will be posted so as to prevent entrance and exit of vessels from the ports aforesaid. If, therefore, with a view to violate such blockade, a vessel shall approach, or shall attempt to leave either of the said ports, she will be duly warned by the Commander of one of the blockading vessels, who will endorse on her register the fact and date of such warning, and if the same vessel shall again attempt to enter or leave the blockaded port, she will be captured and sent to the nearest convenient port, for such proceedings against her and her cargo as prize, as may be deemed advisable.

And I hereby proclaim and declare that if any person, under the pretended authority of the said States, or under any other pretense, shall molest a vessel of the United States, or the persons or cargo on board of her, such person will be held amenable to the laws of the United States for the prevention and punishment of piracy.

In witness whereof, I have hereunto set my hand, and caused the seal of the United States to be affixed.

Done at the City of Washington, this nineteenth day of April, in the year of our Lord one thousand eight hundred and sixty-one, and of the Independence of the United States the eighty-fifth.

ABRAHAM LINCOLN

By the President:

WILLIAM H. SEWARD, Secretary of State

Source: Roy P. Basler, ed., *The Collected Works of Abraham Lincoln*, vol. 4 (New Brunswick, NJ: Rutgers University Press, 1953), pp. 338–339.

4.2.   Lord Lyon, British Minister in Washington, to the Governor of Jamaica, Reviewing the "Trent Issue," December 22, 1861

The note Lyon sent to his colleague in Jamaica offers a clear review of the British position and the extent his government seemed willing to go if the United States did not release Mason and Slidell. Clearly, Britain did not want war with the United States, but it held firm to its position that the United States had acted illegally, and sought redress for that action.

(Confidential)

Sir,   Washington, December 22, 1861

Your Excellency has, no doubt, been already informed that Her Majesty's Government consider that the only adequate redress for the outrage perpetrated on board the packet "Trent" will be the liberation of the . . . gentlemen seized, and their delivery to me to be again placed under British protection; and, moreover, a suitable apology for the aggression.

Her Majesty's Government have expressed a hope that the United States' Government will offer these terms of their own accord; but if they should not be so offered, they are to be proposed by me.

If, upon my proposing them, the United States' Government should ask for delay, in order that this grave and painful matter should be deliberately considered, I am to consent to a delay not exceeding seven days. If at the end of that time no answer is given, or if any other answer is given, than a compliance with the terms, I am instructed to leave Washington with all the members of the Legation, and to repair immediately to London.

I shall, to-morrow morning, make the formal proposition contemplated in my instruction; consequently, I shall, on Monday, the 30th of December, demand my passports, and quit the country, with the whole of Her Majesty's Legation, unless the Government of the United States shall have, before that day, complied with the terms I am ordered to propose to them.

My quitting the United States in this manner would, of course, not amount to an actual declaration of war; and, accordingly, the Commander-in-chief of Her Majesty's ships is directed to refrain, until further orders, from any act of hostility against the sea or land forces of the United States, except in self defence.

Even supposing the Government of the United States should be so ill-advised as to refuse compliance with our terms, I cannot suppose that they will desire to precipitate hostilities. But experience has shown how prone the subordinate officers of this Government are, when they find themselves in superior force, to commit acts of aggression without orders from their superiors. To frustrate such unauthorized acts, therefore, it may be well to at once take reasonable cautions. . . .

Source: *British Documents of Foreign Affairs*, Part 1, Series C, *North America, The Civil War Years, 1862–1865* (New York: University Publications of America, 1986), Document # 7.

4.3. William Seward, Secretary of State, to Lord Lyon, British Minister to the United States, December 26, 1861. Formal United States Response to the *Trent* Affair

---

Seward's response serves as a classic example of diplomatic gamesmanship. In his note, Seward agreed to British demands, but claimed that his reasoning was founded in U.S. policy, policy that began in the early days of America's struggle with Britain over maritime rights. Thus, the note was an admission that Wilkes

*exceeded his authority, but Seward based that conclusion on
American maritime ideology, not Britain's threats.*

The British government has rightly conjectured, what is now my duty
to state, that Captain Wilkes, in conceiving and executing the proceeding
in question, acted upon his own suggestions of duty, without any direction or instruction, or even foreknowledge of it, on the part of this government. No direction has been given to him, or any other naval officer,
to arrest the four persons named, or any of them, on the Trent or on any
other British vessel, or on any neutral vessel, at the place where it occurred or elsewhere. The British government will justly infer from these
facts that the United States not only have had no purpose, but even no
thought, of forcing into discussion the question which has arisen, or any
other which could affect in any way the sensibilities of the British nation. . . .

The question before us is, whether this proceeding [the acts of Captain
Wilkes] was authorized by and conducted according to the law of
nations. It involves the following inquiries. . . .

I address myself to the first inquiry, namely, Were the four persons
mentioned, and their supposed dispatches contraband?

Maritime law so generally deals, as its professors say, *in rem*, that is
with property, and so seldom with persons, that it seems a straining of
the term contraband to apply it to them. But persons, as well as property,
may become contraband, since the word means broadly "contrary to
proclamation, prohibited, illegal, unlawful. . . ."

The second inquiry is, whether Captain Wilkes had a right by the law
of nations to detain and search the Trent.

The Trent, though she carried mails, was a contract or merchant vessel—a common carrier for hire. Maritime law knows only three classes
of vessels—vessels of war, revenue vessels, and merchant vessels. The
Trent falls within the latter class. Whatever disputes have existed concerning a right of visitation or search in time of peace, none, it is supposed, has existed in modern times about the right of a belligerent in
time of war to capture contraband in neutral and even friendly merchant
vessels, and of the right of visitation and search, in order to determine
whether they are neutral, and are documented as such according to the
law of nations.

I assume in the present case what, as I read British authorities, is regarded by Great Britain herself as true maritime law; That the circumstance that the Trent was proceeding from a neutral port to another
neutral port does not modify the right of the belligerent captor.

The third question is whether Captain Wilkes exercised the right of
search in a lawful and proper manner.

If any doubt hung over this point, as the case was presented in the statement of it adopted by the British government, I think it must have already passed away before the modifications of that statement which I have already submitted.

I proceed to the fourth inquiry, namely; Having found the suspected contraband of war on board the Trent, had Captain Wilkes a right to capture the same?

Such a capture is the chief, if not the only recognized, object of the permitted visitation and search. The principle of law is, that the belligerent exposed to danger may prevent the contraband persons or things from applying themselves or being applied to the hostile uses or purposes designed. The law is so very liberal in this respect that when contraband is found on board a neutral vessel which is the vehicle of its passage or transportation, being tainted, also becomes contraband, and is subject to capture and confiscation.

Only the fifth questions remains, namely; Did Captain Wilkes exercise the right of capturing the contraband in conformity with the law of nations?

It is just here that the difficulties of the case begin. What is the manner which the law of nations prescribes for disposing of the contraband when you have found and seized it on board of the neutral vessel? The answer would be easily found if the question were what you shall do with the contraband vessel. You must take or send her into a convenient port, and subject her to a judicial prosecution there in admiralty, which will try and decide the questions of belligerency, neutrality, contraband, and capture. So, again, you would promptly find the answer if the question were, What is the manner of proceeding prescribed by the law of nations in regard to the contraband, if it be property or things of material or pecuniary value? . . .

In the present case, Captain Wilkes, after capturing the contraband persons and making prize of the Trent in what seems to be a perfectly lawful manner, instead of sending her into port, released her from capture, and permitted her to proceed with her whole cargo upon her voyage. He thus effectually prevented the judicial examination which might otherwise have occurred. . . .

I have not been unaware that, in examining this question, I have fallen into an argument for what seems to be the British side of it against my own country. But I am relieved from all embarrassment on that subject. I had hardly fallen into that line of argument when I discovered that I was really defending and maintaining not an exclusively British interest, but an old, honored, and cherished American cause, not upon British authorities, but upon principles that constitute a large portion of the distinctive policy by which the United States have developed the resources of a continent, and, thus becoming a considerable maritime power, have won the respect and confidence of many nations. These

principles were laid down for us in 1804, by James Madison, when secretary of state in the administration of Thomas Jefferson, in instruction
given to James Monroe, our minister to England. Although the case before him concerned a description of persons different from those who
are incidentally the subjects of the present discussion, the ground he
assumed then was the same I now occupy, and the arguments by which
he sustained himself upon it, have been an inspiration to me in preparing
this reply. . . .

If I decide this case in favor of my own government, I must disavow
its most cherished principles, and reverse and forever abandon its essential policy. The country cannot afford the sacrifice. If I maintain those
principles, and adhere to that policy, I must surrender the case itself. It
will be seen, therefore, that this government could not deny the justice
of the claim presented to us in this respect upon its merits. We are asked
to do to the British nation just what we have always insisted all nations
ought to do to us. . . .

The four persons in question are now held in military custody at Fort
Warren, in the State of Massachusetts. They will be cheerfully liberated.
Your lordship will please indicate a time and place for receiving them.

Source: Ruhl J. Bartlett, ed., *The Record of American Diplomacy*, 4th ed. (New York:
Alfred A. Knopf, 1964), pp. 289–292.

4.4.   Excerpt of Letter from A. Dudley Mann, Confederate Diplomatic
Agent in London, to President Jefferson Davis, January 18, 1862

---

*Mann wrote from London to advise the Confederacy's president
regarding the* Trent *Affair and other issues. Unfortunately, his assessment of the incident and its potential consequences proved
inaccurate.*

London, January 18, 1862
MY DEAR MR. PRESIDENT:—

In endeavoring to keep you faithfully advised of all that is transpiring
in Europe, with reference to American affairs, I have incurred a large
amount of risk. I console myself with the belief that all the letters which
I have addressed to you reached their destination. I have employed every
channel of communication which I conceived to be available.

The signal of triumph of this government over the government at
Washington—amounting to disgraceful humiliation—will cause it to ob-
serve, for a short time, a more rigorous neutrality than ever, between the
South and the North. It will act upon the principle that it is cruel to

pursue a coward who runs for his life, exclaiming at the top of his voice, Mercy! Mercy!! Mercy!!!

But a great movement has been reported, the accomplishment of which I regard as positively certain, that will frustrate irremediably, the designs of the Lincolnites:—Louis Napoleon sustained Lord Palmerston, by his moral aid, in the affair of the Trent. The latter, in turn, will sustain the former in the matter of raising the blockade of our ports. As the Yankees yielded unconditionally in the one instance they are quite as likely to yield in the other. *I have the best of reasons for assuring you that there is a cabinet understanding upon the subject; and that all the Powers and States of Europe will cordially become parties to it*. But for the capture and surrender of Messrs. Mason, Slidell, McFarland, and Eustis, Great Britain would have taken the initiative instead of France—as I, from time/to/time informed you would be the case. Already, an urgent remonstrance has been sent to Washington against the sinking of the stone freighted ships in Charleston harbor. In all circles this diabolical proceeding is denounced as an out-lawry upon international and national law. Indeed the manifestation is as universal, as it is unqualified, in condemnation of it.

In defense of our hearth-stones we may still have to endure severe trials and sorrows, but when Peace shall again smile upon our sunny homes, it will also behold us with *unsullied honor*—the essence of all that is noble and elevating on earth, and all that is worth living for to virtuous humanity.

The insolvency of the North, tidings of which arrived last Monday, has dispirited the most clamorous advocates in this metropolis. They perceive that she is now hopelessly ruined—financially as well as morally. Well does the *New Journal of Commerce* remark, that "she has arrived at the beginning of the end."

I can say nothing more [with regard to her] than that the "Nashville" is still in the docks of Southampton. The "Tuscarora" is evidently awaiting her movements. Each have been notified that they are not to proceed to sea within twenty-four hours of the departure of the other.—Never was any navy adorned by a more gallant, discreet, or exemplary commander than Capt. Pegram. As my countryman I am proud of him— both as a gentleman and an officer. He is a general favorite in "Old England."

The *Times* of last Saturday contained a ferocious attack upon Messrs. Mason and Slidell which has very much exasperated our friends. I confess I do not participate in this sensitiveness. The article was positively cruel; but it has been succeeded, day after day, by piercingly excruciating onslaughts upon the Lincoln concern. That journal occasionally strikes at our country, but it seems to do so expressly for the purpose of enabling itself to strike more effectively at our detested and detestable enemy. I shall never lose my temper with it while it thus acts. In its relation to us I may liken it to the sun, which, while its scorching rays blister the cheeks of the fair damsel they also mature the joyous harvest.

Our captured countrymen are daily expected. Their arrival will perhaps not be delayed beyond the 21st or 22nd.

I trust your health continues good. The Northern press has ceased to represent it as bad.

May our friends, on the field and elsewhere, continue as hopeful as ever of the glorious future which awaits the sacrifices which they have made. I am sure that we have seen the last of the darkest days. Bright skies are looming up in the near distance. Ever as Ever, Yours Faithfully—

A. Dudley Mann.

Source: Lynda Laswell Crist, ed., *The Papers of Jefferson Davis*, vol. 8, 1982 (Baton Rouge: Louisiana State University Press, 1995), pp. 20–22.

4.5.   The Emancipation Proclamation, January 1, 1863

Critics in 1863 and after have questioned President Lincoln's famous document for freeing slaves where he could not make it effective (the Confederacy), but continuing the institution where he supposedly could (the border states). Yet, the pronouncement sealed the fate of the institution nationwide. There was little question that, with all of its political overtones, it would lead to the full emancipation of African Americans. With each advance of Union arms after January 1, 1863, slavery as an institution became less secure. And in any case, the slaves did not wait on legal niceties. They fled to Union lines.

A PROCLAMATION

Whereas on the 22nd day of September, A.D. 1862, a proclamation was issued by the President of the United States, containing, among other things, the following, to wit:

"That on the 1st day of January, A.D. 1863, all persons held as slaves within any State or designated part of a State the people whereof shall then be in rebellion against the United States shall be then, thenceforward, and forever free; and the executive government of the United States, including the military and naval authority thereof, will recognize and maintain the freedom of such persons and will do no act or acts to repress such persons, or any of them, in any efforts they may make for their actual freedom.

"That the executive will on the 1st day of January aforesaid, by proclamation, designate the States and parts of States, if any, in which the people thereof, respectively, shall then be in rebellion against the United States; and the fact that any State or the people thereof shall on that day be in good faith represented in the Congress of the United States by members chosen thereto at elections wherein a majority of the qualified voters of such States shall have participated shall, in the absence of strong countervailing testimony, be deemed conclusive evidence that such State and the people thereof are not then in rebellion against the United States."

Now, therefore, I, Abraham Lincoln, President of the United States, by virtue of the power in me vested as Commander-In-Chief of the Army and Navy of the United States in time of actual armed rebellion against the authority and government of the United States, and as a fit and necessary war measure for suppressing said rebellion, do, on this 1st day of January, A.D. 1863, and in accordance with my purpose so to do, publicly proclaim for the full period of one hundred days from the first day above mentioned, order and designate as the States and parts of States wherein the people thereof, respectively, are this day in rebellion against the United States the following, to wit:

Arkansas, Texas, Louisiana (except the parishes of St. Bernard, Plaquemines, Jefferson, St. John, St. Charles, St. James, Ascension, Assumption, Terrebone, Lafourche, St. Mary, St. Martin, and Orleans, including the city of New Orleans), Mississippi, Alabama, Florida, Georgia, South Carolina, North Carolina, and Virginia (except the forty-eight counties designated as West Virginia, and also the counties of Berkeley, Accomac, Northhampton, Elizabeth City, York, Princess Anne, and Norfolk, including the cities of Norfolk and Portsmouth), and which excepted parts are for the present left precisely as if this proclamation were not issued.

And by virtue of the power and for the purpose aforesaid, I do order and declare that all persons held as slaves within said designated States and parts of States are, and henceforward shall be, free; and that the Executive Government of the United States, including the military and naval authorities thereof, will recognize and maintain the freedom of said persons.

And I hereby enjoin upon the people so declared to be free to abstain from all violence, unless in necessary self-defence; and I recommend to them that, in all cases when allowed, they labor faithfully for reasonable wages.

And I further declare and make known that such persons of suitable condition will be received into the armed service of the United States to garrison forts, positions, stations, and other places, and to man vessels of all sorts in said service.

And upon this act, sincerely believed to be an act of justice, warranted by the Constitution upon military necessity, I invoke the considerate judgment of mankind and the gracious favor of Almighty God.

Source: Roy P. Basler, ed., *The Collected Works of Abraham Lincoln*, vol. 6 (New Brunswick, NJ: Rutgers University Press, 1953), pp. 28–30.

4.6.   A Letter from Workers in Manchester, England, to President Lincoln Concerning His Position on Slavery, December 31, 1862

Written shortly before Lincoln issued the Emancipation Proclamation, this letter explains one reason why England was reluctant to support the Confederacy. As much as working people in that nation may have counted on the cotton textile industry, their opposition to slavery served as a powerful force in supporting the Union. President Lincoln responded to the letter on January 19, 1863, with a clear explanation of his ongoing policies following the Emancipation Proclamation.

As citizens of Manchester, assembled at the Free Trade Hall, we beg to express our fraternal sentiments toward you and your country. We rejoice in your greatness as an outgrowth of England, whose blood and language you share, whose orderly and legal freedom you have applied to new circumstances, over a region immeasurably greater than our own. We honor your Free States, as a singularly happy abode for the working millions where industry is honored. One thing alone has, in the past, lessened our sympathy with your country and our confidence in it—we mean the ascendency of politicians who not merely maintained negro slavery, but desired to extend it and root it more firmly. Since we have discerned, however, that the victory of the free North, in the war which has so sorely distressed us as well as afflicted you, will strike off the fetters of the slave, you have attracted our warm and earnest sympathy. . . . We assume that you cannot now stop short of a complete uprooting of slavery. It would not become us to dictate any details, but there are broad principles of humanity which must guide you. If complete emancipation in some States be deferred, though only to a predetermined day, still in [the] interval, human beings should not be counted chattels. . . . Nor must any such abomination be tolerated as slave-breeding States and a slave market—if you are to earn the high reward of all your sacrifices. . . . It is for your free country to decide whether any thing but immediate and total emancipation can secure the most indispensable rights of humanity against the inveterate wickedness of local laws and local executives. We implore you, for your own honor and welfare, not to faint in your providential mission. . . . Our interests, moreover, are identical with yours. We are truly one people, though locally separate. And, if you have any ill-wishers here, be assured they are chiefly those who oppose liberty, at home, and they will be powerless to stir up quarrels between us, from the very day in which your country becomes, undeniably and without exception, the home of the free. Accept our high admiration of your firmness in upholding the proclamation of freedom.

Source: Philip Van Doren Stern, ed., *The Life and Writings of Abraham Lincoln* (New York: Modern Library, 1940), pp. 748–749.

5

The Open Door Notes: America and Asia

The present situation is becoming
daily more difficult. The various
[European] Powers cast upon us looks
of tiger-like voracity, hustling
each other to be first to seize our
innermost territories.

—Tsu Hsi
Dowager Empress of China, 1899

Take up the White Man's burden
   Ye dare not stoop to less
Nor call too loud on Freedom
   To cloke your weariness.

—Rudyard Kipling
Poet Laureate of England, 1898

In the last years of the nineteenth century, the United States expanded
its international perspective dramatically. Following the American Civil
War, between 1865 and 1890 westward expansion settled the transcontinental nation. At the same time, the postwar industrial revolution
moved America from an agrarian, rural, debtor nation to a manufacturing, urban investor in the global marketplace. U.S. manufactured goods,
agricultural products, and capital flooded Europe and Latin America.

The United States had also developed a serious commercial interest in East Asia. The nation had begun to make the moves of a Great Power.

Foreign policy makers in America had shown an interest in Asia for years. As early as the 1850s, Commodore Matthew Perry had visited the isolated nation of Japan and used both diplomacy and naval power to conclude a treaty with the Japanese to open their country to U.S. commerce. The interest that President James Polk showed in California during the Mexican War indicated in part the need to secure San Diego and San Francisco as American ports to trade with the Far East. In a pragmatic sense, the United States envisioned an unlimited market in Asia.

America, however, was not alone in its commercial ambition. In the 1800s, the European nations had sought to acquire as much territory and trade globally as possible. During the new Age of Imperialism, European nations, large and small, gobbled up huge portions of Africa and Asia in a heated competition for empire. In China, European imperialism and U.S. economic interests appeared to collide.

In 1899–1900, Secretary of State John Hay issued two Open Door Notes. That set of letters seemed to challenge the Europeans and Japan to avoid any attempt to prevent the United States from trading in their spheres of influence in China. Hay sought to establish free market opportunities with regard to China. That served as a new, articulated principle in U.S. foreign policy. Through most of the nineteenth century, America lacked the international strength and prestige to carry off such a demand. By 1899, that no longer seemed the case. In a practical sense, the Open Door Notes never achieved their goal. In the mythology of American international affairs, however, the notes signified a policy concept as significant as the Monroe Doctrine.

Americans had traded with China since the 1700s, and in the 1830s and 1840s significant numbers of New England clipper ships sailed into the only open Chinese port at Canton. Great Britain, at the same time, challenged Chinese efforts to keep foreign trade limited to Canton. England defeated China in the Opium War (1839), and the Treaty of Nanking (1842) cleared five additional commercial cities in China to Great Britain. The United States demanded "most favored nation" status, leading the Chinese government to open those facilities to everyone. (This status, granted to most trading partners, means that trade will take place on the same terms that are given to the most favored trading partner.)

The other factor that increased American interest in Asia stemmed from a religious impulse. Missionaries, most representing Protestant denominations, flocked into the region in the nineteenth and twentieth centuries seeking to convert millions of "heathens." In most instances, their motives remained genuine and kind-spirited, but American missionaries also involved themselves in the political and economic issues at stake in the area. That combination of missionary zeal and commercial profit influenced the U.S. position for years.

In the 1850s, Britain and France forced another confrontation with China and, after a brief conflict, negotiated the Treaty of Tientsin (1858). That opened ten more ports and established a diplomatic mission in Peking. Once again, the United States demanded similar treatment. Slowly, the Europeans eroded China's intent to remain isolated from the thrust of Western interference. The Chinese government understood clearly what the foreigners wanted and sought to prevent it. It lacked the military power, however, to block the Western intrusion.

Engrossed in the Civil War, the settlement of the frontier, and its urban-industrial growth between 1860 and 1890, America's primary interest did not extend to Asia. U.S. international concerns focused on Europe and growing trade relations in Latin America. The United States had not, though, forgotten the Pacific and Asia. Global strategists like Alfred T. Mahan saw the maritime benefits of a broad U.S. influence stretching out from the Caribbean to the Far East. While America engaged in a war with Spain over Cuba in 1898, U.S. naval and commercial planners also sought to grab the Philippine Islands from the Spanish as well as the tiny but strategic Pacific island of Guam. With the purchase of Alaska and Midway Island (both in 1867), and with growing control of the island of Hawaii, American interests spread quickly into the Pacific Rim. When President William McKinley annexed the Philippine Islands and Guam from Spain, the United States had an extended series of possessions linking it directly with East Asia. It is difficult to understand Hay's actions in 1899 without an overview of developing American imperialism in the last years of the nineteenth century and the first decade of the twentieth.

The U.S. victory over Spain in 1898 signaled an aggressive American move into the Caribbean and Central America. Between 1898 and 1905, the United States would create its own sphere of influence in that region, and in 1904 President Theodore Roosevelt added a corollary to the Monroe Doctrine basically announcing that American dominance. With the completion of the Panama Canal, under U.S. control, in 1914, a picture of global investment had developed. It stretched from Cuba and Puerto Rico, west through the Caribbean and Central America, across to Hawaii and the islands of the Pacific, and directly into the Philippines. The United States had its "turnpike" to Asia complete.

The obvious expansion beyond the continental United States defined an end-of-century interest in imperialism and provoked a heated debate in America. Pro-expansion advocates offered a variety of justifications for their objectives. The naval strategist Alfred Mahan believed that modern battle fleets, in defense of the nation and its global commerce, needed ports and coaling stations across the oceans of the world. The powerful newspaper magnates Joseph Pulitzer and William Randolph Hearst saw expansion as proof of American power and maturity. Theodore Roosevelt, Albert Beveridge, Henry Cabot Lodge, and other young political leaders envisioned both prestige and commercial profits in new "colonies" that would provide cheap raw resources and consumers for American manufactured goods. President McKinley told a group of clergy at a prayer breakfast that God wanted the United States to expand, a global expression and extension of Manifest Destiny.

The reasoning of pro-imperialists focused on four basic motivations: commercial profits, strategic concerns, pride and jingoism, and the "White Man's Burden." Many Europeans and Americans believed that the "white, Christian, civilized" world owed a responsibility to "uplift its little brown brothers and sisters," even while taking political-economic control of their homes and destroying their existing cultures. Similar to the Manifest Destiny impulses of the nineteenth century, the modern, global version appeared to veneer greed with a shiny, idealistic purpose.

The pro-imperialists held positions of power within the business and government establishment and possessed the ability to market their ideas easily. They faced, however, an equally committed opposition. Significant numbers of Americans, and a variety of political leaders, opposed the direction America had chosen in the late 1800s. Those anti-imperialists also addressed the issues from different perspectives.

Many opponents saw the annexing of foreign territory as a direct betrayal of American democracy and freedom. William Jennings Bryan, of Nebraska, the Democratic presidential candidate in 1896, argued that such colonies could never hope to become states of the Union and would remain perpetual possessions. Mark Twain (Samuel Clemens), Jane Addams, William James, and numerous academics and intellectuals supported the contention.

The anti-democratic position remained the major argument of the Anti-Imperialist League. Founded in Chicago in 1898–1899, and having an estimated membership of 30,000, the league pressed public opinion to question the unchecked growth, particularly into the Pacific, and specifically the Philippines. Those islands posed a particular concern, because the United States became involved in a nasty guerrilla war there. Philippine leaders like Emilio Aguinaldo felt betrayed when America sought to replace Spain as a new colonial power. The vicious war that followed drew criticism from many anti-imperialists unhappy with events in the Philippines and with the direction of U.S. policy in Asia in general.

Some business leaders feared that colonial goods would lower the prices of their own products, but the major economic criticism came from labor leaders in the United States. Samuel Gompers, the head of the

American Federation of Labor, worried that low-paid foreign workers would threaten U.S. wages.

Carl Schurz, one of the few Republican politicians opposed to the imperial growth, asked careful questions about involving the United States in an area of the world far from direct American security interests. It was one thing to defend the nation's security and trade within the hemisphere, even in the Eastern Pacific. Once the United States annexed the Philippines and turned its attention to China, however, might that not involve America in a region it simply lacked the strength and interest to defend? That concern related directly to Hay's development of the Open Door Notes.

The European powers and Japan had focused attention on China and defined spheres of interest there. While those nations had acquiesced regarding U.S. spheres in the Eastern Pacific, they appeared less inclined to accept American foreign policy direction in China. When anti-imperialists in the United States drew attention to America's "sailing into troubled waters," that criticism struck a sound note.

President McKinley, Secretary Hay, and other pro-imperialists saw the Pacific expansion of American territory as a move toward China. To reach from the California coast to the Philippines and then have European or Japanese spheres of influence deny American missionaries and businessmen access to China seemed pointless. Accordingly, Hay prepared his first Open Door Note in September 1899 and forwarded copies to England, Germany, and Russia. A short time later, he sent a similar note to France, Italy, and Japan.

The personal development of the 1899 Open Door Note revolved around three characters. Alfred Hippisley, an Englishman married to an American woman, and involved in the China trade, wanted to promote Anglo-American commercial cooperation in the area. He influenced William W. Rockhill, a serious, formal "China expert" and part-time advisor to Secretary of State Hay. With Hippisley's draft letter encouraging a "free trade" concept, Rockhill worked with Hay to produce the first Open Door Note.

Many Americans came to believe that Secretary Hay warned the Europeans and Japan not to create spheres of influences and to embrace a universal concept of free market economics. Others believed that Hay's directive protected China and found great favor with the Chinese people. Neither interpretation was accurate. Nor was the conclusion that the Open Door Notes produced the desired result.

The secretary of state accepted that spheres of influence already existed in China. He had no intention of challenging those. He simply wanted some concession from the imperial powers that their spheres would not exclude American commerce. In that regard, Hay failed to champion free market international commerce; rather, he simply asked to take advantage of markets that the Europeans and Japanese had already established. While the notes suggest an interest in the territorial integrity of China and a respect for Chinese interests, that was not the case either. Neither the Chinese government nor the Europeans or Japanese who examined Hay's odd request saw any evidence of a sincere interest in preserving Chinese sovereignty.

Secretary Hay's Open Door Note offered an end game in the U.S. move westward across the Pacific. If the aim was to provide bases and territories opening East Asia to U.S. commercial interests, then it followed that China remained the prime goal. To go all the way to the Philippines and have other nations block America at China's door seemed ridiculous, and to allow such a deterrent to American trade, irresponsible.

The European replies to Hay's first note came relatively quickly and proved tactful, but direct. They indicated that America had no need to appear concerned. Their spheres of influence had never excluded the United States or anyone else from commercial access. They would, however, continue to maintain such authority, in their own and everyone else's best interests. In a sense, when one broke down the diplomatic language, the other powers had told Secretary Hay that his note was unnecessary and silly and meant to embarrass the Europeans and Japanese.

Hay seized upon the diplomatic responses to issue, in March 1900, a second Open Door Note claiming that the Great Powers had conceded America's point and agreed to follow the principles established in his first note. Again, diplomatic language aside, the secretary of state announced that the United States had demanded a set policy in China and the other powers had agreed to obey it. He had not! They had not!

Clearly, too, the exchange of notes had no positive impact on the Chinese government. In the midst of the process, the Dowager Empress helped spark, and covertly supported, a violent anti-Western rebellion against the imperial powers—the Boxer Rebellion. Chinese forces trapped and attacked the foreign legations inside their headquarters at Peking for almost two months while Western forces fought to relieve the besieged city.

The end result of that explosive incident led to a stronger foreign military presence in China and the collapse of the Chinese imperial government. China would see a series of internal revolutions and conflict throughout the first half of the twentieth century, leading finally to the Communist Revolution that Mao Zedong (Mao Tse-tung) led to success in 1949. If Secretary Hay aimed at an open commercial opportunity for America and an increasing role in East Asia, that goal existed on precarious and dangerous foundations.

DOCUMENTS

5.1. Albert Beveridge's "March of the Flag" Speech, September 1898

Beveridge gave the speech while campaigning for the U.S. Senate seat from Indiana. He served in the Senate from 1899 to 1911 and remained an ardent imperialist. The speech served as a clear expression of pro-imperialist thinking during the domestic debate following the Spanish-American War.

The March of the Flag

It is a noble land that God has given us; a land that can feed and clothe the world; a land whose coastlines would inclose half the countries of Europe; a land set like a sentinel between the two imperial oceans of the globe, a greater England with a nobler destiny.

It is a mighty people that He has planted on this soil; a people sprung from the most masterful blood of history; a people perpetually revitalized by the virile, man-producing working-folk of all the earth; a people imperial by virtue of their power, by right of their institutions, by authority of their Heaven-directed purposes—the propagandists and not the misers of liberty.

It is a glorious history our God has bestowed upon His chosen people; a history heroic with faith in our mission and our future; a history of statesmen who flung the boundaries of the Republic out into unexplored lands and savage wilderness; a history of soldiers who carried the flag across blazing deserts and through the ranks of hostile mountains, even to the gates of sunset; a history of a multiplying people who overran a continent in half a century; a history of prophets who saw the consequences of evils inherited from the past and of martyrs who died to save us from them; a history divinely logical, in the process of whose tremendous reasoning we find ourselves today.

Therefore, in this campaign, the question is larger than a party question. It is an American question. It is a world question. Shall the American people continue their march toward the commercial supremacy of the world? Shall free institutions broaden their blessed reign as the children of liberty wax in strength, until the empire of our principles is established over the hearts of all mankind?

Have we no mission to perform, no duty to discharge to our fellow man? Has God endowed us with gifts beyond our deserts and marked us as the people of His peculiar favor, merely to rot in our own selfishness, as men and nations must, who take cowardice for their companion and self for their deity—as China has, as India has, as Egypt has?

Shall we be as the man who had one talent and hid it, or as he who had ten talents and used them until they grew to riches? And shall we reap the reward that waits on our discharge of our high duty; shall we occupy new markets for what our farmers raise, our factories make, our merchants sell—aye, and please God, new markets for what our ships shall carry?

Hawaii is ours; Porto Rico is to be ours; at the prayer of her people Cuba finally will be ours; in the islands of the East, even to the gates of Asia, coaling stations are to be ours at the very least; the flag of a liberal government is to float over the Philippines, and may it be the banner that Taylor unfurled in Texas and Fremont carried to the coast.

The Opposition tells us that we ought not to govern a people without their consent. I answer, The rule of liberty that all just government derives its authority from the consent of the governed, applies only to those who are capable of self-government. We govern the Indians without their consent, we govern our territories without their consent, we govern our children without their consent. How do they know what our government would be without their consent? Would not the people of the Philippines prefer the just, humane, civilizing government of this Republic to the savage, bloody rule of pillage and extortion from which we have rescued them?

And, regardless of this formula of words made only for enlightened, self-governing people, do we owe no duty to the world? Shall we turn these peoples back to the reeking hands from which we have taken them? Shall we abandon them, with Germany, England, Japan, hungering for them?

Shall we save them from those nations, to give them a self-rule of tragedy? They ask us how we shall govern these new possessions. I answer: Out of local conditions and the necessities of the case methods of government will grow. If England can govern foreign lands, so can America. If Germany can govern foreign lands, so can America. If they can supervise protectorates, so can America. Why is it more difficult to administer Hawaii than New Mexico or California? Both had a savage and an alien population: both were more remote from the seat of government when they came under our dominion than the Philippines are to-day.

Will you say by your vote that American ability to govern has decayed, that a century's experience in self-rule has failed of a result? Will you affirm by your vote that you are an infidel to American power and practical sense? Or will you say that ours is the blood of government; ours the heart of dominion; ours the brain and genius of administration?

Will you remember that we do but what our fathers did—we but pitch the tents of liberty farther westward, farther southward—we only continue the march of the flag?

The march of the flag! In 1789 the flag of the Republic waved over 4,000,000 souls in thirteen states, and their savage territory which stretched to the Mississippi, to Canada, to the Floridas. The timid minds of that day said that no new territory was needed, and, for the hour, they were right. But Jefferson, through whose intellect the centuries marched; Jefferson, who dreamed of Cuba as an American state, Jefferson, the first Imperialist of the Republic—Jefferson acquired that imperial territory which swept from the Mississippi to the mountains, from Texas to the British possessions, and the march of the flag began!

The infidels to the gospel of liberty raved, but the flag swept on! The title to that noble land out of which Oregon, Washington, Idaho and Montana have been carved was uncertain: Jefferson, strict constructionist of constitutional power though he was, obeyed the Anglo-Saxon impulse within him, whose watchword is, "Forward!": another empire was added to the Republic, and the march of the flag went on!

Those who deny the power of free institutions to expand urged every argument, and more, that we hear, to-day; but the people's judgment approved the command of their blood, and the march of the flag went on!

A screen of land from New Orleans to Florida shut us from the Gulf, and over this and the Everglade Peninsula waved the saffron flag of Spain; Andrew Jackson seized both, the American people stood at his back, and, under Monroe, the Floridas came under the dominion of the Republic, and the march of the flag went on! The Cassandras prophesied every prophecy of despair we hear, to-day, but the march of the flag went on!

Then Texas responded to the bugle calls of liberty, and the march of the flag went on! And, at last, we waged war with Mexico, and the flag swept over the southwest, over peerless California, past the Gate of Gold to Oregon on the north, and from ocean to ocean its folds of glory blazed.

And, now, obeying the same voice that Jefferson heard and obeyed, that Jackson heard and obeyed, that Monroe heard and obeyed, that Seward heard and obeyed, that Grant heard and obeyed, that Harrison heard and obeyed, our President today plants the flag over the islands of the seas, outposts of commerce, citadels of national security, and the march of the flag goes on!

Distance and oceans are no arguments. The fact that all the territory our fathers bought and seized is contiguous, is no argument. In 1819 Florida was farther from New York than Porto Rico is from Chicago today; Texas, farther from Washington in 1845 than Hawaii is from Boston in 1898; California, more inaccessible in 1847 than the Philippines are now. Gibraltar is farther from London than Havana is from Washington; Melbourne is farther from Liverpool than Manila is from San Francisco.

The ocean does not separate us from lands of our duty and desire—the oceans join us, rivers never to be dredged, canals never to be repaired. Steam joins us; electricity joins us—the very elements are in league with our destiny. Cuba not contiguous? Porto Rico not contiguous! Hawaii and the Philippines not contiguous! The oceans make them contiguous. And our navy will make them contiguous.

But the Opposition is right—there is a difference. We did not need the western Mississippi Valley when we acquired it, nor Florida! nor Texas, nor California, nor the royal provinces of the far northwest. We had no emigrants to people this imperial wilderness, no money to develop it, even no highways to cover it. No trade awaited us in its savage vastness. Our productions were not greater than our trade. There was not one reason for the land-lust of our statesmen from Jefferson to Grant, other than the prophet and the Saxon within them. But, to-day, we are raising more than we can consume, making more than we can use. Therefore we must find new markets for our produce.

And so, while we did not need the territory taken during the past century at the time it was acquired, we do need what we have taken in 1898 and we need it now. The resources and the commerce of the immensely rich dominions will be increased as much as American energy is greater than Spanish sloth.

In Cuba, alone, there are 15,000,000 acres of forest unacquainted with the ax, exhaustless mines of iron, priceless deposits of manganese, millions of dollars' worth of which we must buy, to-day, from the Black Sea districts. There are millions of acres yet unexplored.

The resources of Porto Rico have only been trifled with. The riches of the Philippines have hardly been touched by the finger-tips of modern methods. And they produce what we consume, and consume what we produce—the very predestination of reciprocity—a reciprocity "not made with hands, eternal in the heavens." They sell hemp, sugar, cocoanuts, fruits of the tropics, timber of price like mahogany; they buy flour, clothing, tools, implements, machinery and all that we can raise and make. Their trade will be ours in time. Do you indorse that policy with your vote?

Cuba is as large as Pennsylvania, and is the richest spot on the globe. Hawaii is as large as New Jersey; Porto Rico half as large as Hawaii; the Philippines larger than all New England, New York, New Jersey and Delaware combined. Together they are larger than the British Isles, larger than France, larger than Germany, larger than Japan.

If any man tells you that trade depends on cheapness and not on government influence, ask him why England does not abandon South

Africa, Egypt, India. Why does France seize South China, Germany the vast region whose port is Kaou-chou?

Our trade with Porto Rico, Hawaii and the Philippines must be as free as between the states of the Union, because they are American territory, while every other nation on earth must pay our tariff before they can compete with us. Until Cuba shall ask for annexation, our trade with her will, at the very least, be like the preferential trade of Canada with England. That, and the excellence of our goods and products; that, and the convenience of traffic; that, and the kinship of interests and destiny, will give the monopoly of these markets to the American people.

The commercial supremacy of the Republic means that this Nation is to be the sovereign factor in the peace of the world. For the conflicts of the future are to be conflicts of trade—struggles for markets—commercial wars for existence. And the golden rule of peace is impregnability of position and invincibility of preparedness. So, we see England, the greatest strategist of history, plant her flag and her cannon on Gibraltar, at Quebec, in the Bermudas, at Vancouver, everywhere.

So Hawaii furnishes us a naval base in the heart of the Pacific; the Ladrones another, a voyage further on; Manila another, at the gates of Asia—Asia, to the trade of whose hundreds of millions American merchants, manufacturers, farmers, have as good right as those of Germany or France or Russia or England; Asia, whose commerce with the United Kingdom alone amounts to hundreds of millions of dollars every year; Asia, to whom Germany looks to take her surplus products; Asia, whose doors must not be shut against American trade. Within five decades the bulk of Oriental commerce will be ours.

No wonder that, in the shadows of coming events so great, free-silver is already a memory. The current of history has swept past that episode. Men understand, today, the greatest commerce of the world must be conducted with the steadiest standard of value and most convenient medium of exchange human ingenuity can devise. Time, that unerring reasoner, has settled the silver question.

The American people are tired of talking about money—they want to make it. There are so many real things to be done—canals to be dug, railways to be laid, forests to be felled, cities to be built, fields to be tilled, markets to be won, ships to be launched, peoples to be saved, civilization to be proclaimed and the Rag of liberty Hung to the eager air of every sea. Is this an hour to waste upon triflers with nature's laws? Is this a season to give our destiny over to word-mongers and prosperity-wreckers? No! It is an hour to remember our duty to our homes. It is a moment to realize the opportunities fate has opened to us. And so it is an hour for us to stand by the Government.

Wonderfully has God guided us Yonder at Bunker Hill and Yorktown. His providence was above us At New Orleans and on ensanguined seas.

His hand sustained us. Abraham Lincoln was His minister and His was the altar of freedom the Nation's soldiers set up on a hundred battle-fields. His power directed Dewey in the East and delivered the Spanish fleet into our hands, as He delivered the elder Armada into the hands of our English sires two centuries ago. [Author's Note: Beveridge was off by 100 years—the Armada defeat took place in 1588.]

The American people can not use a dishonest medium of exchange; it is ours to set the world its example of right and honor. We can not fly from our world duties; it is ours to execute the purpose of a fate that has driven us to be greater than our small intentions. We can not retreat from any soil where Providence has unfurled our banner; it is ours to save that soil for liberty and civilization.

Source: Indianapolis Journal, September 17, 1898, pp. 47–49, 56–57.

5.2.   First Open Door Note: John Hay to Andrew D. White, September 6, 1899

In his first Open Door Note, Secretary Hay expressed the clear view that colonial spheres of influence in China would threaten the U.S. view on free market opportunities in that country. The message was less anti-imperial and more open market capitalism.

At the time when the Government of the United States was informed by that of Germany that it had leased from His Majesty the Emperor of China the port of Kiao-chao and the adjacent territory in the province of Shantung, assurances were given to the ambassador of the United States at Berlin by the Imperial German minister for foreign affairs that the rights and privileges insured by treaties with China to citizens of the United States would not thereby suffer or be in anywise impaired within the area over which Germany had thus obtained control.

More recently, however, the British Government recognized by a formal agreement with Germany the exclusive right of the latter country to enjoy in said leased area and the contiguous "sphere of influence or interest" certain privileges, more especially those relating to railroads and mining enterprises; but as the exact nature and extent of the rights thus recognized have not been clearly defined, it is possible that serious conflicts of interest may at any time arise not only between British and German subjects within said area, but that the interests of our citizens may also be jeopardized thereby.

Earnestly desirous to remove any cause of irritation and to insure at the same time to the commerce of all nations in China the undoubted benefits which should accrue from a formal recognition by the various powers claiming "spheres of interest" that they shall enjoy perfect equality of treatment for their commerce and navigation within such "spheres," the Government of the United States would be pleased to see His German Majesty's Government give formal assurances, and lend its cooperation in securing like assurances from the other interested powers, that each, within its respective sphere of whatever influence—

First. Will in no way interfere with any treaty port or any vested interest within any so-called "sphere of interest" or leased territory it may have in China.

Second. That the Chinese treaty tariff of the time being shall apply to all merchandise landed or shipped to all such ports as are within said "sphere of interest" (unless they be "free ports"), no matter to what nationality it may belong, and that duties so leviable shall be collected by the Chinese Government.

Third. That it will levy no higher harbor dues on vessels of another nationality frequenting any port in such "sphere" than shall be levied on vessels of its own nationality, and no higher railroad charges over lines built, controlled, or operated within its "sphere" on merchandise belonging to citizens or subjects of other nationalities transported through such "sphere" than shall be levied on similar merchandise belonging to its own nationals transported over equal distances.

The liberal policy pursued by His Imperial German Majesty in declaring Kiao-chao a free port and in aiding the Chinese Government in the establishment there of a customhouse are so clearly in line with the proposition which this Government is anxious to see recognized that it entertains the strongest hope that Germany will give its acceptance and hearty support. The recent ukase of His Majesty the Emperor of Russia declaring the port of Ta-lien-wan open during the whole of the lease under which it is held from China to the merchant ships of all nations, coupled with the categorical assurances made to this Government by His Imperial Majesty's representative at this capital at the time and since repeated to me by the present Russian ambassador, seem to insure the support of the Emperor to the proposed measure. Our ambassador at the Court of St. Petersburg has, in consequence, been instructed to submit it to the Russian Government and to request their early consideration of it. A copy of my instruction on the subject to Mr. Tower is herewith inclosed for your confidential information.

The commercial interests of Great Britain and Japan will be so clearly observed by the desired declaration of intentions, and the views of the Governments of these countries as to the desirability of the adoption of measures insuring the benefits of equality of treatment of all foreign trade throughout China are so similar to those entertained by the United States, that their acceptance of the propositions herein outlined and their cooperation in advocating their adoption by the other powers can be confidently expected. I inclose herewith copy of the instruction which I have sent to Mr. Choate on the subject.

Note: Identical notes, with the necessary changes, were sent on the same day to Germany and Russia. Similar notes went later to Japan, Italy, and France.

Source: Papers Relating to the Foreign Relations of the United States—1899 (Washington, DC: U.S. Government Printing Office, 1947), pp. 129–130 (hereafter referred to as *Foreign Relations Series*).

5.3.   Russian Reply to Secretary Hay's Note, December 18, 1899

In the Russian reply to Secretary Hay appeared the problem that all of the nations interested in China confronted. In a sense, they must agree to the U.S. position or appear overtly contemptuous of Chinese sovereignty. None of the European states were willing to do that.

I had the honor to receive your excellency's note . . . relating to the principles which the Government of the United States would like to see adopted in commercial matters by the powers which have interests in China.

In so far as the territory leased by China to Russia is concerned, the Imperial Government has already demonstrated its firm intention to follow the policy of "the open door" by creating Dalny (Ta-lien-wan) a free port; and if at some future time that port, although remaining free itself, should be separated by a customs limit from other portions of the territory in question, the customs duties would be levied, in the zone subject to the tariff, upon all foreign merchandise without distinction as to nationality.

As to the ports now opened or hereafter to be opened to foreign commerce by the Chinese Government, and which lie beyond the territory leased to Russia, the settlement of the question of customs duties belongs to China herself, and the Imperial Government has no intention whatever of claiming any privileges for its own subjects to the exclusion of other foreigners. It is to be understood, however, that this assurance of the Imperial Government is given upon condition that a similar declaration shall be made by other powers having interests in China.

With the conviction that this reply is such as to satisfy the inquiry made in the aforementioned note, the Imperial Government is happy to have complied with the wishes of the American Government, especially as it attaches the highest value to anything that may strengthen and consolidate the traditional relations of friendship existing between the two countries.

Source: Foreign Relations Series—1899, pp. 340–341.

5.4.   "The Breakup of China and Our Interest in It," *Atlantic Monthly*, **August 1899**

The article provided an excellent contemporary overview of the issues in China with an analysis of European and Japanese policies and agendas as well as the U.S. position on maintaining the territorial integrity of China for commercial purposes.

The literal "cycle of Cathay," or period of sixty years,—not the vague literary expression of Lord Tennyson,—which has just ended, was probably the most momentous for China, if not for the world at large; for it was in 1839 that the difficulties of intercourse between the East and the West came to the first crisis. The year 1899 seems to mark another crisis, which, as regards the integrity of the Chinese problem, may prove final. Yet the situation in Far Eastern Asia was grasped by only a few Western observers before 1895, when the struggle [for] suzerainty over Corea revealed the helplessness of China, and lifted Japan to a seat in the council of Powers. Though worsted in two foreign wars and nearly wrecked by an internal convulsion, the government of the "Son of Heaven" had learned nothing new and forgotten nothing old. The abortive issue of the French attack in 1884 seemed even to give it greater arrogance, and to increase the deference with which it was treated by Europe.

For ten years after the late Jules Ferry had declared Peking to be "une quantite negligeable" events conspired to prove his estimate incorrect. The Burlingame burlesque was forgotten, and the Dragon was again believed to be awakening. He looked very formidable—at a distance. Taking into consideration the blindness of the British, who had been the pioneers of trade, and whose commercial supremacy was still unthreatened, to the political and social conditions of the country, we need not wonder at the ignorance displayed by other peoples. English military experts referred to China as a desirable ally in the struggle, then thought imminent, of Slav and Saxon over India. A succession of muzzled or incompetent envoys represented Queen Victoria at Peking, and set to the consuls throughout the Chinese Empire an example of subservience to native authorities intensely mortifying to the foreign commercial communities which had grown to prosperity under a more vigorous regime.

The lives and property of the Queen's subjects became so cheap that they were the favorite toys of petty mandarins. One China?

During all this period the attitude of the American government and people was different, but hardly more enlightened. The relations of the United States to China were peculiar; the few American resident merchants, who had built up fortunes by exporting Oriental produce, disappeared, and no large importers had arisen. The delusions of a prohibitive tariff and a purely home market paralyzed American enterprise abroad, and the effect of our navigation laws was to deprive us of that share in the carrying trade of Asia which we had enjoy[ed] before our civil war. On the other hand, an enormous influx of Chinese peasants upon the Pacific coast had glutted the labor market, and produced as bitter a racial hostility to them as could be reciprocated by the untraveled multitudes of the Flowery Land. Familiarity with the Chinese individual in our own country had bred contempt for his nation at home, and the interests, missionary rather than commercial, of American citizens in China were more courageously though not more skillfully upheld than those of European subjects.

How long the nations of the West might have indulged in pleasant dreams of a self-instructed Chinese monarchy holding out both hands for the world's commerce and civilization, varied by that strange recurrent nightmare known as "the Yellow Peril," it is difficult to say. But the internal ferment and consequent expansion of Japan hastened the awakening. At first the attention of Europe was concentrated on the naval struggle in the Yellow Sea, from which it was thought possible to learn valuable lessons in armament and tactics. Even after the destruction of Chinese sea power and the occupation of Corea by Japanese troops, the danger threatening the Celestial Empire itself was not realized in Europe. China, it was widely and confidently asserted, could absorb Japanese armies as she would a dust storm. They must simply melt away, leaving their island homes depopulated. The conservative prophets were so rapidly discomfited that bewilderment seized the press and politicians of Great Britain. The Yellow Peril bogey was transferred to Japan, and when Germany, Russia, and France decided to interfere, the authorities of Downing Street seemed willing to be ignored. Had a strong personality ruled the counsels of the Queen something might have been done to save British prestige; but Lord Rosebery was a man of many moods and many minds, hampered by an unpopular domestic policy which he had inherited together with that Elijah's mantle of leadership which was soon to trip him up.

The events which followed the Treaty of Shimonoseki are within the memory of every adult reader of the newspapers. Book after book has been published, professing to give a solution of the Far Eastern question, and often embodying merely the prejudices of a compiler or the per-

functory notes of a flying journalist. The utterances of the Honorable
G. N. Curzon and Mr. Archibald R. Colquhoun were the most important,
until the publication recently of Lord Charles Beresford's report to the
British Associated Chambers of Commerce. (The Break-up of China.
Harpers.) Lord Charles appeals not only to the commercial classes of his
own country, but to the public of the United States as well; he is, like
his predecessors, a believer in a fair field and no favor for all nations in
China, but in addition to this he advocates an Anglo-American entent
[sic], which, with the probable adhesion of Japan and possibly of Germany, he regards as necessary to maintain the "open door." The alternative policy he judges "certain to encompass the doom of China, and
equally certain to produce international strife. Mastery in Asia under a
system of 'spheres of influence' will not be determined by effusion of
ink." The merit of this report lies in the fact that it gives the results of
careful investigations on the spot by a man of world-wide fame in his
profession, having extensive knowledge of human nature and a judgment as open and impartial as robust patriotism and special associations
ever leave to us at maturity. Beresford received the confidence of all
Anglo-Saxon communities in China, as well as assurances of sympathy
from German traders and of hearty support by the people and press of
Japan. He had access to the highest officials of the Chinese government,
and almost every facility for verifying the military and naval collapse of
the empire. He was also interviewed by the fugitive leader of the ill-
fated Reform Party in China, which was overthrown by the coup d'etat
of September, 1898. He saw the Russians at work in Manchuria and the
Germans in Shantung, and he listened to the grievances of Englishmen
against their consular service, to which some reformers in this country
are wont to point as a model. He has studied the treaties, and observed
the administration and effects of the tariff which depends upon them, as
conscientiously as the forts and arsenals which might have more personal interest for a rear admiral who has seen active service. Above all,
he has learned how to assimilate and condense the vast amount of information which he received, how to discard the extreme view, and how
to sift the unfounded assertion. Whether or not one may agree with the
practical utility of the open door policy, the Break-up of China is the
most available and authoritative statement of essential truths for a student of politics or a seller of produce in the Orient.

Lord Charles has assuredly made out a good case against the inaction
or opportunism of the British government amid recent developments,
and he shows how seriously British and American trade is menaced by
the closing of an immense general market. The advent of the United
States to a seat on the court-martial of Powers which is trying the case
of China is likely to be of great moment. Hitherto the majority has been
distinctly inclined to give a sentence of summary decapitation and dis-

section. America, secure in a splendid isolation and confident in the permanent sufficiency of her domestic market, regarded the Oriental problem as academic, and its solution as immaterial to her welfare, until the
guns of Admiral Dewey stirred the masses of his fellow countrymen to
a keen sense of their needs and responsibilities. But other than senti-
mental reasons must be advanced for our undertaking with Great Britain
or a syndicate of Powers to buttress the tottering colossus of China.

Almost all statistics of the foreign trade of China are based upon the
returns of the Imperial Maritime Customs, which do not include the
figures of import or export by overland routes. But the commerce of
Western Europe and America is almost wholly sea-borne, and Lord
Charles Beresford shows how great our export trade to China is, and
how much it increased during the decade which ended with 1897. In free
competition with British plain gray and white cotton goods, the American variety has risen from fourteen and a half per cent of the total import
eleven years ago to twenty-nine and a half per cent during the year
before last. The figures given by Consul-General Jernigan in his report
of October 25, 1895, indicated that the value of the direct sea-borne trade
relations between China and the United States for 1894 was greater than
that between China and the European continent (Russia excepted); that
it was more than double that between Russia and China, and amounted
to nearly five eighths of the direct trade of Great Britain with China. Mr.
A. R. Colquhoun stated that "the volume of the United States trade with
China represented more than one seventh of the entire foreign trade of
the empire in 1896. While the import trade from China has increased
slowly, the export trade to China has increased one hundred times, and
is more than fifty per cent larger than the German exports." A depression
in 1898, due in part to our war with Spain, is more than offset by the
estimates for 1899. And all this notwithstanding the purchasing power
of Chinese silver has fallen thirty per cent since 1893.

Our present rivalry with Russia is in kerosene oil. But the Russian oil
is so much inferior that dishonest methods are employed to introduce it.
Tins and cases which have contained American oil and still bear its trade-
marks are used to pack Russian oil, to the injury of the American exporter and the native consumer. Another branch of American trade, and
one capable in an open market of indefinite development, is the impor-
tation of flour for the northern provinces; but if these regions of China,
where wheat instead of rice is the staple food of the people, should be
acknowledged as the Russian "sphere of influence," the exclusion of
American flour and oil by administrative enactment is sure to follow. It
is, moreover, noteworthy in the statistics of the northern ports that American imports have more generally increased in that section than in the
Yangtse Valley or the southern provinces, where they are not at present
threatened with political discrimination.

Russia has always been served by the best men she has in the career of diplomacy. With her especially it may be said that "a diplomat is an honest man sent abroad to lie for his country." There may be significance in the fact that her present ambassador at Washington has played a great part in the overshadowing influence of the Tsar at Peking. Of course, the cabinet and the press are given to understand, with extreme unctuousness, that Russian influence in Asia is friendly to American interests; but it is well to remember, as a guarantee of Russian good faith, the recent crime against the liberties of Finland.

Lord Charles Beresford's chapters on Railways and Waterways are highly interesting, because it is by facility of travel and transportation that the dough of Cathay must be leavened. But the distinguished defender of the open door is not always consistent in his exposition. He is inclined to surrender in practice a crucial part of his policy for the sake of getting it adopted in theory. "If the open door policy is maintained throughout China," he writes, "the more countries who employ their capital and energy in making railways, the better it will be for British trade; but in order to secure the open door policy, it may be that we shall have to concede to other countries preferential rights or spheres of interest, as far as railway enterprise is concerned. This we have already done with regard to Germany in Shantung and Russia in Manchuria, and the question arises, What is our position in the Yangtse Valley, where other Powers possess railway concessions?

Very pertinent; but if there are to be spheres of railway influence, why should there not be spheres of mining, bridging, conservancy, or other engineering influence? Where are they to cease, and how are they to be regulated? It would be a jungle of jurisdictions, a gnarled knot of privileges which only the sword could cut. We have already, as pointed out by Lord Charles, an example of conflicting courts in the residential concessions at the port of Hankow, where the invalidity of certain titles to real estate is the distress of the occupants, and would be the despair of an American conveyancer.

The trouble is that there has been no definite agreement among the Powers since the collapse of China was made clear to the meanest intellect. Each government has been bullying Peking in its turn, demanding this or that contract or concession with or without the color of a pretext. Where only a harbor or a fringe of seacoast is involved, the disadvantages of the scramble policy may not be immediately patent; but when it is extended to the complicated charters of public carriers, the development of mineral resources, or any enterprise requiring the employment of intricate machinery and skilled labor, the absurdity is manifest. It might reach such proportions that the consent of five Powers would be necessary to construct a breakwater in the Gulf of Pechili, or that one

Power could veto the opening of a switch at a railway junction in the Yangtse Valley.

No such compromise is possible. Either, as Lord Charles Beresford believes and in the main strongly presents to us, "the world must adhere firmly to the open door and equal opportunity policy," with its logical sequence of a revival of the imperial authority in China by injecting stimulants and vigorously chafing the extremities, or there must be accurately surveyed and delimited geographical regions, where Briton, Cossack, Frank, Teuton, Japanese, or Yankee may grow whatever crop of institutions he may prefer and the soil can bear.

Is it for the benefit of the United States to deal with China as a vast unit under her native flag, or as fragments under many flags? That is what we have to decide; and Lord Charles confesses that, when he passed through America, the public mind was partly distracted from his message by the acute stage of the Philippine problem. It is to be hoped that our government is silently exercising the utmost vigilance in behalf of our commercial privileges on the continent of Asia. Failure to do so might not be politically disastrous to the present administration, but posterity will not forgive nor history condone faults of omission or indifference after such warning as have [sic] already been given. Surely, no American administration would seriously contemplate the establishment of a dependency or protectorate on the mainland of China, while our interests there may be safeguarded by international control and reciprocity; but it is difficult to see how these securities can be obtained without more definite engagements on the part of our State Department than our uninformed public opinion now demands. Nevertheless, the signs of a healthy and growing interest are numerous. The American Asiatic Association of those directly interested in the Far East was formed last year, with headquarters at New York, corresponding to the British China Association, and may in time possess equal weight. A very valuable document, Commercial China in 1899, has been issued by the Bureau of Statistics of the Treasury Department at Washington, and gives in a concise and intelligible form the main facts and prospects of the situation. A wide dissemination of this pamphlet is earnestly to be desired; and every factor is to be encouraged that brings home to American manufacturers and merchants the opportunity that awaits them,—an opportunity that, by a wise foreign policy and far-sighted commercial methods, can add immensely to our trade and to our international influence.

Source: "The Breakup of China and Our Interest in It," *Atlantic Monthly* 84, no. 502 (August 1899): 276–280.

6

The Fourteen Points: Woodrow Wilson, the United States, and World War I

The situation is extraordinary. It is militarism run stark mad. Unless someone acting for you can bring about a different understanding, there is someday to be an awful cataclysm. No one in Europe can do it. There is too much hatred, too many jealousies.
—Colonel Edward House to President Woodrow Wilson
May 1914

World War I had a dramatic impact on international affairs and America's role in them. President Woodrow Wilson, following the principle of neutrality that George Washington had advised, hoped to avoid direct U.S. involvement in the conflict. That effort failed, and in April 1917 America declared war on Germany. In making the decision, President Wilson and others hoped to change the nature of diplomacy in the modern era. The widely circulated Fourteen Points served as the game plan for that new age, a progressive concept to make World War I a "war to end all wars." At the heart and soul of those Fourteen Points, the creation of a League of Nations remained the president's major goal.

While American foreign policy may have aimed at commercial interests in Latin America and Asia in the last generation of the nineteenth century, those concerns still included Europe in the broad picture. Looking for markets and advancing security interests in the Caribbean and Central America, the United States saw Great Britain and Germany as competitors. In the Pacific and East Asia, the same concern with European ambitions often colored American policy responses. Fundamentally, the United States, both commercially and politically, viewed Europe as the basis for its international responses. It always had.

When a complex set of issues that included colonial competition, naval arms races, ethnic concerns, nationalism, and economic motivation drove the European nations into war in August 1914, the administration of Woodrow Wilson appeared concerned, but not dumbfounded. The explosion of violence had seemed inevitable for some time.

When war began, many Americans were committed to a domestic reform advocacy known as the Progressive Movement. Many Progressives argued for the perfectibility of society, identified a number of political, economic, and social flaws in urban, industrial America, and worked to resolve those problems. Woodrow Wilson, who served as president from 1913 to 1920, represented and spoke for Progressivism and developed a number of reform policies during his administration.

In a similar fashion, Progressives advocated changes in the foreign policy arena as well. Many professed a strong belief in pacifism, forms of arms control and reduction, and international organizations to prevent war and the exploitation of weak nations by the strong. Progressives tended to conclude that legitimate reform could take place in the international environment as well as in domestic venues. President Wilson and his secretary of state, William Jennings Bryan, while different in background, subscribed to both the broad domestic and international goals of Progressivism. That conviction clearly influenced the development of U.S. policy as the war in Europe continued.

Between August 1915 and April 1917, the president sought to maintain a posture of American neutrality as the war in Europe grew in violence and devastation. A series of events, however, drew the United States into war with Germany. (Germany, Austria-Hungary, and Turkey allied against Britain, France, Italy, and Russia as the key combatants in World War I. The United States joined the latter as an "associated power.") They included German submarine attacks that violated American neutrality, increased U.S. financial investment in the conflict, persuasive use of British propaganda against Germany, and a concern about German threats to American security should it upset the balance of power in Europe. While President Wilson won majority support for his war declaration, 82–6 in the Senate and 373–50 in the House of Representatives, the nation's commitment to the conflict remained, as historian Dan Smith called it, a "great departure."

Wilson understood that America would require enormous sacrifice in a European war, which administrations since George Washington had warned the nation to avoid. While he, and others, believed that German behavior left the United States little choice, the president concluded that a U.S. call to arms demanded a clear expression of self-sacrifice, not self-interest. The "New World" would salvage the "Old" from self-destruction. The Fourteen Points derived from that intention and from a long-standing Progressive belief that international affairs should bear the same reform commitment as domestic issues.

As the nation girded for war, Wilson prepared a January 8, 1918, message to Congress. He offered fourteen points that could serve as both a propaganda vehicle and a possible blueprint for postwar peace negotiations. George Creel, the administration's head of public information, printed more than 60 million copies of the Fourteen Points and distributed them throughout the international community. They came to represent the ideal hopes and goals of people fighting and dying to make the world a safe, peaceful place. President Wilson's prestige soared as his Fourteen Points defined America's intent in the war. In a potent way, the message disarmed and defeated Germany almost as clearly as the arrival of U.S. troops and equipment on the battlefield throughout 1917–1918.

In November 1918, Kaiser Wilhelm abdicated as German emperor and his nation's military leaders asked for an armistice. At 11 A.M. on November 11, 1918, the Great War ended. Ten million had died. Millions more were maimed and scarred in body and spirit. If the great leaders chose to make a "peace as usual," it would discredit the supreme sacrifice of World War I's victims. This peace called for something much different.

Minor criticism and Republican political opposition had challenged some of President Wilson's efforts between 1914 and 1918, but he confronted different circumstances with war's end. The Fourteen Points had done their job, elevating the American leader to a global icon as peacemaker. Wilson announced that he would personally lead the American negotiating team to Paris to engage in meetings with David Lloyd George, Britain's prime minister, Georges Clemenceau, the French premier, and Vittorio Orlando, Italy's premier. While the European victors had, with qualifications, accepted the Fourteen Points, none intended to use Wilson's document as a blueprint for peace. Clemenceau reputedly said, "God gave us Ten Commandments and we've broken all of them! Wilson has Fourteen Points, we shall see!"

The Paris Peace Conference, held between December 1918 and June 1919, became a struggle between Wilson, Clemenceau, and Lloyd George as they sought to advance particular interests. While Premier Orlando attended a number of meetings, key decisions fell to the "Big Three." The victors denied German attendance at the conference until they had decided on peace terms.

The Europeans tended to advocate a "to the victors belong the spoils" approach, traditional diplomacy, particularly after such a brutal, costly war. They wanted specific territory, war reparations, the dismantling of

Germany's and Austria-Hungary's prewar empires, and a total reduction of German military capacity.

While the American leader conceded some of those issues, Wilson hammered at key points in his message, most particularly the Fourteenth Point, an international organization, a League of Nations. And it was around the League of Nations that the Fourteen Points and President Wilson's intent centered. He believed, ultimately, that all of the other issues noted in his various points would take place under the auspices of the League. What occurred at the peace conference would only set the stage for the League's postwar authority.

French and British concerns, however, continued to focus on disarming Germany, confiscating territory both in Europe and colonial areas, and presenting the Germans with a massive reparations bill. Often, those demands clashed with Wilson's desire to initiate a League organization and have that body make determinations about territory, reparations, and other issues at a later date. In the end, the three leaders reached compromises that left them all suspicious and concerned about the future. The French, particularly, believed that the president's naïve, idealistic approach to foreign policy placed them in a severely compromised security position with regard to Germany. Still, the powers agreed to accept the League of Nations as a postwar reality and tied its creation to the Versailles Treaty ending the war with Germany.

President Wilson had struggled for his goal in Paris, but he faced more severe attacks at home. As he left for home on the U.S.S. *George Washington*, the United States Senate had already issued a resolution challenging the League of Nations. In congressional elections in 1918, the Republican Party gained majority control of the Senate. Wilson, a Democrat, had advocated bipartisan politics during America's involvement in World War I. The nation's two-party politics should stop at the water's edge and not distract Americans from winning the war. He appeared, however, to betray that call for unity when he publicly encouraged voters to elect Democratic candidates in 1918. Many Republicans believed that that gave them the option to jettison the bipartisan relationship. Additionally, the president had failed to bring any significant Republican leaders with him to Paris. Ultimately, many of Wilson's political opponents in the Senate disliked him personally and the League of Nations as policy. To its critics, the international organization came to represent the Fourteen Points in general and the self-righteousness, idealism, and naïveté of Progressivism in international affairs.

On March 4, 1919, while the president negotiated the treaty in Paris, the Senate circulated a round-robin resolution. Thirty-nine of its members, incumbent and newly elected, indicated that they would refuse to support the League of Nations "in the form now proposed." Wilson, as a result, lacked the two-thirds majority necessary to approve the treaty and League, as the Constitution required. When he returned to the United States in June 1919, Wilson believed that his moral position and global popularity would alter the March round-robin. His worldwide popularity and his successful efforts at the Paris Peace Conference would surely turn American public opinion against any senator who might challenge his goals. He was wrong.

Between July 1919 and March 1920, a national debate emerged over the League of Nations and the entire concept of the Fourteen Points as a diplomatic agenda for the United States. Basically, three positions surfaced, and they found clear voices in the Senate. *Isolationists* argued that they would vote against any effort to join the League of Nations no matter what the conditions. William E. Borah of Idaho, Hiram Johnson of California, and Robert La Follette of Wisconsin led fourteen "irreconcilables" who opposed the League in any form. Following traditional U.S. theory, they argued that America should pursue its foreign relations unilaterally, as it had since Washington's Farewell Address. The nation must avoid any organization that might drag it into some international crisis that had nothing to do with American security interests. Many isolationists also concluded that America had gone to war to benefit war profiteers and business interests. They saw the treaty and the League as a continuation of that trend.

Reservationists made up a majority of the Republican Senators, about thirty-two members. Henry Cabot Lodge of Massachusetts, the chairman of the Foreign Relations Committee, led one faction, the "strict reservationists," while Frank Kellogg, a Minnesota Republican, spoke for a milder perspective. While a historic debate has developed over the motives of the various reservationists, in basic terms, they sought to amend the League organization to fit particular objections they had regarding the way Wilson had constructed it.

The remaining senators, Democrats, rallied around the leadership of Gilbert Hitchcock. The *pro-Wilson Democrats* supported the president's treaty and the League, but lacked the numbers. Still, public opinion and Wilson's popularity might change some minds in the legislative body, and the reservationists did not agree on every point. In the summer of 1919, the round-robin resolution seemed to spell trouble for the administration, but Wilson had faced naysayers in the past and won them over.

Senator Lodge and opponents of the League realized that public opinion would play a critical role in the battle. In June, most Americans appeared to side with the president. His opponents needed time to change their minds. Lodge, therefore, kept the treaty in his Foreign Relations Committee through the summer and fall of 1919, building a case against the president's efforts and allowing time to weaken Wilson's influence. In the meantime, newspapers, periodicals, and politicians chose sides in the debate as thousands of doughboys returned from France to add their own point of view to the fight. By the end of August, the public's attitude appeared to have shifted. Although there was still support for an American role in a postwar system, a degree of skepticism had emerged questioning the limits of that role. Lodge's tactic had scored points.

President Wilson became agitated over the debate and the apparent loss of momentum for the League. He determined to travel the nation rekindling public support for his position. In early September, the sixty-three-year-old chief executive left Washington on a nationwide train trip. Traveling from city to city, Wilson sought to use his personal conviction and leadership to stimulate public support. Particularly successful in the West, where he spoke to enthusiastic crowds, the president prompted his opponents, specifically the isolationists, to follow behind him giving speeches of their own.

On September 25, Wilson collapsed after a speech in Pueblo, Colorado. Worn out from months of travel, tense negotiations at home and abroad, and the emotion of his personal stake in the issue, Wilson's body failed. Back in Washington, he lay ill and out of the contest for several months. His wife, Edith Bolling Wilson, refused to allow visitors to upset her husband with any serious discussions about the League.

In the meantime, on September 19, the Foreign Relations Committee had added forty-five amendments and four reservations to Wilson's original treaty and League organization. When the Senate defeated those committee amendments, Senator Lodge created, on November 6, fourteen reservations. Essentially, the Senate would have to choose either Wilson's Treaty/League or Lodge's, with amendments, or reject both.

The isolationists (irreconcilables) had no problem. They favored neither Wilson's nor Lodge's options. Opposed to any association with the League, Borah, Johnson, and the others made clear their decision to reject both. Reservationists disagreed about the number and content of the various reservations, but they all agreed on one major concern—Article X of the League Charter or Covenant. It was over that article that America's entry into the League of Nations foundered.

Article X authorized the League to act to enforce its decisions, perhaps with military force. Many senators concluded that it threatened to remove the warmaking power from their body and place it with the international organization. American soldiers might fight wars, not with the Senate's approval, but under League mandate. On that critical point, no reservationist senator would budge. Article X had to go!

The president had argued all along that Article X provided a moral rather than legal requirement for the members of the League. He assured senators that they would keep their constitutional authority. He maintained, however, that some strong executive language was needed to buttress the League's authority. Article X served as that strength. As sick and out of touch as he seemed, Wilson required that Senator Hitchcock and other Democrats stay the course and support his League without removing Article X.

The Senate voted on November 19, 1919. The Wilson Democrats and the irreconcilables combined to defeat the Lodge treaty, with its reservations. Then, the reservationists and irreconcilables voted together to defeat Wilson's treaty. When the Senate voted again, in March 1920, to consider the Lodge treaty, it failed a second time. When one looks at the math, it seems incredible. Fourteen senators had their way! Eighty-two had divided their votes to prohibit any compromise.

Stunned and frustrated, President Wilson considered running for a third term in 1920 and making the election a "solemn referendum" on the League and his accomplishments. That did not occur, but his chosen candidate, James Cox, suffered a major defeat at the hands of Warren G. Harding, a strict reservationist senator from Ohio. And the Republicans held majorities in both houses of Congress. In some sense, the American public had responded. The era of Progressivism, in America and in international relations, appeared to have ended. President-elect Harding had coined the phrase "return to normalcy" during the 1920 campaign. He and the American voters seemed uncomfortable with the nation's new international power status, if that position required an ongoing responsibility to the global community beyond the nation's traditional self-interest. The Fourteen Points and the League of Nations became an uncomfortable reminder of a different time and commitment in U.S. diplomacy.

Even contemporary historians attacked President Wilson's efforts and laid the failure of the League at his doorstep. John Maynard Keynes and Harold Nicolson wrote scathing attacks blaming the whole postwar attitude of cynicism, profiteering, and resentment on Wilson. Those interpretations, along with the political success of the Republicans in 1920, were factors in persuading the American public to turn away from the international responsibilities that many Progressives hoped the nation would take upon itself.

DOCUMENTS

6.1.   President Wilson's Neutrality Proclamation, August 19, 1914

Wilson's proclamation expressed the fundamental U.S. policy as far back as George Washington's earliest diplomatic response. As a pacifist and a clear observer of the American attitude toward Europe, Wilson took a neutral stance that reflected a long-standing U.S. policy, an awareness of the current danger in Europe, and his own convictions.

The effect of the war upon the United States will depend upon what American citizens say and do. Every man who really loves America will act and speak in the true spirit of neutrality, which is the spirit of impartiality and fairness and friendliness to all concerned. The spirit of the nation in this critical matter will be determined largely by what individuals and society and those gathered in public meetings do and say, upon what newspapers and magazines contain, upon what ministers utter in their pulpits, and men proclaim as their opinions upon the street.

The people of the United States are drawn from many nations, and chiefly from the nations now at war. It is natural and inevitable that there should be the utmost variety of sympathy and desire among them with regard to the issues and circumstances of the conflict. Some will wish one nation, others another, to succeed in the momentous struggle. It will be easy to excite passion and difficult to allay it. Those responsible for exciting it will assume a heavy responsibility, responsibility for no less a thing than that the people of the United States, whose love of their country and whose loyalty to its government should unite them as Americans all, bound in honor and affection to think first of her and her interests, may be divided in camps of hostile opinion, hot against each other, involved in the war itself in impulse and opinion if not in action.

Such divisions amongst us would be fatal to our peace of mind and might seriously stand in the way of the proper performance of our duty as the one great nation at peace, the one people holding itself ready to play a part of impartial mediation and speak the counsels of peace and accommodation, not as a partisan, but as a friend. I venture, therefore, my fellow countrymen, to speak a solemn word of warning to you against that deepest, most subtle, most essential breach of neutrality which may spring out of partisanship, out of passionately taking sides.

The United States must be neutral in fact, as well as in name, during these days that are to try men's souls. We must be impartial in thought, as well as action, must put a curb upon our sentiments, as well as upon every transaction that might be construed as a preference of one party to the struggle before another.

Source: *Congressional Records of the United States*, 63rd Congress, 2nd Session, Senate Document #566 (Washington, DC: U.S. Government Printing Office, 1914), pp. 3–4 (hereafter referred to as *Congressional Record*).

6.2.   The Fourteen Points as Stated in Wilson's Speech Before Congress, January 8, 1918

In announcing broad and basic goals for the postwar world, President Wilson brought to bear his generation's progressive attitudes concerning international relations and their sense of what had caused the tragedy seen in World War I. While the specific points did not bind Wilson to actual policies, they set a clear tone for his intentions and acted as a powerful public relations tool in justifying America's selfless commitment to the conflict.

Once more, as repeatedly before, the spokesmen of the Central Empires have indicated their desire to discuss the objects of the war and the possible basis of a general peace. Parleys have been in progress at Brest-Litovsk between Russian representatives and representatives of the Central Powers to which the attention of all the belligerents have been invited [sic] for the purpose of ascertaining whether it may be possible to extend these parleys into a general conference with regard to terms of peace and settlement. The Russian representatives presented not only a perfectly definite statement of the principles upon which they would be willing to conclude peace but also an equally definite program of the concrete application of those principles. The representatives of the Central Powers, on their part, presented an outline of settlement which, if much less definite, seemed susceptible of liberal interpretation until their specific program of practical terms was added. That program proposed no concessions at all either to the sovereignty of Russia or to the preferences of the populations with whose fortunes it dealt, but meant, in a word, that the Central Empires were to keep every foot of territory their armed forces had occupied—every province, every city, every point of vantage—as a permanent addition to their territories and their power.

It is a reasonable conjecture that the general principles of settlement which they at first suggested originated with the more liberal statesmen of Germany and Austria, the men who have begun to feel the force of their own people's thought and purpose, while the concrete terms of actual settlement came from the military leaders who have no thought but to keep what they have got. The negotiations have been broken off. The Russian representatives were sincere and in earnest. They cannot entertain such proposals of conquest and domination. The whole incident is full of significances. It is also full of perplexity. With whom are the Russian representatives dealing? For whom are the representatives of the Central Empires speaking? Are they speaking for the majorities of their respective parliaments or for the minority parties, that military and imperialistic minority which has so far dominated their whole policy and controlled the affairs of Turkey and of the Balkan states which have felt obliged to become their associates in this war?

The Russian representatives have insisted, very justly, very wisely, and in the true spirit of modern democracy, that the conferences they have been holding with the Teutonic and Turkish statesmen should be held within open, not closed, doors, and all the world has been audience, as was desired. To whom have we been listening, then? To those who speak the spirit and intention of the resolutions of the German Reichstag of the 9th of July last, the spirit and intention of the Liberal leaders and parties of Germany, or to those who resist and defy that spirit and intention and insist upon conquest and subjugation? Or are we listening, in fact, to both, unreconciled and in open and hopeless contradiction? These are very serious and pregnant questions. Upon the answer to them depends the peace of the world.

But, whatever the results of the parleys at Brest-Litovsk, whatever the confusions of counsel and of purpose in the utterances of the spokesmen of the Central Empires, they have again attempted to acquaint the world with their objects in the war and have again challenged their adversaries to say what their objects are and what sort of settlement they would deem just and satisfactory. There is no good reason why that challenge should not be responded to, and responded to with the utmost candor. We did not wait for it. Not once, but again and again, we have laid our whole thought and purpose before the world, not in general terms only, but each time with sufficient definition to make it clear what sort of definite terms of settlement must necessarily spring out of them. Within the last week Mr. Lloyd George has spoken with admirable candor and in admirable spirit for the people and Government of Great Britain.

There is no confusion of counsel among the adversaries of the Central Powers, no uncertainty of principle, no vagueness of detail. The only secrecy of counsel, the only lack of fearless frankness, the only failure to make definite statement of the objects of the war, lies with Germany and her allies. The issues of life and death hang upon these definitions. No statesman who has the least conception of his responsibility ought for a

moment to permit himself to continue this tragical and appalling out-
pouring of blood and treasure unless he is sure beyond a peradventure
that the objects of the vital sacrifice are part and parcel of the very life
of Society and that the people for whom he speaks think them right and
imperative as he does.

There is, moreover, a voice calling for these definitions of principle
and of purpose which is, it seems to me, more thrilling and more compelling than any of the many moving voices with which the troubled air
of the world is filled. It is the voice of the Russian people. They are
prostrate and all but hopeless, it would seem, before the grim power of
Germany, which has hitherto known no relenting and no pity. Their
power, apparently, is shattered. And yet their soul is not subservient.
They will not yield either in principle or in action. Their conception of
what is right, of what is humane and honorable for them to accept, has
been stated with a frankness, a largeness of view, a generosity of spirit,
and a universal human sympathy which must challenge the admiration
of every friend of mankind; and they have refused to compound their
ideals or desert others that they themselves may be safe. They call to us
to say what it is that we desire, in what, if in anything, our purpose and
our spirit differ from theirs; and I believe that the people of the United
States would wish me to respond, with utter simplicity and frankness.
Whether their present leaders believe it or not, it is our heartfelt desire
and hope that some way may be opened whereby we may be privileged
to assist the people of Russia to attain their utmost hope of liberty and
ordered peace.

It will be our wish and purpose that the processes of peace, when they
are begun, shall be absolutely open and that they shall involve and permit henceforth no secret understandings of any kind. The day of conquest and aggrandizement is gone by; so is also the day of secret
covenants entered into in the interest of particular governments and
likely at some unlooked-for moment to upset the peace of the world. It
is this happy fact, now clear to the view of every public man whose
thoughts do not still linger in an age that is dead and gone, which makes
it possible for every nation whose purposes are consistent with justice
and the peace of the world to avow. . . .

We entered this war because violations of right had occurred which
touched us to the quick and made the life of our own people impossible
unless they were corrected and the world secure once for all against their
recurrence. What we demand in this war, therefore, is nothing peculiar
to ourselves. It is that the world be made fit and safe to live in; and
particularly that it be made safe for every peace-loving nation which,
like our own, wishes to live its own life, determine its own institutions,
be assured of justice and fair dealing by the other peoples of the world
as against force and selfish aggression. All the peoples of the world are

in effect partners in this interest, and for our own part we see very clearly that unless justice be done to others it will not be done to us. The program of the world's peace, therefore, is our program; and that program, the only possible program, as we see it, is this:

   I. Open covenants of peace, openly arrived at, after which there shall be no private international understandings of any kind but diplomacy shall proceed always frankly and in the public view.

  II. Absolute freedom of navigation upon the seas, outside territorial waters, alike in peace and in war, except as the seas may be closed in whole or in part by international action for the enforcement of international covenants.

 III. The removal, so far as possible, of all economic barriers and the establishment of an equality of trade conditions among all the nations consenting to the peace and associating themselves for its maintenance.

  IV. Adequate guarantees given and taken that national armaments will be reduced to the lowest point consistent with domestic safety.

   V. A free, open-minded, and absolutely impartial adjustment of all colonial claims, based upon a strict observance of the principle that in determining all such questions of sovereignty the interests of the populations concerned must have equal weight with the equitable claims of the government whose title is to be determined.

  VI. The evacuation of all Russian territory and such a settlement of all questions affecting Russia as will secure the best and freest cooperation of the other nations of the world in obtaining for her an unhampered and unembarrassed opportunity for the independent determination of her own political development and national policy and assure her of a sincere welcome into the society of free nations under institutions of her own choosing; and, more than a welcome, assistance also of every kind that she may need and may herself desire. The treatment accorded Russia by her sister nations in the months to come will be the acid test of their good will, of their comprehension of her needs as distinguished from their own interests, and of their intelligent and unselfish sympathy.

 VII. Belgium, the whole world will agree, must be evacuated and restored, without any attempt to limit the sovereignty which she enjoys in common with all other free nations. No other single act will serve as this will serve to restore confidence among the nations in the laws which they have themselves set and determined for the government of their relations with one another. Without this healing act the whole structure and validity of international law is forever impaired.

VIII. All French territory should be freed and the invaded portions restored, and the wrong done to France by Prussia in 1871 in the matter of Alsace-Lorraine, which has unsettled the peace of the world for nearly fifty years, should be righted, in order that peace may once more be made secure in the interest of all.

IX. A readjustment of the frontiers of Italy should be effected along clearly recognizable lines of nationality.

X. The peoples of Austria-Hungary, whose place among the nations we wish to see safeguarded and assured, should be accorded the freest opportunity to autonomous development.

XI. Rumania, Serbia, and Montenegro should be evacuated; occupied territories restored; Serbia accorded free and secure access to the sea; and the relations of the several Balkan states to one another determined by friendly counsel along historically established lines of allegiance and nationality; and international guarantees of the political and economic independence and territorial integrity of the several Balkan states should be entered into.

XII. The Turkish portion of the present Ottoman Empire should be assured a secure sovereignty, but the other nationalities which are now under Turkish rule should be assured an undoubted security of life and an absolutely unmolested opportunity of autonomous development, and the Dardanelles should be permanently opened as a free passage to the ships and commerce of all nations under international guarantees.

XIII. An independent Polish state should be erected which should include the territories inhabited by indisputably Polish populations, which should be assured a free and secure access to the sea, and whose political and economic independence and territorial integrity should be guaranteed by international covenant.

XIV. A general association of nations must be formed under specific covenants for the purpose of affording mutual guarantees of political independence and territorial integrity to great and small states alike.

In regard to these essential rectifications of wrong and assertions of right we feel ourselves to be intimate partners of all the governments and peoples associated together against the Imperialists. We cannot be separated in interest or divided in purpose. We stand together until the end. For such arrangements and covenants we are willing to fight and to continue to fight until they are achieved; but only because we wish the right to prevail and desire a just and stable peace such as can be secured only by removing the chief provocations to war, which this program does remove.

We have no jealousy of German greatness, and there is nothing in this program that impairs it. We grudge her no achievement or distinction of learning or of pacific enterprise such as have made her record very bright and very enviable. We do not wish to injure her or to block in any way her legitimate influence or power. We do not wish to fight her either with arms or with hostile arrangements of trade if she is willing to associate herself with us and the other peace-loving nations of the world in covenants of justice and law and fair dealing. We wish her only to accept a place of equality among the peoples of the world,—the new world in which we now live,—instead of a place of mastery.

Neither do we presume to suggest to her any alteration or modification of her institutions. But it is necessary, we must frankly say, and necessary as a preliminary to any intelligent dealings with her on our part, that we should know whom her spokesmen speak for when they speak to us, whether for the Reichstag majority or for the military party and the men whose creed is imperial domination.

We have spoken now, surely, in terms too concrete to admit of any further doubt or question. An evident principle runs through the whole program I have outlined. It is the principle of justice to all peoples and nationalities, and their right to live on equal terms of liberty and safety with one another, whether they be strong or weak. Unless this principle be made its foundation no part of the structure of international justice can stand. The people of the United States could act upon no other principle; and to the vindication of this principle they are ready to devote their lives, their honor, and everything they possess. The moral climax of this the culminating and final war for human liberty has come, and they are ready to put their own strength, their own highest purpose, their own integrity and devotion to the test.

Source: Ruhl J. Bartlett, ed., *The Record of American Diplomacy*, 4th ed. (New York: Alfred A. Knopf, 1964), pp. 459–461.

6.3. Letter from President Woodrow Wilson to the Senate Foreign Relations Committee Regarding the League of Nations, August 1919

The president sought to defend his clear position on Article X, the most controversial aspect of the League Covenant. In this letter, he took on the Senate's concern over the use of force and justified its moral necessity if the League was to have any real authority in the postwar era.

Mr. Chairman: I have taken the liberty of writing out a little statement that it might facilitate discussion by speaking directly on some points of controversy and upon which I thought an expression of opinion would be not unwelcome. . . .

Nothing, I am led to believe, stands in the way of ratification of the treaty except certain doubts with regard to the meaning and implication of certain articles of the Covenant of the League of Nations; and I must frankly say that I am unable to understand why such doubts should be entertained. . . . It was pointed out that . . . it was not expressly provided that the League should have no authority to act or to express a judgment on matters of domestic policy or that the right to withdraw from the League was not expressly recognized; and that the constitutional right of the Congress to determine all questions of peace and war was not sufficiently safeguarded. . . .

The United States will, indeed, undertake under Article 10 to "respect and preserve as against external aggression the territorial integrity and existing political independence of all members of the League," and that engagement constitutes a very grave and solemn moral obligation. But it is a moral, not a legal, obligation, and leaves our Congress absolutely free to put its own interpretation upon it in all cases that call for action. It is binding in conscience only, not in law.

Article 10 seems to me to constitute the very backbone of the whole Covenant. Without it the League would be hardly more than an influential debating society.

Source: Congressional Record, 65th Congress, 3rd Session, Senate Document #389 (1919), pp. 12–15.

6.4.   Speech by Senator Henry Cabot Lodge Calling for Revisions to the League of Nations, August 1919

The chairman of the Foreign Relations Committee strongly criticized Wilson's attempt to tie the United States to an international organization that might act irresponsibly or without serving the interests of American foreign policy. Lodge may not have agreed with the isolationists, but his speech did express concern for the threat to American unilateral options in the conduct of its relations if the United States joined the League under President Wilson's conditions.

For ourselves, we ask absolutely nothing. We have not asked any government or governments to guarantee our boundaries or our political independence. We have no fear in regard to either. We have sought no territory, no privileges, no advantages, for ourselves. That is the fact. It is apparent on the face of the treaty. I do not mean to reflect upon a single one of the powers with which we have been associated in the war against Germany, but there is not one of them which has not sought individual advantages for their own national benefit. I do not criticize their desires at all. The services and sacrifices of England and France and Belgium and Italy are beyond estimate and beyond praise. I am glad they should have what they desire for their own welfare and safety. But they all receive under the peace territorial and commercial benefits. We are asked to give, and we in no way seek to take. Surely it is not too much to insist that when we are offered nothing but the opportunity to give and to aid others we should have the right to say what sacrifices we shall make and what the magnitude of our gifts shall be. In the prosecution of the war we have unstintedly given American lives and American treasure. When the war closed we had 3,000,000 men under arms. We were turning the country into a vast workshop for war. We advanced ten billions to our allies. We refused no assistance that we could possibly render. All the great energy and power of the Republic were put at the service of the good cause. We have not been ungenerous. We have been devoted to the cause of freedom, humanity, and civilization everywhere. Now we are asked, in the making of peace, to sacrifice our sovereignty in important respects, to involve ourselves almost without limit in the affairs of other nations and to yield up policies and rights which we have maintained throughout history. We are asked to incur liabilities to an unlimited extent and furnish assets at the same time which no man can measure. I think it is not only our right but our duty to determine how far we shall go. Not only must we look carefully to see where we are being led into endless disputes and entanglements, but we must not forget that we have in this country millions of people of foreign birth and parentage.

Our one great object is to make all these people Americans so that we may call on them to place America first and serve America as they have done in the war just closed. We can not Americanize them if we are continually thrusting them back into quarrels and difficulties of the countries from which they came to us. We shall fill this land with political disputes about the troubles and quarrels of other countries. We shall have a large portion of our people voting not on American questions and not on what concerns the United States but dividing on issues which concern foreign countries alone. That is an unwholesome and perilous condition to force upon this country. We must avoid it. We ought to reduce to the lowest possible point the foreign questions in which we involve ourselves. Never forget that this league is primarily—I might say overwhelmingly—a political organization, and I object strongly to having the policies of the United States turn upon disputes where deep feeling is aroused but in which we have no direct interest. It will tend to delay the Americanization of our great population, and it is more important not only to the United States but to the peace of the world to make all these people good Americans than it is to determine that some piece of territory should belong to one European country rather than to another. For this reason I wish to limit strictly our interference in the affairs of Europe and Asia. We have interests of our own in Asia and the Pacific which we must guard upon our own account, but the less we undertake to play the part of umpire and thrust ourselves into European conflicts the better for the United States and the world.

Source: Congressional Record, 66th Congress, 1st Session (1919), pp. 8777–8778.

7

The Kellogg-Briand Pact: Pacificism in the 1920s

They will hammer their swords into plowshares and their spears into pruning hooks. Nation will not take up sword against nation; they will never again be trained for war.

—Micah 4:3

World War I's devastation created disappointment and despair within the international community. The unsatisfactory legacy of the Paris Peace Conference added to the skepticism. In the United States, the emotional struggle between President Woodrow Wilson and the Senate helped to regenerate a traditional homespun addiction to isolationism and pacifism as both public and political expressions. Frustrated and skeptical regarding U.S. involvement in World War I, many Americans came to believe that some form of international disarmament or the diplomatic outlawing of war could prevent another serious conflict.

On August 27, 1928, the major powers signed the Pact of Paris, known informally as the Kellogg-Briand Pact. It outlawed offensive war as an instrument of national policy. Fifteen countries signed the pact, and many others joined shortly thereafter. Within a decade, however, that idealistic belief in an international commitment to pacifism collapsed. The very nations involved in Kellogg-Briand armed for war.

Two broad concepts occupied the attention of diplomats and military analysts following World War I. One advanced the idea that some form of controlled disarmament would create a safer international environment. If nations could limit, on a grand scale, the size and type of weapons, they might avoid the tensions that arm races created, tensions inevitably leading to war. Postwar planners saw the naval arms race between Germany and England as a key cause of World War I. They hoped to prevent such tension and competition in the future through naval disarmament and arms treaties.

The second position suggested that nations might work together to ban war altogether. The idea had existed for years, and in the nineteenth century, the League to Enforce Peace had emerged as a modern attempt to advance the idea. The International Court of Justice, at The Hague, followed the same idea. So, too, did Woodrow Wilson's hope for an active League of Nations.

Following Wilson's League defeat at the hands of the United States Senate, both the government and the American public shifted away from "Wilsonian internationalism." A mood of isolationism and skepticism regarding international involvement surfaced during the postwar decade. Both the government and the public, however, wanted assurances on security and stability. The new Republican administration of President Warren G. Harding worked to accomplish that goal. Secretary of State Charles Evans Hughes developed some limited and marginal U.S. oversight within the League of Nations operations. Those interests, however, never threatened America's unilateral foreign policy. A powerful Republican Senate, led first by Henry Cabot Lodge (1918–1924), then by William E. Borah (1924–1933), chairmen of the Foreign Relations Committee, made sure that the United States avoided any dangerous "entanglements."

While the Harding administration and the Senate did a careful balancing act, Secretary Hughes encouraged a series of naval disarmament conferences to address the danger of a postwar arms race, an issue with both financial and strategic impact. The initial idea for a conference came from Senator Borah, the staunch Republican isolationist who had battled President Wilson so vigorously over the League. The thought of postwar naval disarmament in no way upset Borah's view of unilateral American protection. The United States would occupy the driver's seat in any such multinational system and protect its independent self-interest. Harding and Hughes adopted the concept and invited the major European powers and Japan to meet in Washington in 1921.

After lengthy debate and a variety of internal deals, the Washington Naval Conference agreed to destroy a significant number of existing battleships and establish a future ratio between the powers—5:5:3:1.7:1.7. The United States and Britain could have 5 battleships for every 3 of Japan's and every 1.7 for France and Italy. The Five Power Treaty was signed on February 6, 1922, amid popular acclaim. Its conditions hoped to maintain the ratio until 1936.

The treaty had flaws. It only considered battleships, and while naval strategists still depended on those massive weapons, they also constructed aircraft carriers, cruisers, destroyers, and submarines. Naval expenditures and growth continued. That oversight and others became apparent at the Geneva Naval Conference in 1927, when the original signatories at Washington squabbled over specifics. A new secretary of state, Frank Kellogg, and a new president, Calvin Coolidge, seemed embarrassed at the inability of the United States to achieve any successful results at Geneva. Essentially, another naval arms race began, one that simply avoided battleship construction.

The Geneva Conference led some critics to conclude that war might be prevented by other means than limiting the weapons of war. A number of well-known American intellectuals had argued for some kind of international system to ban war for years. Salmon Levinson, a Chicago attorney, coined the term "outlawry of war" and began a movement to do something about it. In 1921 he organized the American Committee for the Outlawry of War. Nicholas Butler and James Shotwell, at Columbia University, became noteworthy advocates of the idea. So, too, did John Dewey, the most respected of liberal American intellectuals. By the mid-1920s, a powerful lobby of influential scholars, journalists, and business leaders had allied around the issue of outlawing war. The problem centered on how to do it—what machinery, what form of enforcement? On those important details, the advocates disagreed.

In early 1927, Shotwell moved the issue from an intellectual debate to active diplomacy. He met with Aristide Briand, the French foreign minister, and discussed the concept, actually proposing that France and the United States sign some form of agreement that would outlaw war. Briand leaped at the suggestion. Any possibility of having the United States join France in some postwar agreement would protect French security interests in Europe. That remained a critical concern that Briand's government had faced since the failure of the United States to join the League of Nations.

On April 6, 1927, bypassing communication with the U.S. State Department, the French minister sent a letter to the Associated Press proposing a joint Franco-American pact denouncing war as an instrument of international policy. The media provided major coverage of the French proposition.

In the uncertain diplomatic atmosphere of the mid-1920s, the idea of outlawing war caught public and political attention and confronted Frank Kellogg, the secretary of state, with an increasingly popular cause. Kellogg and other American leaders sensed that Briand had attempted to lure the United States into some kind of Franco-American defense treaty, something isolationists would refuse to accept. Kellogg, and official Washington, also disliked the fact that Briand had gone over their heads to the American media and public. Yet, public response to Briand's offer in the United States was favorable. Kellogg had to do something.

Senator Borah provided the answer. Salmon Levinson had earlier convinced Borah that a general outlawing of war could take place without some specific machinery that might drag the United States into a military alliance. In simple terms, America could protect its unilateral foreign policy position (isolationism) and still advocate an international concept based on generating mass public support. It would serve as a moral deterrent to war, based on popular appeal. Rather than a bilateral Franco-American treaty, why not a multilateral agreement? Senator Arthur Capper introduced a resolution in support, and Secretary Kellogg came on board.

Between April and December 1927, while the American public showed an increased interest in the idea, Kellogg worked on an answer to Briand's request. He recommended that the bilateral idea expand to include the other international powers. The French agreed reluctantly. Fifteen nations signed the Pact of Paris on August 27, 1928. It outlawed war as an instrument of foreign policy except in a defensive response. During the next few months, a number of other nations joined the pact, and by the time President Herbert Hoover signed America's ratification of the treaty in 1929, forty-seven countries had entered the Kellogg-Briand Pact. Both Kellogg and Briand won the Nobel Peace Prize for their efforts.

The Senate had approved the treaty by a vote of 85–1, reflecting clearly the public's interest in postwar pacifism and the influence of the lobbyists who had publicized the idea throughout the discussion. Oddly, however, the senators followed the vote with legislation funding the construction of fifteen new naval cruisers. The *New York Evening Post* recognized the irony: "If, after just having signed a peace treaty with twenty-six nations," the editorial argued, "we need fifteen new cruisers, how many would we have needed if we hadn't just signed a peace treaty with twenty-six nations?"[1] The first sign of cynicism had emerged publicly. At the Washington Gridiron Club's annual variety show in 1929, a male chorus needled the naval officers present with a parody of *H.M.S. Pinafore*. The following lyrics were sung to the melody "Little Buttercup":

> Sadder and wiser, of diplomats I'm very shy. Our ships they are slighting. They say "no more fighting." We scarcely dare think what it means; the Navy they're sinking. The Army they're shrinking—Thank God we still have the Marines.[2]

If "the devil is in the details," the Pact of Paris left few details to enforce its basic position. It served frankly as a plea or prayer for peace, not a policy. Critics quickly assessed its weaknesses.

Military officers, both in the army and navy, deplored the thought of pacifism as an alternative to preparedness. They saw it as both a threat to their self-interest and an unrealistic evaluation of a lawless international environment. General Douglas MacArthur considered the Kellogg-Briand Pact "sinister." He spoke against it publicly at the Soldiers and Sailors Club in New York, but his criticism attracted little attention. Other naval and army officers confided to their diaries the conclusion that isolationism and pacifism, manifest in Kellogg-Briand, had drugged Americans into a false sense of security. The military would remind the nation of that stupor in 1940–1941.

In the Congress, both "Big Navy" supporters and pragmatic legislators questioned what Borah advocated and Secretary Kellogg pursued. Senator James Reed of Missouri called the treaty "an international kiss." Carter Glass, the tough senior senator from Virginia, informed his constituents that Kellogg-Briand was not worth the cost of a postage stamp. The criticism centered on the fact that the treaty had so many qualifications, interpretations, and loopholes that it really failed to provide any form of enforcement.

Another group of opponents believed that an Anglo-French conspiracy designed the pact to advance their interests at U.S. expense. While America dismantled its battleships and trusted in a pacifist pact, the European powers and Japan skirted the rules, defined their own terms for defense, and left the United States in the dark, disarmed and naïve.

Kellogg confronted all of those criticisms defending the policy before Congress. Public opinion, Senator Borah, and President Coolidge provided a powerful combination of popular and political muscle and drove the Kellogg-Briand Pact through the Senate easily.

Ultimately, the critics proved accurate. Without a clear mechanism for or commitment to enforcement, the pact had no chance of success. Problems confronted the international community in the 1930s that made moral pledges to outlaw war meaningless. The world depression, the rise of aggressive dictatorships or military regimes in Europe and Asia, and the national and ideological struggles of the 1930s made Kellogg-Briand a sad memory of a more naïve and idealistic decade. The world stormed toward war, and the best hopes of the 1920s had failed to prevent the coming conflict.

NOTES

1. Quoted in Thomas A. Bailey, *A Diplomatic History of the American People*, 10th ed. (Englewood Cliffs, NJ: Prentice-Hall, 1980), p. 650.

2. Quoted in Allan R. Millett and Peter Maslowski, *For the Common Defense: A Military History of the United States* (New York: Free Press, 1994), p. 391.

DOCUMENTS

7.1. Kellogg-Briand Pact of 1928—Treaty between the United States and other Powers providing for the renunciation of war as an instrument of national policy. Signed at Paris, August 27, 1928; ratification advised by the Senate, January 16, 1929

The pact was self-explanatory. It expressed the basic hopes and assumptions of a postwar generation of diplomats and world leaders. The possibility of a multilateral moral statement renouncing war seemed the best hope for peace in an international community lacking the realistic mechanisms to accomplish the task.

BY THE PRESIDENT OF THE UNITED STATES OF AMERICA.
A PROCLAMATION.

WHEREAS a Treaty between the President of the United States of America, the President of the German Reich, His Majesty the King of the Belgians, the President of the French Republic, His Majesty the King of Great Britain, Ireland and the British Dominions beyond the Seas, Emperor of India, His Majesty the King of Italy, His Majesty the Emperor of Japan, the President of the Republic of Poland, and the President of the Czechoslovak Republic, providing for the renunciation of war as an instrument of national policy, was concluded and signed by their respective Plenipotentiaries at Paris on the twenty-seventh day of August, one thousand nine hundred and twenty-eight, the original of which Treaty, being in the English and the French languages, is word for word as follows:

THE PRESIDENT OF THE GERMAN REICH, THE PRESIDENT OF THE UNITED STATES OF AMERICA, HIS MAJESTY THE KING OF THE BELGIANS, THE PRESIDENT OF THE FRENCH REPUBLIC, HIS MAJESTY THE KING OF GREAT BRITAIN, IRELAND AND THE BRITISH DOMINIONS BEYOND THE SEAS, EMPEROR OF INDIA, HIS MAJESTY THE KING OF ITALY, HIS MAJESTY THE EMPEROR OF JAPAN, THE PRESIDENT OF THE REPUBLIC OF POLAND, THE PRESIDENT OF THE CZECHOSLOVAK REPUBLIC,

Deeply sensible of their solemn duty to promote the welfare of mankind; Persuaded that the time has come when a frank renunciation of war as an instrument of national policy should be made to the end that the peaceful and friendly relations now existing between their peoples may be perpetuated; Convinced that all changes in their relations with one another should be sought only by pacific means and be the result of a peaceful and orderly process, and that any signatory Power which shall hereafter seek to promote its national interests by resort to war should be denied the benefits furnished by this Treaty; Hopeful that, encouraged by their example, all the other nations of the world will join in this humane endeavor and by adhering to the present Treaty as soon as it comes into force bring their peoples within the scope of its beneficent provisions, thus uniting the civilized nations of the world in a common renunciation of war as an instrument of their national policy; Have decided to conclude a Treaty and for that purpose have appointed as their respective Plenipotentiaries:

ARTICLE I: The High Contracting Parties solemnly declare in the names of their respective peoples that they condemn recourse to war for the solution of international controversies, and renounce it, as an instrument of national policy in their relations with one another.

ARTICLE II: The High Contracting Parties agree that the settlement or solution of all disputes or conflicts of whatever nature or of whatever origin they may be, which may arise among them, shall never be sought except by pacific means.

ARTICLE III: The present Treaty shall be ratified by the High Contracting Parties named in the Preamble in accordance with their respective constitutional requirements, and shall take effect as between them as soon as all their several instruments of ratification shall have been deposited at Washington.

This Treaty shall, when it has come into effect as prescribed in the preceding paragraph, remain open as long as may be necessary for adherence by all the other Powers of the world. Every instrument evidencing the adherence of a Power shall be deposited at Washington and the Treaty shall immediately upon such deposit become effective as; between the Power thus adhering and the other Powers parties hereto. It shall be the duty of the Government of the United States to furnish each Government named in the Preamble and every Government subsequently adhering to this Treaty with a certified copy of the Treaty and of every instrument of ratification or adherence. It shall also be the duty of the Government of the United States telegraphically to notify such Governments immediately upon the deposit with it of each instrument of ratification or adherence.

IN FAITH WHEREOF the respective Plenipotentiaries have signed this

Treaty in the French and English languages both texts having equal force, and hereunto affix their seals.

DONE at Paris, the twenty-seventh day of August in the year one thousand nine hundred and twenty-eight.

Certified to be a true copy of the signed original deposited with the Government of the United States of America.

FRANK B. KELLOGG

Secretary of State of the United States of America

AND WHEREAS it is stipulated in the said Treaty that it shall take effect as between the High Contracting Parties as soon as all the several instruments of ratification shall have been deposited at Washington;

AND WHEREAS the said Treaty has been duly ratified on the parts of all the High Contracting Parties and their several instruments of ratification have been deposited with the Government of the United States of America, the last on July 24, 1929;

NOW THEREFORE, be it known that I, Herbert Hoover, President of the United States of America, have caused the said Treaty to be made public, to the end that the same and every article and clause thereof may be observed and fulfilled with good faith by the United States and the citizens thereof.

IN TESTIMONY WHEREOF, I have hereunto set my hand and caused the seal of the United States to be affixed.

DONE at the city of Washington this twenty-fourth day of July in the year of our Lord one thousand nine hundred and twenty-nine, and of the Independence of the United States of America the one hundred and fifty-fourth.

HERBERT HOOVER

By the President:

HENRY L. STIMSON

Secretary of State

NOTE BY THE DEPARTMENT OF STATE

ADHERING COUNTRIES: When this Treaty became effective on July 24, 1929, the instruments of ratification of all of the signatory powers having been deposited at Washington, the following countries, having deposited instruments of definitive adherence, became parties to it:

Afghanistan	Finland	China
Albania	Peru	Latvia
Austria	Guatemala	Cuba
Portugal	Hungary	Liberia
Rumania	Iceland	Denmark
Bulgaria	Russia	Lithuania
Serbia	Siam	Croatia & Slovenia

Dominican Republic	Netherlands	Spain
Egypt	Nicaragua	Sweden
Estonia	Norway	Turkey
Ethiopia	Panama	

Source: Charles I. Bevans, ed., *Treaties and Other International Agreements of the United States of America-Multilateral*, vol. 2 (Washington DC: U.S. Government Printing Office 1969), pp. 732–735.

7.2. "The Renunciation of War," an Address by Edwin Borchard, Yale Law Professor and Pacifist, August 22, 1928

The speech given at Williams College in Massachusetts questioned the sincerity of England and France, and the nature of "defensive" war so important in the Kellogg-Briand Pact. Borchard challenged both the intent and the reality of the treaty. Rather than seeing Kellogg-Briand as naïve, Professor Borchard believed that France and England intended to use the concept to manipulate international affairs in their own self-interest.

The origin of the negotiations between the United States and other powers leading to the conclusion of the so-called Briand-Kellogg Pact for the reununciation of war is well known. Beginning with an expression of good-will in M. Briand's note of April 6, 1927, commemorating the entry of the United States into the war and expressing France's willingness to conclude a treaty renouncing war between France and the United States, the negotiations developed rapidly. On June 20, 1927, the French Foreign Minister presented the draft of a treaty embodying his proposal, providing for a condemnation of "recourse to war" and renouncing war as between France and the United States as an "instrument of their national policy." The settlement of all disputes was never to be sought "except by pacific means."

On December 28, 1927, Mr. Kellogg proposed to the French ambassador the extension of the proposed declaration to all the principal Powers. It was argued in the United States that, if the treaty were signed by the United States and France alone, it would be a treaty of alliance. In his accompanying draft of a treaty, Mr. Kellogg recommended the outright and unconditional renunciation of war and the solution of disputes by pacific means only. The French press was critical. It was maintained that France had obligations to the League of Nations and could not make these new commitments. But the criticism was dropped after forty-eight hours on the publication of the French reply undertaking to renounce "wars of aggression." This gave apparently a new turn to the negotiations. The State Department did not reply officially, but officers of the Department pointed out that the term "aggression" changed the entire meaning of the proposition and was not acceptable to the United States. In this position the State Department seems to have had the support of the American press. Editorially it was agreed that "renunciation of aggressive war" was too intricate an expression to define and that the French interpolation of this qualification left Mr. Kellogg's proposition denatured of its vital part and meaningless. Mr. Kellogg pointed out in his new note that the first French note of June 20, 1927, contained no limitation of wars of aggression. In this connection it is well to note that Sir Austen Chamberlain rejected the attempted definition of "aggressor" in the Geneva Protocol as, I believe, one who declines to submit a dispute to discussion in these words: "I therefore remain opposed to this attempt to define the 'aggressor' because I believe that it will be a trap for the innocent and a signpost for the guilty."

Considerable correspondence took place in the early part of 1928 as to the construction to be given to the proposed treaty. In his note of February 27, 1928, in explaining his objection to qualifications on the obligation to renounce war, Mr. Kellogg stated:

> The ideal which inspires the effort so sincerely and so hopefully put forward by your [the French] Government and mine is arresting and appealing just because of its purity and simplicity; and I cannot avoid the feeling that if governments should publicly acknowledge that they can only deal with this ideal in a technical spirit and must insist on the adoption of reservations impairing, if not utterly destroying, the true significance of their common endeavors, they would be in effect only recording their impotence, to the keen disappointment of mankind in general.

The same thought was expressed in Mr. Kellogg's speech to the Council on Foreign Relations on March 15, 1928, in which he said:

> It seems to me that any attempt to define the word "aggression," and by exceptions and qualifications to stipulate when nations are justified in going to war with one another, would greatly weaken the effect of any treaty such as that under consideration and virtually destroy its positive value as a "guaranty of peace."

The subsequent negotiations, however, disclose the unfortunate fact that these very exceptions and qualifications to which Mr. Kellogg objected as so nullifying in effect have, in fact, found their way into the treaty as now universally construed.

The French Government maintained that the treaties must be construed so as not to bar the right of legitimate defense, the performance of obligations under the Covenant of the League of Nations, under the treaties of Locarno, under its treaties of alliance with its allies—now for some unexplainable reason called treaties of neutrality—that the treaty was to become ineffective if violated by one nation, and that it was to be signed by every state before it became effective as to any state.

With the exception of this last reservation, Secretary Kellogg agreed to this interpretation of the French Government—in his speech before the American Society of International Law on April 28, 1928, and incorporated his interpretation of the reservations as to self-defense, wars under the League Covenant, under the treaties of Locarno, and certain undefined and evidently unknown "neutrality" treaties, in his note of June 23, 1928, to the Powers, some fifteen in number, adding that; "none of these governments has expressed any dissent from the above-quoted construction."

In his note of May 19, 1928, accepting the American proposition in principle, Sir Austen Chamberlain for Great Britain expressed his assent to the reservations made by France and added a new one in the following paragraph:

> There are certain regions of the world, the welfare and integrity of which constitute a special and vital interest for our peace and safety. His Majesty's Government have been at pains to make it clear in the past that interference with these regions cannot be suffered. Their protection against attack is to the British Empire a measure of self-defense. It must be clearly understood that His Majesty's Government in Great Britain accept the new treaty upon the distinct understanding that it does not prejudice their freedom of action in this respect. The Government of the United States have comparable interests, any disregard of which by a foreign Power they have declared they would regard as an unfriendly act.

The words in italics were repeated in the British note of July 18, 1928, undertaking to sign the treaty only on the understanding that the British Government maintained this freedom of action with respect to those regions of the world in which it had "a special and vital interest."

II. The original proposition of Mr. Kellogg was an unconditional renunciation of war. The treaty note qualified by the French and British reservations constitutes no renunciation or outlawry of war, but in fact and of late a solemn sanction for all wars mentioned in the exceptions and qualifications. When we look at the exceptions we observe that they include wars of self-defense, each party being free to make its own interpretation as to when self-defense is involved, wars under the League Covenant, under the Locarno treaties, and under the French treaties of alliance. If self-defense could be limited to the terms "to defend its territory from attack or invasion," as suggested by Mr. Kellogg, it would be of some value, but it is understood that no specific definition of self-defense is necessarily accepted.

Considering these reservations, it would be difficult to conceive of any wars that nations have fought within the last century, or are likely to fight in the future, that cannot be accommodated under these exceptions. Far from constituting an outlawry of war, they constitute the most definite sanction of specific wars that has ever been promulgated. War heretofore has been deemed like a disease—neither legal nor illegal. Now by a world treaty, the excepted wars obtain the stamp of legality. This cannot be charged primarily to Secretary Kellogg, whose intentions were of the best, but is a result of the reservations insisted upon by European Powers, which, it is still to be feared, comprehend peace as a condition of affairs achieved through war or the threat of war. The mere renunciation of war in the abstract in the first article of the treaty has but little scope for application, in view of the wars in the concrete, which the accompanying construction of the treaty sanctions. It is idle to suppose that the official construction given to the treaty by all the signatory Powers is not as much an integral part of the treaty as if it had been written into Article 1.

Again it will be noticed that we recognize a British claim to use war as an instrument of national policy in certain undefined "regions of the world," any "interference" with which by anybody, including the United States, will be regarded by Great Britain as a cause of war. To this we subscribe. When the United States at the first Hague Conference secured recognition by our cosignatories for the Monroe Doctrine, it was regarded as an achievement of American diplomacy. But the Monroe Doctrine has geographical limits known to everybody. To this new British claim there are no geographical limits. The vague and expansive terms of the British claim to make war, now recognized by us, covers any part of the world in which Britain has "a special and vital interest." No such broad claim of the right to make war has ever before been recognized.

But the most extraordinary feature of this treaty still remains to be mentioned. It will have been noticed that we recognize the legality of League wars and Locarno wars. As Europe correctly seems to assume, we are now bound by League decisions as to "aggressors" and League policy generally, but without any opportunity to take part in the deliberations leading to League conclusions. We indeed recognize by this treaty the legal right of the League to make war even against us, and it will be observed that Sir Austen Chamberlain in his note of May 19, 1928, frankly admits that respect for the obligations arising out of the Covenant is "the foundation of the policy" of Great Britain. Whether the further European claim that we are bound to support League conclusions as to "aggressor" nations, and other political conclusions, either by joining with the League or by refusing to trade with the League-declared pariah, is sustainable or not, at the very best it places us in the uncomfortable position either of being bound by decisions in the making of which we had no part or of having recriminations leveled against us for refusing to support our treaty.

The new contract begins with diverse interpretations of its obligations, for European views, reflected by Mr. Edwin James of the New York Times, leave no doubt that Europe regards this treaty as a means of involving us in European politics. And we are entangled in the most dangerous way, for we are bound by decisions made in our absence, even decisions made against ourselves—because the recognition of the French and British reservations, now made the authoritative interpretation of the treaty by all the signatories, is a commitment for us. Our hands are tied, not theirs. The reservations are made at our expense, not theirs. Far better and safer would it be had we openly joined the League of Nations and been privileged to take part in deliberations which may lead to most important consequences. We might have been able to prevent undesirable conclusions and use our bargaining power to obtain occasional benefits and advantages instead of disadvantages only. We are now about to sign a treaty in which we expressly recognize the right of the other signatories to make war upon anybody, including ourselves, for the purpose of enforcing, even against us, their mutual obligations under the Covenant of the League of Nations, not to mention individual undefined national interests in any part of the world. They alone will determine the occasion of such action, without our participation.

In justice to Europe, it cannot be said that they have left us in doubt as to their conception of our obligations. Indeed, these obligations are expressly or implicitly contained in the very reservations which the United States has accepted. Should we repudiate these commitments, we shall be denounced as a violator of our own treaty and not without some justification.

It has not been a pleasant task to analyze this Pact of Paris. The original American proposal was progressive, pure and simple, to use Mr. Kellogg's expression. The European amendments transformed the proposal into something entirely different—into a universal sanction for war, into a recognition by us of Europe's right to wage war, even against the United States, whenever the individual interests of certain nations are deemed to require it and whenever the League, in its uncontrolled discretion, decides upon it.

Need more be said? Would it not be far better either to join the League outright and have a share in those deliberations which to us may be so portentous or, better still, make the recourse to arbitration of justifiable issues and the submission to conciliation of non-justifiable issues obligatory at the request of either party? That would be a positive commitment which would make war extremely difficult, whereas the present treaties make war extremely easy. It is to be doubted whether the supposed valuable psychological effects of renunciation of war in the abstract can counterbalance the politic recognition of the legality of war in the concrete—not to speak of its commitments for American foreign policy. If this treaty is ever ratified, the test of its efficacy will be its effect on a limitation of armaments. The President's declaration that it is not expected to have any such effect and the avowed pleasure of certain foreign official newspapers at that promise hardly justify at the moment strong hopes of such a result. The abolition of war will, therefore, have to be pursued along other lines. Possibly in the elimination of the economic causes of conflict, including the attempted monopoly of raw materials and markets, and in the entente of business interests across national boundaries, there lies more hope than in legal efforts to preserve by force the status quo. Other machinery is needed to make changes in existing conditions, when time and circumstances require. To that effort but little attention has yet been paid. These matters are mentioned merely to indicate that, even if the Pact of Paris is not ratified or is accompanied by explanatory reservations on our part, the solution of the problem of war and peace among independent nations has, perhaps, hardly been begun.

Source: Williamstown Institute of Politics, Williams College, Massachusetts, August 22, 1928.

7.3.   Excerpts of U.S. Senate Foreign Relations Committee Hearings with Secretary Kellogg on the Kellogg-Briand Pact, December 7 and 11, 1928

The discussions indicated the senators' interest in obtaining a clear definition of the treaty's intent. Most senators showed a particular concern to retain U.S. options to defend the nation's interests in the hemisphere.

The **CHAIRMAN (William E. Borah of Idaho)**. Mr. Secretary, the committee asked that you be with us to-day for the purpose of going over this treaty. If you desire, you can make any sort of statement you wish, or the committee may ask you questions, whichever you prefer.

Secretary of State Frank KELLOGG. It is immaterial to me. I understood from you the committee wanted to know whether this treaty was a recognition of Russia and the Russian Soviet Government.

The CHAIRMAN. All right. Mr. Secretary, suppose we take up first the question of what are these supposed reservations; the position of France and the position of Great Britain as expressed in their notes, which are referred to in popular parlance as reservations. What is your judgment or what is your view as to the effect of those communications as constituting any changes in the treaty or modifications of the treaty?

Secretary KELLOGG. Any communications made with any of the governments up to the signing of the treaty have been published. I made up my mind when we started negotiations that the only way to obtain this treaty was to publish every note as it was delivered, and I do not think the treaty would ever have been signed if it had not been for the opinion of the world passing on these notes as they appeared, so that every country had full opportunity to discuss the treaty, and if they believed there were any obligations imposed on the United States beyond the agreement not to go to war, I think they would have suggested it. They knew, from the notes that I wrote, that I was not willing to impose any obligation on the United States. I knew that was out of the question. I knew that not many countries would agree to affirmative obligations, if we did.

As you will remember, the British Government refused the security pact because they said it imposed on them certain obligations which some of the governments had claimed existed under Article X of the league; and in consequence of agitation on that question, the fourth assembly of the league with a single negative vote accepted a resolution repudiating any obligation to go to war in defense of any country attacked. But I will not go into the discussion.

Senator SWANSON. As I understand from what you say, if this multilateral treaty is violated by any other nation, there is no obligation, moral or legal, for us to go to war against any nation violating it?

Secretary KELLOGG. That is thoroughly understood. It is understood by our Government; and no other government made any suggestion of any such thing. I knew, from the attitude of many governments, that they would not sign any treaty if there was any moral obligation or any kind of obligation to go to war. In fact, Canada stated that. The other governments never suggested any such obligation. As to the reservations, of course I can not go over all the discussions on this treaty, which lasted many months. There is absolutely nothing in the notes of the various governments which would change this treaty, if the treaty had been laid on the table and signed as it is, without any discussion. It is true, of course, that during this discussion, through these notes with the various nations, many questions were raised as to the meaning of the treaty.

It was for the reason that I did not care to have any private discussions about the matter that I insisted on carrying out the negotiations by notes. I was invited to attend a conference in Europe to negotiate this treaty, which I declined. I was invited to send a lawyer with the lawyers of all the other governments to discuss it. I knew that would be the end of any treaty, and I refused that; so that the negotiation was carried on by notes entirely, and you have got them all. I will illustrate some of the questions. The question was raised by some governments, does this take away the right of self-defense? It seemed to me incomprehensible that anybody could say that any nation would sign a treaty which could be construed as taking away the right of self-defense if a country was attacked. That is an inherent right of every sovereign, as it is of every individual, and it is implicit in every treaty. Nobody would construe the treaty as prohibiting self-defense. Therefore I said it was not necessary to make any definition of "aggressor" or "self-defense." I do not think it can be done, anyway, accurately. They have been trying to do it in Europe for six or eight years, and they never have been able to accurately define "aggressor" or "self-defense."

Senator McLEAN. You stated that the question as to whether action is in self-defense or not, was to be left entirely to the government interested.

Secretary KELLOGG. Left entirely to that government. I knew that this Government, at least, would never agree to submit to any tribunal the question of self-defense, and I do not think any of them would. That is one question that was raised.

Senator SWANSON. The term "self-defense" is not confined to defense of any territory, but any nation may send troops into any territory where it may be necessary for its self-defense.

Secretary KELLOGG. Certainly; the right of self-defense is not limited to territory in the continental United States, for example. It means that this Government has a right to take such measures as it believes necessary to the defense of the country, or to prevent things that might endanger the country; but the United States must be the judge of that, and it is answerable to the public opinion of the world if it is not an honest defense; that is all.

Senator REED of Missouri. The whole of that rule would apply equally to every other country.

Secretary KELLOGG. Certainly; nor do I think it is practicable to do anything else; although there are idealists who say that it is practicable. It is entirely impracticable, in my judgment. Since, however, the purpose of the United States is so far as possible to eliminate war as a factor in international relations, I can not state too emphatically that it will not become a party to any agreement which directly or indirectly, expressly or by implication, is a military alliance. The United States can not obligate itself in advance to use its armed forces against any other nation of the world. It does not believe that the peace of the world or of Europe depends upon or can be assured by treaties of military alliance, the futility of which as guarantors of peace is repeatedly demonstrated in the pages of history.

Senator REED of Missouri. But is it your position that when this treaty was signed, that left it so that the treaty stood there to speak for itself, without regard to any of the negotiations that had gone on, or constructions that had been placed?

Secretary KELLOGG. That is undoubtedly true, except I think they had the right to believe that the legal effect of the treaty is what I state; and they all finally did say that they believed that the question of self defense was answered.

Senator REED of Missouri. I do not want to haggle. I am not trying to haggle, you understand, about this; but I would like to know whether it was your position that when this treaty is signed, when it comes to be put in force, we are to take the treaty by its four corners and consider the language of the treaty, or whether we are to take into consideration, in construing it, certain statements that have been made during the progress of the negotiations; and if certain statements, then what are they, and where do we stop?

I will say this, to make clear my idea. Of course we all know that under the law people may negotiate for six months about a contract and they may write hundreds of letters about it, but finally, when they sign the contract, the contract speaks for itself, and all that has preceded is supposed to be merged in the language of the contract. Now, if that rule applies here, then these negotiations and all these things that took place are unimportant.

Senator REED of Pennsylvania. Mr. Secretary, suppose that some important European power declared war upon Panama, and invaded the Territory of Panama. Would you construe our right of self-defense to authorize us to object to that?

Secretary KELLOGG. Certainly. We have guaranteed the independence of Panama. Outside of that question, we have a right to defend our treaty for maintaining the integrity and independence of Panama just as much as we have a right to defend San Francisco or New York.

Senator REED of Pennsylvania. How about Colombia?

Secretary KELLOGG. South America?

Senator REED of Pennsylvania. Yes.

Secretary KELLOGG. That brings up the Monroe doctrine. The Monroe doctrine is simply a doctrine of self-defense. It does not consist of any agreement between the United States and any country in the Western Hemisphere or anywhere else.

The CHAIRMAN. It is perfectly certain that every nation, when the time arrives, will construe this treaty in the way it regards as justifying self-defense. Every nation will construe the treaty for itself, as to what constitutes self-defense, and it does not make any difference what you said and what was stated afterwards, when the time comes, what she regards as self-defense she will construe as self-defense. Glad to know the Secretary has no sympathy, either.

Senator SWANSON. I understand in your statement giving official interpretation of this treaty, you state there would be no moral obligation for us to use any force.

Secretary KELLOGG. Yes; and furthermore no country suggested it; and no country said anything about it, at all, or made any suggestion at all, except Canada, and Canada said there was no obligation to apply sanctions; if there had been, I am sure she would not have signed it.

The CHAIRMAN. Mr. Secretary, the time has arrived when we have to go on the floor of the Senate. I suppose that is all we can do to-day.

Source: Hearing Before the Committee on Foreign Relations, U.S. Senate, Seventieth Congress, Second Session on The General Pact for The Renunciation of War, signed at Paris August 27, 1928; December 7 and 11, 1928. (Printed for the use of the Committee on Foreign Relations) (Washington DC: U.S. Government Printing Office, 1928), pp. 1–28.

7.4.   Letter from the French Embassy to the U.S. State Department, August 27, 1928

This document provides a short review of the French position regarding the significance of the pact and its impact on French national security.

1. Position of France
NAVAL SITUATION OF FRANCE AND ITALY

1°. No difficulty can arise between France and the United States.

2°. France has no fear to entertain against Great Britain, although the enormous naval superiority of the latter country might create an uneasy feeling on the part of the other.

3°. On the side of Italy France may have serious fears due to the fact that the Government of that country is constitutionally irresponsible and depends entirely upon the will of a single man. Everyday the Italian press, which relies entirely upon Mussolini, addresses threats to France and the whole Italian nation is being

fed with the idea that conquests on the side of her neighbor country
are possible. Likely, such threats are not serious; nevertheless they
constitute a disturbing factor. History shows that an act of madness
is always possible when national feelings have been systematically
raised to a certain pitch.

4°. An alliance between Italy and Germany is not inconceivable and
in that case France, obliged to face two fronts, would be put in a
dangerous situation. In fact, free communications with Africa
where she finds an important proportion of her military contin-
gents, are vital. Italian raids against such an important artery may
be extremely serious.

5°. Is it absolutely sure that in a war of that kind France could
depend upon the unconditional help of Great Britain?

6°. As far as United States are concerned it is true that they have
declared that war is a crime and that consequently the nation which
causes war is criminal. But they have always declined to consider
the consequences of that principle and they seem to claim the right
to furnish supplies indiscriminately to the aggressive nation, and
to her victim under penalty of war.

2. Position of Italy

1°. In case of war with France Italy would be placed in an extremely disadvantageous position. Her enormous length of coast
exposes her to attacks from all sides and her main rail lines might
be cut at any time.

2°. From a strategic point of view, Italy is entirely surrounded by
French possessions (Bizerte, Corsica, Toulon, and on her eastern
coasts, Yugo-Slavia who would probably be an allied [ally] of
France).

3°. Economically speaking, Italy produces no iron, no coal, no
metal, no lumber, no textiles, no oil. Her financial resources are
limited. Her political situation is uncertain.

4°. Italy depends also completely upon foreign help for her food
supplies. A few German submarines almost succeeded in bringing
shortage of food in England. What could numerous French submarines not do?

5°. From the point of view of her resources as well as of her geographic independence, Italy finds herself, as regards France, in serious conditions of inferiority. Naval forces constitute only one
factor of that disparity.

6°. Since Italy lives within the limits of a sea which it would be easy to close entirely, no country could be more attached to the principle of the freedom of the seas, a principle of which America is an ardent defender.

3. Conclusion

For France as well as for Italy, there are questions more vital than proportion of naval armament (neither in fact wants a race for armaments). The question of general security is the most important for them.

For France absolute security lies within a defensive entente with Great Britain and a favorable interpretation of the *Kellogg Pact* by the United States.

For Italy her security lies within the principles of the freedom of the sea.

Consequently nothing could be better for the peace of the Old Continent in which America is so interested, as shown by present negotiations, than an extension by the United States of the principles of Article 7 of the Washington Conference:[1]

The contracting Powers agree that whenever a situation arises which, in the opinion of any one of them, involves the application of the stipulations of the present Treaty (the *Kellogg Pact*), and renders desirable discussion of such application, there shall be full and frank communication between the Contracting Powers concerned.

The United States might object that such a clause is similar to "foreign entanglements." In fact the United States have the right to protect themselves against an event which constitutes for them a serious threat. They have the right to be interested in a conference against war just as they would interest themselves into a conference against plague, against noxious insects, etc. The principle of the foreign policy of the United States was announced by President Coolidge when he said in his Gettysburg speech: Everywhere there is war or threat of war, something happens which is contrary to the interests of the United States.[2] Hence the necessity for them to take measures of prophylactic nature. [WASHINGTON,] September 25, 1929.

NOTES

1. Article VII of the Nine-Power Treaty concerning China, signed at Washington, February 6, 1922; *Foreign Relations*, 1922, vol. 1, p. 280.

2. In his speech delivered on May 30, 1928, President Coolidge said in part: "It is almost impossible to conceive of any conflict anywhere on earth which would not affect us injuriously." *Congressional Record*, vol. 69, pt. 10, p. 10729.

Source: Foreign Relations Series—1929, vol. 1 (1943), pp. 59–61.

8

The Good Neighbor Policy

In the field of world policy I would dedicate this nation to the policy of the good neighbor—the neighbor who resolutely respects himself and because he does so, respects the rights of others.
—Franklin D. Roosevelt
Inaugural Address, March 4, 1933

The Good Neighbor Policy served as a practical effort to improve commercial and political relations with America's neighbors in the hemisphere. Developed by two presidents during the 1930s, the policy acted to alter more than thirty years of U.S. arrogance in its actions toward Latin American states, an arrogance that created deep resentment and distrust. Well meaning in its approach, the Good Neighbor Policy nonetheless aimed to advance and protect the self-interest of the United States.

At the end of the Spanish-American War (1898), U.S. business and security interests in the Caribbean and Central America expanded rapidly. While Great Britain maintained a commercial advantage in the region, the United States accelerated its business interests in competition with England. At the same time, American security concerns led to political strategies designed to make the Caribbean an "American lake," and Central America a U.S. sphere of influence. To pursue those policies, the United States began to intervene directly in the economies and politics of various Caribbean and Central American nations.

In December 1904, President Theodore Roosevelt issued a corollary to the Monroe Doctrine indicating that the United States might, when appropriate, intervene in the internal affairs of Latin American nations:

> Chronic wrongdoing . . . may in America, as elsewhere, ultimately require intervention by some civilized nation, and in the Western Hemisphere the adherence of the United States to the Monroe Doctrine may force the United States, however reluctantly, in flagrant cases of such wrongdoing or impotence, to the exercise of an international police power.[1]

Two years earlier, Luis Drago, Argentina's foreign minister, had publicly protested foreign intervention in Latin America. The Roosevelt Corollary challenged that interpretation and frankly indicated a willingness to disregard it. Most of the nations in the hemisphere agreed with Drago, but the United States proceeded to apply power to enforce its own conclusions.

During the next two decades, four presidential administrations applied military force occasionally, commercial pressure often, and diplomatic influence regularly to promote U.S. interests in the Caribbean and Central America. Broadly termed the "Big Stick" and "dollar diplomacy," the policies of Roosevelt, William H. Taft, Woodrow Wilson, and Calvin Coolidge applied aspects of the Roosevelt Corollary in their relations with hemisphere neighbors. While the more obvious expressions of that intervention persisted in the Caribbean and Central America, U.S. business interests also expanded their control into other Latin American markets and products.

American relations with Mexico, its nearest Latin neighbor, appeared equally unpleasant. Anti-American sentiments had existed in Mexico since the Mexican War (1848). During the early twentieth century, U.S.-Mexican affairs heated. President Wilson insulted the Mexican government during a revolution in that country that saw three presidents struggle to take the place of Porfirio Diaz, a dictator who had ruled Mexico from 1876 to 1911. While Wilson approved of the reform-minded Francisco Madero (1911–1913), the U.S. president refused to acknowledge his successor, Victoriano Huerta, a general who overthrew and murdered Madero.

Traditionally, American policy recognized de facto foreign governments no matter how they had achieved power. That policy had existed since the presidency of Thomas Jefferson. Wilson refused to follow it in Huerta's case and used a variety of political and economic pressures to remove him from office. He told a British visitor, "I am going to teach the South American republics to elect good men!"[2] Eventually, General Venustiano Carranza replaced Huerta (1914), and, to compound an already testy U.S.-Mexican environment, an American military force commanded by John J. Pershing pursued the bandit Pancho Villa into Mexico (1916), violating its territorial sovereignty. While Wilson had never invoked the Roosevelt Corollary to defend his actions (the administration referred to its policy as "watchful waiting"), the United States did not act more aggressively than the term watchful waiting implied.

In 1917, partly in response to the previous issues, the Mexican Constitution of 1917, in Article 27, denied any foreign rights to subsoil land ownership. In simple terms, the government was telling U.S. oil companies that the wealth they were taking out of Mexico no longer belonged to them. For both economic and political reasons, Mexico had decided to send a clear signal to its Yankee neighbor. Enough was enough! Clearly, throughout the hemisphere nations were fed up with U.S. arrogance, exploitation, and intervention.

A number of American anti-imperialists who had criticized U.S. policy in the Philippines and China following the Spanish-American War also turned their attacks on the abuses of the Big Stick. Particularly, those critics assailed the use of U.S. Marines to "pacify" various countries. American troops intervened in Cuba, the Dominican Republic, Haiti, Honduras, Nicaragua, and Panama on a number of occasions. Critics concluded that the Marines protected the business interests of the United Fruit Company, a major U.S. business, at the expense of human rights and international cooperation. Coupled with the economic problems in Mexico, American policy makers found themselves in an unpleasant position. Powerful within the hemisphere, the United States had become feared and despised by its neighbors and attacked at home for its imperialist behavior. None of that worked in the best interests of American foreign policy.

As secretary of commerce, Herbert Hoover pondered the unpleasant situation in the mid-1920s. He had concluded that the United States needed to employ a more cooperative attitude in its business relations with hemisphere neighbors, particularly Mexico. When he became president in 1929, Hoover carried that attitude, plus a Quaker's disaffection for the use of military force, into the White House. To inaugurate the new posture of friendship, Hoover undertook a ten-nation goodwill tour of Latin America between his election in 1928 and his inauguration in the spring of 1929. During his inaugural address, Hoover commented, "It never has been and ought not to be the policy of the United States to intervene by force to secure or maintain contracts between our citizens and foreign states."[3] President Hoover and Secretary of State Henry Stimson shifted U.S. attitudes from intervention to cooperation and initiated the concept of the "good neighbor." In 1930 Hoover ordered the publication of J. Reuben Clark's memorandum. Clark, a State Department official, had written a lengthy analysis of the Roosevelt Corollary and its impact on U.S.–Latin American affairs. The report concluded that U.S. intervention appeared unjustified through any legitimate interpretation of the Monroe Doctrine. In that regard, Clark challenged the past three decades of American foreign policy vis-à-vis the hemisphere. By publishing the document, President Hoover basically endorsed it.

Additionally, Hoover returned to a previous U.S. policy of de facto as opposed to de jure recognition of Latin American governments. As noted above, Woodrow Wilson refused recognition to Latin America governments until they elected "good men." That policy (de jure recognition) smacked of arrogance on America's part, and its hemisphere neighbors resented the approach. Who was the United States to decide what made "good government"? Hoover agreed. He announced that the United States would recognize "in fact" whatever governments the Latin American states chose to represent them, whether those governments gained power at the ballot box or through force. (The de facto policy did not apply in Central America, where the United States had signed a multinational treaty creating a different method of recognition.)

During Hoover's presidency, the basic elements of the Good Neighbor Policy took shape. The concept allowed America to pursue its commercial and security interests, but it served notice that the United States had begun to back away from the Big Stick. President Franklin D. Roosevelt (1933–1945) simply adopted Hoover's ideas and expanded them.

The Roosevelt administration approached "Good Neighborism" from two different perspectives. Between 1933 and 1936, American policy remained unilateral and aimed to improve commercial and political relations on a one-on-one basis with various Latin American nations. Between 1936 and 1940, Roosevelt sought to create a Pan-American or multinational Good Neighborism that would include a coalition of hemisphere states. During 1933, the policy moved from words to action. At the Seventh International Conference of American States, in Montevideo, Uruguay, Secretary of State Cordell Hull supported a Latin American Convention renouncing foreign intervention. In simple terms, he agreed with the Drago Doctrine and rejected the Roosevelt Corollary. Additionally, the secretary's personal presence at the meeting, his friendly attitude, and his obvious "aim to please" behavior sent a favorable signal throughout the hemisphere. It may not have erased memories of America's Big Stick arrogance, but it held out hope that the Yankee Colossus might alter its behavior.

The United States followed its actions at Montevideo with several new responses. Its troops would withdraw from Haiti. The United States suspended the Platt Amendment, which had given it "rights" to intervene in Cuba. America also reduced its role in the internal affairs of Panama and the Dominican Republic. Then the Roosevelt administration extended de facto recognition to governments in Central America. Finally,

The United States in Middle America, 1898–1940

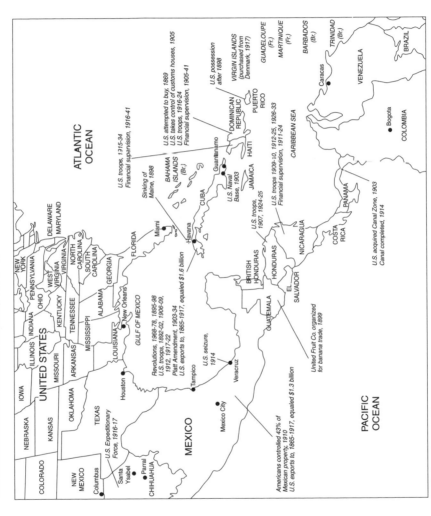

at the Buenos Aires Inter-American Conference in 1936, the United States formally renounced its right to intervene in the internal affairs of any Latin American state.

While U.S. policy sought to reduce political tension between itself and its hemisphere neighbors, America also shored up and advanced its economic interests. Between 1934 and 1941, the United States negotiated thirteen trade agreements with Latin American nations. At the same time, the Export-Import Bank (created during the depression years to provide loans to U.S. businesses) extended that option to assist commercial expansion in Latin America. Roosevelt's policy aimed to reduce America's image under the Big Stick without eliminating U.S. commercial profits and growth in the hemisphere.

As the international situation worsened between 1936 and 1940, with policies and actions that finally led to world war, policy makers in the United States began to shift strategy regarding Latin America. Sensing the possibility of a conflict with either Germany or Japan, Roosevelt had to consider the security implications within the hemisphere. To protect American security interests, Good Neighborism shifted its emphasis to Pan-American cooperation and multinational strategy.

Since its inception in 1823, the Monroe Doctrine had served as a unilateral expression of U.S. intentions to keep others out of the hemisphere. It had, however, always carried the idea that the nations of the Western Hemisphere held a mutual Pan-American need to protect themselves from outside threats. With a major world war looming, Roosevelt resurrected that long ignored idea. We could all work together to ensure our security.

In 1936 Roosevelt had called for a special Inter-American Conference for Peace at Buenos Aires. As noted above, the United States formally rejected its right to intervene in the internal affairs of other states in the Americas. At the same time, however, Secretary Hull received a basic commitment for consultation among the states in the event of a European war. Two years later, at Lima, Peru, the Pan-American nations set up a mechanism to do just that.

As the United States continued to explore and develop various methods to rebuild its image, enhance trade, and develop a multilateral security package with the Latin American states, a serious crisis erupted in Mexico. In 1938 the Mexican government invoked Article 27 of its 1917 Constitution and expropriated all foreign oil holdings. U.S. oil corporations held most of that land, and many Latin Americans held their breath, expecting a resumption of the Big Stick. Business interests used enormous pressure to have Roosevelt's administration do the expected and force Mexico to yield. The government refused. While some advisors in the State Department favored military action, most disagreed. Ultimately, Roosevelt thought it inappropriate. The president recognized Mexico's right of expropriation, demanding only that that government reimburse oil companies for their losses. To many critics, the action, or lack of it, smacked of weakness and inefficiency. To those who supported the decision, both at home and in Latin America, it convinced them that the U.S. government meant what it had said about the "Good Neighbor." The policy had passed a very serious test.

Previous meetings and the good will that resulted from the Mexican crisis led to more cooperation. In September 1939, three weeks after Germany invaded Poland, the hemisphere foreign ministers met in Panama, declared neutrality, and instituted a "safety zone" around the Western Hemisphere. The announcement warned belligerents to conduct no military activities inside that zone. At Havana, Cuba, in 1940, the foreign ministers agreed that any attack on a member of the hemisphere would be viewed as an attack on all of them. The Cuban meeting also led to a decision to prevent Germany from seizing any of the European colonies in the Caribbean owned by the Dutch or French as a result of German conquest of those countries.

Increasingly, Latin American states distanced themselves from Germany diplomatically and commercially. Eventually, nine Caribbean and Central American nations declared war on Germany and Japan, and Colombia, Mexico, and Venezuela broke relations as well. Brazil, the largest country in South America, became an active ally of the United States in World War II. By the 1942 Rio Conference, every nation in the hemisphere except Argentina and Chile had severed diplomatic relations with the enemies of the United States.

In return, the United States provided loans, supplies, and lucrative trade benefits to its neighbors as a form of appreciation and continued commercial involvement. During World War II, the United States became Latin America's principal foreign investor and trader. Latin American raw materials sold to the United States helped support the industrial power that America generated against Germany and Japan. The relationship, both economic and political, played a role in the U.S. victory in World War II in 1945.

The evolution of the Good Neighbor Policy, from its roots with Herbert Hoover in the 1920s to its refinement and expansion under Franklin Roosevelt in the 1930s and 1940s, seemed to alter a relationship that had gone sour. Clearly, the "Good Neighbor" United States served America's interests in the hemisphere far better than the Big Stick. It also appeared to serve Latin American interests as well. As World War II came to a close in August 1945, questions began to emerge in the United States and Latin America as to whether the policies that had worked so well would continue in the postwar international environment.

NOTES

1. Quoted in Thomas A. Bailey, *A Diplomatic History of the American People*, 10th ed. (Englewood Cliffs, NJ: Prentice-Hall, 1980), p. 505.

2. Quoted in ibid., p. 555.

3. Quoted in Wayne S. Cole, *An Interpretive History of American Foreign Relations* (Homewood, IL: Dorsey, 1974), p. 345.

DOCUMENTS

8.1.   Excerpts from the Drago Doctrine, December 29, 1902

*Luis Drago, the Argentine foreign minister, had questioned the
Roosevelt Corollary early in the twentieth century as both illegal
and unethical. His position reflected Latin American resentment
of the U.S. policy of intervention that had dominated U.S–Latin
American policy in the early 1900s.*

Among the fundamental principles of public international law which
humanity has consecrated, one of the most precious is that which decrees
that all states, whatever be the force at their disposal, are entities in law,
perfectly equal one to another, and mutually entitled by virtue thereof
to the same consideration and respect.

The acknowledgment of the debt, the payment of in its entirety, can
and must be made by the nation without diminution of its inherent rights
as a sovereign entity, but the summary and immediate collection at a
given moment, by means of force, would occasion nothing less than the
ruin of the weakest nations, and the absorption of their governments,
together with all the functions inherent in them, by the might of the
earth. The principles proclaimed on this continent of America are otherwise. "Contracts between a nation and private individuals are obligatory according to the conscience of the sovereign and may not be the
object of compelling force," said the illustrious Hamilton. "They confer
no right of action contrary to the sovereign will."

The United States has gone very far in this direction. The eleventh
amendment to its Constitution provided in effect, with the unanimous
assent of the people, that the judicial power of the nation should not be
extended to any suit in law prosecuted against one of the United States
by citizens of another State, or by its citizens or subject of any foreign
State. The Argentine Government has made its provinces indictable, and
has even adopted the principle that the nation itself may be brought to
trial before the supreme court on contract which it enters into with individuals.

What has not been established, what could in no wise be admitted, is
that, once the amount for which it may be indebted has been determined
by legal judgement, it should be deprived of the right to choose the
manner and the time of payment, in which it has as much interest as the

creditor himself, or more, since its credit and its national honor are involved therein.

The collection of loans by military means implies territorial occupation to make them effective and territorial occupation signifies the suppression or subordination of the governments of the countries on which it is imposed.

Such a situation seems obviously at variance with the principles many times proclaimed by the nations of America, and particularly with the Monroe doctrine, sustained and defended with so much zeal on all occasions by the United States, a doctrine to which the Argentine republic has heretofore solemnly adhered.

Among the principles which the memorable message of December 2, 1823, enunciates, there are two great declarations which particularly refer to these republics, viz, "The American continents are henceforth not to be considered as subjects for colonization by any European powers," and "... with the governments ... whose independence we have ... acknowledged, we could not view any interposition for the purpose of oppressing them, or controlling in any other manner their destiny, by any European power in any other light than as the manifestation of an unfriendly disposition toward the United States."

Source: Foreign Relations Series—1902 (1903), pp. 1–5.

8.2.   A Portion of President Herbert Hoover's Inaugural Address, March 4, 1929

The newly elected chief executive discussed his visit to Latin America and offered a brief, if careful, expression of the changing attitude regarding U.S. intervention under the Roosevelt Corollary. Hoover's intent was clear. His country would begin to steer away from the aggressive interventionism that had marked previous administrations.

I have lately returned from a journey among our sister Republics of the Western Hemisphere. I have received unbounded hospitality and courtesy as their expression of friendliness to our country. We are held by particular bonds of sympathy and common interest with them. They are each of them building a racial character and a culture which is an impressive contribution to human progress. We wish only for the maintenance of their independence, the growth of their stability, and their prosperity. While we have had wars in the Western Hemisphere, yet on the whole the record is in encouraging contrast with that of other parts of the world. Fortunately the New World is largely free from the inheritances of fear and distrust which have so troubled the Old World. We should keep it so.

Source: *Inaugural Addresses of the Presidents of the United States* (Washington, DC: U.S. Government Printing Office, 1965), pp. 225–233.

8.3.   *Literary Digest*, December 8, 1928

A Cuban diplomat published a piece questioning President Hoover's true intentions regarding the hemisphere, calling on him to back up his words with specific actions. The article suggested some of the anger and resentment that seethed among Latin Americans in the 1920s toward the Yankee Colossus.

If Mr. Hoover wants to conquer the immediate sympathy of Latin America, he should at once announce a change in the policy of his country, declaring that the Monroe Doctrine does not mean that the American continent is only for the United States, that Haiti will be evacuated, that Nicaragua shall be freed from foreign yoke, that Cuba will see the quick abrogation of the Platt Amendment, that our commercial treaties will cease being one-sided affairs, that our countries will be free to manage their own affairs as they deem fit, and that the United States is a real friend in fact, and not a conqueror.

Source: *Literary Digest*, December 8, 1928, p. 15.

8.4.   President Franklin Roosevelt's Address Before the Special Session of the Governing Board of the Pan American Union Celebrating Pan American Day, Washington, D.C., April 12, 1933

The speech came a month after his inaugural address and served as the first direct response to Latin American listeners regarding the Good Neighbor Policy. Roosevelt had fundamentally adopted the policy conclusions that President Hoover developed during the previous administration.

I rejoice in this opportunity to participate in the celebration of "Pan American Day" and to extend on behalf of the people of the United

States a fraternal greeting to our sister American Republics. The celebration of "Pan American Day" in this building, dedicated to international good-will and cooperation, exemplifies a unity of thought and purpose among the peoples of this hemisphere. It is a manifestation of the common ideal of mutual helpfulness, sympathetic understanding and spiritual solidarity. There is inspiration in the thought that on this day the attention of the citizens of the twenty-one Republics of America is focused on the common ties—historical, cultural, economic, and social—which bind them to one another. Common ideals and a community of interest, together with a spirit of cooperation, have led to the realization that the well-being of one Nation depends in large measure upon the well-being of its neighbors. It is upon these foundations that Pan Americanism has been built.

This celebration commemorates a movement based upon the policy of fraternal cooperation. In my Inaugural Address I stated that I would "dedicate this Nation to the policy of the good neighbor—the neighbor who resolutely respects himself and, because he does so, respects the rights of others—the neighbor who respects his obligations and respects the sanctity of his agreements in and with a world of neighbors." Never before has the significance of the words "good neighbor" been so manifest in international relations. Never have the need and benefit of neighborly cooperation in every form of human activity been so evident as they are today. Friendship among Nations, as among individuals, calls for constructive efforts to muster the forces of humanity in order that an atmosphere of close understanding and cooperation may be cultivated. It involves mutual obligations and responsibilities, for it is only by sympathetic respect for the rights of others and a scrupulous fulfillment of the corresponding obligations by each member of the community that a true fraternity can be maintained.

The essential qualities of a true Pan Americanism must be the same as those which constitute a good neighbor, namely, mutual understanding, and, through such understanding, a sympathetic appreciation of the other's point of view. It is only in this manner that we can hope to build up a system of which confidence, friendship and good-will are the cornerstones.

In this spirit the people of every Republic on our continent are coming to a deep understanding of the fact that the Monroe Doctrine, of which so much has been written and spoken for more than a century was and is directed at the maintenance of independence by the peoples of the continent. It was aimed and is aimed against the acquisition in any manner of the control of additional territory in this hemisphere by any non-American power.

Hand in hand with this Pan American doctrine of continental self-defense, the peoples of the American Republics understand more clearly, with the passing years, that the independence of each Republic must recognize the independence of every other Republic. Each one of us must grow by an advancement of civilization and social well-being and not by the acquisition of territory at the expense of any neighbor.

In this spirit of mutual understanding and of cooperation on this continent you and I cannot fail to be disturbed by any armed strife between neighbors. I do not hesitate to say to you, the distinguished members of the Governing Board of the Pan American Union, that I regard existing conflicts between four of our sister Republics as a backward step.

Your Americanism and mine must be a structure built of confidence cemented by a sympathy which recognizes only equality and fraternity. It finds its source and being in the hearts of men and dwells in the temple of the intellect.

We all of us have peculiar problems, and, to speak frankly, the interest of our own citizens must, in each instance, come first. But it is equally true that it is of vital importance to every Nation of this Continent that the American Governments, individually, take, without further delay, such action as may be possible to abolish all unnecessary and artificial barriers and restrictions which now hamper the healthy flow of trade between the peoples of the American Republics.

I am glad to deliver this message to you, Gentlemen of the Governing Board of the Pan American Union, for I look upon the Union as the outward expression of the spiritual unity of the Americas. It is to this unity which must be courageous and vital in its element that humanity must look for one of the great stabilizing influences in world affairs.

In closing, may I refer to the ceremony which is to take place a little later in the morning at which the Government of Venezuela will present to the Pan American Union the bust of a great American leader and patriot, Francisco de Miranda. I join with you in this tribute.

Source: Samuel Rosenman, ed., *The Public Papers and Addresses of Franklin D. Roosevelt*, vol. 2 (New York: Random House, 1938), pp. 129–132.

8.5.   Mexican Government's Formal Response to U.S. Criticism of Its Decision to Invoke Article 27 Expropriating Subsoil Oil Leases, February 1940

The Sinclair Oil Company and other commercial interests in the United States had lobbied aggressively to persuade the U.S. government and the American people to view Mexico's actions as illegal and harmful. In a forceful response, the Mexican government responded with a sound, clear defense.

The Standard Oil Company of New Jersey has distributed a booklet under the title of "The Mexican Oil Seizure," with the manifest purpose of conveying to the mind of its readers the impression that the government of Mexico, in expropriating the properties of the oil companies, has acted in violation of the laws of Mexico and of the principles of International Law; and also, that in the negotiations conducted with some of the oil companies for the purpose of finding a solution to the problem, the Government of Mexico, from motives which are likely to be misunderstood, has repudiated its offers formally propounded, thereby making impossible any kind of settlement.

Out of respect for public opinion we will set forth in a subsequent special publication the misrepresentations and erroneous interpretations made by the Standard Oil Company in its pamphlet as to the origin of the dispute and as to the negotiations in which the agents of the expropriated companies participated.

For the time being, reference will only be made to the chief misrepresentations which are found in the booklet:

It is stated that the oil companies had an investment in Mexico of several hundred million dollars and that the Mexican Government has admitted its financial inability to pay. The conclusion drawn in the pamphlet is that the companies had no other recourse than to request diplomatic protection from their own governments in support of their claims. These arguments are based on the contention that Mexico could not legally expropriate the properties because of its obvious inability to pay prompt and adequate compensation to the owners. The conclusion is false, because it is based on two premises both of which are equally false:

a). It is not true that the value of the properties of the oil companies lies between 262 million dollars as a minimum and 500 million dollars as a maximum, as is alleged in the pamphlet. Such figures were taken, as therein stated, from an article published in the magazine "Hoy" of July 31, 1939, the author of which is Mr. Luis Cabrera, an attorney of Mexico City. As an instance of the hasty manner in which the writer of that pamphlet proceeds in attempting to establish his assertions, a literal translation of what was really said by Mr. Cabrera follows:

I shall therefore take at random 300 million dollars as representing the value of the various properties of the 17 companies, the expropriation of which has been decreed; and I shall fix the further sum of one hundred million dollars as the value of the properties that must yet be expropriated in order to complete the socialization plan of the oil industry. The total, therefore, is four hundred million dollars which Mexico must pay, theoretically, right down and in cash. If anybody was to tell me that this figure is arbitrary, I would answer to him that indeed it is, and that it is devoid of any scientific basis; but that all the other figures which are mentioned are just as arbitrary, etc. . . .

The writer of the article published in "Hoy" simply figures the sum of 262 million dollars as within Mexico's capacity to pay.

The Mexican Government characterizes as enormously exaggerated the figures which the companies have spread abroad regarding the value of their properties. Inasmuch as there has been no appraisal up to the present time, the only basis available for valuation is the company's own figures in the company's own books. According to the consolidated balance sheets of all the expropriated companies on March 18, 1938, the value of their permanent assets in Mexican pesos amounted to 112,899,890.44. . . .

The companies have systematically refused to discuss the value of their properties. Their representative admits that he proposed during the negotiations with the Government that the question of appraisal should not be considered. Such an attitude on the part of the companies is due to the fact that since they can not deny our right to expropriate private property with, naturally, payment of just compensation, they are actually seeking to create the impression that Mexico could not lawfully carry out the expropriation because of its inability to pay the fantastic sum of millions of dollars which the companies arbitrarily and prematurely assigned to their properties.

b). It is not true that Mexico has recognized her inability to pay, but, quite to the contrary, the Mexican Government has repeatedly declared its willingness to pay to the companies the full value of their properties. The assertion of their representative that the Government of Mexico promised to pay compensation to the companies with only a part of the net proceeds from the oil operations of the expropriated properties, is likewise untrue, for the Government has declared on different occasions its willingness to place at the disposal of the companies a substantial part of all the oil products destined for export, namely, a portion of the total production, including the oil reserves which belonged to the Government of Mexico prior to the expropriation and which have a great potential and actual value.

The fact that Mexico has suspended payment of its foreign debt does not mean, as is suggested in the pamphlet, that Mexico is unable to pay for the oil properties which were expropriated, inasmuch as it actually has at its disposal, an industry obviously productive, the income from which shall be devoted preferentially to the full payment of the compensation.

Among the most important nations of the world there are many who have postponed payment of some of their obligations, and it has not yet occurred to any one to say that such countries are actually suffering a permanent incapacity to meet their obligations.

The pamphlet makes reference to the compensation to American citizens for the value of their agricultural lands. In this particular it is pertinent to point out that an agreement has been reached with the Government of the United States whereby a commission has been created and is already functioning and that the Government of Mexico is making annual payments even before the exact value of the lands has been finally determined.

In the pamphlet an incomplete and malicious narrative of the oil controversy is given, misrepresenting the facts in order to fit them to the conclusion which is sought to be reached, and which conclusion is that the Government of Mexico always entertained the avowed purpose of expropriating the oil companies, taking advantage of various events in the accomplishment of that purpose. The evidence justifies no such conclusion.

It is true, as it is stated in the Standard Oil publication, that the oil companies were always the object of spirited attacks, they being considered as the exploiters of the natural and human resources of the country. In this connection, it should be remembered that the agents of the oil companies, over the years, committed countless rapacious acts such as defrauding the national treasury, bribing officials, seeking to impair the political stability of the government, and that they even made attacks against private property and human life. In fact, they went so far as to disturb at times the friendly relations between the peoples and the governments of the United States and Mexico.

It is also true that the aim of the various Governments of Mexico in the last few years was to place under the control of the Nation, for the benefit of the Mexican people, this important industry on which the national economy depends to a large extent. The methods employed by the oil companies and their attempts to create a political and economic power stronger than the State itself, were deemed prejudicial to public policy in Mexico. Various Mexican administrations, including the present one, have had the purpose in mind of accomplishing such an aim through a slow and gradual process, by creating a national organization to undertake the exploitation of the national reserves, and then gradually increasing the production of the oil lands. This plan was already being developed and important results had already been obtained when the expropriation took place.

Why was the Government compelled to change this plan and to decree the expropriation, placing all the oil properties in Mexico in the hands of a governmental institution? An examination of the events which preceded the expropriation proves that the present Administration had no other course open to it but the one it actually followed, thus being obliged to give a different direction to its policy from that originally intended. These were the actual facts:

I. The workers demanded from the various companies operating in Mexico a revision of their labor contracts. This was a spontaneous act on the part of the labor unions and constituted a normal request, normal not only in Mexico, but in all other countries where the workers are granted freedom and where the workers' right to organize themselves for the defense of their interests is recognized.

II. In view of the fact that the Unions and the companies could not come to an agreement concerning the conditions of the new contract, the workers chose to declare a strike. This is, also, a spontaneous act on the part of the workers and, likewise, a lawful act in any country where the right to strike is recognized.

III. Inasmuch as the strike last for some time and there was no indication of an early agreement between the parties to the controversy, and furthermore, as due to the lack of fuel caused by the strike, it was feared that all economic life in Mexico would be paralyzed, the Mexican Government deemed it its duty to intervene in the dispute, in order to bring about a rapid solution and to prevent a grave danger to the entire Nation. This was the first official or governmental action taken by the Mexican authorities in the controversy between the companies and their workers.

IV. After an unsuccessful attempt was made, first through the Department of Labor and afterwards by the President personally, to obtain a conciliation between the parties, the President suggested to the workers that they should return to their work immediately, and submit their case to the Board of Conciliation and Arbitration which is located in the City of Mexico.

The intervention of the Mexican Government to that end is beyond reproach, from any point of view whatsoever, and was inspired by the highest regard for the public interest.

V. The Board of Conciliation and Arbitration appointed a committee of three experts to study the different aspects of the dispute. After having heard a considerable number of expert witnesses on the questions submitted, chosen both by the companies and the workers, the committee produced a comprehensive and well-reasoned report which served the Board as the basis for its decision.

VI. It is not true that the award rendered by the Board of Conciliation and Arbitration conceded to the workers their full demands. The Board took a reasonable course between the demands of the labor organizations and the concessions the companies were willing to grant. The award, based on the reports of the experts, decrees that the companies must guarantee certain benefits to the workers, by way of increase of wages, medical attention, hygienic dwellings, vacations, payment for extra-time, extra payment for labor in unhealthy regions, etc., amounting to the sum of twenty-six million Mexican pesos, in addition to the amounts covered by the former pay schedules of the workers.

The statement made by the representatives of the companies that the net profit of all the said companies amounted to twenty-three million pesos is false. The experts showed that the companies had previously earned much higher profits and the Mexican Government, which now controls the oil industry, is in a position to declare that the assertion made by the experts is fundamentally correct.

VII. As soon as the decision of the Board of Conciliation and Arbitration was known, the companies announced both in the American and Mexican press, that they were not willing to submit themselves to the decision of the Board and that in case the Supreme Court of Justice, to which they had already appealed, did not grant the application for a review of the award rendered by the Board of Conciliation and Arbitration, they would abandon their fields, plants, and equipment.

The Supreme Court, after a careful study, held that the decision of the Board did not contain any constitutional violations and that, therefore, it could not be reversed.

VIII. Both before and after the Court rendered its decision, several efforts for conciliation were made by various high officials and even by the President himself, offering fair and concrete suggestions to both parties with a view to putting an end to the dispute. Inasmuch as the companies maintained that the decision required an expenditure of more than twenty-six million pesos, the Mexican Government offered to appoint a commission that would supervise, under the guarantee of the Federal Executive, the execution of the Board's decision, in order to insure to the Companies that they would not pay more than the aforesaid twenty-six millions. The Government also suggested that in order to clarify the meaning of some of the provisions of the award, the parties agree to a binding interpretation of those provisions which the companies feared might deprive them of the necessary freedom to manage their business economically and efficiently.

At a meeting held in the President's office the companies' representatives definitely stated that they could not accept the President's suggestion.

Under these circumstances, what alternative was there left to the Government?—Could it permit non-compliance with a decision rendered by a legitimate authority and confirmed by the Highest Tribunal of the Country?—Can anyone imagine that any foreign corporation in any other country would be permitted to look with contempt upon, and refuse to obey the decision of, the highest court of the land?—Could the Mexican Government permit the companies to carry out their threat that they would close down their plants and stop the entire production of the fuel used all over Mexico? The Mexican Government, after carefully weighing its own responsibility, resolved that the public interests demanded that the oil production should not be suspended and that, in view of the fact that the owners were not willing to continue operations, the Government was fully justified in expropriating the oil industry in order that it might be managed by the State.

The above proves conclusively that, contrary to what is stated in the pamphlet, the expropriation was accomplished as the imperative result of a state of national emergency precipitated by the companies themselves. . . .

The pamphlet concludes by stating that it has been written to aid the public in an understanding of the causes which keep the controversy alive. In reality, this is only one more chapter in the propaganda campaign which is supported mainly by Standard Oil in order to create confusion and to disparage the truly high ideals which actuate Mexico. The companies have not made, as they allege, any serious attempt to arrive at a satisfactory solution of the conflict which they themselves brought about, limiting their action, as a simple reading of the pamphlet demonstrates, to making proposals which they knew beforehand to be impossible of acceptance, in order that they might hold themselves out as victims of the obstinacy of the Mexican Government.

Both in the notes from the American Government to the Mexican Government signed July 31 and August 22, 1938, and in the statement made by Undersecretary Welles on August 14, 1939, to which document the pamphlet refers, there is expressed the doctrine that the expropriation of private property, for public use, is legitimate, provided that prompt, just and adequate compensation for such property is granted. This doctrine is concurred in by Mexico. The Government of Mexico, in expropriating the properties of the oil companies and in rejecting the demand for restoration made by the latter, has not declared, as it is falsely stated in the pamphlet, its inability and unwillingness to make prompt, just and adequate compensation.

Therefore, the actual solution of the controversy in accordance with the principles of law, lies in reaching a determination as to what is a just and adequate compensation, namely, in fixing the value of the expropriated properties. Mexico has continuously sought a solution along these lines, but has failed so far due entirely to the persistent refusal of the companies.

The laws of Mexico provide that when a friendly agreement in controversies of this character cannot be reached, the Courts shall be open for the ascertainment of value, after hearing the opinion of experts appointed by both sides. In the event either side fails to appoint such experts, the Courts shall appoint experts for it. The companies, following their inveterate attitude of contempt for the laws of the land in which they have operated, have refused to appoint their own experts, and so, the appraisal must be made by experts appointed by the Mexican Courts.

Without availing themselves of the remedies provided by Mexican law and without resort to the Mexican Courts, the companies are now seeking to becloud the issues for the very purpose of avoiding a settlement by the means prescribed by the laws of Mexico and sanctioned by the principles and doctrines of International Law.

Source: Bureau of Information of the Government of Mexico (Mexico City, Mexico: Distributed by the Consulate General Office of Mexico, New York, August 1940).

9

The Neutrality Acts and American Entry into World War II

It seems to be unfortunately true that an epidemic of world lawlessness is spreading. When an epidemic of physical disease starts to spread, the community approves and joins in a quarantine of the patients in order to protect the health of the community against the spread of disease.
—Franklin D. Roosevelt
Chicago, October 5, 1937

A strong current of isolationism flows beneath the swirls and eddies of U.S. foreign policy. Since George Washington's Farewell Address, the nation has sought to avoid entanglements that might draw it into a war in Europe. The idea of isolationism, in American international affairs, has always centered on Europe and the desire to avoid involvement in a crisis there. Even though the United States had grown in power and influence since the early days of the new nation, the American public and many of its leaders viewed "foreign entanglements" suspiciously. That phrase focused invariably on Europe's dangerous entanglements.

The struggle between Woodrow Wilson and the Senate over the League of Nations, in 1919–1920, centered on potential U.S. involvement in European affairs. Many Americans believed that the president's internationalism would violate the long-held principle of non-entanglement and engage the United States in conflicts that Europeans created. That possibility, isolationists believed, posed only danger and no benefit to American interests. The 1920s, in the United States, witnessed a foreign policy driven by the "isolationist impulse." Republican presidents and Congresses throughout the decade supported the public's desire to remain aloof from international involvement. Secure in a prosperous domestic economy, sensing no imminent foreign threat to U.S. interests, and locked to a foreign policy belief in unilateral options, Americans responded to the problems of the 1930s cautiously.

A severe economic depression at home and developing tension and crises in Europe and Asia during the 1930s posed serious domestic and international problems for the nation. The U.S. Senate legislated a series of laws, the Neutrality Acts, designed to protect America from being drawn into another European war. In response, President Franklin Roosevelt slowly and carefully challenged the Neutrality Acts as he moved the nation toward a more interventionist posture. In the United States, that struggle between isolationists and interventionists dominated international affairs in the decade prior to World War II. As the world became more dangerous in the 1930s, positions on how to respond to the dangers hardened. Isolationists and interventionists confronted the American public with clear choices about the international arena as the world moved toward global conflict.

In 1934, Gerald P. Nye, a Republican senator from North Dakota, chaired the Senate investigation of the munitions industry. After two years of hearings, Nye's committee determined that business interests in the United States, especially bankers and munitions manufacturers, had allowed their drive for profits to lead America into World War I. Additionally, the Nye Committee concluded that European self-interest had duped the United States into war. Finally, the investigation hinted that the president perhaps had too much power in the area of foreign affairs. Potentially, the committee linked the executive branch with business interests and saw some collusion between the two in drawing the United States into World War I, a war the committee concluded served no viable American interests.

Senator Nye's views reflected a broad public disillusionment following World War I. The results of the war dissatisfied many Americans. The Republican Senate still contained members who had fought Wilson over the League of Nations. William E. Borah, who chaired the Senate Foreign Relations Committee, had acted as Wilson's most vigorous opponent in 1919–1920. The Nye Committee's conclusions simply provided focus to what many Americans had already come to believe. U.S. entry into World War I had been a serious mistake.

The Great Depression, which began in 1929, furthered the sense of skepticism and resentment, particularly with regard to big business. As the stock market collapsed, as production declined, and as unemployment rose dramatically, business executives faced the wrath and suspicion of an angry, frightened public. Corporate America had few friends or supporters in the 1930s.

Nye's committee, and its conclusions, responded understandably to the domestic and foreign situation in the decade. The committee report had all of the aspects necessary to condemn what had happened in World War I—conspiracy, corporate greed, war profiteers, perfidious Europeans, and a naïve president. If those conditions had existed, as indicated, prior to World War I, it seemed easy to see similar conditions in the early 1930s.

The press and radio publicized the Senate hearings and helped create popular approval and support for Nye's conclusions. Ultimately, the committee recommended that Congress enact legislation to deal with the problems its investigation had uncovered. Between 1935 and 1937, Congress passed a series of Neutrality Acts. That legislation sought to prevent either American business or European diplomacy from manipulating the United States into entering another war. While the laws had a number of sections dealing with very specific items, those broke down into a few basic protections.

First, the Neutrality Acts created a mandatory American arms embargo in the event of war in Europe. The government forbade arms and munitions manufacturers from selling their products to belligerents. Second, the acts prohibited private financial loans to warring governments. Third, American citizens could not travel on ships belonging to belligerent nations. Finally, if a country at war purchased legal products from the United States, it had to pay cash and transport those goods in its own ships.

The legislation clearly stemmed from the postmortem on World War I that the Nye Committee had defined. The cause and effect connection appeared obvious. Congress looked at what they believed had created that situation and developed laws to prevent the same mistakes. The public generally supported the process and the laws. President Roosevelt reluctantly approved them.

The first two aspects of the Neutrality Acts prevented American businesses or investors from profiting during a European war, or from loaning or crediting European borrowers or buyers. As a result the United States would not incur debts that would threaten its neutrality or self-interest. Since few European nations had repaid debts they still owed the United States as a result of World War I, the issue remained a sore subject. Keeping American citizens off belligerent vessels precluded the possibility of more incidents like the sinking of the *Lusitania* and the *Sussex* where German submarines had inadvertently killed Americans sailing on those vessels. That issue had served as the most volatile and emotional cause of U.S. entry into World War I. Then, the cash and carry laws placed full commercial and transportation responsibilities on belligerents and further safeguarded U.S. interests. In addition, in 1934 Congress also had passed a bill championed by Hiram Johnson, the isolationist senator from California. The Johnson Act banned governments that had defaulted on their debts from borrowing any funds from private U.S. lenders.

Senator Nye and many of his supporters had roots in the Midwest. While not all Midwesterners were isolationists, the strongest support for nonintervention in world affairs during the 1930s was centered there. Many leading isolationist leaders came from the Midwest, and public opinion there tended to support the conclusions Nye had reached and the legislation Congress had passed. Europe could stew in its own juices. Their problems were none of our business.

President Roosevelt, however, grew up a product of Eastern, progressive, internationalist thinking. A protégé of Woodow Wilson, and a leading politician in the Democratic Party, FDR had adopted, both personally and politically, a different outlook than Nye and those who supported him. Between 1932 and 1937, as the Senate developed its neutrality legislation, the president remained preoccupied with the Great Depression and his New Deal domestic policies. He sensed, correctly, that Americans had little interest in the international situation. The president recognized, also, that the Europeans seemed unable to calm a worsening world situation. As an international organization, the League of Nations proved unequal to the task of maintaining peace as well. Roosevelt found, therefore, little sympathy, at home or abroad, for an aggressive, involved U.S. foreign policy. He had determined, however, that the international arena threatened American interests, dangerously so. While the president refused to risk aggressive policy actions when his main focus remained New Deal domestic legislation, he nonetheless had formed clear conclusions regarding the world situation.

The development of powerful dictatorships in Germany and Italy, and the emergence of a challenging military hierarchy in Japan, disturbed the equilibrium created at Versailles in 1919. The Soviet Union also posed potential problems under the leadership of a communist dictator. If isolationists believed that the United States could avoid direct involvement in the brewing confrontations, FDR disagreed. He sensed that Great Britain and France, our associates in World War I, faced new threats they might fail to thwart successfully. America needed viable partners to confront a world at war. The president concluded that the United States had to assist its former associates in some way.

Yet, Roosevelt moved very carefully to advance his internationalist position. The so-called Quarantine Address that he gave in Chicago in 1937 prompted public apathy or criticism and little applause. FDR had openly identified aggressor states, and he called vaguely for some sanctions to be taken against them. His warning fell, for the most part, on disinterested ears. Nye, and the neutrality legislation, appeared to have public support, and, always the deft politician, the president opted to avoid a confrontation. He did sign the Neutrality Acts into law. Effectively, the laws prevented U.S. involvement, of any sort, in the Spanish Civil War or in response to Italy's invasion of Ethiopia in the mid-1930s. That was precisely what noninterventionists hoped to accomplish, and, oddly, Roosevelt agreed in those two instances. Events in Europe and Asia, however, altered the domestic political environment and granted FDR more leverage to begin altering the Neutrality Acts.

In September 1939, World War II erupted with Germany's invasion of Poland. Eight months later, Adolf Hitler's armed forces attacked the Low Countries and stormed across France toward Paris. During the summer of 1940, with France under German occupation, Great Britain battled for its survival as waves of Nazi aircraft attacked the island nation. In September 1940, Germany, Japan, and Italy signed the Tripartite Pact, an alliance aimed directly at the United States, warning it to remain neutral or face the combined arms of the three nations. Finally, Germany's invasion of the Soviet Union in June 1941 convinced many observers that the Nazis would shortly dominate the European continent.

In Asia, Japanese military successes added to a growing concern in the United States. Already dominant in Korea, Japan initiated a military invasion of China in 1937. By 1941 Japanese forces had moved into Indochina and appeared to have created the same kind of sphere of influence in East Asia that Germany sought in Europe. The fact that Germany and Japan had allied in the Tripartite Pact heightened concerns in America. If the president had identified the "bad guys" in his 1937 Quarantine Address, every news bulletin between 1939 and 1941 indicated that those regimes were winning.

Roosevelt's attitude shifted with Germany's and Japan's military successes, and he publicly challenged both the isolationists in general and the Neutrality Acts specifically. A major foreign policy debate exploded in the United States as isolationists and interventionists argued their positions in an attempt to sway public opinion and create different responses to the broadening war. Franklin Roosevelt led the interventionists. As a popular president, an excellent public speaker, and an astute political practitioner, FDR brought all the powerful personal assets he possessed to his foreign policy agenda. Yet, he faced potent opposition.

The America First Committee acted as the strongest pressure group supporting the isolationist position. Begun in 1940 at Yale University, it expanded rapidly. Robert E. Wood, head of the Sears, Roebuck Company, established the committee's headquarters in Chicago. By 1941 it claimed a membership of 850,000 people. Senator Nye became a popular member, as did Charles A. Lindbergh, the famous aviator who had flown the *Spirit of St. Louis* across the Atlantic to international acclaim. The America First Committee offered many of the arguments and conclusions developed during Senator Nye's investigation, and it viewed world events from 1939 to 1941 ominously. Its members maintained that the United States was better served and protected by avoiding the explosive events in Europe and Asia. "America Firsters" believed that President Roosevelt's attempts at interventionism only drew the United States into dangerous and potentially deadly confrontations. Isolationists argued that FDR's position sought simply to help Great Britain and China, and they maintained that such action brought no benefits to the United States. Here was another example of a chief executive that foreigners had duped into fighting their battles. To the America First Committee, and other isolationists, Roosevelt sought to draw the United States down the same ill-conceived path that his mentor, Woodrow Wilson, had in 1916.

Roosevelt, however, could count on supporters as well as critics. If the America First Committee found broad support in the Midwest, Northeasterners tended to view the growing crisis from the president's perspective. Public sentiment there tended to believe that the United States had to help the "good guys" against the "bad guys." Events since 1937 had proved the president's "quarantine" assessment accurate. The Committee to Defend America by Aiding the Allies, and its chairman, William Allen White, served to counter the America First Committee. A more aggressive lobby group, Fight for Freedom, urged Roosevelt to take the strongest possible action against Germany, including a declaration of war.

The problem that confronted the president hinged on public attitudes. While various pressure groups, lobbyists, and public figures argued the particular points and fought over general responsibilities required of the United States, Roosevelt sensed and responded to the ambivalent attitude of American citizens. Opinion polls taken between 1939 and 1941 indicated two clear positions: 85 percent of Americans polled wanted a British victory over Germany; yet, 80 percent refused to believe that the United States should enter the war to ensure that victory. When France fell to the Nazis in the summer of 1940, a majority of Americans believed that defeating Germany remained more important than protecting U.S. neutrality. Fundamentally, the public had chosen sides, and they agreed with FDR. Still, the great majority of Americans prayed that the United States could manage events without an outright declaration of war. In similar fashion, Americans tended to side with China against Japan. The war between Germany and Russia created some problems, since dictators ruled both nations, but, again, public attitudes sided with the lesser of two evils.

Oddly, foreign policy had little impact on the 1940 presidential election. The Republican candidate, Wendell Willkie, of Indiana, identified with the interventionist wing of his party. Associated more with New York bankers and business leaders than small-town farmers from his home state, Willkie actually supported FDR's "aid short of war" policies. Trying to appeal to isolationists late in the campaign, Willkie pledged not to send America's "boys . . . into any foreign wars." He may even have attracted some votes in support of that promise, but essentially, the 1940 presidential election had little to do with clear differences the candidates held. In fact, Roosevelt also had said he would avoid sending Americans into combat.

FDR won an unprecedented third term in November 1940, defeating Willkie by 5 million popular votes. The election results and world events encouraged the administration to push further. The president launched his post-election strategy in a "fireside chat" on December 29. FDR used those famous radio broadcasts to advance both domestic and foreign policy ideas to the American public. In the December address, he used the phrase "great arsenal of democracy" to define the U.S. role in supporting Britain and other nations. A week later, in another radio address, he called on Congress to consider repealing the Neutrality Acts.

Ultimately, and flexibly, the president developed policies that addressed the need to assist Great Britain, China, and Russia and, at the same time, avoid a direct conflict with Germany and Japan. World events occurred in an atmosphere of political reality in the United States. As 1940 was a presidential election year, FDR had to tread carefully. He initiated a slow, studied assault on the Neutrality Acts designed to provide immediate and significant aid and support for England. Additionally, the United States would offer aid and assistance to the other enemies of Germany or Japan.

To begin, the president asked Congress to restructure the Neutrality Acts, allowing the United States to repeal the embargo of munitions sales to belligerents. In November 1939, a Democratic Congress supported FDR's request after a bitter debate. During May 1940, the president began transferring surplus U.S. military equipment and airplanes to England. In June, Roosevelt appointed Henry Stimson and Frank Knox as secretaries of war and the navy, respectively. Both had reputations as outspoken interventionists. Three months later, the administration developed an executive agreement giving fifty U.S. destroyers to Britain in exchange for some military bases on English islands in the Western Hemisphere—the Destroyer-Bases Agreement. In September FDR initiated the first peacetime military draft in U.S. history.

Between January and March 1941, the fundamental debate that had occupied America's foreign policy concerns raged in Congress and across the country. At public meetings, in newspapers, on radio, on college campuses, and in the halls of Congress, isolationists and interventionists waged a battle that would determine the part America would play in the world war. The interventionists won. On February 8, the House of Representatives passed Roosevelt's request by a vote of 260–165. The Senate agreed a month later by a vote of 60–31. Effectively, the Lend-Lease Act FDR signed into law on March 11, 1941, repealed the Neutrality Acts. The long-term effort of Senator Nye and others to prevent U.S. involvement in another misguided conflict had run aground on the reef of a deadly international environment that most Americans now saw as a clear threat to their national security.

The president followed his legislative victory, adding military muscle to the Lend-Lease Act. The U.S. Coast Guard expanded its "security zone" halfway across the Atlantic Ocean, and the navy began to patrol and safeguard merchant vessels well beyond the territorial limits of U.S. waters. The policy released the British navy from sending its vessels across the Atlantic to protect shipping, but it served as a provocative act for a neutral nation. That aggressive and legally questionable decision led eventually to an undeclared naval war between the United States and Germany in 1941.

As the public opinion debate continued, interventionists had found a wedge to counter isolationist pressure groups. The phrases "all aid short of war" and "the great arsenal of democracy" defined their position. The United States could provide the necessary money and equipment to assist those fighting against the Nazis and Japan without the danger of direct American involvement. In that, the interventionists may have developed a double-edged sword. That commitment not only aided the "good guys" without drawing the United States into war, it also kick-started the American economy, as the growing need to produce munitions, arms, and military equipment provided new jobs. In a nation struggling out of the worst depression in history, the potential of reduced unemployment and expanded business had a clear domestic appeal.

Just as President Roosevelt had exploited events in the European war to enhance U.S. support of Great Britain, he began to respond aggressively toward Japan in East Asia. The Japanese had developed the Greater East Asia Co-Prosperity Sphere to define their long-term foreign policy goals. Essentially, Japan aimed to create its own sphere of influence in the region, and that included, ultimately, reducing or eliminating the political and economic influence of Europeans and the United States. Coupled with the Tanaka Memorial, a Japanese military plan, the island nation appeared willing to use aggression to extend its influence. Japan's invasion of Korea (1931), its war with China (1937–1945), the Tripartite Pact (1940) with Germany and Italy, its military attacks against Great Britain's colonies in Asia, and the Japanese invasion of Indochina (1941) left FDR with little doubt as to Japan's threat to the security interests of the United States in the region.

Accordingly, American policy toughened, just as it had toward Germany. Once again, as the president reduced, and then eliminated, the restrictions of the Neutrality Acts, he pushed his interventionist agenda to thwart Japanese aggression in East Asia, particularly toward China. In July 1939, Secretary of State Cordell Hull announced that the United States would end its trade agreement with Japan, effective in January 1940. In September 1940, the government banned the export of scrap iron and steel as well as aviation fuel to Japan. FDR argued that the United States needed those important materials for its own defense needs, but the ban also threatened to weaken Japan, which depended strongly on American supplies. The administration also loaned $125 million to China during 1940.

The United States initiated new military policies as well as economic sanctions. Its Pacific Fleet moved to Pearl Harbor in Hawaii, projecting U.S. naval power well into the Pacific to "warn Japan." In early 1941, Anglo-American military leaders began meetings to plan contingencies in the event of U.S. involvement in war in Europe and/or Asia. With an executive order in April 1941, FDR authorized U.S. pilots to resign their commissions in the American armed forces to fly as volunteers in China—the famed Flying Tigers. The United States sent new fighter aircraft to China for those pilots.

In August 1941, President Roosevelt met secretly with Prime Minister Winston Churchill off the shores of Newfoundland. That meeting produced the Atlantic Charter, a joint Anglo-American eight-point strategy to combat the threats of "Nazi tyranny." It also considered issues in East Asia important to the two nations. While the United States would continue to use diplomatic channels, particularly with Japan, to avoid war, the interventionists had cast the die. The Roosevelt administration dismantled the Neutrality Acts, developed a "great arsenal of democracy," and advanced policies to thwart both German and Japanese military aggression in Europe and East Asia. "All aid short of war" had won the broad approval of the American public. FDR had adroitly persuaded Americans that a serious danger to U.S. security did exist.

Still, in the fall of 1941, public opinion resisted an outright military action on the part of the United States. In that regard, the isolationists could cling to a slim hope that they might win the day. Pearl Harbor destroyed that illusion. The U.S. embargo of fuel and scrap metal so threatened Japan's military options that its leaders felt compelled to act aggressively. U.S. diplomatic warnings to end the war in China or face continued economic sanctions left the Japanese with untenable options. By September 1941, Japan had decided on war. They sought to deliver a strategic military blow to American forces in the Pacific and gain acceptance of their new supremacy in East Asia. In October, General Tojo Hideki and the nation's military assumed control of the Japanese government. Two months later, on December 7, 1941, Japan attacked the

United States at Pearl Harbor. The isolationists had no reasonable response to that "sneak attack."

Franklin Roosevelt did not plan the Pearl Harbor attack to get the United States into World War II. No serious evidence suggests such a conspiracy at any level within the U.S government. The Japanese attack on Hawaii came as the end result of a series of events and policies developed during the period 1939–1941. Clearly, FDR and the interventionists who supported him hoped and planned to see the United States play a more vigorous, aggressive role in defeating the Axis powers. Many of the interventionists did want war with Germany and Japan. Yet, the president sensed that American public opinion would go only so far in its support of his plans. He moved carefully, but clearly, to push the limits of that commitment. The Japanese, not Roosevelt or the interventionists, made the ultimate decision to end the debate that the Neutrality Acts, isolationists versus interventionists, and the events of World War II had created for the American people.

The Neutrality Acts aimed to prevent a recurrence of the conditions that had led the United States into World War I. That legislation stemmed primarily from a basic American belief, articulated in the Nye Committee's report, that war profiteers and selfish European interests had taken Americans into a war that had no real benefit for the United States. Isolationists throughout the 1930s clung to that position until Japan attacked the United States in December 1941. Events between 1939 and 1941, however, differed dramatically from the concerns that confronted American policy makers before World War I. History was not repeating itself. The direct threats to U.S. security and self-interest appeared far more dangerous than they had in 1916. President Roosevelt, and the American public, came to understand the difference and responded accordingly.

DOCUMENTS

9.1.   The Neutrality Acts, May 1, 1937

The first series of legislation Congress passed in response to Senator Gerald P. Nye's committee investigations was the Neutrality Acts. The laws hoped to avoid the situation that had led to U.S. involvement in World War I.

THE NEUTRALITY ACT OF 1937, May 1, 1937
JOINT RESOLUTION To amend the joint resolution, approved August 31, 1935, as amended.

Resolved . . . EXPORT OF ARMS, AMMUNITION, AND IMPLEMENTS OF WAR Section 1. (a) Whenever the President shall find that there exists a state of war between, or among, two or more foreign states, the President shall proclaim such fact, and it shall thereafter be unlawful to export, or attempt to export, or cause to be exported, arms, ammunition, or implements of war from any place in the United States to any belligerent state named in such proclamation, or to any neutral state for transshipment to, or for the use of, any such belligerent state. (b) The President shall, from time to time, by proclamation, extend such embargo upon the export of arms, ammunition, or implements of war to other states as and when they may become involved in such war. (c) Whenever the President shall find that such a state of civil strife exists in a foreign state and that such civil strife is of a magnitude or is being conducted under such conditions that the export of arms, ammunition, or implements of war from the United States to such foreign state would threaten or endanger the peace of the United States, the President shall proclaim such fact, and it shall thereafter be unlawful to export, or attempt to export, or cause to be exported, arms, ammunition, or implements of war from any place in the United States to such foreign state, or to any neutral state for transshipment to, or for use of, such foreign state. (d) The President shall, from time to time by proclamation, definitely enumerate the arms, ammunition, and implements of war, the export of which is prohibited by this section. The arms, ammunition, and implements of war so enumerated shall include those enumerated in the President's proclamation Numbered 2163, of April 10, 1936, but shall not include raw materials or any other articles or materials not of the same general character as those enumerated in the said proclamation, and in the Convention for the Supervision for the International Trade in Arms and Ammunition and in Implements of War, signed at Geneva June 17, 1925. (e) Whoever, in violation of any of the provisions of this Act, shall export, or attempt to export, or cause to be exported, arms, ammunition, or implements of war from the United States shall be fined not more than $10,000, or imprisoned not more than five years, or both ... (f) In the case of the forfeiture of any arms, ammunition, or implements of war by reason of a violation of this Act ... such arms, ammunition, or implements of war shall be delivered to the Secretary of War for such use or disposal thereof as shall be approved by the President of the United States. (g) Whenever, in the judgment of the President, the conditions which have caused him to issue any proclamation under the authority of this section have ceased to exist, he shall revoke the same, and the provisions of this section shall thereupon cease to apply with respect to the state or states named in such proclamation, except with respect to offenses committed, or forfeiture incurred, prior to such revocation.

EXPORT OF OTHER ARTICLES AND MATERIALS Section 2. (a) Whenever the President shall have issued a proclamation under the authority of section 1 of this Act and he shall thereafter find that the placing of restrictions on the shipment of certain articles or materials in addition to arms, ammunition, and implements of war from the United States to belligerent states, or to a state wherein civil strife exists, is necessary to promote the security or preserve the peace of the United States or to protect the lives of citizens of the United States, he shall so proclaim, and it shall thereafter be unlawful, for any American vessel to carry such articles or materials to any belligerent state, or to any state wherein civil strife exists, named in such proclamation issued under the authority of section 1 of this Act, or to any neutral state for transshipment to, or for the use of, any such belligerent states or any such state wherein civil strife exists. The President shall by proclamation from time to time definitely enumerate the articles and materials which it shall be unlawful for American vessels to so transport. . . . (c) The President shall from time to time by proclamation extend such restrictions as are imposed under the authority of this section to other states as and when they may be declared to become belligerent states under the authority of section 1 of this Act. (d) The President may from time to time change, modify, or revoke in whole or in part any proclamations issued by him under the authority of this section. (e) Except with respect to offenses committed, or forfeitures incurred, prior to May 1, 1939, this section and all proclamations issued thereunder shall not be effective after May 1, 1939.

FINANCIAL TRANSACTIONS Section 3. (a) Whenever the President shall have issued a proclamation under the authority of section 1 of this Act, it shall thereafter be unlawful for any person within the United States to purchase, sell, or exchange bonds, securities, or other obligations of the government of any belligerent state or of any state wherein civil strife exists, named in such proclamation, or of any political subdivision of any such state, or of any person acting for or on behalf of the government of any such state, or of any faction or asserted government within any such state wherein civil strife exists, or of any person acting for or on behalf of any faction or asserted government within any such state wherein civil strife exists, issued after the date of such proclamation, or to make any loan or extend any credit to any such government, political subdivision, faction, asserted government, or person, or to solicit or receive any contribution for any such government, political subdivision, faction, asserted government, or person: PROVIDED, That if the President shall find that such action will serve to protect the commercial or other interest of the United States or its citizens, he may, in his discretion, and to such extent and under such regulations as he may prescribe, except from the operation of this section ordinary commercial credits and short-time obligations in aid of legal transactions and of a character customarily used in normal peacetime commercial transactions. Nothing in this subsection shall be construed to prohibit the solicitation or collection of funds to be used for medical aid and assistance, or for food and clothing to relieve human suffering, when such solicitation or collection of funds is made on behalf of and for use by any person or organization which is not acting for or on behalf of any such government, political subdivision, faction, or asserted government, but all such solicitations and collections of funds shall be subject to the approval of the President and shall be made under such rules and regulations as he shall prescribe. . . . (c) Whoever shall violate the provisions of this section or of any regulations issued hereunder shall, upon conviction thereof, be fined not more than $50,000 or imprisoned for not more than five years, or both. Should the violation be by a corporation, organization, or association, each officer or agent thereof participating in the violation may be liable to the penalty herein prescribed. . . .

EXCEPTIONS—AMERICAN REPUBLICS Section 4. This Act shall not apply to an American republic or republics engaged in war against a non-American state or states, provided the American republic is not cooperating with a non-American state or states in such a war.

NATIONAL MUNITIONS CONTROL BOARD Section 5. (a) There is hereby established a National Munitions Control Board (hereinafter referred to as the "Board") to carry out the provisions of this Act. The board shall consist of the Secretary of State, who shall be chairman and executive officer of the Board, the Secretary of the Treasury, the Secretary of War, the Secretary of the Navy, and the Secretary of Commerce. Except as otherwise provided in this Act, or by other law, the administration of this Act is vested in the Department of State. The Secretary of State shall promulgate such rules and regulations with regard to the enforcement of this section as he may deem necessary to carry out its provisions. The Board shall be convened by the chairman and shall hold at least one meeting a year. (b) Every person who engages in the business of manufacturing, exporting, or importing any of the arms, ammunition, or implements of war referred to in this Act, whether as an exporter, importer, manufacturer, or dealer, shall register with the Secretary of State his name, place of business, and places of business in the United States, and a list of the arms, ammunition, and implements of war which he manufactures, imports, or exports. (c) Every person required to register under this section shall notify the Secretary of State of any change in the arms, ammunition, or implements of war which he exports, imports, or manufactures. . . . (d) It shall be unlawful for any person to export, or attempt to export, from the United States to any other state, any of the arms, ammunition, or implements of war referred to in this Act, or to import, or attempt to import, to the United States from any other state, any of the arms, ammunition, or implements of war referred to in this Act, without first having obtained a license therefor. . . . (k) The President is hereby authorized to proclaim upon recommendation of the Board from time to time a list of articles which shall be considered arms, ammunition, and implements of war for the purposes of this section.

AMERICAN VESSELS PROHIBITED FROM CARRYING ARMS TO BELLIGERENT STATES Section 6. (a) Whenever the President shall have issued a proclamation under the authority of section 1 of this Act, it shall thereafter be unlawful, until such proclamation is revoked, for any American vessel to carry any arms, ammunition, or implements of war to any belligerent state, or to any state wherein civil strife exists, named in such proclamation, or to any neutral state for transshipment to, or for the use of, any such belligerent state or any such state wherein civil strife exists. (b) Whoever, in violation of the provisions of this section, shall take, or attempt to take, or shall authorize, hire, or solicit another to take, any American vessel carrying such cargo out of port or from the jurisdiction of the United States shall be fined not more than $10,000, or imprisoned not more than five years, or both; and in addition, such vessel, and her tackle, apparel, furniture, and equipment, and the arms, ammunition, and implements of war on board, shall be forfeited to the United States.

USE OF AMERICAN PORTS AS BASE OF SUPPLY Section 7. (a) Whenever, during any war in which the United States is neutral, the President, or any person thereunto authorized by him, shall have cause to believe that any naval vessel, domestic or foreign, whether requiring clearance or not, is about to carry out of a port of the Untied States, fuel, men, arms, ammunition, implements of war, or other supplies to any warship, tender, or supply ship of a belligerent state, but the evidence is not deemed sufficient to justify forbidding the departure of the vessel as provided for by section 1, title V, chapter 30, of the Act approved June 15, 1917, and if, in the President's judgment, such action will serve to maintain peace between the United States and foreign states, or to protect the commercial interests of the United States and its citizens, or to promote the security or neutrality of the United States, he shall have the power and it shall be his duty to require the owner, master, or person in command thereof, before departing from a port of the United States, to give a bond to the United States, with sufficient sureties, in such amount as he shall deem proper, conditioned that the vessel will not deliver the men, or any part of the cargo, to any warship, tender, or supply ship of the belligerent state. (b) If the President, or any person thereunto authorized by him, shall find that a vessel, domestic or foreign, in a port of the United States, has previously cleared from a port of the United States during such war and delivered its cargo or any part thereof to a warship, tender, or supply ship of a belligerent state, he may prohibit the departure of such vessel during the duration of the war.

SUBMARINES AND ARMED MERCHANT VESSELS Section 8. Whenever, during any war in which the United States is neutral, the President shall find that special restrictions placed on the use of the ports and territorial waters of the United States by the submarines or armed merchant vessels of a foreign state, will serve to maintain peace between the United States and foreign states, or to protect the commercial interests of the United States and its citizens, or to promote the security of the United States, and shall make proclamation therefore, it shall thereafter be unlawful for any such submarine or armed merchant vessel to enter a port or the territorial waters of the United States or to depart therefrom, except under such conditions and subject to such limitations as the President may prescribe. Whenever, in his judgment, the conditions which have caused him to issue his proclamation have ceased to exist, he shall revoke his proclamation and the provisions of this section shall thereupon cease to apply.

TRAVEL ON VESSELS OF BELLIGERENT STATES Section 9. Whenever the President shall have issued a proclamation under the authority of section 1 of this Act it shall thereafter be unlawful for any citizen of the United States to travel on any vessel of the state or states named in such proclamation, except in accordance with such rules and regulations as the President shall prescribe. . . .

ARMING OF AMERICAN MERCHANT VESSELS PROHIBITED Section 10. Whenever the President shall have issued a proclamation under the authority of section 1, it shall thereafter be unlawful, until such proclamation is revoked, for any American vessel engaged in commerce with any belligerent state, or any state wherein civil strife exists, named in such proclamation, to be armed or to carry any armament, arms, ammunition, or implements of war, except small arms and ammunition therefor which the President may deem necessary and shall publicly designate for the preservation of discipline aboard such vessels.

REGULATIONS Section 11. The President may, from time to time, promulgate such rules and regulations, not inconsistent with law, as may be necessary and proper to carry out any of the provisions of this Act; and he may exercise any power or authority conferred on him by this Act through such officer or officers, or agency or agencies, as he shall direct. . . .

Source: Ruhl J. Bartlett, ed., *The Record of American Diplomacy*, 4th ed. (New York: Alfred A. Knopf, 1964), pp. 574–576.

**9.2.   Excerpts from Franklin Roosevelt's "Quarantine Address,"
Chicago, Illinois, October 5, 1937**

---

*Less than a year after his election to a second term, the president
delivered the following speech in order to identify the totalitarian
threats he saw emerging in the 1930s in Europe and Asia. It also
sought to gauge American public opinion to determine whether
he could pursue a more aggressive foreign policy. Initial response
to the speech made it clear that Americans failed to support FDR's
position. The general public wanted the president to focus on
domestic issues and to maintain the Neutrality Acts.*

The political situation in the world, which of late has been growing progressively worse, is such as to cause grave concern and anxiety to all the peoples and nations who wish to live in peace and amity with their neighbors.

Some fifteen years ago the hopes of mankind for a continuing era of international peace were raised to great heights when more than sixty nations solemnly pledged themselves not to resort to arms in furtherance of their national aims and policies. The high aspirations expressed in the Briand-Kellogg Pact and the hopes of peace thus raised have of late given way to a haunting fear of calamity. The present reign of terror and international lawlessness began a few years ago. . . .

Without a declaration of war and without warning or justification of any kind, civilians, including vast numbers of women and children, are being ruthlessly murdered. . . . Innocent people, innocent nations are being cruelly sacrificed to a greed for power and supremacy which is devoid of all sense of justice and humane considerations. . . .

If those things come to pass in other parts of the world, let no one imagine that America will escape, that America may expect mercy, that this Western hemisphere will not be attacked and that it will continue tranquilly and peacefully to carry on the ethics and the arts of civilization. . . .

The peace-loving nations must make a concerted effort in opposition to those violations of treaties and those ignorings of human instincts which today are creating a state of international anarchy and instability from which there is no escape through mere isolation or neutrality. . . .

The peace, the freedom, and the security of 90 per cent of the population of the world is being jeopardized by the remaining 10 per cent who are threatening a breakdown of all international law and order. Surely the 90 per cent who want to live in peace under law and in accordance with moral standards that have received almost universal acceptance through the centuries, can and must find some way to make them prevail. . . .

When an epidemic of physical disease starts to spread, the community approves and joins in a quarantine of the patients in order to protect the health of the community against the spread of the disease.

It is my determination to pursue a policy of peace and to adopt every practicable measure to avoid involvement in war. . . . If civilization is to survive, the principles of the Prince of Peace must be restored. Shattered trust between nations must be revived. Most important of all, the will for peace on the part of peace-loving nations must express itself to the end that nations that may be tempted to violate their agreements and the rights of others will desist from such a course. There must be positive endeavors to preserve peace. . . .

Source: U.S. Department of State, *Addresses and Messages of Franklin D. Roosevelt* (Washington, DC: U.S. Government Printing Office, 1947), pp. 21–24.

9.3.   "Giddy Minds and Foreign Quarrels," Excerpt from an Article by Charles A. Beard Questioning Roosevelt's Interventionism, 1939

Professor Beard was one of America's most distinguished historians. He had written excellent studies of American history, often with an economic interpretation as his focus. In Giddy Minds and Foreign Quarrels *(New York: Macmillan, 1939), most Americans read Beard's views in an abridged version of the book published in* Harper's Magazine *in August 1920. He defended those who questioned Roosevelt's "interventionism." (Beard would later publish* President Roosevelt and the Coming of the War, 1941: A Study in Appearances and Realities, *a critical interpretation of FDR's policies.)*

Those Americans who refuse to plunge blindly into the maelstrom of European and Asian politics are not defeatist or neurotic. They are giving evidence of sanity, not cowardice; of adult thinking as distinguished from infantilism. Experience has educated them and made them all the more determined to concentrate their energies on the making of a civilization within the circle of their continental domain. They do not propose to withdraw from the world, but they propose to deal with the world as it is and not as romantic propagandists picture it. They propose to deal with it in American terms, that is, in terms of national interest and security on this continent. Like their ancestors, who made a revolution, built the Republic, and made it stick, they intend to preserve and defend the Republic, and under its shelter carry forward the work of employing their talents and resources in enriching American life. They know that this task will call for all the enlightened statesmanship, the constructive energy, and imaginative intelligence that the nation can command. America is not to be Rome or Britain. It is to be America.

Source: Robert A. Goldwin, ed., *Readings in American Foreign Policy* (New York: Oxford University Press, 1959), pp. 130–135.

9.4.   Winston Churchill's Telegram to President Franklin Roosevelt Thanking Him for Developing the Destroyer-Bases Deal, August 15, 1940

The British prime minister and the president developed a unique relationship during World War II. In the critical summer of 1940, as German air assaults threatened England, Churchill wrote FDR to thank him for arranging the Destroyer-Bases deal, and to confirm that Great Britain would continue to fight resolutely against Germany and never surrender its fleet. Fighting for their survival, many in Britain neither understood nor sympathized with the political struggle between isolationists and interventionists in the United States. Churchill chafed at the battle himself, but recognized Roosevelt's restrictions.

I need not tell you how cheered I am by your message or how grateful I feel for your untiring efforts to give us all possible help. You will, I am sure, send us everything you can, for you know well that the worth of every destroyer that you can spare us is measured in rubies. But we also need the motor torpedo-boats which you have mentioned, and as many flying boats and rifles as you can let us have. We have a million men waiting for rifles.

The moral value of this fresh aid from your Government and people at this critical time will be very great and widely felt.

We can meet both the points you consider necessary to help you with Congress and with others concerned, but I am sure that you will not misunderstand if I say that our willingness to do so must be conditional on our being assured that there will be no delay in letting us have the ships and flying boats. As regards an assurance about the British Fleet, I am, of course, ready to reiterate to you what I told Parliament on June 4. We intend to fight this out here to the end, and none of us would ever buy peace by surrender or scuttling the Fleet. But in any use you may make of this repeated assurance you will please bear in mind the disastrous effect from our point of view, and perhaps also from yours, of allowing any impression to grow that we regard the conquest of the British Islands and its naval bases as any other than an impossible contingency. The spirit of our people is splendid. Never have they been so determined. Their confidence in the issue has been enormously and legitimately strengthened by the severe air fighting in the past week. As regards naval and air bases, I readily agree to your proposals for ninety-nine-year leases, which are far easier for us than the method of purchase. I have no doubt that once the principle is agreed between us the details can be adjusted and we can discuss them at leisure. It will be necessary for us to consult the Governments of Newfoundland and Canada about the Newfoundland base, in which Canada has an interest. We are at once proceeding to seek their consent.

Once again, Mr. President, let me thank you for your help and encouragement, which means so much to us.

Source: Warren Kimball, ed., *Churchill and Roosevelt: The Complete Correspondence*, (Princeton, NJ: Princeton University Press, 1984), p. 60.

9.5.   Franklin Roosevelt's "Garden Hose" Comments, December 17, 1940

At a press conference, Roosevelt used the analogy of a neighbor's house fire to justify U.S. aid to Great Britain. The brief comments came to symbolize FDR's growing commitment to "all aid short of war." It provided a simple yet powerful statement of the administration's support of Great Britain against Germany. At the same time, less than a year before the Japanese attack on Pearl Harbor, it reflected the American public's desire to help defend Great Britain without America becoming directly involved in the war.

Suppose my neighbor's house catches fire and I have a length of garden hose four or five hundred feet away. If he can take my garden hose and connect it up with his hydrant, I may help him to put out the fire. Now what do I do? I don't say to him before that operation, "Neighbor, my garden hose cost me fifteen dollars; you have to pay me fifteen dollars for it." No! What is the transaction that goes on? I don't want fifteen dollars—I want my garden hose back after the fire is over.

There is absolutely no doubt in the mind of a very overwhelming number of Americans that the best immediate defense of the United States is the success of Great Britain defending itself; and that, therefore, quite aside from our historic and current interest in the survival of Democracy in the world as a whole, it is equally important from a selfish point of view and of American defense that we should do everything possible to help the British Empire to defend itself.

I am trying to eliminate the dollar mark.

Source: Samuel Rosenman, ed., *The Public Papers and Addresses of Franklin D. Roosevelt* (New York Random House, 1940), pp. 604–615.

9.6.   Charles A. Lindbergh's Address Before the America First Committee, April 24, 1941

Lindbergh was the most famous supporter of isolationism during the period prior to Pearl Harbor, and he became a public figure identified with the goals of the America First Committee. The hero who had flown the Spirit of St. Louis *on the first solo flight across the Atlantic in 1927 was an American icon in the 1930s. His support of America First enhanced the committee's influence.*

There is a policy open to this nation that will lead to success—a policy that leaves us free to follow our way of life, and to develop our own civilization. It is not a new and untried idea. It was advocated by Washington. It was incorporated in the Monroe Doctrine. It is based upon the belief that the security of the nation lies in the strength and character of its own people. It recommends the maintenance of armed forces sufficient to defend this hemisphere from attack by any combination of foreign powers. It demands faith in an independent American destiny. This is the policy of the America First Committee today. It is a policy not of isolation, but of independence; not of defeat, but of courage.

War is not inevitable for this country. Such a claim is defeatism in the true sense. No one can make us fight abroad unless we are willing ... to do so. No one will attempt to fight us here if we are ... as a great nation armed. Over a hundred million people in this nation are opposed to entering the war. If the principles of democracy mean anything at all, that is reason enough for us to stay out. If we are forced into war against the wishes of an overwhelming majority of our people, we will have proved democracy such a failure at home that there will be little use of fighting for it abroad.

The time has come when those of us who believe in an independent American destiny must band together and organize for strength. We have been led toward war by a minority of our people. This minority has power. It has influence. It has a loud voice. But it does not represent the American people.

Source: New York Times, April 24, 1941, p. 4.

10

Potsdam: The Last Wartime Conference

Never in history has such an aggregation of victorious military force been represented in one conference, never has there been a meeting which faced graver or more complex issues; and never have three mortal men borne so heavy a responsibility for the welfare of their peoples and mankind.

—*New York Times,*
July 15, 1945

In July 1945, two months after Germany's surrender ended World War II in Europe, President Harry S Truman flew to Berlin. In a suburb of the devastated Nazi capital, the new chief executive met with Prime Minister Winston Churchill of Great Britain and Premier Joseph Stalin of the Soviet Union. The powerful coalition that had defeated Adolf Hitler's Third Reich in May 1945 witnessed its three key leaders in conference for the last time.

At the Potsdam Conference, the "Big Three" discussed and debated issues decided at previous meetings between 1941 and 1945. They also considered policies that would shape the postwar world. As old agendas and new plans confronted the leaders, profoundly important information arrived from the United States. America had successfully detonated an atomic weapon. Still at war with Japan, President Truman made the decision, while at Potsdam, to use the atom bomb to end the conflict in the Pacific.

The meeting in Germany offers a diplomatic overview of the major issues that concerned the allies during World War II. Potsdam also gives some insight into the controversial decision to employ the atom bomb against Japan. Additionally, it provides a glimpse at the beginnings of the Cold War that dominated U.S.-Soviet policies for half a century. Both America and the Soviet Union began to devise strategies responding to the new threats of that bipolar confrontation relatively quickly. Finally, the meeting emphasized the emerging concept of summit diplomacy among the world's powerful states. National leaders, rather than their diplomatic subordinates, had begun to talk face-to-face concerning foreign affairs. That method of international relations had existed in the past, but it became more prevalent during and after World War II.

Even while Franklin Roosevelt battled with isolationists in 1940–1941, he scheduled a secret meeting with Winston Churchill to discuss Anglo-American "war" strategy. Their initial meeting at sea, in August 1941, set the table for future cooperation. While U.S.-British interests often clashed over specific policy decisions, FDR and Churchill worked together well during World War II. The initial meeting produced the Atlantic Charter, common principles proclaiming the Four Freedoms from fear, want, tyranny, and the right to free trade. The Atlantic Charter, like Woodrow Wilson's Fourteen Points, became an ideal as the allies confronted their enemies—noble ideas a postwar world would work to realize. Four months later, Japan attacked Pearl Harbor and America entered the war.

Throughout 1942, the U.S. government strengthened its military forces, developed strategy to fight a two-front war, mobilized its industries, and prepared the American people for a long, costly struggle. In one key decision, Roosevelt agreed to make the war against Germany America's top priority. Many citizens, angry at the Pearl Harbor attack, hoped to see the United States focus on the Pacific. FDR, his advisors, and his allies in London and Moscow all recognized that the Nazis posed the greatest threat to their developing alliance. Accordingly, American forces invaded North Africa in November 1942 and joined Britain in eliminating both German and Italian forces from that area. A modest victory, certainly, but it served as the first against a seemingly invincible Nazi army. At the same time, the Soviet Union had withstood a massive German invasion of its nation and prepared to go on the offensive.

In January 1943, FDR went to Casablanca, Morocco, to meet with Churchill. Premier Stalin did not attend the Casablanca Conference. Russia's war against the Nazis required his full attention. In North Africa, two key issues surfaced that would impact future meetings until the end of the war. First, British and American military leaders determined to direct their next offensive against the Mediterranean island of Sicily, with a future assault on mainland Italy. The Russians had hoped for a quick Anglo-American invasion of France to take pressure off their forces.

While initially inclined to do so, Roosevelt relented when British strategists convinced him that battle losses would be too high to accept. Stalin, suffering hundreds of thousands of casualties against the full force of German might, failed to appreciate the decision.

Additionally, President Roosevelt announced that the allies would demand unconditional surrender from their enemies, a surprise decision he had not discussed with Winston Churchill. That, too, caused concern. While it sent a clear message that the allies refused to negotiate with "evil" leaders, it also precluded the possibility of any compromises with Italy, Japan, or Germany that might have brought an early end to the war. The unconditional surrender decision remained a controversial action even as late as the Potsdam meeting. (Oddly, the United States compromised its unconditional surrender demand when it negotiated with French Vichy forces in North Africa. While the decision aided military operations there, it made the Soviets suspicious of American intentions, an issue that would persist throughout the war.)

During 1943, as military action continued, diplomatic dialogue combined with the clash of armies and navies. Secretary of State Cordell Hull flew to Moscow in October to meet with Russian Foreign Commissar V. I. Molotov and Britain's foreign secretary, Anthony Eden. Hull told the Russians that Roosevelt and Churchill had met in Washington and Quebec during the summer and agreed to a May 1944 invasion of France. At the same time, he discussed Russia's future support against Japan (the Soviet Union and Japan were not at war) and FDR's particular interest in creating a postwar United Nations. Hull remembered the meetings as cordial. The Moscow Conference appeared to have satisfied Stalin's concern about a second front in France, and he agreed to join the war against Japan after the allies defeated Germany.

A month later, in November, the president journeyed to Cairo, Egypt to examine issues related to East Asia and China. FDR met with Churchill and Jiang Jieshi (Chiang Kai-shek), China's Generalissimo. They determined to "divest" Japan of its territorial "conquests" in Asia and reaffirmed the "unconditional surrender" announcement made at Casablanca. From Cairo, FDR and Churchill flew north to Teheran, Iran, to meet, finally, with Premier Stalin. The "Big Three" discussed specific plans for the Allied invasion of France and other military strategy. Importantly, they also had a chance to size each other up. FDR concluded that he could work with the Soviet dictator, whom he casually referred to as "Uncle Joe." Churchill appeared less positive.

At the beginning of 1944, the Grand Alliance had gone over to the offensive on its military fronts. Diplomacy and the conferences reflected the growing optimism and sense of coming victory. While more than a year of war remained, the Normandy invasion in June 1944, and Russia's massive offensive in eastern Europe, put the Germans in a terrible military situation. Island-hopping offensives in the Pacific had begun to push the Japanese back toward their homeland as well.

Again, Churchill and Roosevelt met in Quebec, in September 1944, to decide how the victors would establish an "occupation" of Germany at war's end. They considered a plan by Henry Morgenthau, FDR's Secretary of the Treasury, to dismantle Germany's industry and reconstruct the nation as a small, agricultural country unable to pose any future threat to world peace. A month later the two leaders dropped the so-called Morgenthau Plan as impractical and unnecessary.

Roosevelt's election to a third term as president in 1940 was unprecedented. It had surprised many Americans. His decision to run a fourth time appeared less surprising in 1944. The public seemed to expect FDR to complete the long commitment he had made to winning the world war and establishing peace. Essentially, they did not want to change horses in midstream and expected Roosevelt to finish the job. His opponent, Thomas Dewey of New York, tended to avoid any criticism of the president's wartime policies. An isolationist element within the Republican Party added Governor John Bricker of Ohio to the ticket to balance Dewey's basic sympathy with FDR's postwar commitment to the United Nations. That addition, however, had little import in the campaign or election. An overwhelming number of voters supported FDR's foreign policy views and voted accordingly.

In the final wartime meeting between the Big Three, FDR and Churchill took the long, arduous trip to Yalta, Stalin's vacation resort in the Crimea. In February 1945, the important conference aimed to settle key postwar issues. The allies determined to establish four occupation zones in Germany—under U.S., British, Russian, and French forces—and they would demilitarize the nation and punish its Nazi war criminals. They agreed to create a United Nations, with a preliminary meeting set for April 1945. Stalin stated that the Soviets would oversee free elections in Poland, assuring Roosevelt and Churchill that Russian "liberated" Eastern Europe would have access to government by popular choice.

With regard to East Asia, the Soviet leader said he would join the war against Japan within a reasonable time following Germany's surrender. Finally, the three leaders discussed problems in China relating to the civil war there between communists and Jiang Jieshi's government. Stalin indicated that the Soviets would stay out of the conflict.

Often seen as the key meeting of the war, Yalta served as an ongoing discussion for the allied leaders. Concerns and policies that had surfaced years earlier occupied the attention of the Big Three. Nor did Yalta provide a final chapter to their deliberations. That would occur at Potsdam. On April 12, 1945, Franklin Roosevelt died at his vacation home in Warm Springs, Georgia. Less than a month later, on May 8, Germany surrendered unconditionally. The war against Japan and postwar issues in Europe now fell to Harry S Truman.

Assuming the place of FDR as president seemed to awe Truman. "I don't know whether you fellows ever had a load of hay or a bull fall on you," he remarked to reporters, "but last night the moon, the stars, and all the planets fell on me." Yet, the Missouri politician went to work quickly. He distrusted Russian motives more than Roosevelt had and remained concerned and angry that free elections had not taken place in Eastern Europe. Perhaps the new president's Midwestern roots and lack of foreign policy experience colored his distrust of the Soviets, but he proceeded quickly to voice his concerns. In a tense meeting with the Russian ambassador in Washington, Truman accused the Soviets of violating pledges regarding Poland. He informed the ambassador that the United States had suspended Lend-Lease aid to the war-ravaged Russians. The president told his secretary of state, "[W]e must stand up to the Russians at this point and not be easy with them."[1]

While scholars have debated the importance of Truman's "get tough" position as a cause for Soviet-American discord, the meeting at Potsdam reflected little animosity between the president and Premier Stalin. The American leader arrived for the conference on July 16 to witness firsthand the destruction the allies had brought to bear on Germany's capital. The devastation sobered Truman and made him mindful of the serious issues he would discuss with Stalin and Churchill. The next day, a little after noon, Stalin came to Truman's apartment for an initial meeting. As staff members and interpreters remember, the discussion remained cordial and clear. The Russian leader agreed to declare war on Japan in August, as agreed at Yalta, and Stalin indicated that the Soviets would take no steps to involve themselves in China's civil war, again as decided in February.

The following day, formal meetings began with Winston Churchill present to represent Great Britain. The leader of England's war against the Nazis would not remain in Berlin long. British elections ousted his party from power, and on July 28, Clement Atlee arrived to take Churchill's place as Britain's new prime minister. Both American and Soviet participants noted later that neither Churchill nor Atlee had much influence at the meetings. The chemistry of the "new world order" appeared to recognize a Soviet-American reality.

Truman came to Germany to gain a direct Soviet commitment to join the war against Japan. That he received. He also came to get a personal impression of Stalin. The president left Potsdam convinced that the Russian dictator was tough and serious, but clear in his views. The United States and the Soviet Union could negotiate. The two leaders disagreed over Eastern Europe and promises made at Yalta regarding free elections. While that remained important, it failed to dominate the conference, nor did it seriously affect the relationship between Stalin and Truman. Shortly, the president's view would change.

The other postwar issues the allied leaders discussed ran the gamut from war crimes trials for Nazi officials to the government in Italy. While those concerns demanded attention from Truman, Stalin, and Atlee and their various staffs and advisors, they never proved sufficiently critical to jeopardize U.S.-Soviet discussions. In simple terms, the Potsdam Conference showed the postwar clarity of Soviet and American power and their fundamental differences. Yet, the meetings evidenced no expression of outright animosity. In fact, Truman seemed initially relieved that the Russians would shortly join the war against Japan.

Plans for the atom bomb remained a topic of discussion among Americans at Potsdam. The secret Manhattan Project to develop the weapon in the deserts of New Mexico was in the process of testing its possible military effectiveness. As of July 20, word of the testing had not arrived in Berlin. Yet, the president met, that day, with Generals Dwight Eisenhower and Omar Bradley to discuss using the weapon, if it worked, to end the war with Japan. Eisenhower advised against it, arguing that the Japanese already appeared defeated. Bradley believed that the president had already made up his mind to use the weapon, but conceded that Truman offered no clear decision. The next day, they learned that the test had proved successful. The weapon worked. Two days later, on July 23, a top secret communiqué arrived from Washington informing Truman that the bomb could be used against Japan in early August.

The president decided, at Potsdam, to order the military use of the atom bomb to end the war against Japan. He wrote later that his major diplomatic and military advisors agreed with the decision, and Truman maintained that the primary motive was concern for the loss of American lives if the war continued. There is little reason to doubt that prime motive. Revisionists have argued otherwise. Many believe that the United States used the weapon either to intimidate the Soviet Union or to end the war before the Russians could exercise any serious influence in East Asia through their own military involvement against Japan. Other scholars have suggested that the $2 billion cost of the Manhattan Project required the weapon's use to justify the expense. Still more interpretations maintain that the atom bomb served as retribution for Pearl Harbor and even hint at racial bias as a factor in the decision. Revisionist interpretations believe that Japan was finished anyhow and the atom bomb was unnecessary, or that other less devastating methods were available to the United States.

As David McCullough has pointed out in his biography of Truman, it was not Japan's defeat that concerned Truman; rather, he appeared focused on Japan's surrender. In the three months that he had served as president, U.S. casualties in the Pacific approached half of all American casualties during the preceding three years of war. Every day that Japan remained at war meant more American deaths. Only a quick Japanese surrender would alleviate the ongoing losses. The atom bomb offered that grim alternative.

On August 6, 1945, the United States detonated an atomic bomb over Hiroshima. Two days later, Russia declared war on Japan. The following day, August 9, a second atomic bomb destroyed Nagasaki. A week later, on August 14, Japan formally surrendered, ending World War II. The Potsdam Conference had seen both the dialogues of old issues and concerns and the opening of a new frontier in the field of foreign policy and world affairs for the United States.

The wartime conferences that brought together America, Russia, and Great Britain forged a strategy for victory and an agenda for postwar international relations. While that agenda collapsed amid a dangerous Cold War environment, its intentions nonetheless remained genuine. The three nations had different ideologies, worldviews, and self-interests. Their leaders reflected those differences. Yet, with all of the suspicion, disagreement, and misunderstanding, the conferences managed to conclude at Potsdam with some reasonable sense that the victors had lived up to their agreements, with the exception of Eastern Europe. President Truman may have distrusted Joseph Stalin and sensed that postwar cooperation would prove difficult with the Soviet Union. There is no evidence, however, from his notes, memoirs, or formal meetings that he did not believe that the United States had met the wartime goals and postwar agendas it set out to achieve.

Between 1945 and 1947, both American and Russian policy altered significantly. The noted "long telegram" sent by George Kennan, a U.S. diplomat in Moscow, signaled a clear wariness of Soviet intentions. He returned to the United States to plan, with Truman and Secretary of State George Marshall, a post-Potsdam agenda. On March 12, 1947, the president announced a major foreign aid program designed to assist the government of Greece in dealing with a communist revolution aided, he argued, by the Russians. The Truman Doctrine set the stage for a U.S. commitment to support governments that communist subversion might threaten.

Three months later, on June 5, 1947, Secretary Marshall addressed Harvard University's graduating class. He informed the graduates that the United States would establish a European Recovery Program and offered American financial support to help revive the war-torn continent. The Marshall Plan also aimed clearly to block any possible Soviet penetration of Western Europe by economically stabilizing the countries there. The United States had embarked on a broad policy termed "containment," and it would serve as the basis for the nation's postwar response to perceived Soviet threats to America's security.

Franklin Roosevelt had initiated, with Churchill, the modern era of summit diplomacy, the focused meetings of major heads of state, rather than their foreign ministers, as principal policy leaders. Throughout World War II, the various summits the leaders held tended to reinforce the practice that America's president would act directly at the negotiating table to advance or protect the vital interests of the United States. At Potsdam, Harry Truman accepted the concept of summit diplomacy and carried its conditions into the postwar world. The origins of the Cold War changed both U.S. and Soviet alternatives and would stall summit meetings between their leaders for a decade.

NOTE

1. See David McCullough, *Truman* (New York: Simon and Schuster, 1992), pp. 374–376.

DOCUMENTS

10.1.   President Harry Truman, Diary Entries, July 1945

Two excerpts from President Truman's diary while at Potsdam follow. The first discusses his initial meeting with Premier Stalin. The second entry reflects on the news that the United States had available the atomic bomb and what might be done with it and why.

July 17, 1945

Just spent a couple of hours with Stalin. Joe Davies called on Maisky and made the date last night for noon today. Promptly at a few minutes before twelve I looked up from my desk and there stood Stalin in the doorway. I got to my feet and advanced to meet him. He put out his hand and smiled. I did the same, we shook, I greeted Molotov and the interpreter and we sat down.

After the usual polite remarks we got down to business. I told Stalin that I am no diplomat but usually said yes and no to questions after hearing all the argument. It pleased him. I asked him if he had the agenda for the meeting. He said he had and that he had some more questions to present. I told him to fire away. He did and it is dynamite— but I have some dynamite too which I am not exploding now. He wants to fire Franco, to which I wouldn't object and divide up the Italian colonies and other mandates, some no doubt that the British have. Then he got on the Chinese situation, told us what agreements had been reached and what was in abeyance. Most of the big points are settled. He'll be in the Jap war on August 15. Fini Japs when that comes about. We had lunch, talked socially, put on a real show, drinking toasts to everyone. Then had pictures made in the backyard.

I can deal with Stalin. He is honest, but smart as hell.

July 25, 1945

We met at 11:00 a.m. today. That is, Stalin, Churchill and the U.S. president. But I had a most important session with Lord Mountbatten and General Marshall before that. We have discovered the most terrible bomb in the history of the world. It may be the fire destruction prophesied in the Euphrates Valley era, after Noah and his fabulous ark. Anyway, we think we have found the way to cause a disintegration of the atom. An experiment in the New Mexico desert was startling—to put it mildly. Thirteen pounds of the explosive caused a crater six feet deep and twelve hundred feet in diameter, knocked over a steel tower a half mile away, and knocked men down ten thousand yards away. The explosion was visible for more than two hundred miles and audible for forty miles and more.

This weapon is to be used against Japan between now and August 10. I have told the secretary of war, Mr. Stimson, to use it so that military objectives and soldiers and sailors are the target and not women and children. Even if Japs are savages, ruthless, merciless and fanatic, we as the leader of the world for the common welfare cannot drop this terrible bomb on the old capital or the new. He and I are in accord. The target will be a purely military one and we will issue a warning statement asking the Japs to surrender and save lives. I'm sure they will not do that, but we will have given them the chance. It is certainly a good thing for the world that Hitler's crowd or Stalin's did not discover this atomic bomb. It seems to be the most terrible thing ever discovered, but it can be made the most useful.

Source: Harry S. Truman, *Memoirs* (Garden City, NY: Doubleday, 1955), pp. 372, 394.

10.2.   Excerpts from the Potsdam Conference Report, August 2, 1945

In the final wartime conference at Potsdam, the Big Three agreed to partition Germany and developed the political and economic principles to be implemented in postwar Germany. Also, the Big Three resolved the issue of wartime reparations. In addition, they addressed the postwar problem of restoring a government to Poland. In the document below Stalin guaranteed that Poland would hold free elections.

III. GERMANY

The Political and Economic Principles to Govern the Treatment of Germany in the Initial Control Period.

A. Political Principles

1. In accordance with the Agreement on Control Machinery in Germany, supreme authority in Germany is exercised, on instructions from their respective Governments, by the Commanders-in-Chief of the armed forces of the United States of America, the United Kingdom, the Union of Soviet Socialist Republics, and the French Republic, each in his own

zone of occupation, and also jointly, in matters affecting Germany as a whole, in their capacity as members of the Control Council....

B. Economic Principles

11. In order to eliminate Germany's war potential, the production of arms, ammunitions and implements of war as well as all types of aircraft and sea-going ships shall be prohibited and prevented. Production of metals, chemicals, machinery and other items that are directly necessary to war economy shall be rigidly controlled and restricted....

IV. REPARATIONS FROM GERMANY

1. Reparation claims of the USSR shall be met by removals from the zone of Germany occupied by the USSR, and from appropriate German external assets.

2. The USSR undertakes to settle the reparation claims of Poland from its own share of reparations.

3. The reparation claims of the United States, the United Kingdom and other countries entitled to reparations shall be met from the Western Zones and from appropriate German external assets.

4. In addition to the reparations to be taken by the USSR from its own zone of occupation, the USSR shall receive additionally from the Western zones:

(a) 15 percent of such usable and complete industrial capital equipment, in the first place from the metallurgical, chemical and machine manufacturing industries as is unnecessary for the German peace economy and should be removed from the Western zones of Germany, in exchange for an equivalent value of food, coal, potash, zinc, timber, clay products, petroleum products, and such other commodities as may be agreed upon.

(b) 10 percent of such industrial capital equipment as is unnecessary for the German peace economy and should be removed from the Western Zones, to be transferred to the Soviet Government on reparations account without payment or exchange of any kind in return.

Removals of equipment as provided in (a) and (b) above shall be made simultaneously....

8. The Soviet Government renounces all claims in respect of reparations to shares of German enterprises which are located in the Western Zones of occupation in Germany as well as to German foreign assets in all countries except those specified in paragraph 9 below.

9. The Governments of the UK and USA renounce their claims in respect of reparations to shares of German enterprises which are located in the Eastern Zone of occupation in Germany, as well as to German foreign assets in Bulgaria, Finland, Hungary, Rumania, and Eastern Austria....

IX. POLAND

A. We have taken note with pleasure of the agreement reached among representative Poles from Poland and abroad which has made possible the formation, in accordance with the decisions reached at the Crimea Conference, of a Polish Provisional Government of National Unity recognized by the Three Powers. The establishment by the British and the United States Governments of diplomatic relations with the Polish Provisional Government of National Unity has resulted in the withdrawal of their recognition from the former Polish Government in London, which no longer exists.

The British and United States Governments have taken measures to protect the interest of the Polish Provisional Government of National Unity as the recognized government of the Polish State in the property belonging to the Polish State located in their territories and under their control, whatever the form of this property may be. . . .

The Three Powers note that the Polish Provisional Government of National Unity, in accordance with the decisions of the Crimea Conference, has agreed to the holding of free and unfettered elections as soon as possible on the basis of universal suffrage and secret ballot in which all democratic and anti-Nazi parties shall have the right to take part and to put forward candidates, and that the representatives of the Allied press shall enjoy full freedom to report to the world upon developments in Poland before and during the elections.

B. The following agreement was reached on the western frontier of Poland:

In conformity with the agreement on Poland reached at the Crimea Conference the Three Heads of Government have sought the opinion of the Polish Provisional Government of National Unity in regard to the accession of territory in the north and west which Poland should receive. The President of the National Council of Poland and members of the Polish Provisional Government of National Unity have been received at the Conference and have fully presented their views. The Three Heads of Government reaffirm their opinion that the final delimitation of the western frontier of Poland should await the peace settlement.

The Three Heads of Government agree that, pending the final determination of Poland's western frontier, the former German territories east of a line running from the Baltic sea immediately west of Swinamunde, and thence along the Oder River to the confluence of the western Neisse River and along the western Neisse to the Czechoslovak frontier, including that portion of East Prussia not placed under the administration of the Union of Soviet Socialist Republics in accordance with the understanding reached at this conference and including the area of the former free city of Danzig, shall be under the administration of the Polish State and for such purposes should not be considered as part of the Soviet zone of occupation in Germany. . . .

XIII. ORDERLY TRANSFER OF GERMAN POPULATIONS

The Three Governments, having considered the question in all its aspects, recognize that the transfer to Germany of German populations, or elements thereof remaining in Poland, Czechoslovakia, and Hungary, will have to be undertaken. They agree that any transfers that take place should be effected in an orderly and humane manner. . . .

Source: Raymond Dennett and Robert Turner, eds., Documents on American Foreign Relations, vol. 8 (Princeton, NJ: Princeton University Press, 1948), pp. 925–938.

10.3.   President Harry S Truman's Public Announcement on the Bombing of Hiroshima, August 6, 1945

On August 6, 1945, President Truman announced to the American public the results of the bombing of Hiroshima. The radio message carried military, diplomatic, and scientific messages in its intent.

Sixteen hours ago an American bomber dropped one bomb on Hiroshima, an important Japanese Army base. That bomb had more power than 20,000 tons of T.N.T. It had more than two thousand times the blast power of the British "Grand Slam," which is the largest bomb ever yet used in the history of warfare.

The Japanese began the war from the air at Pearl Harbor. They have been repaid many fold. And the end is not yet. With this bomb we have now added a new and revolutionary increase in destruction to supplement the growing power of our armed forces. In their present forms these bombs are now in production and even more powerful forms are in development.

It is an atomic bomb. It is a harnessing of the basic power of the universe. The source from which the sun draws its power has been loosed against those who brought war to the Far East.

Before 1939, it was the accepted belief of scientists that it was theoretically possible to release atomic energy. But no one knew any practical method of doing it. By 1942, however, we knew that the Germans were working feverishly to find a way to add atomic energy to the other engines of war with which they hoped to enslave the world. But they failed. We may be grateful to Providence that the Germans got the V-1's and the V-2's late and in limited quantities and even more grateful that they did not get the atomic bomb at all.

The battle of the laboratories held fateful risks for us as well as the battles of the air, land, and sea, and we have now won the battle of the laboratories as we have won the other battles. . . . We have spent two billion dollars on the greatest scientific gamble in history—and won. But the greatest marvel is not the size of the enterprise, its secrecy, nor its cost, but the achievement of scientific brains in putting together infinitely complex pieces of knowledge held by many men in different fields of science into a workable plan. And hardly less marvelous has been the capacity of industry to design, and of labor to operate, the machines and methods to do things never done before so that the brain child of many minds came forth in physical shape and performed as it was supposed to do. . . . What has been done is the greatest achievement of organized science in history. It was done under high pressure and without failure.

We are now prepared to obliterate more rapidly and completely every productive enterprise the Japanese have above ground in any city. We shall destroy their docks, their factories, and their communications. Let there be no mistake; we shall completely destroy Japan's power to make war.

It was to spare the Japanese people from utter destruction that the ultimatum of July 26 was issued at Potsdam. Their leaders promptly rejected that ultimatum. If they do not now accept our terms, they may expect a rain of ruin from the air, the like of which has never been seen on this earth. Behind this air attack will follow sea and land forces in such numbers and power as they have not yet seen and with the fighting skill of which they are already well aware. . . .

The fact that we can release atomic energy ushers in a new era in man's understanding of nature's forces. Atomic energy may in the future supplement the power that now comes from coal, oil, and falling water, but at present it cannot be produced to compete with them commercially. Before that comes, there must be a long period of intensive research.

It has never been the habit of the scientists of this country or the policy of this Government to withhold from the world scientific knowledge. Normally, therefore, everything about the work with atomic energy would be made public.

But under present circumstances it is not intended to divulge the technical processes of production or all the military applications, pending further examination of possible methods of protecting us and the rest of the world from the danger of sudden destruction.

I shall recommend that the Congress of the United States consider promptly the establishment of an appropriate commission to control the production and use of atomic power within the United States. I shall give further consideration and make further recommendations to the

Congress as to how atomic power can become a powerful and forceful influence towards the maintenance of world peace.

Source: Raymond Dennett and Robert Turner, eds., *Documents on American Foreign Relations*, vol. 8 (Princeton, NJ: Princeton University Press, 1948), pp. 419–421.

10.4.   Memo to President Truman from Secretary of War Henry L. Stimson, September 11, 1945

One month after Japan's surrender, Stimson recommended that the United States share its atomic secrets with Russia. The signs of the collapsing wartime alliance in an atmosphere of distrust are unclear in the memo. Stimson's six-page memorandum to the president argues the need to work with the Soviets. The results of Potsdam and Hiroshima had not guaranteed Soviet-American animosity.

Dear Mr. President:

In handing you today my memorandum about our relations with Russia in respect to the atomic bomb, I am not unmindful of the fact that when in Potsdam I talked with you about the question whether we would be safe in sharing the atomic bomb with Russia while she was still a police state and before she put into effect provisions assuring personal rights of liberty to the individual citizen.

I still recognize the difficulty and am still convinced of the importance of the ultimate importance of a change in Russian attitude towards individual liberty but I have come to the conclusion that it would not be possible to use our possession of the atomic bomb as a direct lever to produce the change. I have become convinced that any demand by us for an internal change in Russia as a condition of sharing in the atomic weapon would be so resented that it would make the objective we have in view less probable.

I believe that the change in attitude toward the individual in Russia will come slowly and gradually and I am satisfied that we should not delay our approach to Russia in the matter of the atomic bomb until the process has been completed. My reasons are set forth in the memorandum I am handing you today. Furthermore, I believe this long process of change in Russia is more likely to be expedited by the closer relationship in the matter of the atomic bomb which I suggest and the trust and confidence that I believe would be inspired by the method of approach which I have outlined.

Faithfully yours,
[Henry L. Stimson] Secretary of War

Source: Foreign Relations Series—1945, vol. 2, pp. 40–41. See also Department of
   Defense Document #11532, 3E—Declassified April 12, 1974 (Washington, DC:
   National Archives).

10.5.   Excerpts From Winston Churchill's Speech in Fulton, Missouri, March 5, 1946

---

*President Truman invited Churchill to visit the United States, and
by the spring of 1946, both men had become increasingly concerned over Soviet policy in the postwar era. In what came to be
known as the "Iron Curtain" speech, Churchill issued a powerful
attack against Soviet communism.*

From Stettin in the Baltic to Trieste in the Adriatic, an iron curtain has
descended across the Continent. Behind that line lie all the capitals of
the ancient states of Central and Eastern Europe. Warsaw, Berlin, Prague,
Vienna, Budapest, Belgrade, Bucharest and Sofia, all these famous cities
and the populations around them lie in what I must call the Soviet
sphere, and all are subject in one form or another, not only to Soviet
influence but to a very high and, in many cases, increasing measure of
control from Moscow. Athens alone—Greece with its immortal glories—
is free to decide its future at an election under British, American and
French observation. The Russian-dominated Polish Government has been
encouraged to make enormous and wrongful inroads upon Germany,
and mass expulsions of millions of Germans on a scale grievous and
undreamed-of are now taking place. The Communist parties, which were
very small in all these Eastern States of Europe, have been raised to pre-
eminence and power far beyond their numbers and are seeking everywhere to obtain totalitarian control. Police governments are prevailing
in nearly every case, and so far, except in Czechoslovakia, there is no
true democracy. Turkey and Persia are both profoundly alarmed and
disturbed at the claims which are being made upon them and at the
pressure being exerted by the Moscow Government. An attempt is being
made by the Russians in Berlin to build up a quasi-Communist party in
their zone of Occupied Germany by showing special favors to groups of
left-wing German leaders. At the end of the fighting last June, the American and British Armies withdrew westwards, in accordance with an
earlier agreement, to a depth at some points of 150 miles upon a front
of nearly four hundred miles, in order to allow our Russian allies to
occupy this vast expanse of territory which the Western Democracies had
conquered.

If now the Soviet Government tries, by separate action, to build up a pro-Communist Germany in their areas, this will cause new serious difficulties in the British and American zones, and will give the defeated Germans the power of putting themselves up to auction between the Soviets and the Western Democracies. Whatever conclusions may be drawn from these facts—and facts they are—this is certainly not the Liberated Europe we fought to build up. Nor is it one which contains the essentials of permanent peace.

The safety of the world requires a new unity in Europe, from which no nation should be permanently outcast. It is from the quarrels of the strong parent races in Europe that the world wars we have witnessed, or which occurred in former times, have sprung. Twice in our own lifetime we have seen the United States, against their wishes and their traditions, against arguments, the force of which it is impossible not to comprehend, drawn by irresistible forces, into these wars in time to secure the victory of the good cause, but only after frightful slaughter and devastation had occurred.

Twice the United States has had to send several millions of its young men across the Atlantic to find the war; but now war can find any nation, wherever it may dwell between dusk and dawn. Surely we should work with conscious purpose for a grand pacification of Europe, within the structure of the United Nations and in accordance with its Charter. That I feel is an open cause of policy of very great importance.

Source: Robert Rhodes James, *Winston S. Churchill: His Complete Speeches, 1897–1963*, vol. 7 (New York: Chelsea House, 1943–1949), pp. 7285–7293.

10.6.   Excerpts from *Pravda*'s Interview with Joseph Stalin on Winston Churchill's "Iron Curtain" Speech, March 1946

Shortly after Churchill spoke in Missouri, Premier Stalin had an interview with the Russian newspaper Pravda. *He challenged both Britain and the United States in some of the opening rhetoric of the Cold War.*

Mr. Churchill now stands in the position of a firebrand of war. And Mr. Churchill is not alone here. He has friends not only in England but also in the United States of America. . . . There is no doubt that the set-up of Mr. Churchill is a set-up for war, a call to war with the Soviet Union. . . . As a result of the German invasion, the Soviet Union has irrevocably lost in battles with the Germans, and also during the German occupation and through the expulsion of Soviet citizens to German slave labor camps, about 7,000,000 people. In other words, the Soviet Union has lost men several times more than Britain and the United States together.

It may be that some quarters are trying to push into oblivion these sacrifices of the Soviet people which insured the liberation of Europe from the Hitlerite yoke.

But the Soviet Union cannot forget them. One can ask, therefore, what can be surprising in the fact that the Soviet Union. [*sic*] In a desire to insure its security for the future, tries to achieve that these countries [those in Eastern Europe] should have governments whose relations to the Soviet Union are loyal? How can one, without having lost one's reason, qualify these peaceful aspirations of the Soviet Union as "expansionist tendencies" of our Government?

The growth of the influence of communism cannot be considered accidental. It is a normal function. The influence of the Communists grew because during the hard years of the mastery of fascism in Europe, Communists showed themselves to be reliable, daring and self-sacrificing fighters against fascist regimes for the liberty of the peoples. . . .

Source: New York Times, March 14, 1946, p. 4.

10.7.   Excerpts from President Truman's Speech Announcing the Truman Doctrine, March 12, 1947

George Kennan had returned from the Soviet Union to head a long-range policy planning committee to devise a strategy for the Cold War. Implementing a policy termed "containment," the decisions to send aid to Greece and Turkey marked Truman's first salvo in the Cold War. He announced the policy to a joint session of Congress in a radio address to the nation.

The gravity of the situation which confronts the world today necessitates my appearance before a joint session of the Congress. The foreign policy and the national security of this country are involved.

One aspect of the situation, which I wish to present to you at this time for your consideration and decision, concerns Greece and Turkey. . . .

The very existence of the Greek state is today threatened by the terrorist activities of several thousand armed men, led by Communists, who defy the Government's authority at a number of points. . . .

Greece's neighbor, Turkey, also deserves our attention. . . . Since the war Turkey has sought additional financial assistance from Great Britain and the United States for the purpose of effecting that modernization necessary for the maintenance of its national integrity. That integrity is essential to the preservation of order in the Middle East. . . .

One of the primary objectives of the foreign policy of the United States is the creation of conditions in which we and other nations will be able to work out a way of life free from coercion. This was a fundamental issue in the war with Germany and Japan. Our victory was won over countries which sought to impose their will, and their way of life, upon other nations. . . .

At the present moment in world history nearly every nation must choose between alternative ways of life. The choice is too often not a free one.

One way of life is based upon the will of the majority, and is distinguished by free institutions, representative government, free elections, guarantees of individual liberty, freedom of speech and religion, and freedom from political oppression.

The second way of life is based upon the will of a minority forcibly imposed upon the majority. It relies upon terror and oppression, a controlled press and radio, fixed elections, and the suppression of personal freedoms.

I believe that it must be the policy of the United States to support free peoples who are resisting attempted subjugation by armed minorities or by outside pressures. I believe that we must assist free peoples to work out their own destinies in their own way. I believe that our help should be primarily through economic and financial aid which is essential to economic stability and orderly political processes.

The world is not static, and the *status quo* is not sacred. But we cannot allow changes in the *status quo* in violation of the Charter of the United Nations by such methods as coercion, or by such subterfuges as political infiltration. In helping free and independent nations to maintain their freedom, the United States will be giving effect to the principles of the Charter of the United Nations.

It is necessary only to glance at a map to realize that the survival and integrity of the Greek nation are of grave importance in a much wider situation. If Greece should fall under the control of an armed minority, the effect upon its neighbor, Turkey, would be immediate and serious. Confusion and disorder might well spread throughout the entire Middle East. . . .

I therefore ask Congress to provide authority for assistance to Greece and Turkey in the amount of $400,000,000 for the period ending June 30, 1948. . . .

In addition to funds, I ask the Congress to authorize the detail of American civilian and military personnel to Greece and Turkey, at the request of those countries, to assist in the tasks of reconstruction, and for the purpose of supervising the use of such financial and material assistance as may be furnished. I recommend the authority also be provided for the instruction of selected Greek and Turkish personnel.

Finally, I ask that Congress provide authority which will permit the speediest and most effective use, in terms of needed commodities, supplies, and equipment, of such funds as may be authorized. . . .

The seeds of totalitarian regimes are nurtured by misery and want. They spread and grow in the evil soil of poverty and strife. They reach their full growth when the hope of a people for a better life has died. We must keep that hope alive. The free peoples of the world look to us for support in maintaining their freedoms. If we falter in our leadership, we may endanger the peace of the world—and we shall surely endanger the welfare of this nation. . . .

Source: Edward H. Judge and John W. Langdon, *The Cold War: A History Through Documents* (Upper Saddle River, NJ: Prentice-Hall, 1999), pp. 24–25.

10.8. Excerpts from Secretary of State George Marshall's Commencement Address at Harvard University, June 5, 1947

Following President Truman's assistance program to Greece and Turkey, the United States initiated a broader financial assistance package to help rebuild the economies, and hence the political stability of Western Europe to resist Soviet aggression. The European Recovery Program (popularly known as the Marshall Plan) served as a major postwar U.S. policy action in pursuit of the concept of containment.

I need not tell you gentlemen that the world situation is very serious. That must be apparent to all intelligent people. I think one difficulty is that the problem is one of such enormous complexity that the very mass of facts presented to the public by press and radio make it exceedingly difficult for the man in the street to reach a clear appraisement of the situation. Furthermore, the people of this country are distant from the troubled areas of the earth and it is hard for them to comprehend the plight and consequent reactions of long-suffering peoples, and the effects of those reactions on their governments in connection with our efforts to promote peace in the world.

In considering the requirements for the rehabilitation of Europe, the physical loss of life, the visible destruction of cities, factories, mines, and railroads was correctly estimated, but it has become obvious during recent months that this visible destruction was probably less serious than the dislocation of the entire fabric of European economy. For the past

ten years conditions have been highly abnormal. The feverish preparation for war and the more feverish maintenance of the war effort en-
gulfed all aspects of national economies. Machinery has fallen into
disrepair or is entirely obsolete. Under the arbitrary and destructive Nazi
rule, virtually every possible enterprise was geared into the German War
machine. Long-standing commercial ties, private institutions, banks, insurance companies, and shipping companies disappeared, through loss
of capital, absorption through nationalization, or by simple destruction.

In many countries, confidence in the local currency has been severely
shaken. The breakdown of the business structure of Europe during the
war was complete. Recovery has been seriously retarded by the fact that
two years after the close of hostilities a peace settlement with Germany
and Austria has not been agreed upon. But even given a more prompt
solution of these difficult problems, the rehabilitation of the economic
structure of Europe quite evidently will require a much longer time and
greater effort than had been foreseen. . . .

Aside from the demoralizing effect on the world at large and the possibilities of disturbances arising as a result of the desperation of the people concerned, the consequences to the economy of the United States
should be apparent to all. It is logical that the United States should do
whatever it is able to do to assist in the return of normal economic health
in the world, without which there can be no political stability, and no
assured peace.

Our policy is directed not against any country or doctrine but against
hunger, poverty, desperation, and chaos. Its purpose should be the revival of a working economy in the world so as to permit the emergence
of political and social conditions in which free institutions can exist. Such
assistance, I am convinced, must not be on a piecemeal basis as various
crises develop. Any assistance that this Government may render in the
future should provide a cure rather than a mere palliative. Any government that is willing to assist in the task of recovery will find full cooperation. . . . Any government which maneuvers to block the recovery
of other countries cannot expect help from us. Furthermore, governments, political parties, or groups which seek to perpetuate human misery in order to profit therefrom politically or otherwise will encounter
the opposition of the United States.

It is already evident that, before the United States Government can
proceed much further in its efforts to alleviate the situation and help
start the European world on its way to recovery, there must be some
agreement among the countries of Europe as to the requirements of the
situation and the part those countries themselves will take in order to
give proper effect to whatever action might be taken by this Government.
It would be neither fitting nor efficacious for this Government to undertake to draw up unilaterally a program designed to place Europe on its

feet economically. That is the business of the Europeans. The initiative, I think, must come from Europe. The role of this country should consist of friendly aid in the drafting of a European program and of later support of such a program so far as it may be practical for us to do so. The program should be a joint one, agreed to by a number, if not all, of European nations.

An essential part of any successful action on the part of the United States is an understanding on the part of the people of America of the character of the problem and the remedies to be applied. Political passion and prejudice should have no part. . . .

Source: Edward H. Judge and John W. Langdon, *The Cold War: A History Through Documents* (Upper Saddle River, NJ: Prentice-Hall, 1999), pp. 26–28.

11

Joseph McCarthy and the Red Scare

Today we are engaged in a final all-out battle between communistic atheism and Christianity. The modern champions of communism have selected this as the time, and ladies and gentlemen, the chips are down—they are truly down.

—Senator Joseph McCarthy
February 1950

On February 9, 1950, a little-known first-term senator from Wisconsin spoke at a Wheeling, West Virginia, Republican Women's Club luncheon. Senator Joseph McCarthy told his audience that more than two hundred communists or communist sympathizers worked at the State Department seeking to undermine U.S. foreign policy in its postwar confrontation with the Soviet Union. He charged that a conspiracy to destroy American values and support worldwide communism brewed in the very heart of President Harry Truman's diplomatic establishment, the "bright young men" in the foreign service "who have been born with silver spoons in their mouths." McCarthy even implied that Secretary of State Dean Acheson, "a pompous diplomat in striped pants, with a phony English accent," appeared involved.[1]

While McCarthy failed to provide either names or details, his charge shortly caught the public's attention and catapulted him to a position of power and influence remarkable in the period following World War II. Joseph McCarthy came to symbolize the Cold War "Red Scare" in the

United States. Many Americans applauded his efforts to thwart communist aggression at home and abroad. Others saw the senator as a dysfunctional, dangerous threat to free speech and the conduct of realistic foreign policy during the early years of the Cold War. McCarthyism defined a particular style of attack against communism as the nation sought to cope with the complicated concerns that emerged in its international relations. An examination of Senator McCarthy's influence also affords a look at the domestic issues that affected foreign affairs.

Between 1945 and 1949, the United States had responded reasonably quickly to the postwar confrontation with the Soviet Union. The Truman administration determined that Soviet communism posed a clear threat to the security interests of the United States and its allies and moved to confront the danger. When it became clear that America's Western European allies lacked the strength to defend themselves, U.S. policy evolved around the concept of containment. Through the efforts of career foreign services specialists like George Kennan, and with the support of the president and Secretary of State George Marshall, the United States announced the Truman Doctrine (1947) and the European Recovery Program (Marshall Plan, 1947). Those expensive aid programs, designed to revive the political and economic stability of Western Europe, received the support of both Democrats and Republicans, thanks to the bipartisan conclusion that America had to react quickly and dramatically to confront the Russians.

The Marshall Plan helped begin a restoration of Western European security and prosperity, blocking further Soviet expansion in Europe. At the same time, however, a series of nagging issues continued to exacerbate Soviet-American relations. During the summer of 1948, the Russians blockaded access to Berlin (located inside the Soviet zone of occupation). The Berlin Blockade punctuated the growing tension and suspicion between the two world powers, and while the Russians finally removed the hindrance, it confirmed U.S. distrust. In April 1949, America joined with ten Western European nations to form the North Atlantic Treaty Organization (NATO), a mutual defense pact aimed at the Soviet Union. The Russians followed with the Warsaw Pact, an Eastern European response to NATO.

A tense and potentially deadly atomic weapons race also heated the tension between the two states. The United States had considered sharing its nuclear secrets with the United Nations, but by 1946 the Truman administration decided to maintain sole control of the new, awesome weapon. Unfortunately for the United States, the Russians had begun their own efforts to develop atomic weapons. In 1949 the Soviet Union successfully detonated an atom bomb, and the Soviet-American nuclear arms race began. It became apparent shortly that communist spies in both Britain and the United States had provided information to assist the Russians in their efforts.

Across the Pacific, while General Douglas MacArthur organized the military occupation of Japan, a renewed civil war exploded in China. Mao Zedong (Mao Tse-tung) led Chinese communists in a growing assault on the pro-U.S. government of Jiang Jieshi (Chiang Kai-shek). Between 1948 and 1949, it became apparent that the communists were winning the war and, American support notwithstanding, the huge nation would fall to the communists.

All of those crises occurred in the midst of the 1948 presidential election, one the Republicans thought they would win easily. The party already controlled Congress. The presidency would soon follow. Running the popular Governor Thomas E. Dewey of New York against Truman, the Republicans looked forward to reclaiming the White House after sixteen years of Democratic occupancy. "Had Enough?" and "To Err Is Truman!" served as key campaign slogans for political assaults on the president. Most experts predicted a Republican victory, especially after divisions within the Democratic Party produced a major split among its traditional bases of support. The campaign, however, focused more on domestic issues than foreign policy.

To a great extent, both parties had accepted the Marshall Plan and conceded that Truman had acted aggressively to counter Soviet threats. Since former Prime Minister Winston Churchill delivered his Iron Curtain speech in Fulton, Missouri, in March 1946 (see Chapter 10), American foreign policy had moved steadily to confront the Soviet Union. Churchill warned of the Soviet threat of an iron wall separating Europe, and he urged the United States to take up the gauntlet and assume major responsibility to prevent Russia's success. Whether inappropriate or not, given the international situation, most Americans supported Truman's initiatives in foreign policy. Surprisingly, the voters also stuck with the president on domestic concerns as well. In November, Truman narrowly defeated Dewey, shocking the political pundits and the Republicans.

Senator Joseph McCarthy brought his message to a public and government already committed to anti-communist policies. Congress had created the House Un-American Activities Committee (HUAC) in 1945 to investigate domestic subversion and espionage. A year later, Attorney General Thomas Clark warned of a number of communist sympathizers operating in the United States. In March 1947, President Truman signed Executive Order 9835 barring communists and other "radicals" from service in the government. Aimed clearly at postwar communism, the focus gained popular attention during the 1948 Alger Hiss spy trials. Congressman Richard Nixon of California gained national recognition with his public exposure of a conspiracy within the government to sell atomic secrets to the Russians. The Republican congressman had also joined in the general "soft on communism" charges surfacing against the Democrats in the administration.

The clearest expression of an anti-Soviet, anti-communist national policy emerged in National Security Council Document Number 68 (NSC 68), developed in April 1950. Paul Nitze, its main author, argued that the United States faced a dangerous, ongoing confrontation with Soviet communism, a foreign policy threat that challenged American security and the nation's very way of life. The government should, NSC 68 argued, take any action necessary, including a massive military buildup, to thwart communist aggression wherever it appeared.

McCarthy, looking for an issue to enhance his own less than noteworthy first term as senator, may have simply jumped on the bandwagon of postwar anti-communism, but he did so with a resounding thump. One might argue, and many have, that his influence reflected a general and broad American tendency to repression and intolerance. The kind of angry demagoguery exhibited in McCarthy's behavior certainly had occurred in America in the past. Yet, one must ultimately view his popularity and power in light of the particular foreign policy issues that confronted the United States in the decade following World War II. The Cold War caused McCarthy's effect.

Senator McCarthy's explosive charges in West Virginia prompted the Senate to create a subcommittee to investigate the matter. Millard E. Tydings, a Maryland Democrat, chaired the hearings. The subcommittee determined that McCarthy had no evidence to support his allegations, nor could he produce a single name to substantiate them. Promptly, McCarthy stated that Owen Lattimore, a State Department specialist on Far Eastern affairs, was the leader of an "espionage ring" in the government. That accusation proved untenable, and Tydings's subcommittee dismissed the charge as a "fraud and a hoax."

Ironically, Senator McCarthy's popularity grew. Many Republicans saw his allegations as an opportune political weapon to attack the Democrats. Frustrated at Truman's presidential victory in 1948, and confronted with an ongoing New Deal (Truman termed his program the Fair Deal) domestic agenda, the president's political foes saw McCarthy's attacks on the administration as helpful. A number of Southern Democrats, angered at the president's pursuit of civil rights legislation, joined in the attack. Senator McCarthy had begun to draw allies, both in Congress and among the public.

Over President Truman's veto, Congress passed the McCarran Act in September 1950. It required that all communist and communist-front organizations register with the attorney general's office. Additionally, it banned communists from traveling abroad with U.S. passports or working in sensitive defense projects. The outbreak of the Korean War in the summer of 1950 fueled the fire and gave Senator McCarthy another reason to criticize the administration. The North Korean attack across the 38th parallel had caught both the United States and its South Korean allies by surprise. During the summer of 1950, an American-led, United Nations–sponsored military force barely clung to the bottom of the Korean peninsula in what seemed another communist victory.

In the 1950 congressional elections, voters appeared to support McCarthy. Many Americans had concluded that he must be on to something, otherwise why was the United States facing foreign policy setbacks? Perhaps the government had gone soft on communism. The "loss" of China, the nasty, growing conflict in Korea, more spy trials at home, and apparent Soviet threats around the world all seemed to confirm the senator's claims that "fellow travelers" and "pinkoes" in Truman's administration either supported or remained sympathetic to communism. Otherwise, how could a nation as strong as the United States suffer so many failures?

Certainly, American policy between 1945 and 1948 had focused on a Soviet threat in the clearest terms. Senator McCarthy had not invented that issue. His charges, rather, suggested that the administration had failed to counter the threat sufficiently. He stated clearly that New Deal, liberal Democratic "left-overs" probably aided and abetted communism. As America's public morale worsened, McCarthy accelerated his assaults on the State Department, accusing it of losing the Cold War.

When Truman relieved General Douglas MacArthur of command of United Nations forces in Korea in April 1951, McCarthy called for the president's impeachment. General MacArthur had publicly criticized Truman's policy of containment in Korea. Both the president and his advisors concluded that the general's remarks were insubordinate and challenged Truman's position as commander-in-chief. Many Americans, however, agreed with Senator McCarthy's position.

Two months later, in a 60,000 word speech, the senator attacked General George Marshall, the former supreme U.S. commander in World War II, secretary of state, and current chairman of the Joint Chiefs of Staff. The rambling indictment implied that Marshall, both as a diplomat and a military leader, had sided with the New Deal "leftists" who continued to appease the communists. No American leader had made such a commitment to public service as Marshall, yet McCarthy added him to a list of dangerous New Deal liberals.

President Truman struck back, defending his administration's efforts against the communists and criticizing McCarthy's tactics. In a speech before the American Legion, the president warned that the senator's accusations threatened free speech and the exchange of ideas, a danger to any open society. "When any one American—who has done nothing wrong—is forced by fear to shut his mind and close his mouth," Truman said, "then all Americans are in peril."[2]

Newspapers and radio columnists tended to split over the issue. Most supported McCarthy, but others, like the *New York Times* and the *Washington Post*, questioned his methods if not his message. The popular gossip columnist Walter Winchell criticized McCarthy both in print and on his radio program, but the American public continued to support the senator.

McCarthy responded. He attacked anyone who questioned his methods or message. Between 1950 and 1953, his popularity and power grew. He publicly supported Millard Tydings's opponent in the Senate race in Maryland, and Tydings lost his seat. In 1952 McCarthy easily won re-election to the Senate and came back to Congress with Dwight Eisenhower in the White House. Political pundits agreed that McCarthy had helped secure victory for a number of Republicans and even for the new president.

Dwight Eisenhower had carried the Republican banner in the presidential election. Using the criticism K1C2 (Korea, Communism, and Corruption) aimed at the Democrats, and with the support of Senator McCarthy, the former World War II hero easily defeated Adlai Stevenson in November. For the next eighteen months, with Republicans in control of Congress and the White House, Senator McCarthy operated as the second most powerful politician in Washington. In January 1953, he became the chair of the Senate Permanent Investigation Committee, giving him an open-ended vehicle to explore a variety of concerns within the government. During the next fifteen months, McCarthy's committee held 199 days of hearings and called 653 witnesses before it. The senator's loyal aides, Roy Cohn and David Schine, began a series of investigations of State Department Information Libraries overseas. Claiming that many of the books, magazines, and records in the libraries promoted communist values, they succeeded in having more than 30,000 items removed from the shelves.

Eisenhower personally despised McCarthy's methods, but hesitated to criticize the senator publicly. The president hoped to avoid a Republican Party feud, and he realized that the public broadly supported the senator. As late as 1954, 50 percent of Americans polled approved of McCarthy's work. Only 29 percent opposed his actions. Politicians as diverse as John Kennedy and Richard Nixon respected and feared McCarthy's influence and popularity. J. Edgar Hoover, the zealous head of the Federal Bureau of Investigation, also joined the anti-communist hunt. His organization shifted its key focus from chasing organized criminals to tracking communist spies.

Those who took issue with the senator never openly challenged his charges that communism and the Soviet Union threatened the interests and values of America, and that a subversive element in the United States aided and abetted such threats. They questioned his method of leveling unsubstantiated charges and his abrasive, bullying tactics. In college classrooms, editorial boardrooms, or anywhere else, it became difficult, if not impossible, openly to question whether the Soviets or communism were as bad as McCarthy maintained. It seemed equally dangerous to examine whether the United States needed to tone down its aggressive responses in international affairs. A local school board in Indiana went so far as to remove *Robin Hood* from its library shelf. Apparently, the Merry Men of Sherwood Forest supported class warfare similar to communism, because they robbed from the rich to aid the poor.

White House policy under Eisenhower had the effect of limiting McCarthy's impact. The president negotiated an end to the Korean conflict with a cease-fire in the summer of 1953. He developed a massive defense establishment to confront the Soviet Union, including a series of regional security pacts around the globe and an increasing dependence on nuclear weapons. NSC 68 had become more than a document recommending policy; it had become U.S. policy. At the same time, a healthy American economy and Republican Party control of both Congress and the presidency distilled domestic political concerns. If the Wisconsin senator aimed at removing liberal fellow traveler communist sympathizers (buzzwords for New Deal Democrats) from government, Eisenhower's election supposedly had secured that end.

Without obvious targets, McCarthy found his message less than tenable. Still, he continued to look for enemies within the government, and his committee and aides furthered that ambition. In 1954 the senator went after the United States Army. In a dramatic confrontation, McCarthy accused the military of harboring a communist subversive, Major Irving Peress, at its base at Fort Monmouth, New Jersey. The Pentagon refused to cooperate with the senator's investigation, and McCarthy then assaulted the integrity and political loyalty of Peress's commanding officer, General Ralph Zwicker, a highly decorated veteran. The army counterattacked, charging that McCarthy had sought to gain preferential treatment for one of his aides, David Schine, a recent draftee.

In the midst of the brewing controversy, CBS television broadcast a powerful indictment of Senator McCarthy. On March 9, 1954, Edward R. Murrow's *See It Now: Report on Senator McCarthy* aired a stinging editorial questioning McCarthy's methods, his assault on free speech, and his threat to an open exchange of ideas in a free society. Murrow and his producer, Fred Friendly, had televised an earlier program in October 1953 critical of McCarthy. Murrow followed the March program with another attack on McCarthy a week later.

For the first time, a major television network had taken issue with the senator from Wisconsin. By 1954 television had become an important medium of information in America. Twenty-six million viewers had access to the new technology. CBS reported that calls and letters to the studio supported Murrow's views by a 9–1 margin. The Army-McCarthy hearings exploited the same audience. While newspapers and radio still provided news information for most Americans, television had begun to exercise an increasing effect in examining public affairs. Television coverage also began to influence both radio and print journalism.[3]

In April 1954, the Army-McCarthy hearings went on national television. For the next six weeks, millions of Americans viewed firsthand the methods and personality of the senator they had come to admire. The results were unpleasant. McCarthy revealed himself as an ignorant, nasty bully determined to embarrass and harm anyone who disagreed with him. The army's top lawyer, Joseph Welch, consistently undermined McCarthy's charges and humiliated the senator. Senator McCarthy's "point of order" interruptions became the grist for political cartoons and newspaper editorials across the country. In a final personal confrontation, Welch attacked the senator's sense of conscience so poignantly that the hearings ended in a complete victory for the army and a humiliating defeat for the senator.

Ironically, directly after the hearings, polls indicated that McCarthy still had popular support. Yet, that popularity plummeted rapidly. In August, a Senate committee began to investigate McCarthy to consider censuring the senator for his behavior. Shortly, his colleagues voted 67–22 to condemn McCarthy for "contempt" and "abuse." While he still sought publicity, McCarthy had finally lost popular support. More important, the senator had lost the public spotlight—McCarthyism was no longer newsworthy. He died in May 1957, a victim of infectious hepatitis, probably brought on by heavy drinking.

McCarthy's impact has remained the subject of debate for years. If the U.S. government had determined to pursue an anti-Soviet, anti-communist postwar policy, what difference did the senator's charges make? Clearly, Congress and the administration of Harry Truman had acted to do just that. Supporters and critics of McCarthy, then and now, might argue whether the Soviet/communist threat was real and whether the United States overreacted in its perceptions during the early years of the Cold War. That issue has remained a matter of conjecture and scholarly analysis for years. It has, however, little to do with Senator McCarthy's impact. If the senator from Wisconsin did not create or construct American foreign policy between 1945 and 1954, he certainly threatened and probably curtailed an open, thorough debate about U.S. policy during the Cold War.

Within an atmosphere of intolerance, repression, and fear, McCarthyism made healthy skepticism and public critiques of American foreign policy dangerous. The public may have determined, without his influence, that Soviet communism threatened the security interests of the

United States. It was not difficult for immediate postwar events to lead to that conclusion in any event. Certainly, President Truman and his advisors and President Eisenhower's administration reached those conclusions and pursued them with an aggressive foreign policy. McCarthy's influence, however, derived from a darker aspect of public policy creation. He sought to influence public opinion through threats and intimidation, not the solid arguments of empirical evidence or clear events. Critics have termed McCarthyism the "politics of fear." In the dangerous, complicated world of international relations, simple answers, easy villains, and intimidated behavior do not simply reflect the politics of fear, they also create a politics of ignorance.

Additionally, McCarthy's public influence also hindered the government's ability to broaden its foreign policy outlook on the Soviet Union. To appear in any way to pursue policies of moderation left the Truman and Eisenhower administrations open to the charge of being "soft on communism." In that sense, with Senator McCarthy always ready to pounce on the issue, foreign policy remained rigid and confrontational. Options should always remain available to policy makers, who should possess the widest latitude to pursue whatever best suits the public interest. McCarthyism prevented that from occurring. Both the public and administration policy regarding the Soviet Union found limited expression due partly to fear and ignorance.

NOTES

1. Quoted in *Congressional Record*, 81st Congress, 2nd Session (Washington, DC: U.S. Government Printing Offices, 1951), pp. 1954–1957.

2. Eric Goldman, *Rendezvous with Destiny* (New York: Vintage Books, 1977), pp. 330–331.

3. See Erik Barnouw, *The Image Empire* (New York: Oxford University Press, 1970), pp. 46–55.

DOCUMENTS

11.1. Excerpts from National Security Council Document #68, April 1950

In January 1950, President Truman requested a State and War department analysis of the Soviet Union's threat to U.S. security interests. In April, the study arrived on the president's desk. National Security Council Document #68 (NSC 68) served as the basis for the anti-communist Cold War policies that the administration pursued. The conclusion of that lengthy top secret document follows.

Conclusions

The foregoing analysis indicates that the probable fission bomb capability and possible thermonuclear bomb capability of the Soviet Union have greatly intensified the Soviet threat to the security of the United States. This threat is of the same character as that described in NSC 20/4 (approved by the President on November 24, 1948) but is more immediate than had previously been estimated. In particular, the United States now faces the contingency that within the next four or five years the Soviet Union will possess the military capability of delivering a surprise atomic attack of such weight that the United States must have substantially increased general air, ground, and sea strength, atomic capabilities, and air and civilian defenses to deter war and to provide reasonable assurance, in the event of war, that it could survive the initial blow and go on to the eventual attainment of its objectives. In return, this contingency requires the intensification of our efforts in the fields of intelligence and research and development.

Allowing for the immediacy of the danger, the following statement of Soviet threats, contained in NSC 20/4, remains valid:

14. The gravest threat to the security of the United States within the foreseeable future stems from the hostile designs and formidable power of the USSR, and from the nature of the Soviet system.

15. The political, economic, and psychological warfare which the USSR is now waging has dangerous potentialities for weakening the relative world position of the United States and disrupting its traditional institutions by means short of war, unless sufficient resistance is encountered in the policies of this and other non-communist countries.

16. The risk of war with the USSR is sufficient to warrant, in common prudence, timely and adequate preparation by the United States.

a. Even though present estimates indicate that the Soviet leaders probably do not intend deliberate armed action involving the United States at this time, the possibility of such deliberate resort to war cannot be ruled out.

b. Now and for the foreseeable future there is a continuing danger that war will arise either through Soviet miscalculation of the determination of the United States to use all the means at its command to safeguard its security, through Soviet misinterpretation of our intentions, or through U.S. miscalculation of Soviet reactions to measures which we might take.

17. Soviet domination of the potential power of Eurasia, whether achieved by armed aggression or by political and subversive means, would be strategically and politically unacceptable to the United States.

18. The capability of the United States either in peace or in the event of war to cope with threats to its security or to gain its objectives would be severely weakened by internal development, important among which are:

a. Serious espionage, subversion and sabotage, particularly by concerted and well-directed communist activity.

b. Prolonged or exaggerated economic instability.

c. Internal political and social disunity.

d. Inadequate or excessive armament or foreign aid expenditures.

e. An excessive or wasteful usage of our resources in time of peace.

f. Lessening of U.S. prestige and influence through vacillation of appeasement or lack of skill and imagination in the conduct of its foreign policy or by shirking world responsibilities.

g. Development of a false sense of security through a deceptive change in Soviet tactics.

Although such developments as those indicated in paragraph 18 above would severely weaken the capability of the United States and its allies to cope with the Soviet threat to their security, considerable progress has been made since 1948 in laying the foundation upon which adequate strength can now be rapidly built.

The analysis also confirms that our objectives with respect to the Soviet Union, in time of peace as well as in time of war, as stated in NSC 20/4 (para. 19), are still valid, as are the aims and measures stated therein (paras. 20 and 21). Our current security programs and strategic plans are based upon these objectives, aims, and measures:

19.

a. To reduce the power and influence of the USSR to limits which no longer constitute a threat to the peace, national independence, and stability of the world family of nations.

b. To bring about a basic change in the conduct of international relations by the government in power in Russia, to conform with the purposes and principles set forth in the UN Charter.

In pursuing these objectives, due care must be taken to avoid permanently impairing our economy and the fundamental values and institutions inherent in our way of life.

20. We should endeavor to achieve our general objectives by methods short of war through the pursuit of the following aims:

a. To encourage and promote the gradual retraction of undue Russian power and influence from the present perimeter areas around traditional Russian boundaries and the emergence of the satellite countries as entities independent of the USSR.

b. To encourage the development among the Russian peoples of attitudes which may help to modify current Soviet behavior and permit a revival of the national life of groups evidencing the ability and determination to achieve and maintain national independence.

c. To eradicate the myth by which people remote from Soviet military influence are held in a position of subservience to Moscow and to cause the world at large to see and understand the true nature of the USSR and the Soviet-directed world communist party, and to adopt a logical and realistic attitude toward them.

d. To create situations which will compel the Soviet Government to recognize the practical undesirability of acting on the basis of its present concepts and the necessity of behaving in accordance with precepts of international conduct, as set forth in the purposes and principles of the UN Charter.

21. Attainment of these aims requires that the United States:

a. Develop a level of military readiness which can be maintained as long as necessary as a deterrent to Soviet aggression, as indispensable support to our political attitude toward the USSR, as a source of encouragement to nations resisting Soviet political aggression, and as an adequate basis for immediate military commitments and for rapid mobilization should war prove unavoidable.

b. Assure the internal security of the United States against dangers of sabotage, subversion, and espionage.

c. Maximize our economic potential, including the strengthening of our peacetime economy and the establishment of essential reserves readily available in the event of war.

d. Strengthen the orientation toward the United States of the non-Soviet nations; and help such of those nations as are able and willing to make an important contribution to U.S. security, to increase their economic and political stability and their military capability.

e. Place the maximum strain on the Soviet structure of power and particularly on the relationships between Moscow and the satellite countries.

f. Keep the U.S. public fully informed and cognizant of the threats to our national security so that it will be prepared to support the measures which we must accordingly adopt.

In the light of present and prospective Soviet atomic capabilities, the action which can be taken under present programs and plans, however, becomes dangerously inadequate, in both timing and scope, to accomplish the rapid progress toward the attainment of the United States political, economic, and military objectives which is now imperative. A continuation of present trends would result in a serious decline in the strength of the free world relative to the Soviet Union and its satellites. This unfavorable trend arises from the inadequacy of current programs and plans rather than from any error in our objectives and aims. These trends lead in the direction of isolation, not by deliberate decision but by lack of the necessary basis for a vigorous initiative in the conflict with the Soviet Union.

Our position as the center of power in the free world places a heavy responsibility upon the United States for leadership. We must organize and enlist the energies and resources of the free world in a positive program for peace which will frustrate the Kremlin design for world domination by creating a situation in the free world to which the Kremlin will be compelled to adjust. Without such a cooperative effort, led by the United States, we will have to make gradual withdrawals under pressure until we discover one day that we have sacrificed positions of vital interest.

It is imperative that this trend be reversed by a much more rapid and concerted build-up of the actual strength of both the United States and the other nations of the free world. The analysis shows that this will be costly and will involve significant domestic financial and economic adjustments.

The execution of such a build-up, however, requires that the United States have an affirmative program beyond the solely defensive one of countering the threat posed by the Soviet Union. This program must light the path to peace and order among nations in a system based on freedom and justice, as contemplated in the Charter of the United Nations. Further, it must envisage the political and economic measures with which and the military shield behind which the free world can work to frustrate the Kremlin design by the strategy of the cold war; for every consideration of devotion to our fundamental values and to our national security demands that we achieve our objectives by the strategy of the cold war, building up our military strength in order that it may not have to be used.

The only sure victory lies in the frustration of the Kremlin design by the steady development of the moral and material strength of the free world and its projection into the Soviet world in such a way as to bring about an internal change in the Soviet system. Such a positive program— harmonious with our fundamental national purpose and our objectives— is necessary if we are to regain and retain the initiative and to win and hold the necessary popular support and cooperation in the United States and the rest of the free world.

This program should include a plan for negotiation with the Soviet Union, developed and agreed with our allies and which is consonant with our objectives. The United States and its allies, particularly the United Kingdom and France, should always be ready to negotiate with the Soviet Union on terms consistent with our objectives. The present world situation, however, is one which militates against successful negotiations with the Kremlin—for the terms of agreements on important pending issues would reflect present realities and would therefore be unacceptable, if not disastrous, to the United States and the rest of the free world. After a decision and a start on building up the strength of the free world has been made, it might then be desirable for the United States to take an initiative in seeking negotiations in the hope that it might facilitate the process of accommodation by the Kremlin to the new situation. Failing that, the unwillingness of the Kremlin to accept equitable terms or its bad faith in observing them would assist in consolidating popular opinion in the free world in support of the measures necessary to sustain the build-up.

In summary, we must, by means of a rapid and sustained build-up of the political, economic, and military strength of the free world, and by means of an affirmative program intended to wrest the initiative from the Soviet Union, confront it with convincing evidence of the determination and ability of the free world to frustrate the Kremlin design of a world dominated by its will. Such evidence is the only means short of war which eventually may force the Kremlin to abandon its present course of action and to negotiate acceptable agreements on issues of major importance.

The whole success of the proposed program hangs ultimately on recognition by this Government, the American people, and all free peoples, that the cold war is in fact a real war in which the survival of the free world is at stake. Essential prerequisites to success are consultations with Congressional leaders designed to make the program the object of non-partisan legislative support, and a presentation to the public of a full explanation of the facts and implications of the present international situation. The prosecution of the program will require of us all the ingenuity, sacrifice, and unity demanded by the vital importance of the issue and the tenacity to persevere until our national objectives have been attained.

Recommendations

That the President:

a. Approve the foregoing Conclusions.

b. Direct the National Security Council, under the continuing direction of the President, and with the participation of other Departments and Agencies as appropriate, to coordinate and insure the implementation of the Conclusions herein on an urgent and continuing basis for as long as necessary to achieve our objectives. For this purpose, representatives of the member Departments and Agencies, the Joint Chiefs of Staff or their deputies, and other Departments and Agencies as required should be constituted as a revised and strengthened staff organization under the National Security Council to develop coordinated programs for consideration by the National Security Council.

Source: Foreign Relations Series—1950, Vol. 1 (1977), pp. 126–192.

11.2.   Senator Joseph McCarthy's Speech Before the Wheeling, West Virginia, Republican Women's Club, February 1950

This speech, the opening gun in the senator's campaign, demonstrates his adeptness at leveling unsubstantiated charges at his opponents. He accused the Democrats, New Deal liberals, and leftists of being soft on communism and allowing themselves to be infiltrated by communist subversives.

Today we are engaged in a final all-out battle between communistic atheism and Christianity. The modern champions of communism have selected this as the time, and ladies and gentlemen, the chips are down— they are truly down. . . .

Five years after a world war has been won, men's hearts should anticipate a long peace, and men's minds should be free from the heavy weight that comes with war. But this is not such a period—for this is not a period of peace. This is a time of the "cold war." This is a time when all the world is split into two vast, increasingly hostile camps—a time of a great armaments race. . . .

At war's end we were physically the strongest nation on earth—and at least potentially the most powerful intellectually and morally. Ours could have been the honor of being a beacon in the desert of destruction, a shining living proof that civilization was not yet ready to destroy itself. Unfortunately, we have failed miserably and tragically to arise to the opportunity.

The reason we find ourselves in a position of impotency is not because our only powerful potential enemy has sent men to invade our shores, but rather because of the traitorous actions of those who have been treated so well by this Nation. It has not been the less fortunate or members of minority groups who have been selling this Nation out, but those who have had all the benefits that the wealthiest nation on earth has had to offer—the finest homes, the finest college education, and the finest jobs in Government we can give.

This is glaringly true in the State Department. There the bright young men who have been born with silver spoons in their mouths are the ones who have been the worst. . . . In my opinion the State Department, which is one of the most important government departments, is thoroughly infested with Communists.

I have in my hand 205 cases of individuals who would appear to be either card carrying members or certainly loyal to the Communist party, but who nevertheless are still helping to shape our foreign policy.

One thing to remember in discussing Communists in our Government is that we are dealing with spies who get 30 pieces of silver to steal the blueprints of a new weapon. We are dealing with a far more sinister type of activity because it permits the enemy to guide and shape our policy.

Source: Congressional Record, 81st Congress, 2nd Session (1951), pp. 1954–1957.

11.3.   Excerpt from Speech by Senator Margaret Chase Smith, June 1950

Margaret Chase Smith, the first woman elected to the Senate (Republican, Maine), delivered a strong public attack against Senator McCarthy in June 1950, becoming one of the first political leaders to speak out against him. Although McCarthy made her a target in the 1954 Senate elections and tried to have her unseated, Senator Smith won a second term easily. Note that in her speech Smith did not question the evils of communism, but rather the method used to suppress constitutional rights.

I would like to speak briefly and simply about a serious national condition. It is a national feeling of fear and frustration that could result in national suicide and the end of everything we Americans hold dear. It is a condition that comes from the lack of effective leadership either in the legislative branch or the executive branch of our Government.

I think it is high time that we remembered that we have sworn to uphold and defend the Constitution. I think that it is high time that we remembered that the Constitution, as amended, speaks not only of the freedom of speech but also of trial by jury instead of trial by accusation. . . .

Those of us who shout loudest about Americanism in making character assassinations are all too frequently those who, by our own words and acts, ignore some of the basic principles of Americanism—

The right to criticize.

The right to hold unpopular beliefs.

The right to protest.

The right of independent thought.

The exercise of those rights should not cost one single American citizen his reputation or his right to a livelihood nor should he be in danger of losing his reputation or livelihood merely because he happens to know someone who holds unpopular beliefs. Who of us does not? Otherwise none of us could call our souls our own. Otherwise thought control would have set in.

The American people are sick and tired of being afraid to speak their minds lest they be politically smeared as "Communists" or "Fascists" by their opponents. Freedom of speech is not what it used to be in America. It has been abused by some that it is not exercised by others. . . .

Today our country is being psychologically divided by the confusion and the suspicions that are bred in the United States Senate to spread like cancerous tentacles of "know nothing, suspect everything" attitudes.

. . . The Nation sorely needs a Republican victory. But I do not want to see the Republican Party rise to political victory on the Four Horsemen of Calumny—fear, ignorance, bigotry, and smear.

I doubt if the Republican Party could do so, simply because I do not believe the American people will uphold any political party that puts political exploitation above national interest. Surely, we Republicans are not so desperate for victory. . . .

As a United States Senator, I am not proud of the way in which the Senate has been made a publicity platform for irresponsible sensationalism. I am not proud of the reckless abandon in which unproved charges have been hurled from this side of the aisle. I am not proud of the obviously staged, undignified countercharges which have been attempted in retaliation from the other side of the aisle. . . .

As an American, I condemn a Republican Fascist just as much as I condemn a Democratic Communist. They are equally dangerous to you and me and to our country. As an American, I want to see our Nation recapture the strength and unity it once had when we fought the enemy instead of ourselves.

Source: Congressional Record, 81st Congress, 2nd Session, pp. 7894–7895.

11.4.   Excerpt from *See It Now: Report on Senator McCarthy*, March 9, 1954

Edward R. Murrow's popular television show aired a serious criticism of Senator McCarthy and his influence on American opinion and attitudes. Broadcast on March 9, 1954, it reflected a growing apprehension over the senator's method of behavior as he attacked his enemies. Murrow's conclusion to the program follows.

No one familiar with the history of this country can deny that congressional committees are useful. It is necessary to investigate before legislating. But the line between investigation and persecuting is a very fine one, and the junior senator from Wisconsin has stepped over it repeatedly. His primary achievement has been in confusing the public mind as between the internal and the external threat of Communism. We must not confuse dissent with disloyalty. We must remember always that accusation is not proof and that conviction depends upon evidence and due process of law. We will not walk in fear, one of another. We will not be driven by fear into an age of unreason if we dig deep in our history and our doctrine and remember that we are not descended from fearful men, not from men who feared to write, to speak, to associate and to defend causes which were for the moment unpopular.

This is no time for men who oppose Senator McCarthy's methods to keep silent, or for those who approve. We can deny our heritage and our history, but we cannot escape responsibility for the result. As a nation we have come into our full inheritance at a tender age. We proclaim ourselves, as indeed we are, the defenders of freedom—what's left of it—but we cannot defend freedom abroad by deserting it at home. The actions of the junior senator from Wisconsin have caused alarm and dismay amongst our allies abroad and given considerable comfort to our enemies. And whose fault is that? Not really his; he didn't create this situation of fear, he merely exploited it, and rather successfully. Cassius was right. "The fault, dear Brutus, is not in our stars, but in ourselves."

Source: Edward Bliss, Jr., ed., *In Search of Light: The Broadcasts of Edward R. Murrow, 1938–1961* (New York: Avon Books, 1967), pp. 265–266.

12

Vietnam and the Paris Peace Accords: America's Longest War

The President made repeated references to his continuing desire for a negotiated settlement. . . . But he made no move to reactivate the direct channel he already has to Hanoi in Paris. Nor did he make any effort to respond to the openings offered in July by the Viet Cong's seven-point proposal, which has remained largely unanswered for more than four months.

—*New York Times*
November 17, 1971

We fought a military war, our opponents fought a political one. We sought physical attrition; our opponents aimed for our psychological exhaustion. In the process we lost sight of one of the cardinal maxims of guerilla war: the guerilla wins if he does not lose.

—Henry Kissinger
U.S. Secretary of State

America's long and divisive conflict in Southeast Asia ended diplomatically on January 27, 1973. In Paris, France, the representatives of the United States, North Vietnam, South Vietnam, and the Provisional Revolutionary Government (Viet Cong) signed the instruments of peace. President Richard Nixon informed the public of the accords in a televised speech from the Oval Office several hours later. For America, the Vietnam War had ended . . . or had it?

The origins of the conflict and the issues that drew the United States into a war in Southeast Asia took root following World War II. Between 1947 and 1954, two presidential administrations supported France as that nation fought to maintain its colonial control of Indochina in a bloody war that ruined French governments and lost public support.

In 1954, at the Geneva Conference, the superpowers saw the former French colonial system broken up into the countries of Laos, Cambodia, and North and South Vietnam (divided at the 17th parallel). A planned unification of Vietnam would take place in supervised elections in 1956. U.S. support for France had stemmed initially from the conclusion that its European ally appeared engaged in a counterinsurgency war against communist guerrillas. Ho Chi Minh, an avowed communist, provided key leadership for the Viet Minh forces fighting France. It also seemed apparent to American leaders that the Communist Chinese and Russians supported the Viet Minh. In that regard, the war in Indochina served as an extension of the Cold War ideological battle between the United States and the Soviets.

While most Southeast Asia analysts understood that the Viet Minh struggled primarily to free themselves from French colonialism, American leaders stressed the communist rather than nationalist impulse that motivated Vietnamese aggression against France. Essentially, the anchor that moored American policy swung consistently toward an anti-communist, Cold War conclusion. The United States had a global responsibility to thwart communist movements wherever they arose. Truman's and Eisenhower's administrations, therefore, backed France in a dubious relationship that tied the United States to evolving French policy. Additionally, the emerging concept of a "domino theory" concerned American strategists. If one part of Southeast Asia fell to communism, other areas and nations might follow in a neat row, ultimately threatening the loss of the entire region.

At Geneva, the decision to divide Vietnam led to a U.S.-sponsored government in the South that emerged under the presidency of Ngo Dinh Diem and a communist government in the North under Ho Chi Minh's leadership. The U.S. government never formally signed any of the agreements at Geneva, but certainly influenced their outcome. Elections designed to unite the country by 1956 never took place. President Diem, with Eisenhower's support, refused to hold elections, and a renewed conflict between North and South Vietnam began. South Vietnamese and American officials had determined that national unification elections in Vietnam would lead to a communist victory, and that they remained unwilling to allow. North Vietnam's leaders determined that they would win by force what Presidents Diem and Eisenhower had denied them at the ballot box. They allied their interests with the communists in the South (Viet Cong) and attacked Diem's regime.

In simple terms, U.S. diplomacy backed South Vietnam's government and aimed to guarantee its sovereignty. From Dwight Eisenhower to Richard Nixon, four administrations implemented a variety of plans to ensure that goal. Direct and massive military involvement, begun in 1965 under President Lyndon Johnson, escalated that fundamental conclusion into America's longest war.

American military commitment began with aid to the French, followed with assistance to South Vietnam, and expanded when Eisenhower and President John F. Kennedy sent U.S. military advisors into Southeast Asia to back Diem's forces. Additionally, the United States became a member of the Southeast Asia Treaty Organization (SEATO—1954), a regional security pact that placed South Vietnam under its protective umbrella. (SEATO included the United States, Australia, New Zealand, Britain, France, Thailand, Pakistan, and the Philippines.) When President Kennedy was assassinated in Dallas, in November 1963, more than 15,000 U.S. military advisors operated in Vietnam. The U.S. government had also approved a coup that overthrew Diem's unpopular regime and helped replace it with an army general, Doung Van Minh. Growing public criticism of Diem's government in South Vietnam had convinced Kennedy that he had to go. If the United States did not aid in Diem's ouster and assassination, it certainly approved the outcome of those events.

Whether Kennedy would have pursued an aggressive policy in the region remains a matter of debate among historians. His successor, Lyndon Johnson, faced a difficult decision in Southeast Asia. Evidence from a variety of sources warned that without a major U.S. military commitment to the war, the South Vietnamese government would collapse. Johnson may have also feared adopting a weak policy vis-à-vis Vietnam. The new president remained concerned that President Kennedy's advisors might openly question any sign of hesitancy on his part to act aggressively.

Yet, 1964 was a presidential election year, and Johnson hoped to pursue a major domestic program (the Great Society) and a significant civil rights initiative that would occupy his full attention and interest. He won the election pledging to keep America out of war in Southeast Asia. Just prior, the president had asked Congress, in the Gulf of Tonkin Resolution, for a "blank check" to commit American ground combat troops to the region. The Senate voted 48–2 in support of the resolution. The House supported it unanimously. Within a year, U.S. policy had escalated into a full-blown military conflict.

Most Americans supported Johnson's initial request. Whether duped, as some claimed later, convinced the United States could win a quick, decisive victory, or determined to do the right thing, public opinion backed LBJ. Attitudes, however, shifted between 1965 and 1968. As the number of troops grew to half a million and casualties increased, the "communists" fought on, and the Saigon government appeared to lack the support of its people, more and more Americans questioned U.S. policy.

The Tet Offensive (January–February 1968) served as a watershed in decision making. The surprise attack, during which the supposedly defeated communists threw back U.S. and South Vietnamese forces and for a time occupied parts of every key South Vietnamese city, confounded the situation. While the Tet Offensive ended in a resounding U.S.–South Vietnamese military victory in terms of the number of communists killed, it confronted Americans with a grim conclusion. When General William Westmoreland, the U.S. commander in Vietnam, requested 250,000 more troops to follow up the "victory," public opinion in America rebelled at the logic of such a victory. The war would go on, and the North Vietnamese and Viet Cong proved willing to continue the fight. They might fail to win battles, but they appeared dedicated to prolonging the war. U.S. forces, apparently, could not defeat that conviction.

In March, Clark Clifford, the new, but experienced, secretary of defense, sent Johnson a memorandum recommending that the United States find a diplomatic end to the conflict. Several weeks later, on March 25–26, Johnson reconvened a meeting of respected political figures and former policy makers (dubbed the "Wisemen"). In 1967, the group had supported LBJ's policy to build American combat forces. In March, they agreed with Secretary Clifford. The key factors in the shifting points of view stemmed from military, political, and economic concerns.

Militarily, the administration's advisors had concluded that it would take too many more U.S. troops and too much time to win on the battlefield. Politically, the length and sacrifice of such a decision would prove catastrophic to the president. Finally, the cost of the war would prompt a tax increase and was already threatening the international gold standard, based on America's worsening financial condition.

Public opinion polls had shifted months earlier. In a July 1967 Gallup Poll 52 percent of respondents disapproved of Johnson's policies in Vietnam; 56 percent concluded that U.S. forces were engaged in a stalemate war. The Tet Offensive confirmed that view. Protests against American involvement in Vietnam had taken place throughout the 1965–1968 buildup, but remained limited in scope and grew slowly. As early as November 1966, 30,000 peace advocates gathered at the White House. By the following year, the National Coordinating Committee to End the War in Vietnam formed as an umbrella organization to structure and articulate its growing concerns. Political opponents like Eugene McCarthy and George McGovern, and then Robert Kennedy, most coming from Johnson's own Democratic Party, endorsed antiwar policies. After an agonizing self-evaluation, Dr. Martin Luther King, Jr., spoke out against the war. He feared such public criticism would harm his relationship with President Johnson and that the civil rights movement might suffer.

The Vietnam Conflict, 1961–1975

In the end, however, King believed that the moral cost of the war threatened America's soul, just as the financial cost looked to hamstring the anti-poverty programs he supported at home.

Draft-card burnings and antiwar gatherings at the Pentagon and the White House grew throughout 1967 and 1968. In May 1968, protesters led by Catholic priests Daniel and Philip Berrigan entered the Selective Service offices in Catonsville, Maryland, and poured animal blood over draft records. The Students for a Democratic Society (SDS) and its "Weathermen" faction advocated violent antiwar protest. Their leaders orchestrated the confrontation with Chicago police during the Democratic National Convention in 1968. The war, coupled with ongoing civil rights issues, had helped to create an increasingly angry and violent youth movement. Police and government agencies reacted similarly in an escalating confrontation. The war in Vietnam appeared to be tearing America apart.

If most Americans found student protests, marches, and radical views unappealing, they still longed for an end to the conflict and wanted their government to act on that conclusion. Pro-war "hawks" still questioned both the un-Americanism and procommunist leanings of the youth protest movement. "Hawks" also criticized the general public's growing disinterest as misguided. They had, however, lost broad support in the winter and spring of 1968. Most Americans neither supported student protestors, nor agreed with those who wanted to pursue the war with more troops. The broad public wanted an end to the conflict, hopefully salvaging South Vietnamese sovereignty.

The military situation in Vietnam, his meetings with the Wisemen, and the public discontent at home led President Johnson to invite North Vietnam to begin negotiations to end the war. Formal discussions began in Paris on May 13, 1968. Averell Harriman represented the United States, and Xuan Thuy acted for North Vietnam. On the heels of the Tet military defeat, communist leaders appeared uneasy negotiating on the defensive. They recognized, however, that U.S. public opinion afforded them political leverage even if the American military remained strong. The U.S. negotiators saw their military advantage, but understood that attitudes at home were growing increasingly critical. Neither side seemed resolved to end the conflict.

The North Vietnamese had three basic goals—withdrawal of U.S. military forces, the overthrow of the current government in South Vietnam, and the creation of a coalition government in the South with communist representation. The U.S. position sought to preserve the existing government in Saigon and refused to remove American forces until the communists halted the movement of troops and supplies from the North through Cambodia (via the Ho Chi Minh Trail) into South Vietnam. Since neither side would bend, no cease-fire could take place, and the Paris talks reached a stalemate.

The war had exhausted and politically wounded President Johnson, and he announced that he would not seek reelection in 1968. The year brought enormous turmoil and conflict in America. Senator Robert Kennedy, a popular Democratic candidate, war critic, and brother of John

Kennedy, died at the hands of an assassin in California during the primary campaign. Martin Luther King, Jr., the renowned civil rights leader, Nobel Prize recipient, and critic of the war, also fell to an assassin's bullet. Riots confounded American law and order that summer, as the frustration of domestic and foreign policy crises boiled over. At the Democratic National Convention in Chicago, protesters fought with police in an ugly expression of discontent.

The divided Democratic Party chose Hubert Humphrey, LBJ's vice president, as its candidate in a bitter convention battle. The Republicans nominated Richard Nixon. The Californian, Eisenhower's former vice president, had been out of office, but not politics, since the early 1960s. He had advocated a tough position on the war in Vietnam as U.S. involvement grew. By 1968 Nixon had concluded that the nation had to extricate itself from the unpopular, divisive conflict. He saddled Humphrey with Johnson's policies and claimed that he had a timetable to end the war in Vietnam and preserve South Vietnam's independence—"Peace with Honor!" Nixon defeated his opponent narrowly, winning 43.4 percent of the popular vote and 301 electoral votes out of 538, the closest race since 1916.

The new president and his national security advisor, Henry Kissinger, were students and practitioners of realpolitik, a form of foreign policy that pursued national self-interest in a pragmatic form. Both men sought to ease tension and misunderstanding among the United States, the Soviets, and China. To do so required a global strategy that linked various specific issues and hot spots within a grand design. "Linkage" required an end to the war in Vietnam, for both regional and global reasons. Kissinger noted that the administration sought to develop an approach in Vietnam that would make America's withdrawal from the conflict appear more a matter of policy than defeat.

The stalled talks in Paris could continue. The president soon initiated an era of détente with the Soviet Union, and made a historic trip to China to explore new relations with that "enemy." At the same time, in August 1969, he announced the Nixon Doctrine. The United States would assist nations as a helpful friend, not a military guardian. The president also determined to reduce American troop presence in Southeast Asia and have the South Vietnamese assume the major combat role, a policy known as Vietnamization.

Kissinger resumed discussions with Xuan Thuy in August 1969, but the North Vietnamese representative remained resolute. He offered no change in his nation's position, nor did Kissinger for the United States. The American, however, threatened that the stalemate would produce an intensified U.S. military response, including bombing missions and other options. That included an American incursion across the Vietnamese border into Cambodia (April 1970).

The Cambodian "invasion" prompted a new outbreak of protests in the United States. Tragic incidents at Kent State University in Ohio and Jackson State College in Mississippi, where members of the National Guard and state police killed students, amplified the trauma. Still, according to opinion surveys, 40 percent of the public supported the original decision to send troops to Vietnam, and the 52 percent who opposed the decision remained divided. Many supported President Nixon's efforts. The theory that a massive antiwar, anti-administration public movement existed in the United States during 1968–1972 simply fails to bear up under analysis. A Gallup Poll determined that 77 percent of respondents approved of Nixon's policies.

Kissinger began a new round of secret discussions in Paris in February 1970, when he met with Le Duc Tho. Those discussions took place without the knowledge of the delegates meeting formally in the same city. Neither President Nguyen Van Thieu, South Vietnam's leader, nor his representative in Paris, Bui Diem, had any inkling of the discussions. Significantly, Kissinger failed to share information with the American delegation, including Secretary of State William Rogers. He and President Nixon preferred to focus on the clandestine discussions.

During much of the next year, talks in Paris, both secret and formal, continued to stall on the same basic issues—North Vietnamese and American troop withdrawals from South Vietnam. While President Nixon reduced U.S. troop numbers from over 500,000 to fewer than 100,000 during his first term, the North Vietnamese refused to do the same. By October 1970, the president had offered the option of a "standstill" cease-fire. Both sides would simply agree to a military halt while the peace talks continued. The North Vietnamese refused to consider the offer. They realized that the U.S. withdrawal enabled them to negotiate from a growing position of strength. Well into 1971, the meetings, both secret and public, dragged on while Vietnamization continued.

In the midst of the discussions, Daniel Ellsberg, a research specialist in the Defense Department, turned over secret documents to the press outlining U.S. policy in Vietnam. Known as the Pentagon Papers, they revealed a murky, disingenuous series of actions that sought to deceive the public and Congress about the true nature of the conflict. Nixon tried to ban the publication of the documents in the *New York Times*, but the United States Supreme Court ruled in favor of the newspaper. The Pentagon Papers added to the growing disillusionment in the United States regarding the war.

Nixon sought reelection in 1972. The Hanoi government hoped to exploit the election with antiwar advocates in the United States, but Republicans remained confident that most U.S. citizens continued to back the president. During March 1972, the North Vietnamese launched a series of major military assaults throughout South Vietnam. At the time only 70,000 U.S. troops remained in the country, and only 6,000 of those were combat forces. Communist leaders knew that Nixon would not reintroduce American troops and counted on handing the South Vietnamese army a severe beating. Nixon, however, increased air bombardments that escalated into numerous attacks on the North Vietnamese capital at Hanoi and its major port city, Haiphong. In May, Nixon also ordered the mining of Haiphong harbor. Again, critics saw the president's actions as escalation. His supporters argued that the bombings supported the South and served notice at the peace talks that the United States was negotiating from a position of strength. The communist military offensive ran out of steam by early summer 1972.

In the fall, the Hanoi government sought a negotiated settlement to a conflict it determined remained unwinnable on the battlefield. U.S. bombing and South Vietnamese ground forces had stalled the communists' summer offensive. In July and August, Le Duc Tho had met with Kissinger and indicated a more positive attitude toward a negotiated settlement. Meeting between August and October, while President Nixon escalated bombing assaults on the North, the United States reached a breakthrough on October 11. Hanoi agreed to allow the current South Vietnamese government to remain, and the United States conceded that the Provisional Revolutionary Government (Viet Cong) would have representation in that government, thereby ending a political stalemate that had existed since 1968. In the military settlement, the communists agreed to return all U.S. prisoners of war within sixty days of the cease-fire. Kissinger guaranteed the removal of all American forces. One month before the presidential election, Nixon appeared to have brought an end to the Vietnam War.

General Nguyen Van Thieu, the South Vietnamese president, refused to accept the agreement when Kissinger flew to Saigon to discuss it. The South Vietnamese leaders sensed that the United States hoped to get out of the war and abandon them. Thieu considered it a betrayal. Once again, diplomacy stalled.

President Nixon was reelected in November 1972 with a major victory over his antiwar opponent, George McGovern. He believed that his popular mandate would allow the United States to pursue a better position at Paris. Yet, between November and December 13, neither the North nor the South Vietnamese would make any concessions. In the second week of December talks broke off, and President Nixon initiated a new series of extensive bombing raids over the North. While the renewed air attacks sought to convince the North Vietnamese to reach an agreement, they also aimed to persuade President Thieu that U.S. airpower could compensate for the removal of American ground troops. That might lead the South Vietnamese to accept a settlement more readily.

The massive assaults continued until January 8, 1973, when Kissinger and Tho resumed discussions in Paris. In six days, the two diplomats reworked their original October agreement. To placate Thieu, President Nixon pledged that the United States would increase its aid to South Vietnam. He also agreed to halt all American air attacks against the North. America's longest war had ended.

The Paris Peace Accords concluded negotiations that had taken place, off and on, for six years. The agreements allowed the United States to remove its direct military commitment from the area and appeared to recognize South Vietnam's sovereignty. Nixon's "Peace with Honor" pledge had worked! Yet, most observers believed that the South Vietnamese could not survive long without American military support. The war in Southeast Asia continued as both Laos and Cambodia fell to communist regimes. On April 30, 1975, Saigon fell to North Vietnamese forces. Gerald Ford, who had become president following Nixon's resignation as a result of the Watergate scandal, could gain no public support in the United States for renewed military intervention. The communists had reunited Vietnam.

DOCUMENTS

12.1. Memo from Secretary of State Dean Acheson to President Truman on Vietnam, May 1949

In May 1949, Dean Acheson, President Truman's secretary of state, telegraphed an early evaluation of Ho Chi Minh to the U.S. consulate in Vietnam, tying him to the Cold War confrontation between the Soviets and America. The note provided a telling view of emerging U.S. attitudes. The many typos and syntax errors are in the original memo reflecting its informality.

In light Ho's known background, no other assumption possible but that he outright Commie so long as (1) he fails unequivocally repudiate Moscow connections and Commie doctrine and (2) remains personally singled out for praise by internatl Commie press and receives its support. Moreover, US not impressed by nationalist character red flag with yellow stars. Question as to whether Ho as much nationalist as Commie is irrelevant. All Stalinists in colonial areas are nationalists. With achievement natl aims (i.e., independence) their objective necessarily becomes subordination state to Commie purposes and ruthless extermination not only opposition groups but all elements suspected even slightest deviation. On basis examples eastern Eur it must be assumed such wld be goal Ho. . . . It must of course be conceded theoretical possibility exists estab National Communist state on pattern Yugoslavia in any areas beyond reach Soviet army. However, US attitude cld take acct such possibility only if every other possible avenue closed to preservation area from Kremlin control. Moreover, while out of reach of Soviet army it will doubtless be by no means out of reach of Chi Commie hatchet men and and armed forces.

Source: Foreign Relations Series—1949, vol. 7, part 1, The Far East and Australasia (1975), p. 29.

12.2. "The Truth about Vietnam," *New York Times* Editorial, 1962

The New York Times *evolved as a major media critic of the U.S. war in Vietnam during the late 1960s and early 1970s. In 1962,*

however, the newspaper printed an editorial supporting Ameri-
can policy in Vietnam and asking for administration candor in its
public disclosures regarding the conflict.

The question of how to portray the growing American military role in South Vietnam is facing the Administration with a delicate problem.

There are now, news reports say, some 4,000 uniformed Americans in South Vietnam. They are engaged in such activities as training Vietnamese—often in combat situations flying Vietnamese troops into and out of combat and carrying out air reconnaissance and other dangerous intelligence missions. United States ships are patrolling the Vietnamese coast against military infiltration by sea from North to South Vietnam. If Americans are shot at during the course of these activities they are shooting back, and there have already been American combat casualties. . . .

The Administration has been trying to depict the scope of this extensive American involvement in South Vietnam with as much restraint as possible. Some curbs have been put on news coverage of American activities in South Vietnam. The American role in South Vietnam is still primarily confined to assistance to the Vietnamese. . . . Undue publicity might well inflate the American role beyond its true proportions, and this could compromise Washington's efforts to keep the South Vietnam struggle a limited war.

There should, however, be no concealment of the possibility that what we are doing in South Vietnam may escalate into a major conflict. Whether it does will depend on just how extensively and openly Communist North Vietnam and its supporters, Communist China and Russia, choose to intervene in South Vietnam. The United States would find it difficult, if not impossible, to withdraw from the fight if they do decide to throw in major forces. There is reason to believe that they will not do this, that they are also interested in keeping the conflict to a limited one. But the possibility of a major war is still there, and the situation is one about which American officials ought to be candid.

Source: "The Truth about Vietnam," *New York Times*, February 14, 1962.

12.3.   Excerpt from Gulf of Tonkin Resolution, August 1964

At President Johnson's request, Congress passed the Gulf of Ton-
kin Resolution in August 1964. Essentially, the decision author-
ized the president "to take all necessary measures" to respond to
the crisis in Vietnam. The resolution gave LBJ a blank check, and
he cashed it.

To promote the maintenance of international peace and security in Southeast Asia.

Whereas naval units of the Communist regime in Vietnam, in violation of the principles of the Charter of the United Nations and of international law have deliberately and repeatedly attacked United States naval vessels, lawfully present in international waters, and have thereby created a serious threat to international peace; and

Whereas these attacks are part of a deliberate and systematic campaign of aggression that the Communist regime in North Vietnam has been waging against its neighbors and the nations joined with them in the collective defense of their freedom; and

Whereas the United States is assisting the peoples of southeast Asia to protect their freedom and has no territorial, military or political ambitions in that area, but desires only that these people should be left in peace to work out their own destinies in their own way.

Sec. 1. Now, therefore, be it Resolved by the Senate and House of Representatives of the United States of America in Congress assembled, That the Congress approves and supports the determination of the President, as Commander in Chief, to take all necessary measures to repel an armed attack against the forces of the United States and to prevent further aggression.

Sec. 2. The United States regards as vital to its national interest and to world peace the maintenance of international peace and security in Southeast Asia. Consonant with the Constitution of the United States and the Charter of the United Nations and in accordance with its obligations under the Southeast Asia Collective Defense Treaty, the United States is, therefore, prepared as the President determines, to take all necessary steps, including the use of armed force, to assist any member or protocol state of the Southeast Asia Collective Defense Treaty requesting assistance in defense of its freedom.

Sec. 3. This resolution shall expire when the President shall determine that the peace and security of the area is reasonably assured by international conditions created by action of the United States or otherwise, except that it may be terminated earlier by concurrent resolution of the Congress.

Source: The Department of State Bulletin, vol. 51, no. 1313, August 24, 1964, p. 268.

12.4.   Senator J. William Fulbright's Criticism of U.S. Policy in Vietnam, 1966

Senator J. William Fulbright of Arkansas chaired the Senate Foreign Relations Committee, which supported the Gulf of Tonkin

*Resolution. He became, however, a tough critic of administration
policy, and in his noted book,* The Arrogance of Power, *published
in 1966, offers an indictment of U.S. policy. An excerpt from that
book follows.*

Why are Americans fighting in Vietnam? For much the same reason,
I think, that we intervened militarily in Guatemala in 1954, in Cuba in
1961, and in the Dominican Republic in 1965. In Asia as in Latin America
we have given our opposition to communism priority over our sympathy
for nationalism because we have regarded communism as a kind of absolute evil, as a totally pernicious doctrine which deprives the people
subjected to it of freedom, dignity, happiness, and the hope of ever ac-
quiring them. I think that this view of communism is implicit in much
of American foreign policy; I think it is the principal reason for our
involvement in Vietnam and for the emergence of an "Asian Doctrine"
under which the United States is moving toward the role of policeman
for all of Southeast Asia.

It is said that we are fighting against North Vietnam's aggression
rather than its ideology and that the "other side" has only to "stop doing
what it is doing" in order to restore peace. But what are the North Vietnamese doing, except participating in a civil war, not in a foreign country
but on the other side of a demarcation line between two sectors of the
same country, a civil war in which Americans from ten thousand miles
across the ocean are also participating? . . .

The crime of the North Vietnamese . . . is that they are communists,
practitioners of a philosophy we regard as evil. When all the official
rhetoric about aggression and the defense of freedom and the sanctity of
our world has been cited and recited, we are still left with two essential
reasons for our involvement in Vietnam: the view of communism as an
evil philosophy and the view of ourselves as God's avenging angels. . . .

Source: J. William Fulbright, *The Arrogance of Power* (New York: Random House,
    1966), pp. 106–108.

**12.5.   Excerpt from Antiwar Speech by Dr. Martin Luther King, Jr., on
           April 4, 1967**

---

*Martin Luther King, Jr., emerged as the outstanding leader of the
civil rights movement in the 1960s, and he had focused his energies in that area. Increasingly concerned about the war in Vietnam, but hesitant to challenge President Johnson, who supported
the civil rights movement, Dr. King confronted the issue in 1967.*

His antiwar position is stressed in excerpts from the speech below.

Since I am a preacher by trade, I suppose it is not surprising that I have seven major reasons for bringing Vietnam into the field of my moral vision. There is at the outset a very obvious and almost facile connection between the war in Vietnam and the struggle I, and others, have been waging in America. A few years ago there was a shining moment in that struggle. It seemed as if there was a real promise of hope for the poor— both black and white—through the Poverty Program. Then came the build-up in Vietnam, and I watched the program broken and eviscerated as if it were some idle political plaything of a society gone mad on war, and I knew that America would never invest the necessary funds or energies in rehabilitation of its poor so long as Vietnam continued to draw men and skills and money like some demonic, destructive suction tube. So I was increasingly compelled to see the war as an enemy of the poor and to attack it as such.

Perhaps the more tragic recognition of reality took place when it became clear to me that the war was doing far more than devastating the hopes of the poor at home. It was sending their sons and their brothers and their husbands to fight and die in extraordinarily high proportions relative to the rest of the population. We were taking the young black men who had been crippled by our society and sending them 8000 miles away to guarantee liberties in Southeast Asia which they had not found in Southwest Georgia and East Harlem. So we have been repeatedly faced with the cruel irony of watching Negro and white boys on TV screens as they kill and die together for a nation that has been unable to seat them together in the same schools. So we watch them in brutal solidarity burning the huts of a poor village, but we realize that they would never live on the same block in Detroit. I could not be silent in the face of such cruel manipulation of the poor.

If we continue, there will be no doubt in my mind and in the mind of the world that we have no honorable intentions in Vietnam. It will become clear that our minimal expectation is to occupy it as an American colony, and men will not refrain from thinking that our maximum hope is to goad China into a war so that we may bomb her nuclear installations.

The world now demands a maturity of America that we may not be able to achieve. It demands that we admit that we have been wrong from the beginning of our adventure in Vietnam, and that we have been detrimental to the life of her people.

In order to atone for our sins and errors in Vietnam, we should take the initiative in bringing the war to a halt. I would like to suggest five concrete things that our government should do immediately to begin the long and difficult process of extricating ourselves from this nightmare:

1. End all bombing in North and South Vietnam.
2. Declare a unilateral cease-fire in the hope that such action will create the atmosphere for negotiation.
3. Take immediate steps to prevent other battlegrounds in Southeast Asia by curtailing our military build-up in Thailand and our interference in Laos.
4. Realistically accept the fact that the National Liberation Front has substantial support in South Vietnam and must thereby play a role in any meaningful negotiations and in any future Vietnam government.
5. Set a date on which we will remove all foreign troops from Vietnam in accordance with the 1954 Geneva Agreement.

Meanwhile, we in the churches and synagogues have a continuing task while we urge our government to disengage itself from a disgraceful commitment. We must be prepared to match actions with words by seeking out every creative means of protest possible.

As we counsel young men concerning military service we must clarify for them our nation's role in Vietnam and challenge them with the alternative of conscientious objection. I am pleased to say that this is the path now being chosen by more than 70 students at my own Alma Mater, Morehouse College, and I recommend it to all who find the American course in Vietnam a dishonorable and unjust one. Moreover, I would encourage all ministers of draft age to give up their ministerial exemptions and seek status as conscientious objectors. Every man of humane convictions must decide on the protest that best suits his convictions, but we must all protest. . . .

Source: Robert J. McMahon, ed., *Major Problems in the History of the Vietnam War* (Lexington, MA: D. C. Heath, 1995), pp. 470–475. Dr. King's major speeches are in Clayborne Carson, and Kris Shepard, eds., *A Call for Conscience: The Landmark Speeches of Martin Luther King, Jr.* (New York: Warner Books, 2001).

12.6.   Excerpt of Letter from President Nixon to President Nguyen Van Thieu, January 5, 1973

In January 1973, President Nixon sought to convince President Nguyen Van Thieu that the agreement Henry Kissinger had

worked out in Paris would not sacrifice the current South Viet-
namese government. Thieu remained skeptical and angry. In a
series of letters the two leaders argued their positions. Nixon's
January 5 letter was indicative of the discussions.

There is nothing substantial that I can add to my many previous messages, including my December 17 letter, which clearly stated my opinions
and intentions. With respect to the questions of North Vietnamese
troops, we will again present your views to the Communists as we have
done vigorously at every other opportunity in the negotiations. The result is certain to be once more the rejection of our position. We have
explained to you repeatedly why we believe the problem of North Vietnamese troops is manageable under the agreement, and I see no reason
to repeat all the arguments.

We will proceed next week in Paris along the lines that General [Al-
exander] Haig explained to you. Accordingly, if the North Vietnamese
meet our concerns on the two outstanding substantive issues in the
agreement, concerning the DMZ and the method of signing, and if we
can arrange acceptable supervisory machinery, we will proceed to conclude the settlement. The gravest consequences would then ensue if your
government chose to reject the agreement and split off from the United
States. As I said in my December 17 letter, "I am convinced that your
refusal to join us would be an invitation to disaster—to the loss of all
that we together have fought for over the past decade. It would be in-
excusable above all because we will have lost a just and honorable alternative."

As we enter this new round of talks, I hope that our countries will
now show a united front. It is imperative for our common objectives that
your government take no further actions that complicate our task and
would make more difficult the acceptance of the settlement by all parties.
We will keep you informed of the negotiations in Paris through daily
briefings of Ambassador Lam.

I can only repeat what I have so often said: The best guarantee for the
survival of South Vietnam is the unity of our two countries which would
be gravely jeopardized if you persist in your present course. The actions
of our Congress since its return have clearly borne out the many warnings we have made.

Should you decide, as I trust you will, to go with us, you have my
assurance of continued assistance in the post-settlement period and that
we will respond with full force should the settlement be violated by
North Vietnam. So once more I conclude with an appeal to you to close
ranks with us.

Source: Robert J. McMahon, ed., *Major Problems in the History of the Vietnam War*
   (Lexington MA: D. C. Heath, 1995), pp. 564–565.

12.7.   Excerpts from Paris Peace Accords, January 27, 1973

On January 27, 1973, the United States concluded the Paris Peace Conference with a formal agreement involving North and South Vietnam. Essentially, this was the diplomatic conclusion to the Vietnam War.

Chapter I

The Vietnamese People's Fundamental National Rights

Article 1

The United States and all other countries respect the independence, sovereignty, unity, and territorial integrity of Vietnam as recognized by the 1954 Geneva Agreements on Vietnam.

Chapter II

Cessation of Hostilities—Withdrawal of Troops

Article 2

A cease-fire shall be observed throughout South Vietnam as of 2400 hours G.M.T., on January 27, 1973.

At the same hour, the United States will stop all its military activities against the territory of the Democratic Republic of Vietnam by ground, air and naval forces, wherever they may be based, and end the mining of the territorial waters, ports, harbors, and waterways of the Democratic Republic of Vietnam. The United States will remove, permanently de-activate or destroy all the mines in the territorial waters, ports, harbors, and waterways of North Vietnam as soon as this Agreement goes into effect.

The complete cessation of hostilities mentioned in this Article shall be durable and without limit of time.

Article 3

The parties undertake to maintain the cease-fire and to ensure a lasting and stable peace.

As soon as the cease-fire goes into effect:

a. The United States forces and those of the other foreign countries allied with the United States and the Republic of Vietnam shall remain in-place pending the implementation of the plan of troop withdrawal. The Four-Party Joint Military Commission described in Article 16 shall determine the modalities.

b. The armed forces of the two South Vietnamese parties shall remain in-place. The Two-Party Joint Military Commission described in Article 17 shall determine the areas controlled by each party and the modalities of stationing.

c. The regular forces of all services and arms and the irregular forces of the parties in South Vietnam shall stop all offensive activities against each other and shall strictly abide by the following stipulations:

—All acts of force on the ground, in the air, and on the sea shall be prohibited;

—All hostile acts, terrorism, and reprisals by both sides will be banned.

Article 4

The United States will not continue its military involvement or intervene in the internal affairs of South Vietnam.

Article 5

Within sixty days of the signing of this Agreement, there will be a total withdrawal from South Vietnam of troops, military advisors, and military personnel, including technical military personnel and military personnel associated with the pacification program, armaments, munitions, and war material of the United States and those of the other foreign countries mentioned in Article 3 (a). Advisors from the above-mentioned countries to all paramilitary organizations and the police force will also be withdrawn within the same period of time.

Article 6

The disarmament of all military bases in South Vietnam of the United States and of the other foreign countries mentioned in Article 3 (a) shall be completed within sixty days of the signing of this Agreement.

Article 7

From the enforcement of the cease-fire to the formation of the government provided for in Articles 9(b) and 14 of this Agreement, the two South Vietnamese parties shall not accept the introduction of troops, military advisors, and military personnel, armaments, munitions, and war material into South Vietnam.

The two South Vietnamese parties shall be permitted to make periodic replacement of armaments, munitions, and war material which have been destroyed, damaged, worn out or used up after the cease-fire, on the basis of piece-for-piece, of the same characteristics and properties, under the supervision of the Joint Military Commission of the two South Vietnamese parties and of the International Commission of Control and Supervision.

Chapter III

The Return of Captured Military Personnel and Foreign Civilians, and Captured and Detained Vietnamese Civilian Personnel.

Article 8

a. The return of captured military personnel and foreign civilians of the parties shall be carried out simultaneously with and completed not later than the same day as the troop withdrawal mentioned in Article 5. The parties shall exchange complete lists of the above-mentioned captured military personnel and foreign civilians on the day of the signing of this Agreement.

b. The parties shall help each other to get information about those military personnel and foreign civilians of the parties missing in action, to determine the locations and take care of the graves of the dead so as to facilitate the exhumation and repatriation of the remains, and to take any such other measures as may be required to get information about those still considered missing in action.

c. The question of the return of Vietnamese civilian personnel captured and detained in South Vietnam will be resolved by the two South Vietnamese parties on the basis of the principles of Article 21 (b) of the Agreement of the Cessation of Hostilities in Vietnam of July 20, 1954. The two South Vietnamese parties will do so in a spirit of national reconciliation and concord, with a view to ending hatred and enmity, in order to ease suffering and to reunite families. The two South Vietnamese parties will do their utmost to resolve this question within ninety days after the cease-fire comes into effect. . . .

Chapter VII

Regarding Cambodia and Laos

Article 20

a. The parties participating in the Paris Conference on Vietnam shall strictly respect the 1954 Geneva Agreement on Cambodia and the 1962 Geneva Agreements on Laos, which recognized the Cambodian and the Lao peoples' fundamental national rights, i.e., the independence, sovereignty, unity, and territorial integrity of these countries. The parties shall respect the neutrality of Cambodia and Laos.

The parties participating in the Paris Conference on Vietnam undertake to refrain from using the territory of Cambodia and the territory of Laos to encroach on the sovereignty and security of one another and of other countries.

b. Foreign countries shall put an end to all military activities in Cambodia and Laos, totally withdraw from and refrain from reintroducing into these two countries troops, military advisors and military personnel, armaments, munitions and war material.

c. The internal affairs of Cambodia and Laos shall be settled by the people of each of these countries without foreign interference.

d. The problems existing between the Indochinese countries shall be settled by the Indochinese parties on the basis of respect for each other's independence, sovereignty, and territorial integrity, and noninterference in each other's internal affairs.

Source: Weekly Compilation of Presidential Documents, Vol. 9, No. 4 (Washington DC: U.S. Government Printing Office, 1973), pp. 45–46, 49.

13

The Camp David Accords: The Search for Peace in the Middle East

Behold, I have set the land before you: go in and possess the land which the Lord swore unto your fathers, Abraham, Isaac, and Jacob, to give unto them and to their seed after them.

—Deuteronomy 1:8

We are convened here at a moment of historic opportunity for the cause of peace in the Middle East, and for the cause of peace in the world. For the first time in a generation the people of the Middle East are sitting together to turn their talents to the challenge of a lasting peace.

—Henry Kissinger
December 21, 1973

When President Jimmy Carter met with Anwar Sadat of Egypt and Menachem Begin of Israel in late summer 1978, the three leaders sought peace in a troubled region of the world. At Camp David, the presidential retreat in Maryland, the United States exercised its influence to create the opportunity. For thirty years, war had dominated affairs in the Middle East. The Camp David Accords, signed September 17, 1978, offered a fragile commitment to use diplomacy, not armed conflict, to resolve issues in the region. Yet, those issues seemed so complex and so intense, and American interests and understanding so new to the area, that even the participants appeared concerned that the agreements developed at Camp David might falter. U.S.-assisted resolution of the Arab-Israeli conflict remained tenuous.

America's focus on the Middle East developed following World War II. Several concerns propelled U.S. interests in the region. First, the influence of Great Britain and France declined in the area after 1945, and the United States began to occupy that Western power vacuum. Additionally, the United States hoped to expand its access to the increasing oil resources in the Middle East. Third, America supported the creation of an independent Jewish state in Palestine. Finally, the evolving global character of the Cold War led the United States to view with suspicion Soviet involvement in the Middle East. Unfortunately, those various interests collided.

The Arab nations opposed any attempt to create an independent Jewish state in Palestine. (*Arab* is a generic term used to describe the various nations in the Middle East. Its use here identifies states whose people practice Islam as a principal religious faith and speak Arabic as a national language.) Freed of Turkish power following World War I and developing their own sense of nationalism and identity, a number of Arab states viewed Jewish aspirations as dangerous. Whatever territory the Jewish nation might occupy in the region of Palestine would derive from land most Arabs believed belonged to them. When the United Nations declared the nation of Israel sovereign, on May 14, 1948, war between the fledgling country and its angry neighbors became inevitable. Committed to the support of Israel, President Harry Truman's administration found itself at odds with Egypt, Syria, and Jordan.

The First Arab-Israeli War (1948–1949) witnessed a clear U.S. commitment to support Israel. That support grew dramatically during the next thirty years and served as a key source of tension between America and the Arab community. An American-Israeli partnership of any sort dampened relations between the United States and Arab states, and, practically, it threatened America's oil interests in the region. As the nation's dependence on foreign oil increased, U.S. policy regarding the Arab-Israeli conflict became more focused. By 1947 American oil companies owned more than 40 percent of Middle Eastern petroleum supplies, all of it in Arab nations. Support of Israel threatened that commercial reality.

The Soviet Union had originally backed Israel's independence, and, in fact, assisted the young nation with weapons during the 1948–1949 war. In the 1950s, however, Russian policy shifted in response to American initiatives in the region. By 1955 the Cold War had come to the Middle East. In 1952 Gamal Abdel Nasser led a group of young Egyptian military officers who overthrew the ineffective, pro-Western King Farouk. Nasser sparked a new era of Arab nationalism in the Middle East and worked to lead that broadly defined concept. At the same time, the Baath Party developed in Syria as another expression of pan-Arab sentiment. Loosely, both concepts rejected colonialism, imperialism, and Zionism. (Zionism generally describes the Jewish movement to establish a homeland in the Middle East. Arabs use it to define Israeli aggression.) To their adversaries, those terms signified Europeans, Americans, and Israelis. While individual Arab states and leaders sometimes disagreed about methodology, and while some tended to work amicably with the United States and Western European nations on a host of issues, all seemed united around opposition to the existence of Israel.

Just as a sense of unity began to emerge within the Arab community, the United States negotiated a regional security pact in the Middle East. In 1955 Secretary of State John Foster Dulles signed the Baghdad Pact (CENTO). America joined with Britain, Turkey, Iran, Iraq, and Pakistan to guard against Soviet "adventurism" in the Middle East. The action threatened President Nasser's position, and it concerned the Russians. The Soviets had already begun to supply Syria with weapons, and they courted Egypt as well. The superpowers appeared to be choosing sides, and an arms race of sorts developed in the region.

In rapid succession, events heated. Israel and Egypt clashed over territory in the Gaza Strip and the Sinai. Fearing a combined Arab assault into their territory, Israel attacked first, in October 1956. Rapidly, its armed forces moved through the Sinai into Egypt. In retaliation, Nasser nationalized and closed the Suez Canal. Britain and France, sensing a threat to their commercial interests, joined Israeli forces. The military action caught both the Americans and Russians by surprise, yet both nations reacted quickly and condemned it. The two superpowers forced a cease-fire that discredited the Europeans and stopped Israel from further action. On November 7, 1956, the war ended.

The results of the Sinai conflict enhanced Nasser's influence and prestige, reduced the role of Britain and France in the Middle East, and brought the United States more directly into affairs in the region. At the same time, the Soviet Union improved its relations with Egypt and Syria. Israel returned to its 1949 borders, and all of the active participants took time to recover and reassess their positions.

An overview of the diplomatic situation in the Middle East in the mid-1950s left a mixture of issues for the United States. Clearly, it had determined to ally its interests with the defense of Israeli sovereignty. At the same time, American policy identified what it called "moderate" and "radical" Arab states. Saudi Arabia and Iran fell into the former category, Egypt and Syria the latter. It appeared as if the Soviet Union sought to work with and exploit the "radical" states to undermine American policy in the region, so U.S. responses tended to steer a course designed to back Israel and accommodate moderate Arab governments as well.

While the various players in the complicated landscape jockeyed to advance their interests, another critical problem surfaced. The Jewish state in Palestine had created a refugee situation involving numbers of Palestinian Arabs who migrated out of Israel into Jordan, Syria, and Lebanon. Estimates suggest that between 600,000 and 700,000 Palestinians left the territory by 1949. Those refugees failed to play a major role in the Arab-Israeli tension for many years, but shortly, the "Palestinian question" would surface as a major sticking point in the Middle East.

From its inception, America's policy in the Middle East generated little public debate in the United States. In the aftermath of World War II, most Americans supported the establishment of a Jewish homeland in Palestine. A debate developed between pro-Arab, pro-oil experts in the State Department and the Truman administration decision to support Israeli sovereignty in 1947. The debate was, however, neither spirited nor particularly divisive.

Jewish lobbyists in the United States appealed to President Truman. Jewish voters had supported the Democratic Party during the Roosevelt era, and 1948 was an election year. The Zionist Organization of America's aggressive leader, Rabbi Abba Hillel Silver, advised, argued, and threatened the administration, seeking support for Israel's independence.

As public and political attitudes in the United States began to react to the global demands of the Cold War, the Middle East became simply another piece of the evolving and complicated mosaic. The Soviet-American postwar confrontation remained the driving force in U.S. foreign policy. The Middle East offered no legitimate exception to that outlook, and public opinion tended to see the issues there in that broad focus.

Between 1956 and 1967, relative peace existed in the Middle East. President Nasser remained the hero of Arab nationalism. He had convinced Syria and Yemen to join with Egypt in the creation of the United Arab Republic (1958). Iraq left the Baghdad Pact, and its own Baath Party shifted outside the so-called moderate orbit to align its interests with the "radicals." U.S. Marines landed in Lebanon in 1958 to suppress a revolt in that nation, sparked, its president warned, by Egyptian influence. The Soviet Union continued to pour arms and support into Syria and Egypt, and it also began to supply Iraq with military equipment. While peace existed in the region, a serious, localized arms race continued.

In response to Russian policy, the United States armed Israel, Saudi Arabia, and Iran. The Soviets provided close to $2 billion in military supplies to Egypt between 1958 and 1967. The United States gave Israel about $850 million between 1949 and 1965. In some respects, the two superpowers had grabbed hold of the tiger's tail, and their client states drew them further into a dangerous and emotional environment. In 1967 the region exploded.

The Six-Day War began on June 5, 1967. Again, sensing a possible attack and outnumbered, Israel launched a surprise assault against Egypt and Syria. The action caught Israel's enemies off guard and rewrote the map of the Middle East. In less than a week, Jewish forces had reoccupied the Sinai Peninsula and had seized the Golan Heights, the West Bank of the Jordan River, the Gaza Strip, and East Jerusalem.

Defending themselves against accusations that they had launched an unprovoked assault, Israeli leaders argued that Egypt and Syria, as well as the Jordanians, had massed forces preparing to annihilate Israel. They also maintained that the Syrians sponsored and protected terrorist attacks into Jewish territory. Arab supporters viewed the conflict as another example of Israeli aggression (Zionism aimed at territorial expansion). Israelis maintained that they sought to defend their sovereignty against Arab neighbors pledged to destroy their nation.

The war served as a stunning example of Israeli military prowess and made clear the reality of the Jewish state's will to survive amid hostile neighbors. The conflict, however, had added 1.3 million Palestinian Arabs inside the expanded Israeli borders. The growth of Palestinian nationalism, the status of the Palestine Liberation Organization (PLO; founded in 1964), and the expansion of terrorism in support of Palestinian "liberation" from Israel became commonplace following the Six-Day War.

In response to the conflict, the United Nations passed UN Resolution 242, an ambiguous but important document. It called for Israel to return territories taken during the war, but failed to say what territories, or how that process might occur. The resolution also recognized the right of all nations to exist in peace in the region. Israel, Egypt, and Jordan signed Resolution 242. Syria refused, and, at a meeting of Arab leaders in Khartoum, Sudan, the majority of Arab states proclaimed that they would support "no peace, no recognition, and no negotiations" with Israeli. Military preparedness, not diplomacy, continued to dominate affairs in the Middle East.

While U.S. policy and public opinion remained basically unchanged regarding the region, most Americans and their leaders recognized the increased significance of Middle Eastern policy for the United States after the Six-Day War. American policy appeared to back the right horse, as Israeli military superiority indicated. Yet, Western dependence on Arab oil, the expensive and dangerous arms race, and the superpower confrontation in the area had all grown significantly in the late 1960s. As events in Southeast Asia drew the United States into a questionable conflict in Vietnam, American interests in the Middle East appeared equally dangerous, even though Israel proved a stable and tenacious client. When President Richard Nixon assumed office in 1969, he and his national security advisor, Henry Kissinger, added the Arab-Israeli conflict to their agenda of diplomatic initiatives.

During Nixon's first administration, while he worked to extricate the United States from the Vietnam War, the president initiated a policy of détente with the Soviet Union, seeking to relax tension and clarify superpower problems. In May 1972, Nixon met with Soviet Premier Leonid Brezhnev in Moscow and discussed their joint concerns regarding the Middle East. The two leaders pledged to cooperate in reducing military tension in the area. They also agreed to "freeze" the territorial issues. In simple terms, Israel would hold onto the land it had taken in the Six-Day War. Neither Nixon nor Brezhnev wanted tensions in the Middle East accidentally to draw them into a war. The Soviets, however, continued to supply Egypt and other Arab states with weapons, and the United States did the same for Israel and Shah Reza Pahlavi's pro-Western regime in Iran. American interests sought to use Israel and Iran as allies and buffers in the region, both geopolitically and economically.

Meanwhile, Palestinian terrorist organizations expanded their activities with the support and encouragement of Syria and other Arab states. And Egypt's new president, Anwar Sadat, came to power determined to recover territory his nation had lost in the Six-Day War. Increasingly dissatisfied with the Soviet-Egyptian alliance, Sadat sought discussions with U.S. leaders, but Kissinger told Egyptian diplomats that their country would have to make concessions in exchange for Israel's withdrawal from the Sinai. President Sadat determined to win militarily what previous wars had failed to accomplish. Only this time, Egypt would attack first.

On October 6, 1973, during the Muslim observance of Ramadan and the Jewish celebration of Yom Kippur, Egyptian and Syrian forces attacked Israel. Initially successful, the Arab attacks almost accomplished their objectives. The Soviets rushed massive aid into Egypt and Syria as their military supplies dwindled. President Nixon responded with a similar dispatch of equipment for Israel's depleted military hardware. Ultimately, Israel went on the offensive, and its troops recaptured lost territory and threatened Damascus and Cairo. U.S. and Soviet forces went on alert, apparently squandering Nixon's and Brezhnev's efforts at détente. Tensions between the superpowers cooled, however, and the conflict ended when a Soviet-American initiative led to a UN-sponsored cease-fire on October 24. For the fourth time, Israel had defeated Arab armies, but on this occasion just barely.

In the midst of the war, the Organization of Petroleum Exporting Countries (OPEC) embargoed the sale of oil to any nation it believed supported Israel in the Yom Kippur War. Even Saudi Arabia, a traditional U.S. ally, joined the embargo. Then, on December 23, OPEC announced a huge increase in the price of crude oil. Petroleum had finally bubbled to the surface as a weapon in the Arab-Israeli conflict. Arab oil accounted for 37 percent of petroleum consumed in the West. OPEC's embargo and price increase hurt the U.S. economy. A 1974 Department of Energy report argued that the five-month embargo cost 500,000 jobs and close to a $20 billion loss in the gross domestic product. The political and economic repercussions seemed serious, and Americans began to sense more acutely their relationship with the Arab states and Middle East policy. Gas lines at service stations, increased transportation costs, and other inconveniences made the issues personal. Perhaps, American policy makers mused, the wholehearted backing of Israel might require rethinking.

Public opinion in the United States also shifted slightly over the Palestinian issue. In November 1975, the United Nations issued a resolution that described Israel as a racist regime and Zionism in Palestine as oppressive to the Palestinian people. The UN's position (mostly Third World states supported the resolution) may have had little impact on public attitudes in the United States, but it gave pause to reconsider past policy. While most Americans opposed terrorism and its Arab supporters, the idea of a Palestinian state for refugee Arabs held some appeal. The U.S. media, including popular movies, portrayed Arab terrorism in a negative light, and pro-Israel lobby groups continued to hold sway in the public debate. Oil, the Palestine liberation message, and a basic weariness with the unresolved crisis in the Middle East, however, had created an environment that led some Americans to demand a more balanced U.S. policy.

Henry Kissinger agreed with the need to redirect American interests in the Middle East. He traveled to Cairo in November 1973, and began what journalists dubbed "shuttle diplomacy." Kissinger had served as Nixon's national security advisor in the president's first term. With Nixon's reelection in 1972, he appointed Kissinger secretary of state. The new secretary flew among Cairo, Tel Aviv, and Washington, working to leverage a diplomatic resolution to more than twenty-five years of conflict. Between 1973 and 1975, Kissinger laid the groundwork for the Camp David meeting. Importantly, Anwar Sadat had concluded that some form of negotiation with Israel had to occur, and the United States appeared the most likely broker to mediate. Things moved slowly, however, and no action took place until 1977.

As Jimmy Carter came to the presidency in 1977, little had changed in the Middle East except the willingness of Sadat to negotiate. PLO and Arab-sponsored terrorism continued. Israeli reaction to those acts remained swift and usually took the form of military reprisals. Syria, Libya, Iraq, and other Arab states showed little interest in peace. Even the moderate Arab leadership kept silent. Sadat, however, moved forward and exchanged a series of notes with President Carter indicating his interest in a diplomatic solution. In March 1977, Carter publicly endorsed the idea of a Palestinian homeland. A month later, President Sadat came to Washington and indicated his interest in normalizing relations with Israel. Again, Carter supported a Palestinian homeland.

Both Israel and the American Jewish community criticized the presi-

The Middle East Since 1945

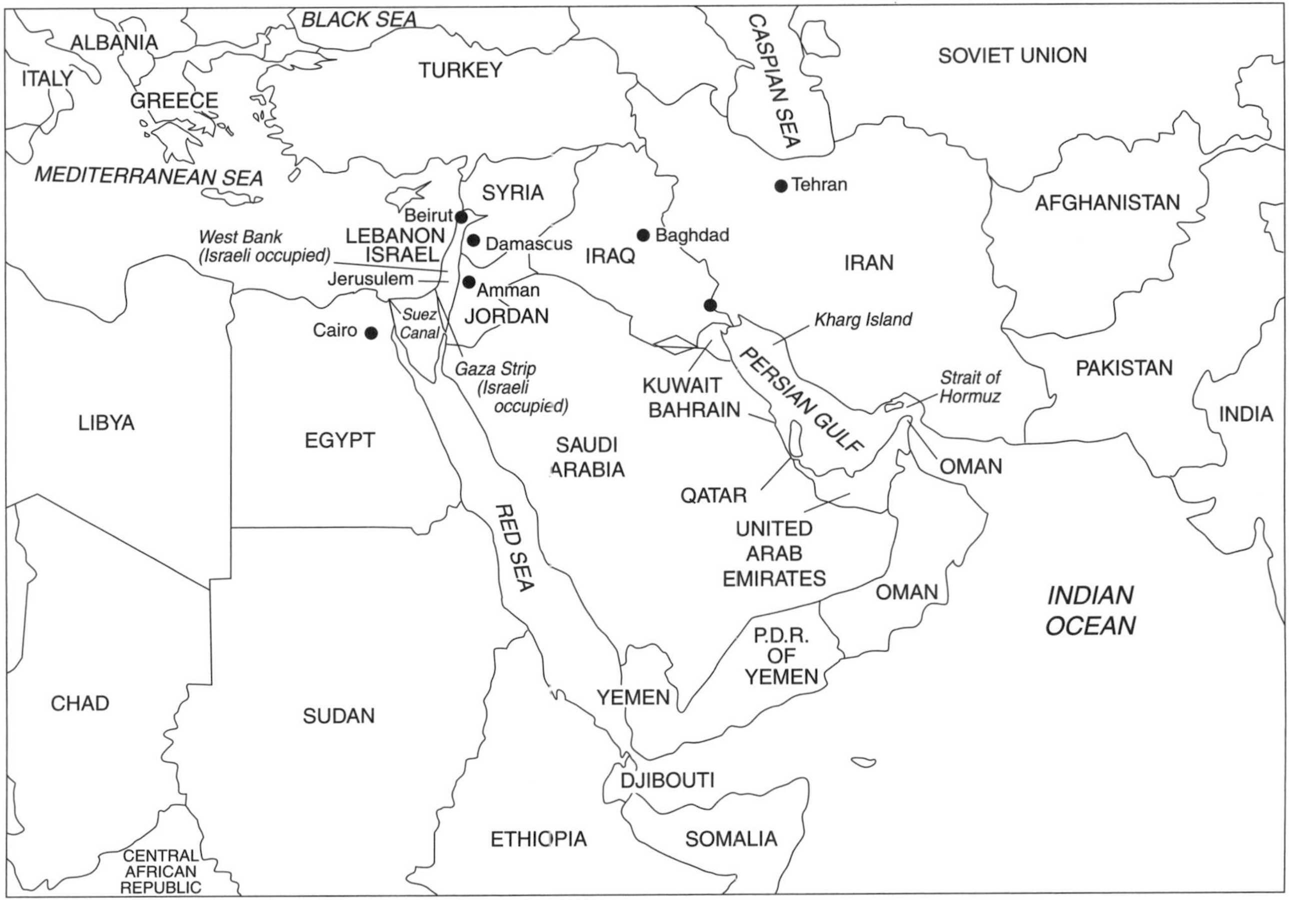

dent's position, and Carter toned down the Palestine sentiment, but his attitude remained clear. Returning to Cairo, Sadat initiated secret discussions between Egyptian and Israeli diplomats. The actual discussions took place in Morocco, in preparation for a meeting in Geneva that the Americans had brokered. Shuttle diplomacy appeared to have infected everyone involved. Problems continued to hinge on the PLO. Sadat wanted their leaders present at the Geneva meeting, but the Israeli government refused.

Aggressively, President Sadat told his National Assembly that he would personally go to Israel to discuss peace, surprising both Carter and the Israeli premier, Menachem Begin. With little choice but to respond, Begin invited the Egyptian leader, and Sadat arrived in Tel Aviv on November 19, 1977. Carter went to Egypt in January 1978 and committed the United States to mediate any Egyptian-Israeli negotiation. For the next seven months, the two governments deadlocked on details and specifics. Then, in August, President Carter invited Sadat and Begin to come to Camp David.

In a series of personal, emotional, and choreographed meetings between the three leaders at the presidential retreat in Maryland, they hammered out the Camp David Accords. The United States had to threaten to cut off aid to both Israel and Egypt to force resolution, and President Carter's personal, persuasive style also helped in the settlement. Additionally, both Anwar Sadat and Menachem Begin wanted a diplomatic conclusion to their decades of strife. On September 17, 1978, Israel and Egypt signed two accords.

The first agreement called for negotiations among Egypt, Jordan, Israel, and representatives of the Palestinian people to settle the territorial concerns regarding the West Bank and the Gaza Strip. The second accord called for an Israeli withdrawal from the Sinai Peninsula during a three-year period and full restoration of the territory to Egypt. Sadat agreed to permit Israeli shipping through the Suez Canal. Egypt would also begin normal commercial relations with Israel.

Since neither Syria nor Jordan could make war against Israel without an Egyptian alliance, the accords, to a great extent, guaranteed the Jewish state freedom from attack in the foreseeable future. The PLO and other Arab states, however, condemned the Camp David Accords, isolated Sadat, and may have even intensified Arab opposition to peace with Israel. Certainly, any analysis of Middle East affairs since 1978 would not lead an observer to conclude that the Camp David Accords had brought peace to the region. Yet, Egypt, Israel's implacable enemy for a generation, had recognized the Jewish state and, for the first time, agreed to deal with their differences diplomatically. So much of the postwar history of the area had centered on war and violence that a legitimate peace negotiation offered the possibility that diplomacy, not war, could become the norm.

The United States had played a pivotal role in bringing the meeting to fruition. While advancing or protecting U.S. interests between 1945 and 1978, American leaders had worked carefully to do so, always with an eye to diplomacy rather than conflict. Critics might condemn American motives, and many have, both at home and abroad. Certainly, many of the terrorist and anti-Western attitudes of Arab states stem directly from the conclusion that U.S. support of Israel appears wrong-headed and even evil. Arab Americans have argued for years that their position goes largely unheard in the United States. Yet, the United States remained the peace broker notwithstanding all other issues. Henry Kissinger's shuttle diplomacy and President Carter's work at Camp David took advantage of the heroism of Anwar Sadat and Menachem Begin to attempt that whispered hope for peace in the Middle East. When Egypt and Israel signed their peace treaty on March 26, 1979, U.S. mediation could claim a role in that hopeful conclusion.

The decisions reached at Camp David had far-reaching consequences in the Middle East. Essentially, Egypt had realigned its interests and moved away from the policies of hard-line Arab states regarding Israel. While Sadat found more support among Arab moderates, such radical states as Iraq and Syria sought to isolate Egypt. Sadly, the Egyptian president's efforts cost him his life. In October 1981, an assassin killed him. Hosni Mubarek, Egypt's new president, vowed to pursue Sadat's agenda.

While the United States had played a major role in the Middle East following World War II, its focus and priorities expanded dramatically in the 1970s. Camp David solidified America's principal role as mediator and peace broker in the region. It tied U.S. policy inexorably to the ill-will of those who opposed the efforts at peace and enhanced America's responsibility to continue brokering agendas toward conciliation for those in the region who sought peace. In either case, the United States became a target for attack. That position has remained, to the present, an American foreign policy consideration.

The fundamentalist Muslim revolution that overthrew the Shah of Iran in 1979 and replaced him with a government hostile to the United States stemmed from continued American initiatives in the region. Additionally, the U.S./UN conflict with Saddam Hussein of Iraq in 1990–1991 also evolved from the same American diplomatic presence in the Middle East. Arabs, Israelis, petroleum, and the regional security of the area remain key issues for U.S. policy makers to an extent that few would have envisioned following World War II.

DOCUMENTS

13.1.   Department of State Note on American Policy Regarding Jewish State in Palestine, September 30, 1947

A debate may have developed in the State Department, and a pro-Arab, pro-oil position did question U.S. support of an independent Jewish state in the region. That did not significantly affect the Truman administration's position to support the creation of Israel. This memorandum expresses the formal American position.

The position taken by the United States Delegation in the General Assembly on the Palestine question should take full account of the following principal factors:

1. The Near Eastern area is of high strategic significance in overall American policy. Consequently the maintenance of good will toward the United States on the part of the Moslem world is one of the primary goals of American foreign policy.

2. The policy of the United States toward Palestine over the span of the years since the First World War shows a consistent interest in the establishment of a Jewish National Home. The United States has frequently stated its support of large-scale Jewish immigration into Palestine and has indicated that it might look with favor upon some arrangement providing for a partition of Palestine, provided that such an arrangement gave promise of being workable.

3. The position taken by the United States with regard to the report of the Special Committee on Palestine must indicate the confidence of this government in the United Nations and United States support of the procedures for which, in this case, it assumed a large initiative.

4. The plan for Palestine ultimately recommended by the General Assembly should be a United Nations solution and not a United States solution. It is essential that the basic position to be taken by the United States Delegation to the General Assembly with regard to the Palestine report and the specific tactics followed

by the Delegation be such that the final recommendation of the General Assembly cannot be labeled "the American plan."

5. It is a matter of urgency that the General Assembly should agree at this session upon a definitive solution of the Palestine problem. The only immediate hope of restoring order in Palestine and thus promoting stability in the whole Near East lies in agreement by the United Nations upon a solution which the interested parties cannot expect by agitation and violence to alter.

6. It is essential that any plan for Palestine adopted by the General Assembly be able to command the maximum cooperation of all elements in Palestine.

Source: Foreign Relations Series—1947, vol. 5, pp. 1166–1170.

13.2.   United Nations Security Resolution 242, November 22, 1967

Following the Six-Day War, the United Nations adopted the resolution that served as a basis for all future diplomatic considerations involving the Arab-Israel conflict. While ambiguous in key areas, it established a foundation for future foreign policy initiatives for all of the participants.

Expressing its continued concern with the grave situation in the Middle East.

Emphasizing the inadmissibility of the acquisition of territory by war and the need to work for a just and lasting peace in which every State in the area can live in security.

Emphasizing further that all member States in their acceptance of the Charter of the United Nations have undertaken a commitment to act in accordance with Article 2 of the Charter. [The United Nations]

1. Affirms that the fulfillment of Charter principles requires the establishment of a just and lasting peace in the Middle East which should include the application of both the following principles;

    (i) Withdrawal of Israeli armed forces from territories occupied in the recent conflict.

    (ii) Termination of all claims or states of belligerency and respect for and acknowledgement of the sovereignty, territorial integrity and political independence of every State in the area and their right to live in peace within secure and recognized boundaries free from threats or acts of force;

2. Affirms further the necessity
   (a) For guaranteeing freedom of navigation through international waters in the area;
   (b) For achieving a just settlement of the refugee problem;
   (c) For guaranteeing the territorial inviolability and political independence of every State in the area, through measures including the establishment of demilitarized zones;
3. Requests the Secretary-General to designate a Special Representative to proceed to the Middle East to establish and maintain contacts with the States concerned in order to promote agreement and assist efforts to achieve a peaceful and accepted settlement in accordance with the provisions and principles in this resolution;
4. Requests the Secretary-General to report to the Security Council on the progress of the efforts of the Special Representative as soon as possible.

Source: Congressional Quarterly, *The Middle East*, 7th ed. (Washington, DC: Congressional Quarterly, 1990), p. 301.

13.3.   Arab Summit Resolution, Khartoum, Sudan Conference, September 1, 1967

As the United Nations worked to provide a resolution to respond to the Six-Day War, the Arab states already had issued their own resolution refusing to concede or recognize any attempt to pursue a diplomatic solution to the recently concluded crisis. Israel would cite the Khartoum Resolution as evidence of Arab intransigence regarding a peaceful solution in the region. U.S. reaction remained similarly critical.

1. The conference has affirmed the unity of Arab ranks, the unity of joint action and the need for coordination and for the elimination of all differences. The Kings, Presidents, and representatives of the other Arab Heads of State at the conference have affirmed their countries' stand by an implementation of the Arab Solidarity Charter which was signed at the third Arab conference at Casablanca.

2. The conference has agreed on the need to consolidate all efforts to eliminate the effects of the aggression on the basis that occupied lands are Arab lands and that the burden of regaining these lands falls on the Arab States.

3. The Arab Heads of State have agreed to unite their political efforts at the international and diplomatic level to eliminate the
effects of the aggression and to ensure the withdrawal of the
aggressive Israeli forces from the Arab lands which have been
occupied since the aggression of 5 June. This will be done within
the framework of the main principles by which the Arab States
abide, namely no peace with Israel, no recognition of Israel, no
negotiations with it, and insistence on the rights of the Palestinian people in their own country.

4. The conference of Arab Ministers of Finance, Economy, and
Oil recommended that suspension of oil pumping be used as a
weapon in the battle. The summit conference has come to the
conclusion that the pumping of oil can itself be used as a positive
weapon, since oil is an Arab resource which can be used to
strengthen the economy of the Arab States directly affected by
the aggression. The conference has, therefore, decided to resume
the pumping of oil, since oil is a positive Arab resource that can
be used in the service of Arab goals.

Source: T. G. Fraser, *The Middle East, 1914–1979* (New York: St. Martin's Press,
1980), pp. 115–116.

**13.4.   United Nations Security Council Resolution 338, October 22,
1973**

---

*In the midst of the Yom Kippur War, the United Nations issued
Resolution 338 calling for a cease-fire and implementation of
Resolution 242 of 1967 (see Document 13.2.). The two UN resolutions are often linked as expressions of that body's attempt to
implement some basis for peace negotiations in the Middle East.*

The Security Council

1. Calls upon all parties to the present fighting to cease all firing
and terminate all military activity immediately, no later than 12
hours after the moment of the adoption of this decision, in the
positions they now occupy;

2. Calls upon the parties concerned to start immediately after the
cease-fire the implementation of Security Council Resolution 242
(1967) in all of its parts;

3. Decides that, immediately and concurrently with the cease-fire,

negotiations start between the parties concerned under appropriate auspices aimed at establishing a just and durable peace in the Middle East.

Source: Congressional Quarterly, *The Middle East*, 7th ed. (Washington, DC: Congressional Quarterly, 1990), pp. 301–302.

13.5.   Declaration by Arab Heads of State at Rabat, Morocco, October 28, 1974

In a major pronouncement on Palestinian claims for statehood, the leaders at the Arab summit issued a manifesto supporting that position. It served as a key backing for the Palestine Liberation Organization. U.S. policy appeared initially skeptical.

The Conference of the Arab Heads of State:

1. Affirms the right of the Palestinian people to return to their homeland and to self-determination.
2. Affirms the right of the Palestinian people to establish an independent national authority, under the leadership of the PLO in its capacity as the sole legitimate representative of the Palestinian people, over all liberated territory. The Arab States are pledged to uphold this authority, when it is established, in all spheres and at all levels.
3. Supports the PLO in the exercise of its national and international responsibilities, within the context of the principles of Arab solidarity.
4. Invites the kingdoms of Jordan, Syria, and Egypt to formalize their relations in light of these decisions and in order that they may be implemented.
5. Affirms the obligation of all Arab States to preserve Palestinian unity and not to interfere in Palestinian internal affairs.

Source: Yehuda Lukacs, *Documents on the Israeli-Palestine Conflict 1967–1983* (Cambridge: Cambridge University Press, 1984), pp. 96–97.

13.6.   Excerpt from Prime Minister Yitzhak Rabin's Statement Before the Israeli Knesset Regarding the Rabat Declaration, November 5, 1974

Prime Minister Rabin's response to the Arab position on Palestine indicates how significant the issue had become in Arab-Israeli

relations and how directly it impacted on any future resolution
to the conflict that had existed in the region for so long.

The meaning of [the Rabat] Resolution is clear. The Rabat Conference decided to charge the organizations of murderers with the establishment of a Palestinian State, and the Arab countries gave the organizations a free hand to decide on their mode of operations. The Arab countries themselves will refrain, as stated in the Resolution, from intervening in the "internal affairs" of this action.

We are not fully aware of the significance of the fourth Resolution, which refers to "outlining a formula" for the coordination of relations between Jordan, Syria, Egypt and the PLO. It is by no means impossible that it is also intended to bring about closer military relations between them.

The significance of these Resolutions is extremely grave. The aim of the terrorist organization is well known and clear. The Palestine National Covenant speaks bluntly and openly about the liquidation of the State of Israel by means of armed struggle, and the Arab States committed themselves at Rabat to support this struggle. Any attempt to implement them will be accompanied by at least attempts to carry out terrorist operations on a large scale with the support of the Arab countries.

The decisions of the Rabat Conference are merely a continuation of the resolutions adopted at Khartoum. Only further to the "no's" at Khartoum, the root organization of the terrorists has attained the status conferred upon it by the presidents and kings at Rabat. Throughout this conference was the aspiration to destroy a member-state of the United Nations. The content of this gathering has nothing whatsoever in common with social progress or the advancement of humanity among the Arab nations or in relations with the peoples in the region and throughout the world.

There is no indication of any deviation from the goal and policy of the terrorist organizations, so let us not delude ourselves on this score. The terrorist organizations had no success in the administered territories, but the successes they achieved at the U.N. General Assembly and at Rabat are encouraging them to believe that the targets they had so confidently set themselves are now within reach.

The policy laid down at Khartoum and Rabat shall not be executed. We have the power to prevent its implementation. The position of the government of Israel in the face of these resolutions at the Rabat Conference is unequivocal:

A) The government of Israel categorically rejects the conclusions of the Rabat Conference, which are designed to disrupt any progress towards peace, to encourage the terrorist elements, and to foil any step which might lead to peaceful coexistence with Israel.

B) In accordance with the Knesset's resolutions, the government of Israel will not negotiate with terrorist organizations whose avowed policy is to strive for Israel's destruction and whose method is terrorist violence.

C) We warn the Arab leaders against making the mistake of thinking that threats or even the active employment of the weapon of violence or of military force will lead to a political solution. This is a dangerous illusion. The aims of the Palestinian National Charter will not be achieved, either by terrorist acts or by limited or total warfare.

Source: Ian J. Bickerton and Carla L. Klausner, *A Concise History of the Arab-Israeli Conflict* (Upper Saddle River, NJ: Prentice-Hall, 1998), p. 184.

13.7. **Excerpts from the First Camp David Accord, September 17, 1978**

Signed at the White House, the first Camp David Accord accepted the principles in UN Resolutions 242 and 338. The lengthier and more detailed of the two accords, it spelled out the basis for peace between Israel and Egypt.

Preamble.

The search for peace must be guided by the following:

The agreed basis for a peaceful settlement of the conflict between Israel and its neighbors is United Nations Security Council Resolution 242, in all its parts.

To achieve a relationship of peace, in the spirit of Article 2 of the United Nations Charter, future negotiations between Israel and any neighbors prepared to negotiate peace and security with it, are necessary for the purpose of carrying out all the provisions and principles of Resolutions 242 and 338.

Peace requires respect for the sovereignty, territorial integrity and political independence of every state in the area and their right to live in peace within secure and recognized boundaries free from threats or acts of force. Progress toward that goal can accelerate movement toward a new era of reconciliation in the Middle East marked by cooperation in promoting economic development, in maintaining stability, and in assuring security.

Security is enhanced by a relationship of peace and by cooperation between nations which enjoy normal relations. In addition, under the terms of peace treaties, the parties can, on the basis of reciprocity, agree to special security arrangements such as demilitarized zones, limited armaments areas, early warning stations, the presence of international forces, liaison, agreed measures for monitoring and other arrangements that they agree are useful.

Framework:

Taking these factors into account, the parties are determined to reach a just, comprehensive, and durable settlement of the Middle East conflict through the conclusion of peace treaties based on Security Resolutions 242 and 338 in all their parts. Their purpose is to achieve peace and good neighborly relations. They recognize that, for peace to endure, it must involve all those who have been deeply affected by the conflict. They therefore agree that this framework is intended by them to constitute a basis for peace not only between Egypt and Israel, but also between Israel and each of its other neighbors which is prepared to negotiate peace with Israel on this basis. With that objective in mind, they have agreed to proceed as follows:

A. West Bank and Gaza

　1. Egypt, Israel, Jordan and the representatives of the Palestinian people should participate in negotiations on the resolution of the Palestinian problem in all its aspects. To achieve that objective, negotiations relating to the West Bank and Gaza should proceed in three stages.

　　(a) Egypt and Israel agree that, in order to ensure a peaceful and orderly transfer of authority, and taking into account the security concerns of all parties, there should be transitional arrangements for the West Bank and Gaza for a period not exceeding five years. In order to provide full autonomy to the inhabitants under these arrangements the Israeli Military Government and its civilian administration will be withdrawn as soon as a self-governing authority has been freely elected by the inhabitants of these areas to replace the existing military government. To negotiate the details of a transitional arrangement, the Government of Jordan will be invited to join the negotiations on the basis of this framework. These new arrangements should give due consideration both to the principle of self-government by the inhabitants of these territories and to the legitimate security concerns of the parties involved.

(b) Egypt, Israel, and Jordan will agree on the modalities for establishing the elected self-governing authority in the West
Bank and Gaza. The delegations of Egypt and Jordan may include Palestinians from the West Bank and Gaza or other Palestinians as mutually agreed. The parties will negotiate an
agreement which will define the powers and responsibilities
of the self-governing authority to be exercised in the West
Bank and Gaza. A withdrawal of Israeli armed forces will take
place and there will be a redeployment of the remaining Israeli
forces into specified security locations. The agreement will also
include arrangements for assuring internal and external security and public order. A strong local police force will be established, which may include Jordanian citizens. In addition,
Israeli and Jordanian forces will participate in joint patrols and
in the manning of control posts to assure the security of the
borders.

(c) When the self-governing authority (administrative council) in
the West Bank and Gaza is established and inaugurated, the
transitional period of five years will begin. As soon as possible, but not later than the third year after the beginning of the
transitional period, negotiations will take place to determine
the final status of the West Bank and Gaza and its relationship with its neighbors, and to conclude a peace treaty between Israel and Jordan by the end of the transitional period.
These negotiations will be conducted among Egypt, Israel,
Jordan, and the elected representatives of the inhabitants of
the West Bank and Gaza. . . . the negotiations will resolve,
among other matters, the location of the boundaries and the
nature of security arrangements. The solution from the negotiations must also recognize the legitimate rights of the Palestinian people and their just requirements. In this way, the
Palestinians will participate in the determination of their own
future through:

1) The negotiation among Egypt, Israel, Jordan and the representatives of the inhabitants of the West Bank and Gaza
   to agree on the final status of the West Bank and Gaza and
   other outstanding issues by the end of the transitional period.

2) Submitting their agreement to a vote by the elected representatives of the inhabitants of the West Bank and Gaza.

3) Providing for the elected representatives of the inhabitants
   of the West Bank and Gaza to decide how they shall govern
   themselves consistent with the provisions of their agreement.

       4) Participating as stated above in the work of the committee negotiating the peace treaty between Israel and Jordan. . . .

   4. Egypt and Israel will work with each other and other interested parties to establish agreed procedures for a prompt, just and permanent implementation of the resolution of the refugee problem.

B. Egypt-Israel

   1. Egypt and Israel undertake not to resort to the threat or the use of force to settle disputes. Any disputes shall be settled by peaceful means in accordance with the provisions of Article 33 of the charter of the United Nations.

   2. In order to achieve peace between them, the parties agree to negotiate in good faith with a goal of concluding within three months from the signing of this framework a peace treaty between them, while inviting other parties to the conflict to proceed simultaneously to negotiate and conclude similar peace treaties with a view to achieving a comprehensive peace in the area. The framework for the conclusion of a peace treaty between Egypt and Israel will govern the peace negotiations between them. The parties will agree on the modalities and the timetable for the implementation of their obligations under the treaty.

C. Associated Principles.

   1. Egypt and Israel state that the principles and provisions described below should apply to peace treaties between Israel and each of its neighbors—Egypt, Jordan, Syria and Lebanon.

   2. Signatories shall establish among themselves relationships normal to states at peace with one another. To this end, they should undertake to abide by all the provisions of the charter of the United Nations. Steps to be taken in this respect include:

      a) Full recognition

      b) Abolishing economic boycotts

      c) Guaranteeing that under their jurisdiction the citizens of other parties shall enjoy the protection of due process of law.

For the Government of the Arab Republic of Egypt: Al-Sadat
For the Government of Israel: M. Begin
Witnessed by: Jimmy Carter, President of the United States

Source: Elaine P. Adam, *American Foreign Relations: A Documentary Record* (New York: New York University Press, 1979), pp. 288–293.

13.8.   Excerpts from the Second Camp David Accord, September 17, 1978

The second set of agreements at Camp David focused on the specific issues between Egypt and Israel with particular emphasis on territorial, military, and economic provisions.

In order to achieve peace between them, Israel and Egypt agree to negotiate in good faith with a goal of concluding within three months of the signing of the framework, a peace treaty between them. . . .

The following matters are agreed between the parties:

A. The full exercise of Egyptian sovereignty up to the internationally recognized border between Egypt and mandated Palestine,

B. The withdrawal of Israeli armed forces from the Sinai,

C. The use of airfields left by the Israelis near El Arish, Rafah, Ras en Naqb, and Sharm el Sheikh for civilian purposes only, including possible use by all nations.

D. The right of free passage by ships of Israel through the Gulf of Suez and the Suez Canal on the basis of the Constantinople Convention of 1888 applying to all nations, the Straits of Tiran and the Gulf of Aqaba are international waterways to be open to all nations unimpeded. . . .

E. The construction of a highway between Sinai and Jordan near Eliat with guaranteed free and peaceful passage by Egypt and Jordan,

F. The stationing of forces listed below.

After a peace treaty is signed, and after the interim withdrawal is complete, normal relations will be established between Egypt and Israel, including: Full recognition, including diplomatic, economic and cultural relations, termination of economic boycotts and barriers to the free movement of goods and people, and mutual protection of citizens by the due process of law.

Interim withdrawal:

Between three months and nine months after the signing of the peace treaty, all Israeli forces will withdraw east of a line extending from a point east of El Arish to Ras Muhammed, the exact location of this line to be determined by mutual agreement.

For the Government of the Arab Republic of Egypt: A. Sadat

For the Government of Israel: M. Begin
Witnessed by: Jimmy Carter, President of the United States.

Source: Congressional Quarterly, *The Middle East*, 7th ed. (Washington, DC: Congressional Quarterly, 1990), pp. 303–304.

13.9.   Communiqué Excerpts from the Arab Summit in Baghdad, Iraq, March 31, 1979

The summit's rejection of the Camp David Accords made clear that the Arab-Israeli crisis remained unresolved and potentially dangerous. While Egypt and Israel had taken a giant step, any analysis of events between 1978 and the present recognizes that concerns in the region remain unresolved. A Muslim "extremist" assassinated Anwar Sadat in October 1981, and terrorist activities have increased significantly since 1978.

As the Government of the Arab Republic of Egypt has ignored the Arab summit conferences' resolutions, especially those of the sixth and seventh conferences held in Algiers and Rabat: as it has at the same time ignored the ninth Arab summit conference resolutions—especially the call made by the Arab kings, presidents, and princes to avoid signing a peace treaty with the Zionist enemy—and signed the peace treaty on 26 March 1979;

It has thus deviated from the Arab ranks and has chosen, in collusion with the United States, to stand by the side of the Zionist enemy in one trench; has behaved unilaterally in the Arab-Zionist struggle affairs; has violated the Arab nation's rights; has exposed the nation's destiny, its struggle and aims to dangers and challenges; has relinquished its pan-Arab duty of liberating the occupied Arab territories, particularly Jerusalem, and of restoring the Palestinian Arab people's inalienable rights, including their rights to repatriation, self-determination and establishment of the independent Palestinian state on their national soil. . . . The Arab League Council, on the level of Arab foreign ministers, has decided the following:

1. A. To withdraw the ambassadors of the Arab states from Egypt immediately.

   B. To recommend the severance of political and diplomatic relations with the Egyptian Government. The Arab governments will adopt the necessary measures to apply this recommendation within a maximum period of one month from the date of issuance of this decision, in accordance with the constitutional measures in force in each country.

2. To consider the suspension of the Egyptian Government's membership in the Arab League as operative from the date of the Egyptian Government's signing of the peace treaty with the Zionist enemy. This means depriving it of all rights resulting from this membership.

3. To make the city of Tunis, capital of the Tunisian Republic, the temporary headquarters of the Arab League. . . .

Source: Walter Laquer and Barry Rubin, eds., *The Arab-Israeli Reader: A Documentary History of the Middle East Conflict* (New York: Penguin Books, 1984), pp. 616–617.

14

The Reagan-Gorbachev Summit in Reykjavik: The End of the Cold War

Mr. Gorbachev, tear down this wall!

—Ronald Reagan
Speech at the Berlin Wall, June 12, 1987

During the 1980s a series of events led to several key summit meetings between President Ronald Reagan and Soviet Premier Mikhail Gorbachev. The results of those important discussions helped to end the Cold War, the dangerous Russian-American confrontation that had dominated world affairs since the end of World War II. When the two leaders met in Reykjavik, Iceland, October 11–16, 1986, that summit served to anchor both the personal and political relationship that would lead the superpowers to suspend the animosity that had marked their foreign policy for four decades. While the Reykjavik meeting produced no specific agreement, the summit evidenced a genuine, sincere commitment on the part of both President Reagan and Premier Gorbachev to bring an end to the Cold War. The inability of the two leaders to reach specific conclusions on a treaty disappointed both sides, but Reagan and Gorbachev shortly did resolve the troublesome details that they had been unable to agree upon in Iceland.

The confrontation between the United States and the Soviet Union dominated American foreign policy in the last half of the twentieth century. Historians and politicians have debated how seriously Soviet policy threatened the national security interests of the United States. Whether such threats were real or perceived, however, American policy and public opinion saw the Soviet Union as an ominous, persistent enemy and acted accordingly.

Ronald Reagan was a product of that anti-Soviet, anti-communist conclusion. From his days as president of the Screen Actors Guild to his years as governor of California, he grew to believe that both the ideology (communism) and the nation-state (the Soviet Union) represented dangerous threats to American democracy and capitalism. Others shared his views, and it became a mainstream conservative political position in U.S. politics. The Republican Party, throughout the era, adopted strong diplomatic and military platform positions aimed at challenging Russia in the Cold War clash of the superpowers. Democrats had also supported Cold War policy and rhetoric. In fact, its leaders had developed the strategies to confront Russia. By the 1980s, however, many Democrats had toned down that approach in the aftermath of the Vietnam conflict.

Richard Nixon, an ardent, outspoken anti-communist in the 1950s, surprised Americans when he moved to develop clearer, more peaceful communication with the Soviets and Communist China in the late 1960s and early 1970s. As the Republicans' standard bearer, he appeared to betray their basic position. Yet, his efforts at détente and rapprochement with the two great communist states received general support from the American public and his party. The Watergate scandal and Nixon's resignation as president, in 1974, hindered his efforts to create a more peaceful relationship with the Soviets and China, but the Nixon "diplomatic revolution" survived Nixon.

In Moscow, Kremlin leaders had worked equally carefully with the United States to look at new ways of dealing with their conflicting interests. Neither nation wanted a confrontation to lead to war, a possibility fraught with destructive potential based on the massive growth of nuclear weapons in the 1960s and 1970s. Yet, the Soviets sensed an opportunity to improve their position. Consistently behind the United States in nuclear weapons capacity and other strategic military options, the Russians concluded that America's dissatisfaction with its loss in Vietnam and Nixon's political scandal would afford the Soviets a chance to expand their military development and reach parity with the United States.

Throughout the 1970s, the Soviet military establishment enhanced its nuclear weapons systems, both in numbers and in sophistication. At the same time, the Russian navy grew dramatically to become a global blue-ocean power. Russia's land forces received new weapons as well, and the Russians came to believe that they had achieved parity with or even superiority over the United States. While estimates vary, the Soviet government may have devoted anywhere from 20 to 50 percent of the gross domestic product (GDP) to defense.

In the aftermath of Vietnam and Watergate, U.S. military readiness and spending declined. Public antipathy toward the military, as well as cautious political leaders both in Congress and in the White House, added to the conclusion that the United States had begun to lose momentum in the long struggle with the Soviet Union. Coupled with a worsening economic situation in America, including the energy crisis that OPEC prompted, pundits and observers saw U.S. foreign policy as flawed and failing.

The presidency of Jimmy Carter (1977–1981) seemed to further jeopardize U.S. self-perception. His ambivalent response to events in Latin America and the Middle East, the Soviet invasion of Afghanistan, and the Iran hostage crisis all defined the Carter presidency as a continuation of America's inability to effectively influence world affairs. With the exception of the Camp David Accords, the United States had proved unable to pursue a coherent foreign policy agenda. Things appeared bad and getting worse. President Carter may have initiated a U.S. arms buildup that Ronald Reagan inherited and expanded, but the new president saw both America's "enemy" and the potential application of a renewed military resource differently than his predecessor.

Ronald Reagan came to the presidency with a simple, clear, and provocative foreign policy position. Communism and the Soviet Union remained America's mortal enemy, and he pledged to use every effort to confront and defeat that ideology and the "Evil Empire" that Russia personified. He would employ every diplomatic and military effort possible to meet that goal. Critics saw Reagan as a "cowboy" diplomat, a throwback to the McCarthy era of wild, "shoot from the hip" anticommunism that had dominated the 1950s. His rhetoric sounded threatening and thoughtless. Additionally, his decision to rebuild America's military strength alarmed both cost-conscious observers and those who believed it would prompt a dangerous confrontation with the Soviet Union.

At the beginning of the 1980s, a series of events began to work toward a surprising conclusion to those initial concerns. First, the Soviet Union had spent too much money and GDP on its military growth in the 1970s, at the expense of the rest of the Russia economy. Soviet leaders were coming to conclude that they simply remained incapable of competing economically with the United States. Russia lacked the capacity to maintain a stable society so long as it devoted so much to defense. At the same time the Russian war in Afghanistan had failed to produce the desired results. The Soviets found themselves in a nasty war (their Vietnam), and the situation grew worse each year.

Second, a series of political and economic upheavals in Poland, a longstanding Soviet satellite, generated a labor movement, Solidarity, that began to challenge the communist government in Warsaw and its continued allegiance to Moscow. Lech Walesa's Solidarity "rebellion" threatened to disrupt the largest nation in Eastern Europe and pull it from the Soviet orbit. In 1956 and 1968, Soviet troops had stormed into Hungary and Czechoslovakia, respectively, to suppress such upheaval. In the 1980s, Russian leaders hesitated. Soviet authority and influence had waned, and other Iron Curtain states watched events in Poland carefully, even hopefully.

Third, President Reagan's decision to rebuild America's military power occurred with rapidity and conviction. While begun during Jimmy Carter's presidency, the buildup reached major proportions in the first half of the 1980s. The United States literally challenged the Russians to a renewed arms race, spending billions of dollars on advanced nuclear, naval, and ground weapons. When the president announced a decision to begin research and eventual deployment of the Strategic Defense Initiative (SDI), a space-based defense concept designed to intercept and destroy incoming nuclear weapons, it frightened the Soviets and many Americans as well.

Critics laughed at Reagan's SDI concept, deeming it unfeasible, provocative, and expensive. In America, editorials ridiculed the administration's "Star Wars" project. The Russians saw neither humor nor stupidity in the proposed idea of SDI.

The Soviets perceived the U.S. buildup and SDI as a direct challenge to their national security. As much money as the Russians had spent in the 1970s, the Americans outspent them in the 1980s. At the same time, U.S. technological sophistication produced more and better weapons and more effective means to deliver them to their targets. The U.S. deployment of a new generation of medium-range missiles in Europe merely heightened Soviet concerns regarding American arms.

The Reagan administration appeared interested in negotiating with Soviet leaders, but, as the president remarked to his wife, Nancy, they kept dying. Between 1982 and 1985, Russian general secretaries changed four times. (Those Soviet leaders included Leonid Brezhnev [1982], Yuri Andropov [1984], and Konstantin Chernenko [1985]. Mikhail Gorbachev replaced Chernenko in March 1985. The previous leaders had all died of natural causes.) When Mikhail Gorbachev assumed power in March 1985, both leaders showed an interest in a summit meeting to discuss arms control. The Russian premier advocated three basic initiatives as new policy—glasnost (openness), perestroika (restructuring), and "new thinking" (diplomatic collaboration). Whether those ideas hinged on the internal problems confronting the Soviet Union or stemmed from a personal commitment of the new premier, they helped open the door to a meeting with Ronald Reagan.

The U.S. president invited Gorbachev to meet with him in Washington, but the Russian leader opted for a neutral site. The two men, with their advisors, gathered in Geneva, Switzerland, on November 19–21, 1985. While the media sought to make high drama of the two personalities and their styles, even hinting at a potential incompatibility, the latter failed to occur. The Geneva Summit produced no specific results, but it proved significant. Reagan and Gorbachev managed to have a private meeting at a small lakeside beach house on the grounds of the estate where the formal sessions took place. The youthful former KGB officer talked openly and privately with a classic, aging American "Cold Warrior." Ironically, the two men left that discussion with a sense of mutual trust and respect, thereby setting the stage for future success.

During 1986, the Russians indicated an interest in the so-called zero option for theater nuclear forces, essentially the elimination of medium- and short-range nuclear missiles on both sides. At the same time, Gorbachev agreed to a new round of talks designed to reduce strategic weapons (START). Those discussions had occurred during Reagan's first administration, but stalled. Basically, the Russians indicated a plan that would do a number of things. It called for the elimination of all nuclear weapons, in three stages, during a period of fifteen years. At the same time, the United States and Russia would remove their intermediate-range missiles from Europe, supporting President Reagan's zero option proposal. Finally, Gorbachev suggested a major ban on nuclear weapons testing and a serious cut in conventional military forces on the part of NATO and the Warsaw Pact. The proverbial ball landed in America's court for President Reagan's response.

The Soviets appeared to have grabbed the initiative in arms reduction issues, and that placed the U.S. administration in a domestic bind. Liberal critics attacked the president for not moving quickly enough to limit and even end the nuclear arms race. Nuclear nonproliferation advocates had formed a strong public presence in the 1980s, both in the United States and Western Europe. In 1982, more than a million protesters had gathered in Central Park in New York City to attack the government's position. Most saw Reagan as a relic of the confrontational policies of the early Cold War. They believed his military expenditures, missile deployment, and SDI indicated a dangerous trend in policy.

At the same time, conservative critics questioned the president's willingness and interest in dealing with the Soviets. They pointed out that Russia had never lived up to any of its deals with the United States. Gorbachev appeared to lead Reagan down a primrose path that would threaten America's security. Any attempt to reduce U.S. military strength in the face of Russian threats betrayed, to conservatives, the lessons of Cold War history. George Will, a respected conservative columnist, castigated President Reagan for his ignorance in even considering discussions with Gorbachev.

A second meeting did occur. Again, Reagan wanted the Soviet leader to come to Washington, but their staffs finally agreed to a summit in Reykjavik, Iceland. The discussions took place on October 12, 1986, and came very close to a major breakthrough in U.S.-Soviet arms reduction. The Americans saw the meeting as preliminary to a summit that would take place in Washington and lead to a treaty. Mikhail Gorbachev came to Reykjavik prepared to make a deal, and the Soviet premier offered a sweeping proposal. The superpowers would reduce their nuclear weapons by 50 percent, eliminate all intermediate-range missiles from Europe, abide by an anti-ballistic missile treaty for ten years, and ban nuclear weapons testing altogether. (The United States and the Soviet Union had signed the Anti-Ballistic Missile Treaty [ABM] in 1972.) The U.S. delegation responded with a counterproposal. Reagan called for the elimination of all strategic missiles within ten years. Gorbachev went further, proposing the destruction of all nuclear weapons, regardless of their delivery system, by 1996. It seemed clear that both delegations, especially their two leaders, seriously intended to work out a proposal. Reagan and Gorbachev, specifically, showed a genuine pacifist intent, and, regardless of their political self-interest, they hoped legitimately to make the world a safer place. The talks, however, stalled over the Strategic Defense Initiative. Gorbachev wanted the Americans to confine SDI to laboratory testing only. That Reagan refused to concede, and the Reykjavik Summit ended in a mood of disappointment on both sides.

When the particulars emerged in the press, the same critics assailed the president from the same postures. Liberals condemned Reagan for being so close to a major arms limitation treaty and throwing it away over SDI. Conservatives worried that "their" president had come too close to surrendering the U.S. defense position to Soviet guile. An atmosphere of bitterness and a sense of lost opportunity appeared to affect world opinion, as well as the people who had actually met in Iceland. While pundits, politicians, and professors assailed the failure, 72 percent of the American people polled approved of President Reagan's efforts. Only 17 percent blamed him for the failed summit.

As Premier Gorbachev returned to Moscow to operate affairs of state within the new tripartite guidelines he had established, the U.S. government went about its own business. START, SDI, and weapons deployment remained key issues of concern. Yet, as disappointing as Reykjavik appeared, Reagan and Gorbachev still trusted and respected each other. The possibility existed that something might come of that personal rapport. As always, world events impacted on the personalities and influenced their continued desire to conclude a meaningful treaty.

The Soviet Union's economic woes, the worsening war in Afghanistan, problems in Eastern Europe, and the new openness in Russia all kept pushing Gorbachev to a resolution of Soviet relations with the United States. In June 1987, President Reagan visited Berlin, Germany. Reflecting on the momentous changes occurring in the Soviet Union and throughout Eastern Europe, he focused his speech in Berlin on one of the most infamous symbols of the Cold War, the Berlin Wall. He asked Premier Gorbachev to "open this gate . . . to tear down this wall." The Iron Curtain's fabric appeared to be shredding from without and within.

For years, American politicians had stood at the Berlin Wall and railed against communist aggression. President John Kennedy's "Ich bin ein Berliner" pronouncement in 1963, shortly after the wall had been erected, lingered as a major sign of U.S. commitment to many West Germans. In 1987, however, President Reagan's comment had the sound of inevitability.

Five months after Reagan's visit to Germany, the Soviet premier arrived in Washington, D.C., for a third meeting with his adversary. If the Americans refused to budge on SDI, the superpowers could still progress with an intermediate-range nuclear forces (INF) treaty. Gorbachev had suggested that possibility in February, ten months earlier. In December, he came to America to seal the agreement. Known as "global zero-zero," the INF Treaty eliminated all missiles with ranges of 300–3,400 miles by the year 2000. Reagan and Gorbachev signed the treaty in a ceremony at the White House on December 8, 1987.

Again, critics noted that the INF Treaty reduced nuclear armaments by only 4 percent. While accurate, this criticism overlooked the long-term consequences and the significance of the two leaders involved in the treaty. Geneva, Reykjavik, and Washington had established a personal relationship between the superpower leaders. For the first time since the beginning of the Cold War, the United States and the Soviet Union had actually agreed to go beyond the limitation of nuclear weapons to the abolition of a whole class of weapons. Clearly, the broad and complex issues that confronted both nations in the 1980s might well have led to such a conclusion in any event. The particular relationship that had developed between Ronald Reagan and Mikhail Gorbachev, however, also played a key role in the results.

Their three summit meetings, but particularly the bitter failure in Reykjavik, tied Reagan and Gorbachev to a joint conclusion. The Cold War had created an environment that made the world too dangerous a place. Premier Gorbachev commented that as angry as he had been at the failure to achieve a settlement in Iceland, particularly regarding SDI, he believed without question that President Reagan remained a leader dedicated to making a safer world, as he did. That left the door ajar for all of the events that would follow—from INF, to the collapse of the Berlin Wall (1989), to the complete restructuring of the Soviet system and contemporary Russia efforts to create a democratic government and a market economy.

At Reykjavik, two superpower leaders saw an opportunity to end the

Cold War and opened the door to their personal diplomacy that, in many respects, succeeded in defusing the single most dangerous international issue since the end of World War II. Soviet-American animosity coupled with the joint development of their massive nuclear forces had served as the nightmare of the international community for almost half a century. To be sure, other issues and concerns occupied the attention of the world community as well as the United States and the Soviet Union. The Cold War, however, and its potential destructive impact overshadowed everything else. The two superpower leaders knew that when they met in Iceland, and they also realized that they had an obligation to seize the moment to reorient U.S.-Soviet relations from confrontation to consultation and cooperation. Such a shift required personal, mutual trust at the highest level. In the cold of Reykjavik, the two leaders gained that.

DOCUMENTS

14.1.   President Ronald Reagan's Speech Before the British House of Commons, June 8, 1982

Early in his presidency, Reagan defined his Cold War position on the Soviet Union and communism clearly and provocatively in his speech to Britain's Parliament. The so-called Evil Empire speech, given in March 8, 1983, in Orlando, Florida, is less specific, but both those remarks and these define Reagan's classic attitude regarding America's long-standing enemy.

We're approaching the end of a bloody century plagued by a terrible political invention—totalitarianism. Optimism comes less easily today, not because democracy is less vigorous, but because democracy's enemies have refined their instruments of repression. Yet optimism is in order because day by day democracy is proving itself to be a not at all fragile flower. From Stettin on the Baltic to Varna on the Black Sea, the regimes planted by totalitarianism have had more than thirty years to establish their legitimacy. But none—not one regime—has yet been able to risk free elections. Regimes planted by bayonets do not take root. The strength of the Solidarity movement in Poland demonstrates the truth told in an underground joke in the Soviet Union. It is that the Soviet Union would remain a one-party nation even if an opposition party were permitted because everyone would join the opposition party. . . .

Historians looking back at our time will note the consistent restraint and peaceful intentions of the West. They will note that it was the democracies who refused to use the threat of their nuclear monopoly in the forties and early fifties for territorial or imperial gain. Had that nuclear monopoly been in the hands of the Communist world, the map of Europe—indeed, the world—would look very different today. And certainly they will note it was not the democracies that invaded Afghanistan or suppressed Polish Solidarity or used chemical and toxin warfare in Afghanistan and Southeast Asia.

If history teaches anything, it teaches self-delusion in the face of unpleasant facts is folly. We see around us today the marks of our terrible dilemma—predictions of doomsday, antinuclear demonstrations, an arms race in which the West must, for its own protection, be an unwilling participant. At the same time we see totalitarian forces in the world who seek subversion and conflict around the globe to further their barbarous assault on the human spirit. What, then, is our course? Must civilization perish in a hail of fiery atoms? Must freedom wither in a quiet, deadening accommodation with totalitarian evil?

Sir Winston Churchill refused to accept the inevitability of war or even that it was imminent. He said, "I do not believe that Soviet Russia desires war. What they desire is the fruits of war and the indefinite expansion of their power and doctrines. But what we have to consider here today while time remains is the permanent prevention of war and the establishment of conditions of freedom and democracy as rapidly as possible in all countries."

Well, this is precisely our mission today: to preserve freedom as well as peace. It may not be easy to see; but I believe we live now at a turning point. In an ironic sense Karl Marx was right. We are witnessing today a great revolutionary crisis, a crisis where the demands of the economic order are conflicting directly with those of the political order. But the crisis is happening not in the free, non-Marxist West but in the home of Marxism-Leninism, the Soviet Union. It is the Soviet Union that runs against the tide of history by denying human freedom and human dignity to its citizens. It also is in deep economic difficulty. The rate of growth in the national product has been steadily declining since the fifties and is less than half of what it was then. The dimensions of this failure are astounding: a country which employs one-fifth of its population in agriculture is unable to feed its own people. Were it not for the private sector, the tiny private sector tolerated in Soviet agriculture, the country might be on the brink of famine. These private plots occupy a bare 3 percent of the arable land but account for nearly one-quarter of Soviet farm output and nearly one-third of meat products and vegetables. Overcentralized, with little or no incentives, year after year the Soviet system pours its best resources into the making of instruments of destruction. The constant shrinkage of economic growth combined with the growth of military production is putting a heavy strain on the Soviet people. What we see here is a political structure that no longer corresponds to its economic base, a society where productive forces are hampered by political ones.

The decay of the Soviet experiment should come as no surprise to us. Wherever the comparisons have been made between free and closed societies—West Germany and East Germany, Austria and Czechoslovakia, Malaysia and Vietnam—it is the democratic countries that are prosperous and responsive to the needs of their people. And one of the simple but overwhelming facts of our time is this: of all the millions of refugees we've seen in the modern world, their flight is always away from, not toward the Communist world. Today on the NATO line, our military forces face east to prevent a possible invasion. On the other side of the line, the Soviet forces also face east to prevent their people from leaving. The hard evidence of totalitarian rule has caused in mankind an uprising of the intellect and will. Whether it is the growth of the new schools of economics in America or England or the appearance of the so-called new philosophers in France, there is one unifying thread running through the intellectual work of these groups—rejection of the arbitrary power of the state, the refusal to subordinate the rights of the individual to the superstate, the realization that collectivism stifles all the best human impulses. . . .

Chairman Brezhnev repeatedly has stressed that the competition of ideas and systems must continue and that this is entirely consistent with relaxation of tensions and peace. Well, we ask only that these systems begin by living up to their own constitutions, abiding by their own laws, and complying with the international obligations they have undertaken. We ask only for a process, a direction, a basic code of decency, not for an instant transformation.

We cannot ignore the fact that even without our encouragement there has been and will continue to be repeated explosion against repression and dictatorships. The Soviet Union itself is not immune to this reality. Any system is inherently unstable that has no peaceful means to legitimize its leaders. In such cases, the very repressiveness of the state ultimately drives people to resist it, if necessary, by force.

While we must be cautious about forcing the pace of change, we must not hesitate to declare our ultimate objectives and to take concrete actions to move toward them. We must be staunch in our conviction that freedom is not the sole prerogative of a lucky few but the inalienable and universal right of all human beings. So states the United Nations Universal Declaration of Human Rights, which, among other things, guarantees free elections.

The objective I propose is quite simple to state: to foster the infrastructure of democracy, the system of a free press, unions, political parties, universities, which allows a people to choose their own way to develop their own culture, to reconcile their own differences through peaceful means. This is not cultural imperialism; it is providing the means for genuine self-determination and protection for diversity. Democracy already flourishes in countries with very different cultures and historical experiences. It would be cultural condescension, or worse, to say that any people prefer dictatorship to democracy. Who would voluntarily choose not to have the right to vote, decide to purchase government propaganda handouts instead of independent newspapers, prefer government to worker-controlled unions, opt for land to be owned by the state instead of those who till it, want government repression of religious liberty, a single political party instead of a free choice, a rigid cultural orthodoxy instead of democratic tolerance and diversity?

Since 1917 the Soviet Union has given covert political training and assistance to Marxist-Leninists in many countries. Of course, it also has promoted the use of violence and subversion by these same forces. Over the past several decades, West European and other social democrats, Christian democrats, and leaders have offered open assistance to fraternal, political, and social institutions to bring about peaceful and democratic progress. Appropriately, for a vigorous new democracy, the Federal Republic of Germany's political foundations have become a major force in this effort.

We in America now intend to take additional steps, as many of our allies have already done, toward realizing this same goal. The chairmen and other leaders of the national Republican and Democratic party organizations are initiating a study with the bipartisan American Political Foundation to determine how the United States can best contribute as a nation to the global campaign for democracy now gathering force. They will have the cooperation of congressional leaders of both parties, along with representatives of business, labor, and other major institutions in our society. I look forward to receiving their recommendations and to working with these institutions and the Congress in the common task of strengthening democracy throughout the world. It is time that we committed ourselves as a nation—in both the public and private sectors—to assisting democratic development. . . .

What I am describing now is a plan and a hope for the long term— the march of freedom and democracy which will leave Marxism-Leninism on the ash heap of history as it has left other tyrannies which stifle the freedom and muzzle the self-expression of the people. And that's why we must continue our efforts to strengthen NATO even as we move forward with our zero-option initiative in the negotiations on intermediate-range forces and our proposal for a one-third reduction in strategic ballistic missile warheads. Our military strength is a prerequisite to peace, but let it be clear we maintain this strength in the hope it will never be used, for the ultimate determinant in the struggle that's now going on in the world will not be bombs and rockets but a test of wills and ideas, a trial of spiritual resolve, the values we hold, the beliefs we cherish, the ideals to which we are dedicated.

The British people know that, given strong leadership, time, and a little bit of hope, the forces of good ultimately rally and triumph over evil. Here among you is the cradle of self-government, the Mother of Parliaments. Here is the enduring greatness of the British contribution to mankind, the great civilized ideas: individual liberty, representative government, and the rule of law under God. I've often wondered about the shyness of some of us in the West about standing for these ideals that have done so much to ease the plight of man and the hardships of our imperfect world. This reluctance to use those vast resources at our command reminds me of the elderly lady whose home was bombed in the blitz. As the rescuers moved about, they found a bottle of brandy she'd stored behind the staircase, which was all that was left standing. And since she was barely conscious, one of the workers pulled the cork to give her a taste of it. She came around immediately and said, "Here now—there now, put it back. That's for emergencies." Well, the emergency is upon us. Let us be shy no longer. Let us go to our strength. Let us offer hope. Let us tell the world that a new age is not only possible but probable.

During the dark days of the Second World War, when this island was incandescent with courage, Winston Churchill exclaimed about Britain's adversaries, "What kind of people do they think we are?" Well, Britain's adversaries found out what extraordinary people the British are. But all the democracies paid a terrible price for allowing the dictators to underestimate us. We dare not make that mistake again. So, let us ask ourselves, "What kind of people do we think we are?" And let us answer, "Free people, worthy of freedom and determined not only to remain so but to help others gain their freedom as well." Sir Winston led his people to great victory in war and then lost an election just as the fruits of victory were about to be enjoyed. But he left office honorably and, as it turned out, temporarily, knowing that the liberty of his people was more important than the fate of any single leader. History recalls his greatness in ways no dictator will ever know. And he left us a message of hope for the future, as timely now as when he first uttered it, as opposition leader in the Commons nearly twenty-seven years ago, when he said, "When we look back on all the perils through which we have passed and at the mighty foes that we have laid low and all the dark and deadly designs that we have frustrated, why should we fear for our future? We have," he said, "come safely through the worst."

Well, the task I've set forth will long outlive our own generation. But together, we too have come through the worst. Let us now begin a major effort to secure the best—a crusade for freedom that will engage the faith and fortitude of the next generation. For the sake of peace and justice, let us move toward a world in which all people are at last free to determine their own destiny.

Source: New York Times, June 8, 1982, p. A–160.

14.2.   Premier Mikhail Gorbachev's Remarks at the Conclusion of the Geneva Summit, November 21, 1985

The Soviet premier provided a short, careful statement concerning his first meeting with the U.S. president, but in Gorbachev's remarks one notes the beginnings of mutual respect between the two world leaders.

You've already been handed the joint statement. The President and I have done a huge amount of work. We've gone into great detail; we've really done it in depth. And we've done it totally openly and frankly. We've discussed several most important issues. The relations between our two countries and the situations in the world in general today— these are issues and problems the solving of which in the most concrete way is of concern to both our countries and to the peoples of other countries in the world. We discussed these issues basing our discussions on both sides' determination to improve relations between the Soviet Union and the United States of America. We decided that we must help to decrease the threat of nuclear war. We must not allow the arms race to move off into space and we must cut it down on earth.

It goes without saying that discussions of these sorts we consider to be very useful, and in its results you find a clear reflection of what the two sides have agreed together. We have to be realistic and straightforward, and therefore the solving of the most important problems concerning the arms race and increasing hopes of peace we didn't succeed in reaching at this meeting. So of course there are important disagreements on matters of principle that remain between us. However, the President and I have agreed that this work of seeking mutually acceptable decisions for these questions will be continued here in Geneva by our representatives.

We're also going to seek new kinds of developing bilateral Soviet-American relations. And also we're going to have further consultations on several important questions where, for the most part, our positions again are completely different. All this, we consider these forthcoming talks to be very, very useful.

But the significance of everything which we have agreed with the President can only, of course, be reflected if we carry it on into concrete measures. If we really want to succeed in something, then both sides are going to have to do an awful lot of work in the spirit of the joint statement we have put out. And in this connection, I would like to announce that the Soviet Union, for its part, will do all it can in this cooperation with the United States of America in order to achieve practical results to cut down the arms race, to cut down the arsenals which we've piled up and give—produce the conditions which will be necessary for peace on earth and in space.

We make this announcement perfectly aware of our responsibility both to our own people and to the other peoples of the earth. And we would very much hope that we can have the same approach from the Administration of the United States of America. If that can be so, then the work that has been done in these days in Geneva will not have been done in vain.

Source: New York Times, November 22, 1985, p. A–16.

14.3.   "But Arms Dangers Lurk," Excerpts from Senator Albert Gore's Op-Ed Article in the *New York Times*, November 24, 1985

Senator Gore (D-Tenn.) served as a member of the Senate Armed Services Committee. This op-ed piece in the New York Times *is an example of criticism of President Reagan's failure to create a settlement at the Geneva Summit from the liberal perspective.*

On one level, the summit meeting appears to have been a triumph of form over substance. . . . it was our failure to respond with an appropriate and intelligent counterproposal that doomed any chance of substantial progress at Geneva.

First of all, the United States showed not the slightest flexibility on strategic defense, even though the negotiating situation virtually screamed for it. Following on the heels of our preposterous reinterpretation of the Anti-Ballistic Missile Treaty—we asserted that the treaty was compatible with Star Wars testing and development—this rigidity surely signaled to Moscow that the Administration probably has no intention of stopping the rush toward a defensive arms race.

The second nail in the coffin was our proposal to ban mobile intercontinental missiles. With that idea, we abruptly reversed the logic of the bi-partisan Scowcroft Committee of 1983—particularly its suggestion that we move away from multiple-warhead missiles. It didn't seem to matter to the Administration that we had been urging this idea upon the Russians for the last three years—and that they were beginning to accept it.

This bewildering switch can only have reinforced Soviet suspicions. It is hard to imagine a more serious blow to the arms control process or to the fragile strategic consensus built up so painfully in this country over defining strategic reductions. . . .

Both sides make a serious mistake in assuming that the improved tone of relations can prevent a deterioration in the underlying strategic equation. There has been no formal extension of the understandings of the second strategic arms limitation accord. The erosion of the A.B.M. treaty continues unabated. And the President still proposes to substitute the Strategic Defense Initiative for deterrence.

Simple faith in the President's vision of strategic defense will not magically prevent an all-out defensive or offensive arms race—no more than simple faith in supply-side economics has prevented a doubling of the national debt.

Source: "But Arms Dangers Lurk," *New York Times*, November 24, 1985, sec. 4, p. 23.

14.4.   **"Why Hurry into a Weapons Accord," Richard Pipes's Op-Ed Column in the *New York Times*, October 10, 1986**

A day before the summit in Reykjavik, Richard Pipes, a former member of the National Security Council and a history professor at Harvard University, questioned the whole concept of arms control negotiations with the Soviets. His position reflected the conservative view that President Reagan appeared too eager to make a deal with the communists.

Washington and Moscow seem to be well on the way toward reaching some sort of accord on nuclear arms. Conservatives worry that the President is about to make one-sided concessions and settle for a disadvantageous deal. This may or may not be likely, but this is not the real issue. Even a good deal would be a mistake, for the root of the problem is not nuclear weapons. . . .

Mr. Reagan now receives his advice on policy toward Moscow from a single source, Secretary of State George P. Shultz. The National Security Council has been reduced to near impotence and the White House staff lacks the expertise to offer alternative views. Mr. Shultz seems as firmly in control of American foreign policy as Henry A. Kissinger was at the height of his powers, and he has used his authority quietly to turn the President's Soviet policy around by 180 degrees.

The rationale behind the Administration's shift and its sense of urgency is the belief that Mikhail S. Gorbachev faces a profound internal crisis and is therefore genuinely eager for some sort of "deal." In the Administration's view, this opportunity must not be missed, lest "hardline" Stalinists take over in Moscow.

It is undeniable that the Soviet Union faces a crisis and that if its economy is not reformed it risks forfeiting the status of a great political and military power. But it is equally true that the Soviet elite wishes to carry out these reforms in the manner that least upsets the existing Stalinist system and the advantages it gives them. The deal it is prepared to strike thus calls for minimal concessions in its domestic and foreign policies in exchange for maximum assistance from the West in upgrading the Soviet economy.

This, in effect, means that the deal the Russians prefer is a new arms accord. The Russians badly want progress on arms control, and have pursued such progress for more than two decades now, because it gives foreigners the illusion that the risk of war is being reduced, inhibits American defensive programs, and, above all, allows the true cause of international tension—Soviet aggression abroad and lawlessness at home—to be relegated into the background. Arms control thus helps Moscow preserve the Stalinist system intact and continue its expansion while giving the appearance of good will. . . .

In this endeavor, Mr. Gorbachev is assisted by Anatoly Dobrynin. An official with unique American experience, Mr. Dobrynin was the Kremlin's ambassador to Washington for nearly a quarter of a century and is now head of the International Department of the Communist Party's Central Committee, the true source of Soviet foreign policy decisions.

Unlike Mr. Shultz, whose interest in the Soviet Union is limited to its external conduct—with occasional rhetorical complaints about human rights violations—Mr. Dobrynin understands very well the relationship between American domestic and foreign policies. He can advise Mr. Gorbachev on how to manipulate American public and Congressional opinion with gestures and arms agreements that create an atmosphere of good will at minimum cost.

The question, therefore, is not whether Mr. Reagan and his Administration have grown "soft" on Communism but rather whether Mr. Reagan's advisor has as good an insight into Soviet political conditions and strategy as his opposite number has into ours. Even an equitable and verifiable arms control agreement would not affect the nature of the Soviet system and thus would not eliminate the principal source of friction between the superpowers. But such a deal could well create a spurious atmosphere of better relations, which would in turn mean that the desperately needed Western financial and technical resources would flow freely to Moscow. The Soviet Union would retain its political and economic regime and probably make it even more efficient—and thus much more dangerous in the future. In the meantime, the Kremlin would be able with impunity to continue its genocidal policies in Afghanistan and to inflame international conflicts through terrorism and proxy warfare.

Mr. Reagan once instinctively understood these realities. He was the first President to challenge not only Soviet behavior but also the Communist philosophy and institutions behind the behavior. With this approach, he had gained the psychological initiative in the East-West confrontation. He is about to lose this initiative, thanks to his desire and rather meaningless agreements. It is said he has allowed the State Department to divert him from his original path because of concern about his place in history. It is always dangerous for statesmen to allow this consideration to lead them to act out of character: history is best left to historians. And intuition tells me that Mr. Reagan will be remembered better for the "evil empire" than for yet another arms control agreement.

Source: "Why Hurry into a Weapons Accord," *New York Times*, October 10, 1986, sec. 1, p. 39.

14.5.   "The March of Folly," Tom Wicker's Editorial in the *New York Times*, October 17, 1986

Wicker, a respected liberal columnist, added to the chorus of attacks on Ronald Reagan's failure to achieve a settlement at the Reykjavik Summit. His editorial provides another example of concern over U.S. policy from the perspective of the left in American politics.

At Iceland, Ronald Reagan missed the best chance any President has had in the last two decades to eliminate the central security concern expressed by every Administration of the period: the fear that heavy, accurate Soviet missiles might be able, in a first strike, to destroy the land-based segment of the American nuclear triad.

Mr. Reagan missed that opportunity by failing to nail down the Soviet offer to reduce by 50 percent the strategic offensive weapons of both sides—land-based, submarine-based and air-based.

Instead of thus closing the so-called "window of vulnerability," against which he himself had so frequently warned, Mr. Reagan opted to protect a research program in which some of the most distinguished American scientists have no faith, and for which the necessary computers and software do not and may never exist.

This program, the so-called Strategic Defense Initiative, at best cannot produce a deployed weapons system for more than 10 years or for less than perhaps $3 trillion; and to be effective even then, the S.D.I. still would require the kind of offensive arms treaty that Mr. Reagan passed up in the Iceland talks.

The best the President himself could say for his having insisted on the S.D.I. was that it was needed as an "insurance policy" against Soviet cheating on the 50 percent reductions in land-, sea- and air-based missiles that might have been had. That policy may bear the most expensive premium Americans have ever been required to pay for "insurance."

The S.D.I., Administration spokesmen say, is the threat that brought the Russians back to the bargaining table in a compromising mood; and that may well be right. The S.D.I., Administration propagandists insist, is what will keep Mr. Gorbachev compromising and bargaining until—

these propagandists must expect us to believe—he will knuckle under to American strategic superiority. Nothing in the history of the nuclear era supports the notion that he or any Soviet leader ever will do so.

Mr. Gorbachev, most Kremlinologists believe, does not want to have to match whatever research and deployment costs might grow out of the S.D.I. He prefers, and desperately needs, to devote such huge investments to improvements in the Soviet economy and living standard—a priority many Americans may wish their President would adopt for his own society. That doesn't mean Moscow won't or can't match the United States in military development; it always has, and in this case would have no other choice.

The Soviet leader knows what Mr. Reagan, in his insistence that the S.D.I. is "purely defensive," cannot seem to grasp—though the thesis was developed in the Johnson Administration by Secretary of Defense Robert S. McNamara: *a defensive system adds to a nation's offensive capacity*.

As President Nixon once put it, if two gladiators are fighting with swords, and one is handed a shield, the shield is not just a defensive instrument but an aid to the offensive ability of the gladiator who possesses it. Similarly, if one of the superpowers launches a first strike from behind a defensive system, it may destroy enough of the other's weapons so that its own defense cannot be penetrated by a retaliatory strike.

In the higher realms of technology in which S.D.I. research is proceeding, moreover, it's always possible that some discovery would convert a "purely defensive" concept into a deadly offensive weapon. In his speech after Iceland, Mr. Gorbachev showed himself well aware of that, as he did when he said after the Geneva summit conference that Americans were "just itching to get this world domination and look down on the world from on high."

Such speculations cannot be set to rest by Mr. Reagan's personal word. He will not always be in office, and Moscow can no more know what future course United States policy may take than Washington can be sure of the Kremlin's intentions.

And so, in Barbara Tuchman's phrase, the march of folly proceeded inexorably to Hofdi House. But Mr. Reagan's fault was not merely in his having opted for the dubious vision of strategic defense over the historic reality of strategic arms reduction. As will be explored in another article, he failed as a negotiator to see how he might have had those reductions and still have retained a reasonable possibility of pursuing necessary research on S.D.I.

Source: "The March of Folly," *New York Times*, October 17, 1986, sec. 1, p. 39.

14.6.   "The Opiate of Arms Control," George Will's Column in *Newsweek* Magazine, April 27, 1987

Will, a noted, articulate exponent of conservative opinion, expressed concern several months after the Reykjavik Summit that the "antinuclear left" had seduced President Reagan into a belief in their misguided arms control outlook.

The prudent person's answer to Mr. Gorbachev's question—"What are you afraid of?"—is: "You—and perhaps Ronald Reagan." The President who pledged to close the "window of vulnerability" may be opening a barn door of danger and encouraging attitudes that will impede compensating defense efforts.

People are conservative about what they understand: they have the caution that comes from appreciation of complexity, and anxiety about abrupt departures from settled arrangements. The current danger has become acute because of the radicalism of Reykjavik, where Reagan suddenly endorsed dismantling the strategic arrangements that have kept the peace during four decades of technological evolution. For years we have relied on the strategic "triad" of land-, air- and sea-based nuclear forces. The triad was endorsed by the Scowcroft commission, which Reagan endorsed. Yet with the idea of eliminating ballistic missiles, Reagan approved sawing off two legs (land and sea) of the triad. The administration has shelved the idea of eliminating ballistic missiles, but the idea is alive and well in the European theater and cannot easily be confined here. . . .

Reagan seems to accept the core of the catechism of the antinuclear left, the notion that the threat to peace is technological, not political—the notion that the threat is the existence of nuclear weapons, not the nature of the Soviet regime. Reagan seems to believe that peace necessarily becomes more secure as the number of nuclear weapons declines. But that is false. The lower the levels in any arms control agreement, the larger the leverage gained from cheating, and cheating is a Soviet constant (the difference between the number of SS-20's the Soviets say they have deployed and the number they have produced suggests several hundred may be hidden). However, even assuming Soviet compliance with an agreement, withdrawal of the Pershing II's in exchange for the SS-20's would be unwise. It took three years of delicate dealings to produce the allies' decisions to deploy Pershings. The Soviets could redeploy SS-20's in Europe in a few weeks. The Soviets act on national decisions; we react on alliance decisions. Besides, SS-20's deployed east of the Urals could strike London.

The grave danger is not the Pershings-for-SS-20's deal. It is the subliminal message that this is just the first step and that a "nuclear-free world" is possible and desirable. Reagan should stipulate: NATO is committed to integrated nuclear and conventional forces. Gorbachev, with his eye on more than 4,000 nuclear bombs, artillery shells, and short-range missiles, has raised the ante by asking, Why not a de-nuclearized Europe? That would leave the United States with no "graduated response" to Soviet aggression. Confronting the overwhelming Soviet advantage in conventional and chemical forces, the U.S. choice in a crisis would be to surrender Europe or use strategic weapons. Europeans would reasonably doubt America's readiness to sacrifice Chicago to protect, or avenge, Hamburg. We are sleepwalking back to the 1950's, when U.S. troops in Europe were a "tripwire" to trigger massive retaliation by U.S. strategic forces. But in the 1950's we had overwhelming strategic superiority. Today we are strategically inferior.

The West needs reductions to equal levels not only of intermediate and short-range missiles, but also of conventional forces. In those forces, the Soviet advantage is not only numerical but geographic. However, the time for reaching agreements grows exponentially as the number of matters being negotiated grows arithmetically. And the West leads the Soviet Union in impatience. Eugene Rostow notes that "a nearly mystical faith in arms control has become the opiate of Western opinion," especially American opinion. From the 1783 proposal to demilitarize the Great Lakes, to the Baruch plan for giving an international agency control of all nuclear energy, and beyond, U.S. policy has been driven by faith in law as the tamer of the world. Henry Kissinger notes an asymmetric result: "No new Soviet weapons program has ever been challenged or stopped by Western efforts. But from the neutron weapon to medium-range missiles in Europe to SDI, the Soviet Union has sought to stop—and has succeeded in slowing down—new Western technology by the simple device of declaring it an 'obstacle' to the 'arms-control process.' "

What happened in the United States first as farce may be recurring as tragedy. Despising Eisenhower was the liberal's hobby—until the final hours of his presidency, when he warned against "the military-industrial complex." Reagan, too, may leave office basking in the approval of former despisers. If so, his successors will have to cope with his handiwork, which will include the advancement of two central Soviet goals—the denuclearization of Europe and the stigmatization of nuclear weapons.

Source: "The Opiate of Arms Control," *Newsweek*, April 27, 1987, p. 86.

15

Epilogue

What's past is prologue.

—William Shakespeare
The Tempest, Act II, Scene 1

In 1992, as the Cold War between the United States and the Soviet Union ended, Francis Fukuyama published *The End of History and the Last Man*. Printed in twenty-two languages, the work had a significant impact on foreign policy observers. A number of readers interpreted the author's argument to suggest that the collapse of Soviet communism and America's "victory" concluded the broad issues that had divided and afflicted the world community during the previous centuries. With the end of the Cold War the issues of conflict that had plagued civilization, namely, colonialism, imperialism, nationalism, and ideological struggles, no longer occupied the attention and concern of the global community. In a sense, our historic focus on such things no longer had meaning.

Scholars, political leaders, and observers began to question how the United States might address world affairs as the sole superpower. Did it have new worlds to conquer? Might the nation opt to pursue foreign policy goals and objectives unrelated to its former commitments? What would those strategies and policies seek to accomplish? The American public, freed of the tensions and dangers of the U.S.-Soviet confrontation, experienced a degree of euphoria and pride. Surely, the world would become a safer place, and America's role in it could take on aspects of a Pax Americana, a protector of the new stability. Those with a classical background spoke eloquently about the Roman Empire's similar position in the first and second centuries. They hoped for the possibility of a Golden Age of peace, cooperation, and prosperity under the shield of America's singular strength. Others, however, warned that unilateral power breeds arrogance and misjudgment. In any event, a "New World Order" seemed to emerge in the aftermath of the Cold War, and the United States clearly held center stage.

Perhaps the United Nations might begin to play a broader role in addressing more directly the variety of issues that confront the world community. In that case, America would manage its interests in concert with and in support of a world organization. Soviet-American confrontation, in the past, had generally limited the ability of the UN to respond aggressively to international crises. Since the two superpowers could utilize their vetoes in the United Nations Security Council to prevent collective decisions, the UN remained somewhat limited in its responses. In the new century, however, examples of cooperation and direct United Nations actions appear more prevalent.

From the Gulf War in the 1990s to international responses to crises in East Africa and East Timor, the UN has assumed a more direct response to international concerns. Critics of that UN involvement claim that the international organization has become the tool of U.S. interests. An alternate view argues that the United States might surrender its own foreign policy options to a "one world government" organization that could work against American interests.

World affairs, and the U.S. role in those diplomatic arenas, remain as challenging as ever. From Colombia to Somalia, from Bosnia to the straits of Formosa, and in Iraq and East Timor, the United States must respond and react to numerous ongoing crises and concerns that may or may not directly affect American security interests and the future of the world community.

EUROPE

The United States formulated its foreign policy in the crucible of eighteenth-century European power politics. Many of the nation's diplomatic principles evolved responding to the dangers of "entanglements" in the political affairs of Europe, often as a defensive reaction. While America's rise to world power in the twentieth century altered former approaches to U.S.-European affairs, the region has and will continue to demand critical attention.

The deadly zeal of nationalism and balance of power diplomacy created many of the crises that produced the European wars of the nineteenth and twentieth centuries. While recent history suggests a growing commercial and political unity in Europe, indicating a possible reduction of that cause for tension, the region still confronts issues that warrant the interests and focus of the United States.

The explosion of violence and war in the Balkans caught the international community by surprise in the late 1980s, and the deadly conflicts there appear to defy resolution. The 1990s witnessed a brutal, genocidal war in the former Yugoslavia, pitting religious, ethnic, and national enemies against each other fighting over issues that have their roots deep in the cultural history of the people who live in the area.

The United Nations, NATO, and the United States took the lead in trying to find a peaceful resolution to the conflict in the Balkans, and the Dayton Accords, signed in December 1995, helped to restore a vestige of peace in Bosnia. Yet, conflict expanded into Kosovo, a province of Serbia seeking autonomy and independence. NATO forces, with heavy U.S. military involvement, resorted to armed force to stop Serbian aggression in the region. At present, a multinational military "police force" patrols the area in a dangerous and unresolved environment. An international war crimes tribunal in the Netherlands has convened to prosecute political and military officials from Serbia accused of genocide in scenes that evoke memories of the postwar trials of Nazi officials.

What of the role of the North Atlantic Treaty Organization? Originally designed and implemented to protect Western Europe against Soviet military threat, NATO's purpose is now a matter of scrutiny and concern. As several former Warsaw Pact nations have joined NATO, its mission has changed, as it appears to have in the Balkans. A key debate has developed regarding the continued U.S. role in the organization. Can the Europeans protect themselves? Do they need or want continued dependence on American military force now that the Soviet threat no longer exists? The most powerful regional security pact of the modern era, NATO's mission seems unclear. Critics argue that NATO forces have no business being involved in policing missions in the Balkans. Others contend that the regional security force must adopt a new mission and support the effort. In either case, the U.S. role in decisions remains important.

The Reagan-Gorbachev era produced a remarkable shift in diplomacy and helped precipitate the demise of the Soviet Union. Yet, Russia and the former Socialist Republics that made up the USSR have made an unsteady and uneasy transition toward democracy and successful market economics. Few but the most optimistic observers believed such a transition would occur rapidly and without problems. Civil war in Chechnya and elsewhere, a stagnant economy, gangsterism, and other problems confront the former superpower. Russia, however, remains geographically the largest nation on earth. It still possesses powerful nuclear capabilities that require a diplomatic respect for the country's position in the world community. The United States must continue to work carefully with Russian leaders to assist in the difficult transition that has occurred there.

THE WESTERN HEMISPHERE

The United States maintains its historic and ambivalent relationship with Latin America into the twenty-first century. From the Monroe Doctrine to the "Big Stick" to the Good Neighbor Policy, U.S. interests aim to keep foreign threats, both political and ideological, out of the hemisphere while preserving the region to advance U.S. political and commercial objectives. If Latin Americans fail to appreciate the special sphere of interest the United States defines for itself in the hemisphere, it nonetheless remains a significant part of U.S. foreign policy. The support for the Contras in Nicaragua and the continued decision to isolate Cuba suggest recent U.S. commitments to counter perceived threats to its security and business interests.

In Latin America, a majority of the military juntas and dictatorships, left and right, have disappeared. Democratic governments emerged in the last two decades of the century throughout the region, sometimes, but not always, with the support and encouragement of the United States. But problems linger in the hemisphere. Staggering poverty still exists in broad areas of Latin America, and much of that misery is tied to race and the continued exploitation of majority populations of color. The democracies are fragile, and dictatorial alternatives have a long history of success in the region. Civil strife in Mexico, Peru, Colombia, and elsewhere continue to threaten stability in the region.

The United States has a key security and economic interest in Latin America. In 1993, the North American Free Trade Agreement (NAFTA) opened the door to new commercial possibilities amid heated debate in the United States as to its benefits. The Organization of American States should continue to exercise influence in the region, and U.S. involvement in Haiti and elsewhere seeks to function with OAS support. Perhaps the economic results of that cooperation may result in a Western Hemisphere "common market." How the United States will continue to pursue its unique relationship with the many and complex Latin American concerns will remain a key issue in U.S. foreign policy.

THE MIDDLE EAST

American foreign policy concerns came relatively late to the Middle East. Yet, following World War II, the exploding Arab-Israeli conflict and enhanced U.S. dependence on Middle East petroleum drew the United States into a volatile yet also subtle arena. Perhaps the most optimistic achievement of that involvement resulted in President Carter's meeting with Anwar Sadat and Menachem Begin. The Camp David Accords, however, failed to secure a lasting peace in the Middle East. The Egyptian-Israeli agreement may have resolved a basic, specific military confrontation between those two states, but concerns in Lebanon, Palestine, and elsewhere continue to plague the area.

Its role as a broker in the Middle East ties the United States to the continuing unrest and seething tension there. The Arab-Israeli confrontation appears destined to warrant continued U.S. diplomatic involvement, and public attitudes in America remain cautious concerning the broker's role the United States plays in the region.

A lengthy war between Iraq and Iran in the 1980s shaped a situation that led Iraq's leader, Saddam Hussein, to invade Kuwait and threaten Saudi Arabia in 1990. U.S. leadership, in a United Nations–endorsed resolution, produced a dramatic and quick military defeat of Iraq and its removal from Kuwait. That victory, however, remains tenuous. Fear of "rogue" states like Iraq developing chemical and biological weapons of terrorism continues to haunt diplomats and security officials throughout the world. Saddam Hussein remains in power, and American aircraft still patrol no-fly zones in the area.

Terrorism, regardless of who sponsors or encourages it, creates an additional foreign policy concern for the United States. For a variety of reasons, and from different regions, anger and frustration with American policy and behavior continue to provoke isolated acts of violence against the United States. Those who perpetrate attacks that Americans consider to be acts of terrorism view themselves as patriots or religious martyrs. A clear and coherent policy approach to terrorism remains a difficult and challenging responsibility.

While the traditional political issues noted above remain, a recent increase in the cost of petroleum has resurrected a critical economic concern. America and Western Europe depend heavily on oil to drive their industrial, free market economies. A new oil crisis might threaten U.S. commercial interests and require a forceful response as costs increase. Finally, attempts at a diplomatic resolution to the Palestinian issues have failed to occur and confront the administration of President George W. Bush in the new century.

ASIA

When American naval vessels, traders, and missionaries arrived in East Asia in the mid-nineteenth century, they sought to open the region to U.S. religious and commercial profit. Those goals drew the United States across the Pacific and have engaged the nation in critical foreign policy issues ever since. The United States has fought three wars in Asia in the past half century in pursuit of its perceived security interests. Ironically, former allies became enemies and previous enemies became friends.

Japan, America's nemesis in the 1940s, has become a major trading partner of the United States. South Korea has American troops stationed along its borders with North Korea to guard the 38th parallel. Yet, China, the embattled nation that provoked Secretary of State John Hay's protective Open Door Notes in the 1890s, came to represent the greatest contemporary threat to American interests in Asia. While current U.S. administrations work carefully to develop better political and commercial relations with China, critics continue to warn of human rights violations in that country. Others predict that China may pose serious threats to U.S. security interests. Recent military developments in China, and its ongoing tenuous relationship with Taiwan, have U.S. security analysts concerned.

Other places in Asia also exist in potentially dangerous environments that have global implications. The ongoing conflict between India and Pakistan, with the availability of nuclear weapons on both sides, verges on war regularly. In the past, the United States has maintained a friendly relationship with Pakistan, at the expense of its relationship with India. The stakes remain high, and while the United States has attempted to play a broker's role similar to its strategy in the Middle East, that has failed to produce any resolution to the tension.

America's direct involvement in Korea and the legacy of Vietnam also continue to demand diplomatic attention. The Korean peninsula remains divided, as it has since 1953. All of Southeast Asia still seeks to recover from the devastation of a generation of war there. Both areas warrant U.S. scrutiny and diplomatic interest.

Few Americans had heard of East Timor or the situation in the Indonesian archipelago that brought the region to national attention in 2000, but efforts to resolve that crisis also occupy the attention of U.S. foreign policy. Another opportunity and responsibility may need American attention.

AFRICA

Africa remained peripheral in the context of American foreign policy throughout most of the nation's history. During much of the nineteenth and twentieth centuries, most of the continent remained under the domination of European imperialism. The national security interests of the United States focused in other regions and considered other issues. Yet, the African continent faces enormous problems and possibilities in the modern era that require the attention of any serious foreign policy observer. The long-term impact of colonialism, political strife and corruption, disease, and famine tend to overshadow the many examples of success in Africa. U.S. policy acted slowly to support Desmond Tutu, Nelson Mandela, and others in South Africa as they fought to undo white minority rule. That tended to define U.S. policy in general during the years that African colonial systems broke free of European control and declared their independence. Prompted partly by growing public sentiment in America, the United States ultimately backed majority rule in South Africa and joined a world chorus applauding Mandela's new government.

Yet, the United States appears to have no basic foreign policy construct for the African continent, as the 1991 fiasco in Somalia suggested. U.S. military forces arrived in that East African nation, a country devastated by starvation and political turmoil, ostensibly to provide famine relief. The military, however, became embroiled in a political struggle between warring factions in the country. That ended in a violent confrontation that left a number of American soldiers dead and resulted in a hasty, embarrassing U.S. withdrawal from the region. Public and scholarly opinion debated whether America should have become directly involved in Somalia at all. Whether one supported the humanitarian effort or saw no critical interests involved for the United States, most agreed that American foreign policy in the region lacked any clear sense of focus or purpose.

Famine and exploding AIDS/HIV epidemics throughout sub-Saharan Africa may demand both international and U.S. commitment. The twin crises of hunger and disease ravage many areas of Africa, and humanitarian agencies plead for concentrated action from the world community. In a region that appears to have little impact on the security or economic interests of the United States, however, it seems unrealistic to expect a priority policy to emerge. That type of commitment may, however, serve to define the Pax Americana of the twenty-first century.

The African continent has many nations, with different issues and concerns, and it may seem simplistic to address the area as one entity. Yet, whether individually or collectively, the nations and peoples of the region should become a focus of U.S. attention.

PUBLIC ATTITUDES

No matter how the United States responds to world affairs in the twenty-first century, domestic concerns and opinion will continue to direct and foster foreign policy options. Like the proverbial backseat driver, the American public sees little problem in nudging the arm of the driver (the president) and indicating what direction it seeks to travel. Often, broad public sentiment tends to support government policy, and, in many instances, it shapes the government's responses. In cases where that has not occurred, the public debate remains spirited and even contentious.

For the past half-century, U.S. public opinion and administration policies have worked together somewhat supportively on the Cold War. From the early days of bilateral cooperation between Congress and the president to produce the Marshall Plan to more recent events leading to the INF Treaty, Americans generally conceded that the Soviet Union posed clear security threats to U.S. interests. Critics and skeptics existed, and issues like the war in Vietnam tested the will and patience of public attitudes, but for the most part the focus remained consistent and clear. That clarity has ended. Importantly, public opinion in the United States appears unclear as to what direction the government ought to go in the future. Pundits, politicians, and experts seem to be searching for approaches and options that appeal to the American constituency. As yet, no clear principles or formats have appeared.

New ideas and approaches to foreign policy can certainly replace the old formulas and issues. Perhaps national and regional concerns may subside into more general global responses. Concerns over the environment, disease, age and gender issues, population growth and movement, and poverty cut across national and regional borders and involve the world community at large. How the United States might assume the lead in defining those topics and responding to them serves as an additional challenge to the diplomacy of the twenty-first century. Quite often, it is impossible to predict what global issues might emerge to demand America's foreign policy attention. Nations can anticipate potential concerns and focus on those, but history suggests that an unexpected crisis or issue often appears to confound the most intelligent foresight. That is why a set of broad diplomatic principles tends to offer some limited focus in a world of complex and changing particulars.

In the final analysis, the defined self-interest of a nation generally drives its foreign policy agendas. Since nation-states continue to serve as the existing political institutions that conduct foreign policy, it appears likely that the United States will continue to operate within that framework. That has been the case throughout American history just as it has with other nations. The particular issues and events described in the preceding chapters emerged from concepts and goals established early in America's relations with the world community. Some had to alter with the demands and opportunities of twentieth-century U.S. power. That will remain the case in the future. Thomas Jefferson noted that "the condition upon which God hath given liberty is eternal vigilance." It seems an appropriate caution for those who observe and practice U.S. foreign policy in the new century.

Annotated, Selected Bibliography

The volumes listed here do not constitute a comprehensive bibliography. That would require a section as lengthy as the book itself. Rather, they are key works that will help students locate additional information, arguments, and details on the history of U.S. international relations. Additionally, there is a separate section on web sites that should prove helpful to readers as well as a section on CD-ROMs and videos.

BOOKS

Adams, E. D. *Great Britain and the American Civil War*. 2 vols. New York: Longmans, Green, 1925. A careful study, but dated.

Adler, Selig. *The Isolationist Impulse: Its Twentieth Century Reaction*. New York: Abelard-Schuman, 1957. An excellent analysis that carefully examines the idea of isolationism.

———. *The Uncertain Giant, 1921–1941: American Foreign Policy Between the Wars*. New York: Macmillan, 1965. The best general review of diplomacy during the era.

Alperovitz, Gar. *Atomic Diplomacy: Hiroshima and Potsdam*. New York: Vintage Books, 1967. A noted revisionist interpretation that offers a critical view of the U.S. decision to use the atom bomb.

Alteras, Isaac. *United States–Israeli Relations, 1953–1960*. Gainesville: University of Florida Press, 1995. The book offers a clear study of the early period in America's relationship with Israel.

Ambrose, Stephen. *Nixon: The Triumph of a Politician, 1962–1972*. New York: Simon and Schuster, 1989. One volume in Ambrose's excellent study of President Richard Nixon.

Ambrosius, Lloyd E. *Woodrow Wilson and the American Diplomatic Tradition: The Treaty Fight in Perspective.* Cambridge: Cambridge University Press, 1987. The work offers a sound and interesting overview of President Wilson's concept of the Fourteen Points and the League of Nations.

Ammon, Harry. *James Monroe: The Quest for National Identity.* Charlottesville: University of Virginia Press, 1990. A careful study that sees President Monroe as a practiced foreign policy leader.

Anderson, David. *Imperialism and Idealism: American Diplomats in China, 1861–1898.* Bloomington: Indiana University Press, 1985. The author studies eight diplomats who set the stage for Sino-American relations at the turn of the century.

Bailey, Thomas A. *A Diplomatic History of the American People.* 10th ed. Englewood Cliffs, NJ: Prentice-Hall, 1980. Perhaps the most popular and extensive general study of American foreign policy history.

———. *Wilson and the Peacemakers.* New York: Macmillan, 1947. The book is a combined edition of Bailey's two-volume study of the Paris Peace Conference and President Wilson's fight with the Senate over the League of Nations.

Bancroft, Frederic. *The Life of William Seward.* 2 vols. New York: Harper and Bros., 1900. The biography remains an excellent analysis even though dated.

Bartlett, Ruhl J. *The League to Enforce Peace.* Chapel Hill: University of North Carolina Press, 1944. A sound study of the origins of Woodrow Wilson's Fourteen Points and the League of Nations.

Beard, Charles A. *President Roosevelt and the Coming of the War.* Hamden, CT: Archon, 1968. A critical analysis that questions Franklin Roosevelt's "interventionist" policies.

Beisner, Robert L. *From the Old Diplomacy to the New, 1865–1900.* Arlington Heights, IL: Harlan Davidson, 1986. A good review of foreign policy changes in the last half of the nineteenth century.

———. *Twelve Against Empire: The Anti-Imperialists, 1898–1900.* New York: McGraw-Hill, 1968. The study offers a careful look at those who opposed U.S. expansion.

Bemis, Samuel Flagg. *The Diplomacy of the American Revolution.* Bloomington: Indiana University Press, 1957. Still one of the best studies of the issue.

———. *John Quincy Adams and the Foundations of American Foreign Policy.* Westport, CT: Greenwood Press, 1980. A must for anyone interested in the early period of American international relations.

———. *The Latin American Policy of the United States: An Historical Interpretation.* New York: Harcourt, Brace and World, 1943. While dated and pro-U.S. in its interpretation, the book still provides a clear review of the issues.

Benedetti, Charles, and Charles Chatsfield. *An American Ordeal: The Antiwar Movement of the Vietnam Era.* Syracuse, NY: Syracuse University Press, 1990. A solid, careful look at public dissent during the Vietnam War.

Berman, Larry. *Lyndon Johnson's War: The Road to Stalemate in Vietnam.* New York: Norton, 1989. A critical review of President Johnson's Vietnam policies.

Beschloss, Michael, and Strobe Talbott. *At the Highest Level: The Inside Story of the End of the Cold War.* Boston: Little, Brown, 1994. An interesting look at the era. Beschloss is a presidential historian, and Talbott served as deputy secretary of state during the period.

Bickerton, Ian J., and Carla L. Klausner. *A Concise History of the Arab-Israeli Conflict.* Upper Saddle River, NJ: Prentice-Hall, 1998. As the title suggests, a concise, clear overview of the developing conflict.

Boyd, Bill. *Bolivar: Liberator of a Continent.* New York: S.P.I. Books, 1998. Boyd's work is a dramatized biography of the Venezuelan leader, but worth a look to examine Bolivar's attitudes regarding the United States.

Braestrup, Peter. *Big Story: How the American Press and Television Reported and Interpreted the Crisis of Tet 1968 in Vietnam and Washington.* 2 vols. Boulder, CO: Westview, 1977. The book provides a careful analysis of the media's role in presenting the war and diplomacy to the American public.

Buckley, Thomas H. *The United States and the Washington Conference, 1921–1922.* Chattanooga: University of Tennessee Press, 1970. A careful, scholarly look at the conference and disarmament.

Bundy, William. *A Tangled Web: The Making of Foreign Policy in the Nixon Presidency.* New York: Hill and Wang, 1998. The book gives a clear, critical review of President Nixon's foreign policy.

Burns, James M. *Roosevelt: Soldier of Freedom.* New York: Harcourt Brace Jovanovich, 1970. One of the best FDR biographies. Volume two of Burns's study of the president is useful for an analysis of foreign policy throughout the period 1933–1945.

Burns, William. *Economic Aid and American Policy Toward Egypt, 1955–1981.* Albany: State University of New York Press, 1985. A specialized study, but one that shows how the United States used its economic policies to influence Egypt's position in the Middle East.

Callahan, James M. *The Diplomatic History of the Southern Confederacy.* Baltimore: Johns Hopkins Press, 1901. Classic older study of the South's foreign policy during the war.

Cambell, Charles. *Special Business Interests and the Open Door Policy.* New Haven, CT: Yale University Press, 1951. A sound look at the business factors involved in Sino-American policy at the end of the nineteenth century.

———. *The Transformation of American Foreign Relations, 1865–1900.* New York: Harper and Row, 1976. A good review.

Carter, Jimmy. *Keeping Faith.* New York: Bantam, 1982. The president's own review of his foreign policy initiatives.

Clemens, Diane Shaver. *Yalta.* New York: Oxford University Press, 1970. The book gives a sound, clear look at the conference.

Clymer, Kenton J. *John Hay: The Gentleman as Diplomat.* Ann Arbor: University of Michigan Press, 1975. A favorable look at the secretary of state who issued the Open Door Notes.

Cohen, Michael J. *Palestine and the Great Powers.* Princeton, NJ: Princeton University Press, 1982. The author develops a scholarly study of the early background of the Palestine issue.

Cole, Wayne S. *America First: The Battle Against Intervention, 1940–1941.* Madison: University of Wisconsin Press, 1953.

———. *Charles A. Lindbergh and the Battle Against American Intervention in World War II.* New York: Harcourt Brace Jovanovich, 1974.

————. *An Interpretive History of American Foreign Policy.* Homewood, IL: Dorsey, 1974. Offers a good look at domestic and external byplay in the development of U.S. foreign policy.

————. *Roosevelt and the Isolationists, 1932–1945.* Lincoln: University of Nebraska Press, 1983.

————. *Senator Gerald P. Nye and American Foreign Relations.* Minneapolis: University of Minnesota Press, 1962. Professor Cole's books provide an outstanding analysis of foreign policy during the critical national debate prior to World War II.

Crook, David Paul. *The North, the South, and the Powers, 1861–1865.* New York: Wiley, 1974. Crook has written a quality study of the relationship of the two sides with Great Britain and France during the Civil War.

Dallek, Robert. *Franklin D. Roosevelt and American Foreign Policy, 1932–1945.* New York: Oxford University Press, 1995. An excellent look at Roosevelt's attitude and actions.

Dayan, Moshe. *Breakthrough: A Personal Account of the Egypt-Israeli Peace Negotiations.* New York: Alfred A. Knopf, 1981. Dayan, a participant in the events, provides a firsthand account.

Deconde, Alexander. *Entangling Alliance: Politics and Diplomacy Under George Washington.* Westport, CT: Greenwood Press, 1974. One of the best studies of the early years in American foreign policy.

Dippie, Brian. *The Vanishing American: White Attitudes and U.S. Indian Policy.* Lawrence: University of Kansas Press, 1982. The author provides a careful review of U.S. "foreign policy" regarding the American Indian peoples.

Divine, Robert. *The Reluctant Belligerent: American Entry into World War II.* New York: John Wiley and Sons, 1965. A classic study of the events and policies leading the United States into the war.

————. *Roosevelt and World War II.* New York: Penguin, 1970. The companion piece to Divine's *Reluctant Belligerent* takes FDR's policies through the war.

Donald, David. *Lincoln.* New York: Simon and Schuster, 1995. Of the many wonderful books about President Lincoln, Donald's is one of the best.

Dozer, Donald. *Are We Good Neighbors? Three Decades of Inter-American Relations, 1930–1960.* Gainesville: University of Florida Press, 1959. The author credits Franklin Roosevelt more than Herbert Hoover with developing and pursuing the Good Neighbor Policy.

Duberman, Martin. *Charles Francis Adams.* Boston: Houghton Mifflin, 1961. The most complete and careful study of the U.S. ambassador to Great Britain during the Civil War.

Dull, Jonathan. *A Diplomatic History of the American Revolution.* New Haven: Yale University Press, 1985. Provides a sound review of Revolutionary War diplomacy.

Dulles, Foster Rhea. *China and America: The Story of Their Relationship Since 1784.* Princeton: Princeton University Press, 1946. The book remains a standard, if dated, analysis and overview.

Duroselle, Jean Baptiste. *From Wilson to Roosevelt: Foreign Policy of the United States, 1913–1945.* New York: Harper and Row, 1968. A clear, thorough analysis of foreign policy during the first half of the twentieth century.

Ellis, Lewis. *Frank B. Kellogg and American Foreign Relations, 1925–1929.* New Brunswick, NJ: Rutgers University Press, 1961. The best study of Secretary of State Kellogg with particular analysis of the disarmament negotiations.

———. *Republican Foreign Policy, 1921–1933.* New Brunswick, NJ: Rutgers University Press, 1968. A general review of basic policy during the period.

Ezer, Weizman. *The Battle for Peace.* New York: Bantam, 1981. Weizman gives a clear account of the Egyptian-Israeli negotiations.

Feis, Herbert. *The Atomic Bomb and the End of World War II.* Princeton, NJ: Princeton University Press, 1966. An objective analysis of the U.S. policy decision to use the atomic bomb.

———. *Between War and Peace: The Potsdam Conference.* Princeton: Princeton University Press, 1960. Perhaps the best study of the Potsdam Conference.

———. *Churchill, Roosevelt, and Stalin: The War They Waged and the Peace They Sought.* Princeton: Princeton University Press, 1967. Excellent examination of the wartime conferences.

Ferrell, Robert. *American Diplomacy in the Great Depression: Hoover-Stimson Foreign Policy, 1929-1933.* New York: Norton, 1970. A scholarly study of a period often dismissed in U.S. diplomacy.

———. *Peace in Their Time: The Origins of the Kellogg-Briand Pact.* New York: Norton, 1969. The book is a must read for those interested in the details of the peace pact.

———. *Woodrow Wilson and World War I, 1917–1921.* New York: Harper and Row, 1985. A good look at Wilson's foreign policy.

Fleming, D. F. *The Cold War and Its Origins, 1917-1960.* Garden City, NY: Doubleday, 1969. An excellent, clear study of the origins of U.S.-Soviet relations.

Fraser, T. G. *The Middle East, 1914–1979.* New York: St. Martin's Press, 1980. A good basic review of the developing issues in the Middle East that shows U.S. involvement.

Fried, Richard M. *Nightmare in Red: The McCarthy Era in Perspective.* New York: Oxford University Press, 1990. The book provides a balanced, objective look at the anti-communist sentiment following World War II, tied to other domestic issues and concerns in the United States.

Gaddis, John. *The United States and the End of the Cold War.* New York: Oxford University Press, 1992.

———. *The United States and the Origins of the Cold War, 1941–1947.* New York: Columbia University Press, 1972. Gaddis's two works provide a wonderful review of U.S.-Soviet relations in the last half of the twentieth century.

Gelb, Leslie, and Richard K. Betts. *The Irony of Vietnam: The System Worked.* Washington, DC: Brookings Institute, 1979. A controversial but significant interpretation.

Gellman, Irwin F. *Good Neighbor Diplomacy: United States Policies in Latin America.* Baltimore: Johns Hopkins University Press, 1979. The author stresses Roosevelt's interest in expanding U.S. global power into the region.

Gilbert, Felix. *To the Farewell Address: Ideas of Early American Foreign Policy.* Princeton: Princeton University Press, 1970. A scholarly analysis of the origins of U.S. diplomatic concerns and goals.

Glad, Betty. *Charles Evans Hughes and the Illusion of Innocence: A Study in American*

Diplomacy. Urbana: University of Illinois Press, 1966. The author stresses the influence of Secretary of State Hughes on the entire era between the wars, especially U.S. interest in disarmament.

Goldman, Eric. *The Crucial Decade and After, 1945–1960*. New York: Random House, 1965. Goldman's book offers a lively analysis of the postwar period with some excellent chapters on U.S. foreign policy, particularly his look at Senator Joseph McCarthy's role in the Red Scare.

Gorbachev, Mikhail. *Memoirs*. New York: Doubleday, 1996. The Russian premier's personal account of events is both interesting and studied.

Green, David. *The Containment of Latin America: A History of Myths and Realities of the Good Neighbor Policy*. Chicago: Quadrangle Books, 1971. The author argues that the policy simply devised another way to protect and advance U.S. commercial and security interests throughout the hemisphere.

Griffith, Robert. *Politics of Fear: Joseph McCarthy and the Senate*. Amherst: University of Massachusetts Press, 1987. One of the best studies of Senator Joseph McCarthy and his impact on U.S. policy.

Griswold, A. Whitney. *The Far Eastern Policy of the United States*. New York: Harcourt, Brace, 1938. A dated, but complete, review of evolving U.S. policy in Asia.

Guerrant, Edward O. *Roosevelt's Good Neighbor Policy*. Albuquerque: University of New Mexico Press, 1950. An older study that credits Roosevelt.

Haig, Alexander. *Caveat: Realism, Reagan, and Foreign Policy*. New York: Macmillan, 1984. Haig acted in a variety of positions in the White House and offers a reasonable interpretation of President Reagan's foreign policy.

Halberstam, David. *The Best and the Brightest*. New York: Random House, 1969. A critical view of U.S. policy in Southeast Asia that argues that anticommunism and a lack of Asian specialists in the U.S. government led to the mistaken involvement in Vietnam.

Hallin, Daniel C. *The Uncensored War: The Media and Vietnam*. New York: Oxford University Press, 1986. An excellent look at the role of media coverage of the war in Vietnam.

Harris, Thomas L. *The Trent Affair*. Indianapolis, IN: Bowen-Merrill Co., 1986. The best work on the key incident during the Civil War.

Herring, George C. *America's Longest War: The United States and Vietnam, 1950–1975*. Philadelphia: Temple University Press, 1986. The author offers a thorough, balanced look at the conflict in both military and diplomatic terms.

Hicks, John D. *Republican Ascendancy, 1921–1933*. New York: Harper and Row, 1960. Hicks provides a comprehensive and critical review of Republican politics and diplomacy during the period.

Hill, Dilys. *The Reagan Presidency: An Incomplete Revolution*. New York: St. Martin's Press, 1990. The book has a good chapter on foreign policy issues.

Hoff-Wilson, Joan. *Herbert Hoover: Forgotten Progressive*. Boston: Little, Brown, 1975. Hoover's principal biographer, the author portrays the president's role in the Good Neighbor Policy far more favorably than other scholars.

Hunt, Michael. *The Making of a Special Relationship: The United States and China to 1914*. New York: Columbia University Press, 1983. A recent scholarly review of the background to U.S.-China relations with particular emphasis on the Open Door Notes and other late nineteenth-century issues.

Iriye, Akira. *The Cold War in Asia: A Historical Introduction*. Englewood Cliffs, NJ: Prentice-Hall, 1974. Iriye has long been considered an expert in the field. His work is always thoughtful and thorough.

Israel, Jerry. *Progressivism and the Open Door: America and China, 1905–1921*. Pittsburgh, PA: University of Pittsburgh Press, 1971. A solid, clear look at the development and influence of the Open Door Policy.

Kaplan, Lawrence. *Colonies into Nation: American Diplomacy, 1763–1801*. New York: Macmillan, 1972. A clear, thorough review of the origins of American foreign policy.

Kaplan, Morton, et al. *Vietnam Settlement: Why 1973, not 1969?* Washington, DC: American Enterprise Institute, 1973. This collection of works has some excellent analysis on the conduct of U.S. policy in Vietnam.

Karnow, Stanley. *Vietnam: A History*. New York: Viking Press, 1983. The book served as the companion for the Public Broadcasting System's television history of the war. Both the book and the televised series should be in every library.

Kattenburg, Paul M. *The Vietnam Trauma in American Foreign Policy, 1945–1975*. New Brunswick, NJ: Transaction, 1980. A sound general review of policy and action.

Kaufman, Robert G. *Arms Control During the Pre-Nuclear Era: The United States and Naval Limitation Between the Two World Wars*. New York: Columbia University Press, 1990. An interesting look at the 1920s and disarmament with battleships as the ultimate weapons of that era.

Keynes, John Maynard. *The Economic Consequences of the Peace*. New York: Harcourt, Brace, 1920. The economist's criticism of President Wilson's "failures and flaws" at the Paris Peace Conference influenced that negative view of Wilson for a generation.

Kimball, Jeffrey. *Nixon's Vietnam War*. Lawrence: University of Kansas Press, 1998. The author provides an excellent look at the role of Nixon, Henry Kissinger, and the peace negotiations.

Kimball, Warren. *The Juggler: Franklin Roosevelt as Wartime Statesman*. Princeton: Princeton University Press, 1991. A scholarly, clear recent look at FDR's wartime policies.

Kryzanek, Michael J. *U.S.–Latin American Relations*. New York: Praeger, 1990. The author provides a sound general look at relations in the hemisphere.

Kutler, Stanley. *The American Inquisition: Justice and Injustice in the Cold War*. New York: Hill and Wang, 1982. The book gives a good current study of the evolution of anti-communism in the United States following World War II.

Kyvig, David, ed. *Reagan and the World*. New York: Praeger, 1990. The work has two sound chapters on arms negotiations.

LaFeber, Walter. *America, Russia, and the Cold War, 1945–1992*. New York: McGraw-Hill, 1991. A recent edition of the author's classic study of the Cold War. LaFeber is balanced in his scholarly study, but sees the United States as principally responsible for the struggle between the two nations.

————. *The American Age: United States Foreign Policy at Home and Abroad Since 1750*. New York: Norton, 1989. The author examines the commercial drive and stresses economic factors in his thoughtful study of U.S. foreign policy.

————. *The New Empire: An Interpretation of American Expansion, 1860–1898*. Ithaca, NY: Cornell University Press, 1963. LaFeber reviews the post–Civil War period with a similar interest in American economic motivation in its foreign policy.

Langer, William, and S. Everett Gleason. *The Challenge to Isolation, 1937–1940*. New York: Harper and Bros., 1952. An old standby introduction to the issues.

Latham, Earl. *The Communist Controversy in Washington: From the New Deal to McCarthy*. Cambridge, MA: Harvard University Press, 1966. One of the best books examining U.S. attitudes on communism, with good analysis of the McCarthy era.

Link, Arthur. *Wilson the Diplomatist: A Look at His Major Foreign Policies*. Baltimore: Johns Hopkins University Press, 1957. Professor Link is Wilson's major biographer and has written extensively about the president.

————. *Woodrow Wilson: Revolution, War and Peace*. Arlington Heights, IL: Harlan Davidson, 1979.

Lucaks, John. *A History of the Cold War*. Garden City, NY: Doubleday and Co., 1961. The book is another good, broad review of the Soviet-American confrontation.

Maddox, Robert J. *William E. Borah and American Foreign Policy*. Baton Rouge: Louisiana State University Press, 1969. The best book that examines the career of the powerful Idaho senator.

Masur, Gerhard. *Simon Bolivar*. Albuquerque: University of New Mexico Press, 1948. The book is dated, but, in English, still provides a good biography of the Latin American leader.

May, Earnest. *Imperial Democracy: The Emergence of America as a World Power*. New York: Harper and Row, 1973. The author provides thorough analysis of U.S. policy at the turn of the century.

————. *The Making of the Monroe Doctrine*. Cambridge, MA: Harvard University Press, 1975. A classic and critical history of the Monroe Doctrine.

McCann, Frank D. *The Brazilian-American Alliance, 1937–1945*. Princeton: Princeton University Press, 1973. The book provides an excellent case study on the Good Neighbor Policy and the relationship between Getulia Vargas, Brazil's president, and Roosevelt.

McCormick, Thomas J. *China Market: America's Quest for Informal Empire, 1893–1901*. Chicago: Dee, 1990. A careful economic interpretation of U.S. interests in East Asia.

McCullough, David. *Truman*. New York: Simon and Schuster, 1992. The best biography of the president, with excellent chapters on Truman's foreign policy decisions.

Mecham, J. L. *The United States and Inter-American Security, 1889–1960*. Austin: University of Texas Press, 1961. Provides a comprehensive review of the various hemisphere conferences.

Merk, Frederick. *Manifest Destiny and Mission in American History: A Reinterpretation.* Westport, CT: Greenwood Press, 1984. Merk offers one of the best studies of the controversial issue in American history.

Miller, D. H. *The Peace Pact of Paris: A Study of the Kellogg-Briand Pact.* New York: G. P. Putnam's Sons, 1928. A scholarly, contemporary look at the treaty.

Millett, Allan R., and Peter Maslowski. *For the Common Defense: A Military History of the United States.* New York: Free Press, 1994. The book is a good text for students of military history, and it provides sound analysis of foreign policy issues as well.

Millis, Walter. *Arms and Men: A Study in American Military History.* New York: G. P. Putnam's Sons, 1956. Millis's book remains a classic study of the evolution of American military policy and behavior.

Morris, Benny. *The Birth of the Palestine Refugee Problem, 1947–1949.* Cambridge: Cambridge University Press, 1987. The book studies the early origins of the problem that continues to threaten peace in the Middle East.

Morris, Edmund. *Dutch: A Memoir of Ronald Reagan.* New York: Random House, 1999. Much has been made of Morris's biography, both highly critical and positive. The author does, however, offer a clear analysis of Reagan's approach to arms negotiations and Soviet-American relations.

Morris, Richard. *The Peacemakers: The Great Powers and American Independence.* Boston: Northeastern University Press, 1965. To study the diplomacy of the American Revolution, students need to consider Morris.

Newman, John M. *JFK and Vietnam: Deception, Intrigue, and the Struggle for Power.* New York: Warner, 1992. The author argues that President Kennedy would have removed U.S. presence in Vietnam after the 1964 election.

Nitze, Paul. *From Hiroshima to Glasnost.* New York: Grove Weidenfeld, 1989. Nitze served as one of the leading U.S. arms negotiators and has written a careful review of American policy.

Oberdorfer, Dan. *The Turn: From the Cold War to a New Era. The United States and the Soviet Union.* London: Jonathan Cape, 1992. A sound analysis of the critical period in arms negotiations and the changes in the Soviet Union and the United States.

O'Connor, Raymond. *Diplomacy for Victory: FDR and Unconditional Surrender.* New York: Norton, 1971. An excellent study of the Casablanca Conference.

O'Reilley, Kenneth. *Hoover and the Un-Americans: The FBI, HUAC and the Red Menace.* Philadelphia: Temple University Press, 1983. A critical, careful analysis of J. Edgar Hoover's role during the McCarthy era.

Ovendale, Ritchie. *The Origins of the Arab-Israeli Wars.* New York: Longman, 1992. The book is a good study of the early confrontation.

Owsley, Frank L. *King Cotton Diplomacy: Foreign Relations of the Confederate States of America.* Chicago: University of Chicago Press, 1966. A clear, thorough review of Confederate policy and its failures.

Paterson, Thomas G., ed. *Kennedy's Quest for Victory: American Foreign Policy, 1961–1963.* New York: Oxford University Press, 1989. The recognized diplomatic historian has compiled an excellent review of President Kennedy's foreign policy approach.

Pells, Richard. *The Liberal Mind in a Conservative Age: American Intellectuals in the*

1940's and 1950's. Middletown, CT: Wesleyan University Press, 1989. Pells provides a thoughtful look at the academic response to McCarthyism.

Perkins, Dexter. *Hands Off: A History of the Monroe Doctrine*. Boston: Little, Brown, 1963. Interested readers should start a study of the Monroe Doctrine with Perkins.

———. *The United States and Latin America*. Baton Rouge: Louisiana State University Press, 1961. An older work, it still provides a comprehensive look at the history of the relationship.

Persico, Joseph E. *Edward R. Murrow: An American Original*. New York: McGraw-Hill, 1988. Easy to read, Persico delivers an interesting biography of the journalist that stresses the emerging role of television in national events.

Porter, David L. *The Seventy-Sixth Congress and World War II, 1939–1940*. Columbia: University of Missouri Press, 1979. A scholarly look at the role of Congress during the critical battle between isolationists and interventionists.

Powell, James Roy. "Going for Broke: Richard Nixon's Search for 'Peace with Honor.' " Doctoral dissertation, University of Kansas, 1998. Clear focus on the Paris negotiations.

Purifoy, Lewis M. *Harry Truman's China Policy: McCarthyism and the Diplomacy of Hysteria, 1947–1951*. New York: New Viewpoints, 1976. The author focuses on Sino-American relations, but offers a critical view of McCarthyism's impact on U.S. policy.

Quandt, William. *Decade of Decisions: American Policy Toward the Arab-Israeli Conflict, 1967–1976*. Berkeley: University of California Press, 1977. Quandt presents a thorough review of U.S. policy.

Randall, J. G., and David H. Donald. *The Civil War and Reconstruction*. Lexington, MA: D. C. Heath, 1969. There are a number of quality texts on the American Civil War. This is one of the best.

Reagan, Ronald. *An American Life*. New York: Simon and Schuster, 1990. The president's autobiography offers insight into his perceptions and policies.

Reeves, Thomas. *The Life and Times of Joe McCarthy*. New York: Stein and Day, 1982. This is a sound biography of the Wisconsin senator.

Rich, Norman. *Great Power Diplomacy: 1814–1914*. New York: McGraw-Hill, 1992. A revealing study of European diplomatic attitudes regarding the United States as it grew in strength and influence.

Sachar, Howard. *A History of Israel: From the Aftermath of the Yom Kippur War*. Vol. 2. New York: Oxford University Press, 1987. Sachar provides an extensive analysis of modern Israel.

Sadat, Anwar. *In Search of Identity: An Autobiography*. New York: Harper and Row, 1978. The book provides a wonderful perspective told by one of the principal participants in the peace process.

Savelle, Max. *The Origins of American Diplomacy*. New York: Macmillan, 1967. A lengthy, demanding study that one should only undertake with care and deliberation.

Schaller, Michael. *Reckoning with Reagan: America and Its President in the 1980's*. New York: Oxford University Press, 1992. The book offers an additional study of the president with thoughtful views on his foreign policy positions.

Schrecker, Ellen W. *No Ivory Tower: McCarthyism and the Universities*. New York: Oxford University Press, 1986. This serves as a wonderful companion piece to Pells's work on American intellectuals.

Sherwin, Martin J. *A World Destroyed: The Atomic Bomb and the Grand Alliance*. New York: Vintage, 1977. As the title suggests, the book offers a critical analysis of U.S. decisions at the end of World War II.

Shotwell, J. T. *War as an Instrument of National Policy; and Its Renunciation in the Pact of Paris*. London: Constable, 1929. Along with D. H. Miller's contemporary study of Kellogg-Briand, Shotwell provides a similar hopeful view of disarmament.

Smith, Dan. *The Great Departure: The United States and World War I, 1914–1920*. New York: Wiley, 1965. One of the best books on American entry into World War I.

Smith, Gaddis. *American Diplomacy During the Second World War*. New York: Alfred A. Knopf, 1985. Smith presents a scholarly, balanced review.

Stone, Ralph. *The Irreconcilables: The Fight Against the League of Nations*. New York: W. W. Norton, 1973. The author presents a favorable and fair treatment of those who fought against President Wilson's League of Nations.

Talbott, Strobe. *The Russians and Reagan*. New York: Council on Foreign Relations, 1984. The career diplomat has written a careful review of the president's dealings with the Soviet Union.

Tansill, Charles. *Backdoor to War: The Roosevelt Foreign Policy, 1933–1941*. Westport, CT: Greenwood Press, 1975. Tansill maintains that FDR provoked the war with Japan in order to confront a more dangerous threat in Germany.

Taubman, William. *Stalin's American Policy: From Entente to Détente to Cold War*. New York: W. W. Norton, 1982. The book is a very good look at Soviet policy under Joseph Stalin.

Tillman, Seth. *The United States and the Middle East*. Bloomington: Indiana University Press, 1982. The author presents a broad, clear overview of U.S. policy as it evolved in the region.

Tompkins, E. Berkeley. *Anti-Imperialism in the United States: The Great Debate, 1890–1920*. Philadelphia: University of Pennsylvania Press, 1970. Tompkins examines, with care, those who opposed growing U.S. expansion.

Trask, David. *The United States in the Supreme War Council: American War Aims and Inter-Allied Strategy, 1917–1918*. Westport, CT: Greenwood Press, 1978. The author offers a clear look at Wilson's Fourteen Points in the context of allied war aims against the Central Powers.

Van Deusen, Glydon G. *William Henry Seward*. New York: Oxford University Press, 1967. Still the best biography of the secretary of state.

Vinson, John. *The Parchment Peace: The United States Senate and the Washington Naval Conference, 1921–1922*. Athens: University of Georgia Press, 1955. An older study that provides good insight into congressional attitudes on disarmament.

———. *William E. Borah and the Outlawry of War*. Athens: University of Georgia Press, 1957. Vinson looks at Senator Borah's key influence in driving the disarmament agenda.

Warren, Gordon H. *Fountain of Discontent: The Trent Affair and Freedom of the Seas.* Boston: Northeastern University Press, 1981. A sound, in-depth review of the critical incident.

Webster, C. K., ed. *Britain and the Independence of Latin America.* London: Oxford University Press, 1938. A collection of British Foreign Office documents that makes the argument that Britain, not the United States, made the Monroe Doctrine work.

Weinberg, Albert K. *Manifest Destiny: A Study of National Expansionism in American History.* New York: AMS Press, 1979. A traditional, thorough study.

Whitaker, Arthur. *The United States and the Independence of Latin America, 1800–1830.* New York: Norton, 1964. The author provides a clear, studious look at Latin American attitudes regarding the Monroe Doctrine.

Widenor, William C. *Henry Cabot Lodge and the Search for an American Foreign Policy.* Berkeley: University of California Press, 1980. Widenor argues that both Senator Lodge and President Wilson were idealists who clashed over legitimate political views.

Williams, William A. *The Tragedy of American Diplomacy.* 2nd ed. New York: W. W. Norton, 1988. There are a number of revisionist, critical books on American foreign policy. This remains the standard.

Wiltz, John. *From Isolation to War, 1931–1941.* New York: Crowell, 1968. A balanced, careful study of the key issues during the critical decade before Pearl Harbor.

Wittner, Lawrence S. *Rebels Against War: The American Peace Movement, 1933–1983.* Philadelphia: Temple University Press, 1984. Examines pacifist attitudes in detail and with balance.

Wood, Bryce. *The Dismantling of the Good Neighbor Policy.* Austin: University of Texas Press, 1985. A wonderful follow-up to Wood's first work that examines the evolution of the Good Neighbor Policy following World War II.

———. *The Making of the Good Neighbor Policy.* New York: W. W. Norton, 1967. Originally published in 1954, the work is well documented and discounts Hoover's contributions.

Yergin, Daniel. *Shattered Peace: The Origins of the Cold War and the National Security State.* Boston: Houghton Mifflin, 1977. The book seeks to analyze the impact of Cold War tension on domestic policies.

Young, Marilyn. *The Rhetoric of Empire: American China Policy, 1895–1901.* Cambridge, MA: Harvard University Press, 1968. A studious, thorough look at U.S. policy as it developed in China.

INTERNET WEB SITES

There are a number of easy to use web sites with extensive information on American history in general and diplomatic history in particular. A basic site for history that allows the reader to search by time period, topic, and/or region is http://dir.yahoo.com/Arts/Humanities/History. Also see http://www.looksmart.com. Another general web site is http://www.hyperhistory.com. All three offer access to various fields and eras in history, United States and general. They are subcategorized by century, area, and topic. The general information is credible and reasonably comprehensive. Good arts and humanities sections can be found at http://home.about.com/education/history/index.htm. Readers should remember that not all the sites on the general webs are going to carry objective and accurate information. The following two sites have excellent general resources: http://www.hamline.edu/~kfmeyer/history.html and http://www.ukans.edu/history.

The best source on the web for information, documents, and other information specifically on diplomatic history is http://Faculty.tamu-commerce.edu/sarantakes/stuff.html. It is an "A to Z" site essential to the diplomatic historian. Mount Holyoke College's program, http://www.mtholyoke.edu/acad/intrel, remains an excellent resource for documents pertaining to international relations. Also, Yale University Law School offers an excellent site for treaties and other international documents in its Avalon project. Look in http://www.yale.edu/lawweb/avalon/diplomacy.htm. North Carolina University's excellent site for a variety of historical material and documents is http://www.ibiblio.org. An additional site that specializes in foreign policy is the American diplomacy web site at http://www.unc.edu/depts/diplomat. Finally, readers may consult the Department of State's web site at http://www.state.gov and search in its electronic research collection.

VIDEOS AND CD-ROMs

CD-ROMs and videos are readily available on general topics in American, European, and world history. Most textbooks now include CD-ROMs along with a written text. See, for example, John M. Faragher et al., *Out of Many: A History of the American People*, 3rd ed. (Princeton, NJ: Prentice-Hall, 2000), and Robert Divine et al., *America: Past and Present* (New York: Addison-Wesley, 1999). While designed primarily to serve as study guides, the CD-ROMs also provide additional access to information, outside readings, primary documents, and so on. Several good commercial sources sell CD-ROMs and videos, among them http://socialstudies.com and http://www.learner.org/collections/multimedia/history.

The Arts and Entertainment Network (A&E) has produced a series of biographies of American leaders from George Washington to Henry Kissinger. Many of them are excellent, short reviews of the key figures and examine their role in foreign policy issues. The best video review of the Cold War era was produced in 1998 by Cable News Network (CNN). The twenty-four episodes (50 minutes; 8 volumes) remain an excellent analysis. The classic film *Point of Order* serves as a wonderful visual look at the Army-McCarthy hearings and shows Welch's famous assault on McCarthy.

In 1983, WGBH Boston produced *Vietnam: A Television History* for PBS. The eleven-part series offers the best video history of the conflict, with good portions devoted to foreign policy at its best. A PBS Video documentary on President Dwight Eisenhower, in its "American Experience" series (1997), looks at the issue, but gives too much credit to the president for "destroying" McCarthy. "A Walk Through the 20th Century," a nineteen-part PBS series narrated by Bill Moyers, also looks at McCarthy's impact.

As part of its "American Experience" series, WGBH Television, Boston, produced an excellent biographical study of Ronald Reagan in 1998. The second half of the two-part program offers a careful, interesting review of foreign policy issues during the Reagan years, and it takes a focused look at arms negotiations.

Index

Acheson, Dean, 189
Adams, Charles Francis, 46, 48, 49, 51, 52
Adams, John, 10, 13, 25
Adams, John Quincy, 3, 28–29, 36
Adams-Onis Treaty (1819), 31
Addams, Jane, 68
African Americans, 50, 51
Age of Imperialism, 66
Aguinaldo, Emilio, 68
Alaska: Russia in, 28, 30; 34; purchase of, 67
Alexander I, Tsar, 29
"All aid short of war," 152–153
Amendment, Thirteenth (1865), 51
America First Committee, 149–150
"America Firsters," 150
Andropov, Yuri, 258
Anglo-French Wars, 5, 10–12
Anti-Imperialist League, 68
Antietam, Battle of (1862), 49, 50, 52
Arab-Israeli Conflicts, 231–233, 234–235, 236–237
Article X, 90–91
Articles of Confederation, 11

Atlantic Charter (1941), 153

Baath Party, 232, 234
Baghdad Pact (CENTO) (1955), 233, 234
Bailey, Thomas A., 2
"Balance of Power," 86
Begin, Menachem, 231, 239, 240
Belgium, 80
Benjamin, Judah P., 52
Berlin Blockade (1948), 190
Berrigan, Daniel, 214
Berrigan, Philip, 214
Beveridge, Albert, 68, 71
"Big Stick" Diplomacy, 126–128
"Big Three," 87
Blockade, Naval, 2, 5; in Civil War, 46
Bolivar, Simon, 3, 29–30
Bonaparte, Napoleon, 13, 27
Borah, William E., 89, 90, 104, 106, 107, 146
Border states, 50
Boxer Rebellion (1900), 70

Bradley, Omar, 172
Brezhnev, Leonid, 258
Briand, Aristede, 105, 106
Bricker, John, 170
Bright, John, 78
Bryan, William J., 68
Bull Run, Battle of (1861), 49
Butler, Nicholas, 105

Cairo Conference (1943), 169
Calhoun, John C., 5
Camp David Accords (1978), 231, 239–
   240; text of, 247–253
Canada, 5, 10, 31, 72, 123
Canning, George, 28, 35–36
Capper, Arthur, 106
Carranza, Venustiano, 126
Carter, Jimmy, 231, 237–239, 257
Casablanca Conference (1943), 168–
   169
Cherokee Nation v. Georgia (1831), 31
China: and Open Door Notes, 65–67,
   69–70; trade with, 69; in World War
   II, 149–150, 152–153, 169–170; 191,
   282
Churchill, Winston, 153, 167–168, 169–
   171, 174, 182, 191
Clark, J. Reuben, 127–128
Clay, Henry, 5
Clemenceau, Georges, 87
Clifford, Clark, 212
Cobden, Richard, 50
Cohn, Roy, 194
Cold War, 168, 173, 174, 183, 184, 189,
   190, 196, 198, 210, 219, 232, 255,
   256, 259, 261, 262, 277, 284
Committee to Defend America by
   Aiding the Allies, 150
Confederate States of America, 45–46
Congress of Vienna (1815), 28
Constitutional Convention (1787), 11
Coolidge, Calvin, 105, 126
Cox, James, 91
Creel, George, 87

Davis, Jefferson, 46, 47, 52
Dayton, William, 51

Destroyer-Bases Agreement (1940),
   151
Dewey, John, 105
Diaz, Porfirio, 126
"Dollar diplomacy," 126
Drago Doctrine (1902), 126, 133
Dulles, John Foster, 233

Egypt, 49, 182, 231–238
Eisenhower, Dwight D., 172, 194–195,
   197, 210–211
Ellsberg, Daniel, 216
Emancipation Proclamation (1863), 50–
   51, 52
England. *See* Great Britain
European Recovery Program (1947),
   173, 186, 190
"Evil Empire" speech, 263
Executive Order 9835 (1947), 191
Export-Import Bank, 130

Fairfax, Lieutenant D.M., 47–48
Farouk, King, 232
Ferdinand VII, 28, 30
Five Power Treaty (1922), 104
Flying Tigers, 153
Ford, Gerald, 218
Fort Sumter, 46
Fourteen Points, 85, 87–88
France: in eighteenth and nineteenth
   centuries, 11–13, 46, 49, 67; in the
   1920s, 105–107; in World War I, 86–
   87; in World War II, 169, 170, 209,
   210, 232, 233
Franklin, Benjamin, 10
Freedom of the Seas, 2, 5
French Revolution, 11, 27
Friendly, Fred, 195
Fukuyama, Francis, 277

Genet, Edmond, 12
Geneva Conference (1954), 210
Geneva Naval Conference (1927), 105
Geneva Summit (1985), 259, 261
Germany: in World War I, 85–88; in
   World War II, 147–154, 167–172,
   261

Ghent, Peace of (1814), 27
Glasnost, 258
Glass, Carter, 107
Golan Heights, 235
Gompers, Samuel, 68–69
Good Neighbor Policy, 125, 127–130, 131
Gorbachev, Mikhail, 255, 258–261
Great Britain: in Civil War, 46–52; in eighteenth and nineteenth centuries, 2, 5, 9–11, 12–14, 28–29; in Middle East, 232–233; and Open Door Notes, 66–67; in World War I, 86–88; 125; in World War II; 148–150, 151–152, 167–168, 170–173
Great Depression, 146
Great Society, the, 211
Guadalupe Hidalgo, Treaty of (1848), 33
Gulf of Tonkin Resolution (1965), 211; text of 220–221

Hamilton, Alexander, 11
Harding, Warren G., 91, 104
Harriman, Averell, 214
Harvey, George, 1
Hay, John, 3, 66, 69–70, 76
Hearst, William Randolph, 68
Hidecki, Tojo, 153
Hippisley, Alfred, 69
Hitchcock, Gilbert, 89, 91
Hitler, Adolf, 149, 167, 184
Ho Chi Minh Trail, 214, 219
Holland, 15
Holy Alliance, 28
Hoover, Herbert, 106, 127–128, 131
House Un-American Activities Committee (HUAC), 191
Huerta, Victoriano, 126
Hughes, Charles Evans, 104
Hull, Cordell, 128, 130, 153
Humphrey, Hubert, 215
Hussein, Saddam, 240, 281

Imperialism, 3, 67–69
Impressment, 12
Indian Removal Act (1830), 31

Inter-American Conference (1936), 130–131
Interventionism, 146
Iran, 182, 232–239, 240, 281
Iraq, 232–240, 281
Iron Curtain, Churchill speech on; 182–184, 191, 258
Irreconcilables, 89, 90, 91
Isolationism, 2, 7, 89–90, 104, 145–146
Isolationists, 104–105, 145, 148, 149–150, 151, 152, 153, 154
Israel, 231–240, 280–281

Japan, 3, 66, 104; in World War II, 149, 151–154, 167–168, 170–173; 282
Jay, John, 10
Jay's Treaty (1794), 13
Jefferson, Thomas, 7, 11, 12, 13, 22, 126
Jewish Homeland, 232–233
Jieshi, Jiang (Chiang Kai-shek), 169, 191
Johnson, Hiram, 89, 90
Johnson, Lyndon, 211–214
Johnson Act (1934), 148

Kai-shek, Chiang (Jiang Jieshi), 169, 191
Kellogg-Briand Pact (1928), 103–104, 105–107, text of, 108–111
Kellogg, Frank, 89, 105–107; excerpts of testimony before Senate, 116–120
Kennan, George, 173, 190
Kennedy, John F., 194, 211, 214–215, 261
Kennedy, Robert, 212, 214
Kent State, 216
Keynes, John Maynard, 91
King Cotton, 50
Kissinger, Henry, 209, 215–216, 217–218, 235, 237
Knox, Frank, 151
Korea, 149, 193
Korean War, 193

LaFollette, Robert, 89
League of Nations, 2, 88–91, 97, 99, 100, 145

Lebanon, 233–234, 281
Lee, Robert E., 49
Lend Lease Act (1941), 152
Levinson, Salmon, 105, 106
Lincoln, Abraham, 33, 45, 46, 47, 49,
  50, 51, 52, 53
Lindbergh, Charles, 149, 164–165
Lloyd-George, David, 87
Lodge, Henry Cabot, 68, 89, 90, 91
Lodge Treaty (1919), 91
Louis XVI, 11
Louisiana Territory (Louisiana Pur-
  chase, 1803), 13
Lusitania, 147

MacArthur, Douglas, 107, 193
Madero, Francesco, 126
Mahan, Alfred, 67
Mandela, Nelson, 283
Manhattan Project, 172
Manifest Destiny, 27, 30–34, 41, 68
Marshall, George, 173, 186, 190, 193
Marshall, John, 31
Marshall Plan, 173, 186, 190, 191
Mason, James, 46, 47, 48, 59
McCarran Act (1950), 192
McCarthy, Joseph, 189–197, 203–204,
  257
McCarthyism, 189–197
McCullough, David, 172
McGovern, George, 212, 217
McKinley, William, 67, 69
Mexican Constitution, 127
Mexican War, 33, 34, 47, 66, 126
Millis, Walter, 3
Minh, Ho Chi, 210
Missouri Compromise, 33
Moir, James, 47
Molotov, V.I., 169
Monroe, James, 2–3, 6, 27, 29–30, 31,
  38
Monroe Doctrine, 2–3, 6, 27–30, 31,
  34, 280; text of 38–40, 66, 67, 126,
  128, 130
Morgenthau, Hans, 5
Morgenthau, Henry, 170
Mubarek, Hosni, 240
Murrow, Edward, 195, 206–207

NAFTA (North American Free Trade
  Agreement) (1993), 3, 280
Nanking, Treaty of (1842), 66
Napoleon III, 47
Napoleonic Wars, 2, 27
Nasser, Gamal Abdel, 232, 233, 234
National Security Council Document
  68 (NSC 68) (1950), 192, 195; text of
  198–203
Naval Blockade, 2, 5; in Civil War, 46;
  text of, 53–54
Neutrality, 9–12; in Civil War, 46, 49–
  50; during the 1930s, 145–148; in
  World War I, 85–86, 92–93
Neutrality Acts, 145, 146–148, 149, 151–
  154; passage of 146–148, 149; repeal
  of 151–152, 154
Neutrality Proclamation, 9; text of, 15
New Deal, 148, 192
"New World Order," 278
Nicolson, Harold, 91
Nitze, Paul, 192
Nixon, Richard, 191–192, 194, 209,
  215, 216–218, 235–236, 256
Nixon Doctrine, 215
North Atlantic Treaty Organization
  (NATO) (1949), 190, 259, 279
Nye, Gerald P., 146–147, 148, 149, 152
Nye Committee, 146–147, 154

Oil Producing and Exporting Coun-
  tries (OPEC), 236, 257
Open Door Notes (1899–1900), 3, 66–
  67, 69–70; text of 76–77
Opium War (1839), 66
Organization of American States
  (United Nations), 4, 130, 280
Orlando, Vittorio, 87

Pahlavi, Shah Reza, 236
Pakistan, 376
Palestine, 232–234, 236–240, 281
Palestine Liberation Organization
  (PLO), 236–240
Palmerston, Lord, 48–49, 51, 52
Pan-Americanism, 2, 3
Panama Canal, 67

Paris Peace Conference (1918–1919),
    87.
Pax Americana, 278
Pearl Harbor, 154
Pentagon Papers, 216
Peress, Irving, 195
Perestroika, 258
Perry, Matthew, 66
Pershing, John, 127
Platt Amendment, 128
Polk, James K., 33
Potsdam Conference (1945), 167–168,
    171–172, 174
Potsdam Declaration (1945), 176–179
Progressive Movement, 86
Progressivism, 86
Pulitzer, Joseph, 68

Quarantine Address (1937), 148, 149,
    150; text of, 160–161
Quebec Conference (1944), 169, 170

Reagan, Ronald, 255–256, 257–259,
    260, 261, 263, 279
Realpolitik, 215
"Red Scare," 189
Reed, James, 107
Revolutionary War, 3, 10
Reykjavik Summit (1986), 255, 260,
    261–262
Rockhill, William W., 69
Rogers, William, 216
Roosevelt, Franklin D., 6; and Good
    Neighbor Policy, 125, 128, 129–130;
    and Neutrality Acts, 146, 148–150,
    152–154; and World War II, 168–170
Roosevelt, Theodore, 6, 68, 126
Roosevelt Corollary (1904), 6, 126–127,
    128, 133
Round-robin resolution, 88–89
Rush, Richard, 28, 35
Russia, 28–30, 78–79, 86. See also So-
    viet Union (Russia)

Sadat, Anwar, 231, 236, 237, 239, 240
San Jacinto, U.S.S., 47, 48
San Lorenzo, Treaty of (1795), 13
Schine, David, 194, 195

Schurz, Carl, 69
Senate Foreign Relations Committee,
    89, 90, 104, 146
Seward, William, 46, 48, 49, 51, 55–58
Shotwell, James, 105
Silver, Abba Hillel, 234
Six-Day War (1967), 234–235, 236
Slidell, John, 46, 47, 48, 49
Solidarity Movement, 257
Southeast Asia Treaty Organization
    (SEATO), 211
Soviet Union (Russia): and McCarthy-
    ism, 189–191, 194, 196–197; and
    Middle East, 232–233, 234, 236; and
    Reagan, 255–262, 279; and Vietnam,
    210, 215; in World War II, 167–169,
    170–174
Spain, 10, 11, 13, 27–28, 30, 67
Spanish-American War (1898), 67, 125
Spanish Civil War, 149
Spheres of influence, 67, 69, 70
Spheres of interest, 70
Stalin, Joseph, 167, 168, 169, 170, 171,
    183–184
Stevenson, Adlai, 194
Stimson, Henry, 127, 151, 181
Strategic Defense Initiative (SDI), 258,
    260, 261
Suez Canal, 233, 239
Summit Diplomacy, 168, 174, 255
Sussex, 147
Syria, 232–237, 239

Taft, William, 126
Tet Offensive (1968), 212, 214
Third Reich, 167
Tho, Le Duc, 216, 217, 218
Thoreau, Henry David, 33
Thuy, Xuan, 214, 215
Tientsin, Treaty of (1858), 67
Tonkin Gulf Resolution (1964), 211
Trent Affair, 45, 46, 48, 49, 52
Tripartite Pact (1940), 149, 152
Truman Doctrine, 173; text of, 184–
    186, 190
Truman, Harry S: during McCarthy
    period, 190, 191, 192, 193; and Mid-
    dle East, 232; at Potsdam Confer-

ence, 167, 171–173, 175–176, 179–
181; text of Truman Doctrine, 173,
184–186; Vietnam policy, 210
Tse-tung, Mao (Mao Zedong), 70, 191
Tutu, Desmond, 283
Twain, Mark (Samuel Clemens), 68
Tydings, Millard E., 192

Unconditional Surrender, 169, 171
United Nations, 4, 170, 190, 193, 232,
235, 237, 240, 242–243, 244–245

Vanderbilt, Cornelius, 34
Versailles, Treaty of (Paris Peace Con-
ference) (1918–1919), 87–88, 89, 90,
91
Vietnam (North and South), 209–218
Vietnamization, 215, 216
Villa, Pancho, 127

Walesa, Lech, 258
War: "all aid short of," 151, 152;
"Hawks," 5, 14. See also individual
wars
Warsaw Pact (1949), 190, 259, 279
Washington, George, 6, 7, 9, 11, 12,13,
14, 15; text of Farewell Address, 16–
22; 23–24, 85, 89, 145
Washington Naval Conference (1921),
104

Watergate, 218
Welch, Joseph, 196
Westward Expansion, 30–34
White, William Allen, 150
"White Man's Burden," 68
Wilhelm, Kaiser, 87
Wilkes, Captain Charles, 47, 48
Williams, William A., 3
Willkie, Wendell, 150–151
Wilmot, David, 33
Wilson, Edith Bolling, 90
Wilson, Woodrow, 2, 6, 85, 86–87, 88–
89, 90–91; text of Neutrality Procla-
mation, 92–93; text of Fourteen
Points, 93–98; 99, 103, 104, 126, 145,
146, 148
Worcester v. Georgia (1832), 31
World War I, 6, 85, 86, 87, 103, 146,
147
World War II, 149, 154, 167, 168, 173,
174, 189, 193, 210, 232, 255, 280

XYZ Affair, 13

Yalta Conference (1945), 170–171
Yom Kippur War, 236–237, 244

Zedong, Mao (Mao Tse-tung), 70,
191
Zwicker, Ralph, 195

About the Author

JOLYON P. GIRARD is Professor in the History and Political Science Department at Cabrini College in Radnor, Pennsylvania, where he received the Lindbach Award for Excellence in Teaching. He is currently researching a history of American prisoners of war from 1763 to the present.